COST ESTIMATING
WITH
MICROCOMPUTERS

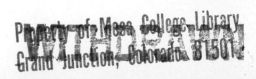

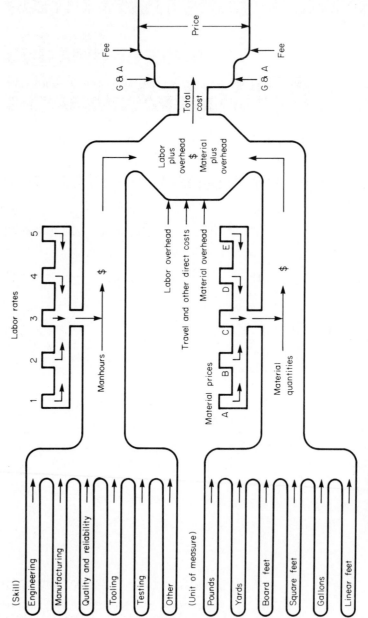

Figure 1 The anatomy of an estimate. (*Courtesy of John Wiley and Sons, Cost Estimating, 1982, and the National Estimating Society, Estimator Magazine, Winter 1983.*)

COST ESTIMATING WITH MICROCOMPUTERS

Rodney D. Stewart, PE, CCA, CPE

and

Ann L. Stewart

MCGRAW-HILL BOOK COMPANY

New York St. Louis San Francisco Auckland
Bogotá Hamburg Johannesburg London
Madrid Mexico Montreal New Delhi
Panama Paris São Paulo Singapore
Sydney Tokyo Toronto

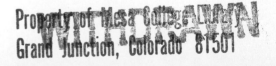

Library of Congress Cataloging in Publication Data

Stewart, Rodney D.
  Cost estimating with microcomputers.

  Includes index.
  1. Costs, Industrial—Estimates—Data processing.
  2. Microcomputers. I. Stewart, Ann L. II. Title.
  HD47.S763 1986   658.1′552′02854   85-12807
  ISBN 0-07-061462-8

234567890   DOC/DOC 8987

ISBN 0-07-061462-8

The editors for this book were Tyler G. Hicks and Jim Bessent, the designer was Naomi Auerbach, and the production supervisor was Thomas G. Kowalczyk. It was set in Century Schoolbook by Achorn Graphics.

Printed and bound by R. R. Donnelley & Sons Company.

Software Trademarks Mentioned in Manuscript

AutoCAD	Autodesk Systems, Inc.
Best Bid	Concord Management Systems, Inc.
COSTFORM	Diversified Data Systems, Inc.
CalcStar	MicroPro International Corp
Cost Plus	Construction Software Systems, Inc.
Costware	Mobile Data Services
DATACOST	Mobile Data Services
Data Base/Assembly Estimating CMIS	Construction Data Control, Inc.
ESPRI	Contractors Management System
EasyPlanner	Information Unlimited Software Inc.
Framework	Ashton Tate
Galaxy	R.S. Means
Harvard Project Manager	Harvard Software
InSearch	Menlo Corporation
KnowledgeMan	Micro Data Base Systems, Inc.
Lotus 1-2-3	Lotus Systems, Inc.
MICA/JC	Micro Associates, Inc.
MacProject	Apple Computer
Microplan	Digital Research
Microsoft Project	Microsoft
Multiplan	Microsoft
PFS File	Software Publishing, Inc.
PFS Report	Software Publishing, Inc.
Peachcalc	Peachtree Software Inc.
Personal Consultant	Texas Instruments, Inc.
Pertmaster	Westminister Software
Project Scheduler 5000	Scitor Corporation
Summit	Software Resources Center
Super-Calc 3	Sorcim Corp.
Symphony	Lotus Systems, Inc.
The Financial Planner	Ashton Tate
Visi-Calc IV	Visi-Corp

To our Father
The One Who Is More Than Enough!

CONTENTS

PREFACE

Cost Estimating with Microcomputers was written primarily for three categories of individuals:

1. Those who own a microcomputer and want to apply it to cost estimating

2. Those who are cost estimators and want to use microcomputers to help do their job

3. Those who know little about either microcomputing or cost estimating but want to enter the field or initiate the practice of cost estimating with microcomputers

The book contains the basics of cost estimating combined with the basics of microcomputing to show how these two disciplines can be melded together to start using the computer for cost estimating in a very short time. The results are increased speed and accuracy and a professionally prepared cost estimate.

The techniques in this book will be equally useful for the practicing estimator who wants to substantially improve his or her cost estimates by using commercially available microcomputing software and hardware tools, and for the estimator employed in a university, industrial firm, or government organization. The definitions, steps, and suggestions in this book will allow you to acquire a beginning set of tools for computerized estimating that can be built upon and expanded as you increase your knowledge, skill, and understanding of the use of microcomputers for your specific cost estimating situations.

Estimators who work in large organizations with mainframe or larger multiple-user computers will find that many of the functions of cost estimating for even very large jobs can be done on microcomputers. The use of a desktop, personal, or portable microcomputer can offer a readily available, rapid-response, "standalone" capability that can individualize, professionalize, and improve the efficiency of the day-to-day estimating process. Estimators in small businesses, contracting, or the professions will find the microcomputer to be an economical cost estimating tool that will produce cost estimates of professional quality rivaling those of much larger organizations; and with the purchase of the proper applications software packages, this same tool can be used concurrently for such other functions as accounting, word processing, and mailing lists, as well as others functions that involve the handling, storing, sorting, computing, and reporting of information.

The business, engineering, or architectural student who wants to become familiar with the most advanced tools available in the estimating profession will find this book helpful. It will familiarize the student with microcomputing and estimating definitions, terms, techniques, and data, and will form a base for rapid understanding of the application of computers to the estimating tasks that are increasingly confronting the business, technical, and professional communities. *Cost Estimating with Microcomputers* is filled with software program listings, examples, and scenarios that will help students become familiar with microcomputer estimating. Appendix I contains a glossary of microcomputer terms and Appendix II contains a glossary of cost estimating terms that will assist the user in becoming familiar with either field.

Since it is the nature of computers and computing that the uses expand exponentially as the user becomes more familiar with the available tools, the reader will find that this book only begins to cover the microcomputer's potential in estimating and related disciplines. The fundamentals provided build a solid foundation for some of the more important initial uses of microcomputers for cost estimating and suggest ways of further expanding the use of the same knowledge and equipment to tasks related to estimating as the user's skills and knowledge increase.

We believe the reader will find this book valuable in deciding whether to use "off-the-shelf," commercially available applications software programs, templates for these off-the-shelf programs, vertical market systems, or specially programmed software for specific estimating applications.

The handy and helpful examples of programs, spreadsheet templates, and database techniques found throughout the book are designed to familiarize the reader with the concepts as well as the details of cost estimating with microcomputers. The examples can be used "as is" or modified to fit specific estimating situations. Careful entry, checking, and use of the examples will be necessary to achieve the best results.

There are literally hundreds of useful software packages or products on the market at this writing, and many more are being introduced into the marketplace every day. To make an informed decision in selecting software or hardware to be used in cost estimating, we recommend that the reader subscribe to one of the many excellent periodicals on microcomputers and computing; combine the knowledge gained in these magazines with knowledge gained from this book; and talk to a Certified Professional Estimator (CPE), Certified Cost Engineer (CCE), or Certified Cost Analyst (CCA) and your computer dealer about your specific applications before purchasing new software or new microcomputer hardware.

When you acquire a new microcomputer or apply your existing microcomputer to cost estimating, you will find that you have acquired a new friend and professional partner that will substantially increase productivity, professionalism, and business prosperity.

Rod Stewart

Annie Stewart

ACKNOWLEDGMENTS

We would like to express our appreciation to all of those who supplied information and assistance in the preparation of this book. Among those who supplied help, support, and permission to use material are Mr. Ron Sketo of the United States Army Corps of Engineers; Mr. Michael F. Yarlick of the Scitor Corporation; Mr. Jeff Bell of the National Estimating Society; Mr. Truman Howard of the United States Army Missile Command; Ms. Nona Whatley of John M. Cockerham Associates, Inc.; Ms. Toni Pacak of Estimation, Inc.; Mr. Frank Cerra of John Wiley and Sons; Mr. Quenten Hensely of Micro-Associates, Inc.; Mr. Duane Uken of Engineering Economics Research, Inc.; and Mr. Richard Stern of Construction Data Services, Inc.

We would also like to express our gratitude to Mr. Kenneth Brooks of The Computer House in Andalusia, Alabama, and Mr. Terry McMullen and others of Texas Instruments, Inc., for keeping us up to date and informed about emerging developments and advances in the fields of microcomputer hardware, microcomputer software, and microcomputer systems.

WHY COST ESTIMATING WITH MICROCOMPUTERS?

The modern desktop, personal, professional, or portable microcomputer, coupled with the appropriate software and with skills in cost estimating, can provide a sizable improvement in productivity and profitability for any venture. Microcomputers can increase the speed and accuracy of the estimating process. Because of their adaptability and flexibility, microcomputers, using a variety of available and custom-tailored software products, can be used to advantage in virtually any estimating situation. Estimates prepared using microcomputers can possess the qualities of high visibility, credibility, and increased professionalism.

Developing accurate estimates for work activities and work outputs will assist a company in two ways. First, jobs are less likely to be underestimated. Underestimating a job may result in winning a competition without allocating sufficient resources to perform the work. The result of an underestimated job is a cost overrun or a loss of profits by the performing company. Second, companies that bid too high as a result of an inaccurate cost estimate may not be selected to do the work because of their high bid. Both of these results have an adverse effect on the profitability of an organization that is selling a product or service in today's marketplace. Not only is profitability increased through the use of the latest microestimating techniques, but productivity in the estimating process itself is also increased. This productivity reduces overhead costs, bid costs, bidding times, and the accompanying labor and resource expenditures.

The Field of Cost Estimating

Cost estimating is rapidly evolving into a profession that will eventually be treated in much the same way as accounting, law, medicine, or engineering. High-technology tools such as the microcomputer are being used in all of these professions. Why is this happening? As John Naisbitt points out in his 1982 best-seller *Megatrends,* several subtle but distinct changes are occurring as a result of the introduction of high technology into our everyday lives. The number of choices an individual or business can make in acquiring a product or service is increasing at a seemingly exponential rate. We are moving from an era of "either-or" decisions into an age of "multiple-choice" decisions. Growth of the number of choices has a twofold effect on the field of cost estimating: (1) cost estimates must be developed to cover all of the new products, services, and options thereof; and (2) customers, buyers, purchasing agents, and consumers are becoming more discerning, cost conscious, and selective in making economic decisions. The former effect brings about an increase in the number of cost estimates made by suppliers, and the latter results in the need for more independent cost estimating and cost analysis tools to be used by the procurers to make an informed decision.

Another trend is the move to more highly complex and sophisticated products and services. These more complex work outputs and work activities contain a greater number of systems, components, parts, or work tasks, making the estimating job itself more complex. The rapid communications capabilities that are evolving as part of the information age are making it imperative for business and industry to use the products of high technology themselves—one of the principal products being the computer.

In many years of work with industry, government, and in supporting the academic community with books, handbooks, and seminars, the authors have discovered that there is a common thread of methodology that runs through virtually every cost estimating situation. The methodology used in this book can be applied to small, medium-sized, or large work activities and work outputs in many fields; and the microcomputer programs, software, and techniques discussed are applicable in a wide variety of settings. The examples given range from home construction to multimillion dollar high-technology missile system development projects, but the applicability of many of the techniques is virtually universal, with the complexity or depth of the example corresponding to the complexity or depth of the project itself.

Microcomputers for Cost Estimating

The microcomputer's characteristics of speed, accuracy, and adaptability to a wide range of uses make it an ideal tool for the estimator in this age of high technology. How do these characteristics cause the microcomputer to be an ideally suited tool for the cost estimator? We will discuss each characteristic below and show why the new tool will provide improved visibility of estimating data with all of the attendant advantages of this improved visibility, and why the new tool provides increased cost estimate credibility, which is a prerequisite for running a profitable venture.

Speed

Speed is the principal benefit that the microcomputer can provide to the cost estimating process. Cost estimates are almost always required in a very short time. The reason for this is that in a process that includes concept formulation, planning, design, scheduling, and then estimating, the cost estimating step is usually the last step before a bid, quote, or proposal is submitted. It is the last domino in the bidding process and, therefore, must take up any "negative slack" that has been created by the slippage of preceding steps. The microcomputer can perform routine estimating computations at a speed at least several orders of magnitude higher than any hand or semiautomated estimating process. The increased speed brought about by computerized cost estimating will not only be a significant factor in producing estimates on time but will (1) permit prior iterations based on preliminary or fragmentary cost or resource inputs; (2) allow rapid production of variations, options, or alternative estimates; and (3) permit the use of the latest available labor rates, unit material costs, and estimating factors through on-line or stored databases of actual costs for similar work.

Not only is the speed in computation capability brought about by microcomputers of advantage to the cost estimator, but the speed in producing high-quality, legible, error-free typed or printed reports is of significant benefit in converting the cost estimate and its supporting rationale into a usable document. Depending on the kind of printer or plotter used to produce estimate outputs, the actual production speed of producing a typed (printed) document can be considerably faster than conventional typing. Graphic outputs by microcomputers can be done in seconds or minutes instead of the hours or days required for conventional artwork. Speed is a principal benefit to the cost estimator, but there are also other significant benefits that the microcomputer brings to the estimating process.

Accuracy

In a cost estimate a small error usually gets a disproportionally large negative vote from evaluators. Unfortunately, it is true that no matter how meticulously an estimate is put together, if there are mathematical or typographical errors, the credibility of the whole estimate is brought under question. The microcomputer brings with it an uncanny ability to produce error-free computations as well as error-free typing (provided that it is supplied with the correct initial inputs or subsequent corrections). The use of direct keyboard entry into the microcomputer by the estimator can eliminate one large potential source of error: that of faulty transcribing of handwritten notes or data. Improved accuracy of unit prices for materials and labor hours can be a result of on-line access through hard-wired or telecommunication links. The big accuracy advantage comes in multifaceted, matrix-type estimates where multiple sheets or even multiple volumes of cost data must be submitted with a cost estimate. The computer can cross-check these large estimates in seconds or minutes. The cross-checking would take hours or days to accomplish by hand or by semiautomated methods.

Adaptability

The adaptability or flexibility of a microcomputer with the proper software to accomplish a wide variety of estimating functions and to provide outputs in many different formats is a principal advantage because: (1) varying estimating methods are used in different situations; (2) customers usually either demand or are more efficiently served by providing some selectivity and individualism in estimate reporting formats; (3) each estimating situation and estimator has specific needs for estimate output content and format.

Another sizable advantage of the use of microcomputers in cost estimating situations is that the microcomputer can be used for functions other than the estimating process itself. If, for example, a small business or professional person were to acquire a computer for cost estimating purposes and if the cost estimating function did not require full-time use of the computer for cost estimating, the computer could be used for other functions such as accounting, word processing, mailing lists, etc., during the time it is not being used for cost estimating. In Chapter 10 we will discuss the desirability of considering this factor in the microcomputer evaluation and acquisition process.

Because of its relatively small size (compared to mainframe and most minicomputers), the microcomputer is easily transportable. This transportability feature is of significant value to the cost estimator if on-site collection of data, cost estimating, or cost-to-complete analysis is required. Some estimators mount their microcomputers in vans, trucks, motor homes, or temporary portable offices and locate them directly on or near the job or client's work area or plant. Others use the portable versions of microcomputers and carry them on airplanes, buses, trains, or cars.

Visibility

A principal characteristic that microcomputers bring to cost estimating is the trait of visibility. By visibility, we mean the capability of either viewing the entire estimate at the top level or delving deeply into the various components that make up the cost estimate. In-depth visibility is required to provide traceability of costs. Through an in-depth look at a cost estimate, the estimator can identify major cost drivers and determine their potential effect on the overall project. The various spreadsheet, database, and vertical market software programs that are available or that can be programmed on the microcomputer are ideally suited to provide both an overall view of an estimate and an in-depth look at the estimate components.

Because of the visibility and traceability provided by the microcomputer, estimate resource values can be modified easily. Most microcomputer estimating software programs provide a means of rapidly going to a specific point in the estimate, making a modification, and then viewing the effects of the change on the overall estimate. The ability to see the "trees" as well as the entire "forest," permits selectivity in making modifications, deletions, additions, and updates.

The capability of in-depth visibility provides a means for tracking, on a time-schedule basis, actual costs of various activities within a project compared to the original cost estimate. Costs can be managed, controlled, directed, reported, and modified as the project proceeds.

Credibility

Microcomputers provide a sizable improvement in estimate *credibility*. Credibility in estimating is improved through the use of a systematic, organized, methodical, and logical approach. The microcomputer estimating applications programs that are available and that can be developed require a systematic approach to estimating.

Credibility is also enhanced by the *timeliness* of the data (pricing data and labor productivity data) that is used in the estimate. Use of frequently updated on-line databases assures the estimator as well as the potential customer that the very latest pricing and productivity data have been included in the estimate; thus the estimate is both more doable and more competitive. Combining word processing and database features in an estimating software package or an estimating process permits the incorporation of work descriptions, definitions, and detailed cost estimating rationale along with the resource numbers that they support. This built-in rationale helps to keep the estimated dollars in line with the work scope, since any change in one should be accompanied by a corresponding change in the other.

The use of microcomputers in cost estimating provides a degree of professionalism that is necessary to assure competence and comprehension. With the microcomputer, the small business owner, contractor, or professional person with limited resources can provide an attractive, organized, professional-looking, credible cost estimate for a minimum of resources expended.

Features of Microcomputers and How They Apply to Estimating

Computation Ability

With the advent of in-depth, systematic, organized cost estimating, the computation speed and accuracy of the microcomputer are becoming a necessity in the modern business, engineering, and professional worlds. The sheer size of the databases involved in even small projects, the larger number of skill categories and skill levels involved, the increased number of work elements in even simple tasks, and the constant demands of customers for more details in making economic decisions all make speed of computation a fundamental requirement. The job of computing and cross-checking even a small estimate by hand or semiautomated means (using pocket or desktop calculators) has become unwieldy for all but the very simplest single-function tasks. Rapid changes and fluctuations in labor rates, material prices, factors, price indexes, and government and company laws, rules, and regulations often make it necessary to recompute the entire estimate more than once or twice. Also, many customers are requiring that one or more alternatives or options be priced as well as the primary option. The work required to provide these alternative estimates, once a cumbersome job when done by hand, is made simple by the microcomputer. Figure 1-1 is a printout of a simple and brief BASIC computer program that will replace a huge volume of learning-curve handbook tables (more about this in Chapter 3).

Report Generation Ability

One of the jobs that most clerk-typists and secretaries enjoy the least is the typing of numerical figures in tabular form. Most typists who do an excellent job on text material are slowed considerably when it comes to a table, formula, or figure containing text plus numerical data. Hand typing of cost estimates, unless only the bottom-line cost is presented, is rapidly becoming a thing of the past with the advent of microcomputerized cost estimating. The field of accounting, having relied on handwritten pen-and-ink entries into journals and general ledgers for generations, was one of the first professions to adopt computers for their work on

```
10 CLS
20 COLOR 7
30 REM   THIS PROGRAM IS NAMED "CURVEL"
40 PRINT TAB(20) "LEARNING CURVE FOR SMALL NO. OF UNITS"
50 PRINT
60 PRINT "DATE:";DATE$
70 PRINT "TIME:";TIME$
80 PRINT
90 REM   THIS PROGRAM COMPUTES THE XTH UNIT HOURS, CUMULATIVE TOTAL HOURS,
100 REM   AND CUMULATIVE AVERAGE HOURS FOR THE CRAWFORD LEARNING CURVE SYSTEM
110 REM   WHERE:
120 REM      "N" IS THE LEARNING CURVE PERCENTAGE
130 REM      "K" IS THE MAN-HOURS REQUIRED FOR THE FIRST UNIT
140 REM      "Z" IS THE TOTAL NUMBER OF UNITS TO BE EVALUATED
150 REM      "Y1" IS THE HOURS REQUIRED TO PRODUCE THE XTH UNIT
160 REM      "Y2" IS THE CUMULATIVE HOURS
170 REM      "Y3" IS THE CUMULATIVE AVERAGE HOURS
180 INPUT "PUT IN THE LEARNING CURVE PERCENTAGE ";N:PRINT
190 PRINT "IF ONE (1) IS USED FOR THE FIRST UNIT HOURS, A LEARNING CURVE"
200 PRINT "FACTOR TABLE WILL RESULT":PRINT
210 INPUT "PUT IN THE HOURS REQUIRED FOR THE FIRST UNIT ";K:PRINT
220 INPUT "PUT IN THE NUMBER OF UNITS ";Z:PRINT
230 IF K>1 THEN 260:IF K=1 THEN 250
240 PRINT
250 PRINT "LEARNING CURVE FACTORS FOR A CURVE OF";N;"PERCENT ARE:"
260 PRINT "UNIT, CUM, & CUM AVG HRS FOR A L.C. OF";N;"% & TFU HRS OF";K;":"
270 PRINT
280 PRINT "UNIT NO.    XTH UNIT HRS.    CUM TOTAL    CUM AVERAGE"
290 Y2 = 0:FOR X=1 TO Z
300 Y1=K*X^(LOG(N/100)/LOG(2))
310 Y2=Y1+Y2:Y3=Y2/X:PRINT X,Y1,Y2,Y3:NEXT X
320 INPUT "DO YOU WANT THIS PRINTED ON THE PRINTER?(YES/NO)";P$
330 IF P$ = "NO" THEN GOTO 470
340 IF P$ = "N" THEN GOTO 470
350 LPRINT TAB(20) "LEARNING CURVE FOR SMALL NO. OF UNITS"
360 LPRINT
370 LPRINT DATE$,TIME$
380 LPRINT
390 IF K>1 THEN 410:IF K=1 THEN 400
400 LPRINT "LEARNING CURVE FACTORS FOR A CURVE OF";N;"PERCENT ARE:"
410 LPRINT "UNIT, CUM, & CUM AVG HRS FOR A L.C. OF";N;"% & TFU HRS OF";K;":"
420 LPRINT
430 LPRINT "UNIT NO.    XTH UNIT HRS.    CUM TOTAL    CUM AVERAGE"
440 Y2 = 0:FOR X=1 TO Z
450 Y1=K*X^(LOG(N/100)/LOG(2))
460 Y2=Y1+Y2:Y3=Y2/X:LPRINT X,Y1,Y2,Y3:NEXT X
470 INPUT "PROCESS ANOTHER CURVEL (YES/NO) ";A$
480 IF A$="YES" THEN GOTO 10
490 IF A$="Y" THEN GOTO 10
500 COLOR 7
510 CLS
520 LOCATE 12,35:PRINT "THANK YOU"
530 RUN "DATACOST.BAS"
540 END
```

Figure 1-1 Listing for CURVEL computer program.

a wholesale basis. The field of estimating, up to now not so established or formalized, is adopting the same capability.

The wide variety of printers, both of the letter-quality type and the dot matrix type, as well as a large number of print styles or fonts, makes high-speed, quality printing available to print the outputs of an estimate. The capability of printing nice-looking, accurate, and professional tabular numerical reports is of as great an advantage to the estimator as is the rapid computation capability. Dot matrix printers have an advantage in that they can print compressed print reports with up to 255 character columns along an 11 by 14 inch table. This type of display gives the estimator a capability of viewing a large page of numbers at one time and of producing detailed but legible spreadsheets to include in estimate reports.

Storage of Information

Microcomputer magnetic diskettes can hold 360,000 characters (letters or numbers) or more, meaning that a good-sized cost estimate (or several small cost estimates) can be stored on one floppy diskette. Many microcomputers come equipped with Winchester or hard disks that hold from 5 million characters up to 20 million or more characters of information. With these large data storage capacities, the cost estimator has available enough space to store very large cost estimates that go down to very low levels of detail. In addition to number storage, these character capacities can allow for the storage of accompanying text or rationale that describes the product or service being estimated and how the cost numbers were derived. Chapter 9 contains quantitative numbers that will help size the required storage capacities to the types and sizes of estimates to be performed.

On-Screen Visibility

Before the advent of microcomputers and related on-line terminals for mainframe computers, the estimator had to input numbers via card decks keypunched according to a coded input sheet and then wait until the computer completed its batch processing of data. The output usually came in the form of a printout or stack of pages containing the cost output numbers in spreadsheet format. There was no opportunity to review the estimate inputs in an on-line fashion before the computations were started or to view the estimate results before the printout was produced.

Now, with the capability to view, in real time, organized and sorted estimate information on a microcomputer or terminal screen before computing or printing an estimate, last-minute changes and corrections in the inputs can be made before computing or printing the estimate.

Most estimating software permits quick access to any part of the input data which allows the estimator to check inputs for accuracy, consistency, and reasonableness. Often the software will also allow the estimator to review the *results* of the computations on a video screen or monitor *before* these results are printed. This real-time capability to view, change, re-compute, check, and modify the estimate fulfills one of the requirements of the estimating process itself: the ability to iterate and reiterate re-source and work content values to match the requirements of the job.

The use of color monitors for numerical or graphic screen displays adds yet another dimension to the preprinting visibility available to the estimator. The choice of a computer terminal with large well-defined characters and high resolution or character definition, and the use of scrolling techniques to access remote portions of the estimate spreadsheet rapidly will enhance the estimator's ability to use the monitor's display screen as a preliminary worksheet to make preliminary or final changes, deletions, or additions to the estimate.

Communications and Networking

Where cost estimates are prepared by a team of two or more estimators, communications between two or more microcomputers or between the microcomputers and a mainframe computer may be helpful to the overall estimating process. Some of the possibilities of this networking arrange-ment are: (1) preparation and input of a section or element of an estimate by each member of the estimating team; (2) viewing of the total estimate by each team member; (3) access to company databases of *unit cost* and *unit quantity* information (these terms are defined in Chapter 2 and Ap-pendix II); and (4) real-time monitoring of the estimate's progress by the estimate manager or team leader. Some of the simpler of these functions are already operational in some companies. There are many more pos-sibilities, such as integration of the cost estimating system with company financial, purchasing, payroll, and job-tracking systems as described in Chapter 7.

Microestimating and Organizational Trends

New organizational concepts and trends in business and industry have accompanied the introduction of the information age. Greater emphasis is being placed on the individual worker and on giving this worker a more identifiable task or place in the organization. Workers in administrative or white-collar settings as well as in manufacturing or production set-tings are being recognized as key members of a group or cell which pro-duces an identifiable element of work. This cellular concept lends itself to specialization within the cell. These same trends that are designed to increase the productivity of individuals and small work groups beg the use of the low-cost, high-technology information systems and hardware that are now available. The work specialty of cost estimating, coupled with the use of the microcomputer, can provide individual cells with their own cost information system. The individual estimator or small group of estimators, armed with excellent microcomputer software and hardware tools, can be an integral part of the trend toward increased personal and group productivity.

Standardization of Estimating Methods and Techniques

The microcomputer itself is playing a vital role in the more effective use of existing estimating methods and techniques and is focusing a spotlight on the need for standardization and simplification of the estimating process. The increased computation capability and improved productivity that the microcomputer gives to every cost estimator, as well as the need to communicate the results of the estimating process to other estimators and to management, are providing incentives to develop a better understanding of the estimating process.

As stated previously, we have found that the estimating methods or techniques can be applied to virtually any estimating situation; hence, families of cost estimating software products can be adopted that will conform to a wide variety of estimating situations. Chapters 3 through 8 describe six principal groups of software types that are available to the estimator, and these chapters show how a relatively standard and proven estimating methodology can be used in their application.

Taking Advantage of Speed and Storage Capacity

The estimating process, sequence, and methodology itself can be structured to take advantage of the speed and storage capacity of microcomputers. Once the estimating computer hardware and software have been acquired and placed in operation, the computer can be used during the estimating process in an iterative fashion to provide rough, preliminary, or interim estimates as a basis for a final, finely tuned estimate. The use of computer power is cheap once it is installed. Therefore, the estimating organization should take full advantage of the computer's speed in doing computations at points in the estimating process other than the very end. Since many computer estimates can be generated in a short time period, the estimator has an opportunity to explore more options, to repeat the estimate with different assumptions and input parameters, and to do sensitivity analysis studies. Therefore, the estimating process itself should be organized and scheduled to fully use the great speed and accuracy of the microcomputer. Check-estimates should be interspersed in the estimating cycle; provision should be made for partial estimates or estimates of work elements as the inputs are received; and estimate options that may be desirable in the final estimate should be computed.

Because larger storage capacities are becoming available on hard disks and streamer tape backups, multiple estimates of the same project with slightly different assumptions, ground rules, and inputs can be computed and stored for later use in the bid cycle or the contract negotiation cycle if required.

The larger memory capacities becoming available on microcomputers can be put to good use by employing software packages that use as much of the computer's memory capacity (random access memory, RAM) as possible. Some applications software packages are built to use the available memory capacity of the machine automatically. Using the available memory capacity will speed up estimate generation because access to information residing in memory is faster than access to information residing on computer storage media such as magnetic disks or tapes. In Chapter 9, more is said about the sizing of speed, memory capacity, and storage capacity to the estimating job.

Acquiring the Skills, Techniques, and Equipment

You have taken the first step in acquiring microestimating skills by purchasing this book. Because of the huge amount of information that is available in the estimating and microcomputing fields, the wide variety of estimating situations that are encountered in business and industry today, and the diversity of microcomputer hardware and software products available in the marketplace, you will undoubtedly supplement your knowledge in several ways before acquiring a microcomputer. You will find that the required information is readily available from a number of sources for a person who is genuinely interested in becoming fully informed on microestimating as it is applied to his or her profession.

The Technical Literature

There are a number of good books (see the bibliography) and several periodicals covering the general subject of cost estimating. Still, one of the best sources of cost estimating information is the technical, professional, or trade association or society representing your field or discipline.

Since cost estimating methodology is (sometimes erroneously) considered to be a sensitive subject because of the competitive nature of business, very little information is available from other organizations, particularly competitors. Often, your suppliers or customers of long standing will provide estimating data, techniques, and tools. The very best estimating data and information are usually found within one's own organization, since it is the performers who know best how to estimate their own work.

Literature on microcomputing is much more readily available. Suppliers of microcomputers and software are usually very happy to deluge you with information about their products and services. The problem is more of too much information than not enough. Trying to sort out which computer is best for your application based on a list of 30 to 50 computer and software specification and description items is like trying to find a dogwood tree in a redwood forest of California. But computer store owners will help you decide; and if you can afford an independent, unbiased computer consultant, you can usually get some good sound advice on which system to select without resorting to comparisons of manufacturer-supplied brochures and specification sheets.

Technical and Professional Societies

The best way to decide which type, style, size, and capacity microestimating system to acquire is to approach the problem from the viewpoint of your own technical or professional estimating needs rather than on a comprehensive review of all of the microcomputer options available in the marketplace. Again, the professional estimating and cost analysis societies can be of considerable help in determining what type of system to acquire. Three of the leading estimating and analysis societies are:

The National Estimating Society; Washington, D.C.

The American Association of Cost Engineers; Morgantown, West Virginia.

The Institute of Cost Analysis; Alexandria, Virginia.

Each of the these societies has a strict list of qualifications and tests that must be passed in order to award certifications, respectively, as follows:

Certified Professional Estimator (CPE)

Certified Cost Engineer (CCE)

Certified Cost Analyst (CCA)

Enlist someone who has one or more of these certifications to help you. They are experienced, qualified experts in their field. To supplement this advice, as mentioned above, you should solicit help from the technical, professional, or trade society that represents your specific industry, business, or profession.

Availability of the Technology of Microestimating

A final answer to the question of "Why cost estimating with microcomputers?" is that the technology of cost estimating and the technology of microcomputing are both steadily improving and becoming more economical and readily obtainable by the average business and even by the average individual. The situation here brings to mind the question posed to mountain climbers as to why they want to climb a particular peak; their classic answer, "Because it is there." Not only do microcomputers, properly applied, have a capability of improving productivity as a result of more accurate estimates, but the user has the satisfaction and all of its peripheral benefits of using the very latest in technology to perform one of the most important functions in business and industry today: cost estimating.

In microcomputer terminology, the microcomputer *system* is comprised of two basic categories of products: (1) the *software* and (2) the *hardware*.

In the remainder of this book we will provide some important background on the basics of cost estimating; we will discuss single or multipurpose software packages (simple user-entered BASIC programs, spreadsheet programs, database systems, scheduling and estimating packages, and integrated software packages), and vertical market systems. We will then discuss microcomputer hardware for cost estimating; comparison, analysis, and economic justification of systems; and some future expectations in the world of microestimating.

Note that a common example is used to demonstrate several of the cost estimating techniques and methods. The common example is a software development project with several names, depending on the system used in the demonstration. The trademark names used for these systems are as follows:

COSTPLAN: Estimating Software Template for Multiplan.

COSTWARE: Estimating software estimated using a database system (PFS File and PFS Report).

COSTTIME: Estimating software estimated using a scheduling system (Project Scheduler 5000).

SOFTWARE: Estimating software estimated using a scheduling system (Project Scheduler 5000).

The same basic example is used to demonstrate several systems in order to give the reader an idea of the treatment of the same problem inputs and outputs by various software packages.

2

THE FUNDAMENTALS
OF ESTIMATING

A good cost estimate depends on the quality of the input data. The best types of input data are those that come from actual experience. What types of input data are required for a cost estimate? How and from whom are these data elements collected? How are they organized and verified? What are the prerequisites to getting good data in the first place? We will address these questions in this chapter.

Definition: Who, What, When, Why, Where, and How

Probably the most serious hindrance to creating successful cost estimates is the failure to define fully the work activity or work output before the estimating process is started. Costs are influenced by: (1) *who* is going to do the work, (2) *what* the work content is (detailed specifications), (3) *when* the work is going to be done (scheduling), (4) *why* the work is being done (estimate rationale), (5) *where* the work is going to be performed (in your plant, on site, or another geographical location), and (6) *how* the work is going to be performed. It is amazing how many estimators are asked to estimate the costs of a job or task without being supplied with the answers to these basic questions. Because lack of definition is a universal problem in cost estimating, the cost estimator always has to assume the role of a questioner, prober, and searcher for deeper and more specific definition of the work. In many instances the requirement for a cost estimate actually *initiates* or *drives* the need for initial or further definition. Now that you know you will inevitably run into this problem, you must be courageous enough to ask these questions both of yourself and of those who are designing the work activity or work output. The estimator has a right to know and a need to know detailed answers to these questions.

Many times it is taken for granted that knowledge and information exist on a product's planned characteristics, delivery schedule, method of manufacture, place of manufacture, and skills needed, when in fact very little information about some of these vital facts exists at all. The key to a credible and accurate cost estimate is to link the estimated costs with the most probable work characteristics; therefore the cost estimator must, in many instances, actually take the lead in forcing further definition before the estimating process is started. This requires a great deal of tact and diplomacy because product definition is usually not in the realm of the estimator's responsibility. A willingness to use what is available is always a desirable trait in the cost estimator, and to demand information that does not exist would be presumptuous. But the questions are there and need to be asked because the thought process of the designer does not always consider the factors needed to make a cost estimate—such as *how* the product or service is going to be produced or rendered. It is an estimator's obligation and duty to probe and to dig out as much information as possible regarding these work characteristics before starting the estimating process. Estimators who do this will, in the long term, gain a reputation for high professionalism in their work as well as a track record for producing highly credible and accurate cost estimates. The managers, technicians, engineers, and other professionals in the company or organization will, after the initial irritation of having to answer more questions or do more work, thank the estimator for probing and searching the depths of the project.

The Anatomy of an Estimate

The types of input data required for a cost estimate are:

1. *Production units.* The number of pounds, yards, board feet, square feet, gallons, miles, blocks, drawings, parts, pages, etc., to be produced. Typical production units used are shown on Table 2-1.

2. *Labor unit quantities.* The number of labor time units (hours, days, weeks, months) required to produce a unit of output (e.g., welding

**TABLE 2-1 Typical Production Units Used in Estimating
(Courtesy of U.S. Army Corps of Engineers.)**

	Abbreviation	Description
Area:	SI	Square inch
	SF	Square foot
	SY	Square yard
	CSF	100 square feet
	ARC	Acre
Distance:	IN	Inch
	FT	Foot
	LF	Linear foot
	VLF	Vertical linear foot
	YD	Yard
	CLF	100 linear feet
	MLF	1000 linear feet
	MI	Mile (statute)
Flow:	CFM	Cubic feet/minute
	MCF	1000 cubic feet/minute
Liquid:	GAL	Gallon (U.S.)
Time:	MIN	Minute
	HR	Hour
	DAY	Day
	WK	Week
	MTH	Month
	YR	Year
Volume:	CI	Cubic inch
	CF	Cubic foot
	CY	Cubic yard
	BF	Board foot
	MBF	1000 board feet
Weight:	OZ	Ounce
	LB	Pound (avoirdupois)
	TON	Ton (short)
Misc:	BBL	Barrel
	EA	Each
	FLR	Floor
	LAN	Lane
	LS	Lump sum
	OPN	Opening
	PCT	Percent
	PR	Pair
	RSR	Riser
	SEA	Seat
	SET	Set
	SQ	Square (roofing)

time per foot; paving time per mile; labor hours per block laid; drafting time per drawing; writing, editing, or typing time per page; etc.). These are labor productivity factors.

3. *Labor rates.* The dollar cost per time of each labor skill category and skill level (otherwise known as wage rate or salary).

4. *Labor unit prices.* Labor unit prices equal labor unit quantities multiplied by labor rates. Hence, the labor unit price is the labor cost per unit of production.

5. *Material unit quantities.* The numbers of units of material required for a given amount of completed work (i.e., welding rod usage per inch or foot of weld; tons of asphalt used per each mile of highway paving; number of blocks per foot of wall; number of pounds of sheet metal per foot of ductwork; etc.). These are material usage factors.

6. *Material price.* The cost per unit of material quantity such as dollars per pound or ton, dollars per yard, dollars per board foot, etc.

7. *Material unit prices.* Material unit prices equal material unit quantities multiplied by material prices. Hence, the material unit price is the material cost per unit of production.

8. *Cost of subcontracts and purchased parts.* The costs of processes, products, projects, or services outside of the producing company or organization.

9. *Labor overhead percentage.* A percentage multiplied by labor costs to cover labor burden costs and labor overhead costs.

10. *Material burden percentage.* A percentage multiplied by material costs to cover material burden costs.

11. *Travel and other direct costs.* Costs attributable to the job that do not fit into one of the above categories (travel, transportation, computer services, reproduction services, training, etc.).

12. *General and administrative percentage.* A percentage multiplied by total direct and indirect costs to cover general and administrative expenses.

13. *Profit or fee percentage.* A percentage multiplied by total costs to derive the profit or fee to be earned on the work.

These input data are assembled into an estimate in the manner shown in Figures 2-1 through 2-3:

1. Labor unit prices (dollars per production unit) are obtained by multiplying the labor unit quantity (hours per production unit) by the labor rate (dollars per hour).

2. Labor costs are obtained by multiplying the production units by the labor unit price.

3. Material unit prices (dollars per production unit) are calculated by multiplying the material unit quantity (unit of measure per completed production unit) by the material price (dollars per material unit of measure).

4. Material costs are calculated by multiplying the production units by the material unit price.

5. Labor overhead costs are computed by multiplying labor costs by the labor overhead percentage divided by 100.

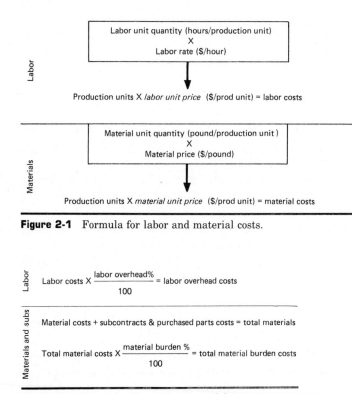

Figure 2-1   Formula for labor and material costs.

Figure 2-2   Formulas for total costs and fee.

Subtotal costs = labor plus labor overhead costs
                 + total material plus total material burden costs
                 + travel and other direct costs

General and administrative costs = general and administrative percentage
                                    X subtotal costs

Total costs = subtotal costs + general and administrative costs

Profit or fee = profit or fee percentage X total costs

Figure 2-3   Formulas for total costs and fee.

6. Total material and subcontract costs are equal to material costs plus subcontract and purchased parts costs. Material burden costs are found by multiplying total material costs by the material burden percentage divided by 100.

7. Subtotal costs include labor plus labor overhead costs, total material and total material burden costs, and travel and other direct costs.

8. General and administrative (G&A) costs are found by multiplying the subtotal costs by the G&A percentage. Total costs are the subtotal costs plus G&A costs.

9. The profit or fee is computed by multiplying the total costs by the profit or fee percentage.

Organizing the Estimate: The Work Element Structure

To provide a framework for collecting and organizing cost estimate data, it is often convenient if not necessary to develop a work element structure or task structure that arranges the various facets of the job in a logical and convenient hierarchy. The work element structure (or work breakdown structure as it is often called) uses a numbering or coding system that makes it easier to process resource data once the estimate computations begin. Development of a detailed work element structure containing the tasks or jobs that make up the total project and definition of the content and interrelationship between the work elements should take place early in the planning phase of any project; refinement and updating of the work element structure should continue throughout the project. Two typical work element structures, one for a hardware development project and one for a software development project, are shown in Figures 2-4 and 2-5, respectively. In developing the work element structure, the estimator should take care to identify the major elements of the project, then subdivide these into minor elements, subminor elements, and so on, as far as the job definition will allow. Since the work element structure will be the basis on which cost data are collected, it is important to identify the work content of each element to prevent duplications, overlaps, or omissions of important resources needed to do the job. This is done through the preparation of a work element structure "dictionary" that describes the work content of each element and identifies interfaces with other work elements. This work element structure dictionary can also be used as the basis for a contract proposal or contract work statement. Notice on Figure 2-4 that the work element structure is broken down into levels 1, 2, and 3. Levels can go down as far as the estimator desires but usually no lower than level 8.

The Project Schedule

As shown on Figure 2-6, estimating is preceded by the planning and scheduling. These preliminary steps are needed to generate programmatic and technical ground rules, assumptions, specifications, and criteria that will be used by the estimator in developing labor and material unit quantities.

Carrying out work activities or producing work outputs involves mul-

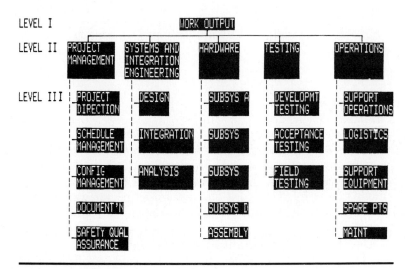

Figure 2-4   Typical work element structure, product or project.

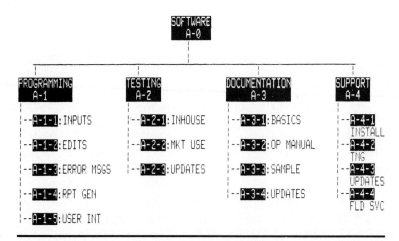

Figure 2-5   Work element structure, process or service.

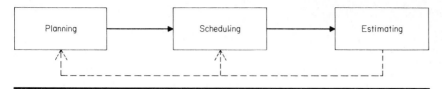

Figure 2-6 Estimating is preceded by planning and scheduling.

tiple events and actions on the part of the producer that fall in series, in parallel, or in accordance with an optimum time-oriented flow with both sequential and concurrent milestones and activities. In all but the very simplest job it is necessary to lay out a time-based schedule against which resources can be estimated because: (1) the labor and material unit prices may vary with time, (2) the funding profile and payment schedule may be critical to project approval, and (3) human and material resources must be planned to synchronize with other work activities and work outputs of the same producer.

The estimator must develop schedule elements, task or work element durations, precedence relationships, and key milestone dates for the project being estimated. From this information, critical path networks, critical path bar charts, Gantt charts, and event-activity timetables can be generated either manually or with the microcomputer.

There are a number of excellent microcomputer scheduling and estimating tools already available in the applications software market (see Chapter 6) and additional microcomputer scheduling and estimating applications software tools are becoming available.

Techniques Used in Schedule Planning

There are a number of analytical techniques used in developing an overall schedule of a work activity that help assure the correct allocation and sequencing of schedule elements. Among these techniques are the use of precedence and dependency networks, arrow diagrams, critical path bar charts, and project evaluation and review technique (PERT). These scheduling techniques use graphical and mathematical methods to develop the best schedule based on the sequencing of schedule activities in a way that each activity is performed only when the required predecessor activities are accomplished. A simple example of how these techniques work is shown on Figure 2-7.

In this schedule, eight schedule elements have been chosen, the length of each schedule activity has been designated, and a relationship has been established between each schedule activity and its predecessor activity as follows:

Schedule Relationships

Schedule element	Title of schedule element	Time required for completion, months	Percent completion required*
A	Study and analysis	6	33⅓
B	Design	8	50
C	Procurement	8	50
D	Fabrication	12	66⅔
E	Assembly	12	100
F	Testing	8	100
G	Delivery	4	100 plus 4 months
H	Operation	36	100

*Percent completion required before subsequent activity can be accomplished.

Notice several things about the precedence relationships: (1) some activities can be started before their predecessor activities are completed; (2) some activities must be fully completed before their follow-on activities can be started; (3) and some activities cannot be started until a given number of months after the 100 percent completion date of a predecessor activity. Once these schedule interrelationships are established, a total program schedule can be laid out by starting either from a selected begin-

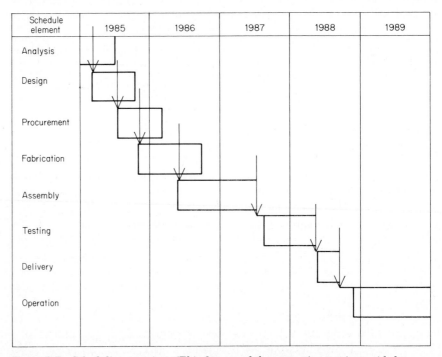

Figure 2-7 Scheduling a project. *(This figure and the supporting text is provided through the courtesy of John Wiley and Sons, COST ESTIMATING by Rodney D. Stewart, 1982, pp. 62–64.)*

ning point and working forward in time until the completion date is reached, or by starting from a desired completion date and working backward in time to derive the required schedule starting date. In many instances, you will find that both the start date and completion date are given. In that instance, the length of schedule elements and their interrelationships must be established through an iterative process to develop a schedule that accomplishes a job in the required time period. If all schedule activities are started as soon as their prerequisites are met, the result is the shortest possible time schedule to perform the work.

Most complex work activities have multiple paths of activity that must be accomplished parallel with each other. The longest of these paths is called a *critical path,* and the schedule critical path is developed by connecting all of the schedule activity critical paths. Construction of a schedule such as that shown on Figure 2-7 brings to light a number of other questions concerning a schedule. The first of these is, How do I establish the length of each activity? This question strikes at the heart of the overall estimating process itself, since many costs are incurred by the passage of time. Labor costs of an existing work force, overhead costs (insurance, rental, and utilities), and material handling and storage costs continue to pile up in an organization whether there is a productive output or not. Hence, it is important to develop the shortest possible overall schedule to accomplish a job and to accomplish each schedule element in the shortest time and in the most efficient method possible. The length of each schedule activity is established by an analysis of that schedule activity and the human and material resources available and required to accomplish it. Human resource and material estimating techniques are used extensively by the estimator in establishing the length of calendar time required to accomplish a schedule activity as well as the work-hours and materials required for its completion.

A second question is, What do I do if there are other influences on the schedule such as availability of facilities, equipment, and human resources? This is a factor that arises in most estimating situations. There are definite schedule interactions in any multiple-output organization that must be considered in planning a single work activity. Overall corporate planning must take into account these schedule interactions in its own critical path chart to assure that facilities, labor, and funds are available to accomplish all work activities in an effective and efficient manner. A final question is, How do I establish a credible "percent-complete" figure for each predecessor work activity? This is accomplished by breaking each activity into subactivities. For instance *design* can be subdivided into conceptual design, preliminary design, and final design. If the start of the procurement activity is to be keyed to the completion of preliminary design, then the time that preliminary design is complete determines the percentage of time and corresponding design activity that must be completed prior to the initiation of procurement.

Collecting Resource Data and Supporting Rationale

Since the resource information that goes into your cost estimate has a greater bearing on its accuracy and credibility than any other aspect of the estimate, we will devote considerable attention in this section as to where and how cost estimating data can be obtained. As mentioned earlier, one's own actual experience in producing like work activities or work outputs is the most valuable database available for estimating. Accumulation of a database with at least the following fields would be most helpful in an environment of continual needs for cost estimates:

1. Title and subtitle of the job
2. Date(s) work was performed
3. Location of work performance
4. Names of the skill categories used
5. Names of skill levels used within each category
6. Labor hours of each skill category and level used
7. Listing of materials types used
8. Quantities of each material used
9. Equipment and facilities used
10. Derived labor and material unit quantities
11. List of costs of subcontracts and purchased parts
12. Efficiency factor based on delays and problems encountered

Continual collection of data like the above through either manual or computer means will provide a basis for the development of estimating relationships that can be continually upgraded so that you will be prepared for just about any estimating situation.

Production Units

When specified in the contract or work statement, the number of units to be produced can be merely a matter of adding the percentage or number of units expected to be rejected in production or scrapped to the quantity to be delivered. But the estimation of the number of units of measure to be produced is often not that straightforward. For example, the numbers of engineering drawings required to document completely a subsystem or component design or the number of program statements required to write a computer software package may not be readily available in your database or easily and quickly estimated. Here is the place where the cost estimator must go directly to the person or persons who will be performing the job to determine the most likely production unit quantity. Careful drawing takeoff for quantities of subsystems, components, or parts; piping; wiring; fasteners; feet or inches of weld; etc.; will result in a good estimate of actual production output requirements.

Labor Unit Quantities

Labor unit quantities or *productivity factors* can be derived from your own in-house database of labor units required to complete various jobs. Be sure to take into account the actual efficiencies encountered and adjust these against the desired or predicted efficiencies to be expected in the new work. Where there are handbooks or standards available of the labor units needed to complete a unit of production based on machine feed and speed rates, etc., these can be used if adjusted appropriately for your organization.

Many organizations use a *realization factor* at this point in the estimating process to adjust what is theoretically possible to what can actually and more realistically be achieved. For example, one handbook shows that it is theoretically possible to weld sheet metal at a rate of 0.25 minutes per inch, while in actual practice, the JKL company experienced a capability of 0.40 minutes per inch, resulting in a realization factor of 1.60.

Labor unit quantities can be estimated at the lowest possible level (i.e., minutes or seconds per soldering connection) or at a higher level (minutes of soldering time per printed circuit board). At a higher level yet, the job can simply be *work-loaded* or staffed.

Handbooks such as *Machinery's Handbook,* published by Industrial Press, Inc., New York, contains speeds for milling, boring, drilling, and other metalworking operations on various metals and alloys with various Brinell hardness numbers. The U.S. Army Corps of Engineers periodically publishes a mammoth multivolume *unit price book* which gives labor hours and materials required for innumerable commercial construction tasks. Battelle's Columbus, Ohio, Laboratories has published a large multivolume handbook of work hours and dollars required to manufacture various aircraft structural components. Craftsman Book Company of Solana Beach, California, issues a whole series of data books each year with labor and materials costs for both residential and commercial construction tasks. An exhaustive literature search on almost every product or service line will undoubtedly bring to light more data than you really need on labor unit quantities. Do not forget to consult with your local university's engineering, industrial management, and business departments as there may be graduate students collecting productivity data in a number of fields for use in theses. (We recently ran across an exhaustive survey of highway maintenance productivity factors that was done as part of a master's thesis.) But keep in mind that your own company's productivity data are probably the best indicator of how it is going to perform on a job. So use other people's data, but do so cautiously.

Labor Rates

As is the case in labor unit quantities, labor unit prices must be based principally on your own in-house skill category and skill level salary structure. Tying down even which specific individuals will perform on a job will help lend realism to your wage rate assumptions in the proposal or cost estimate. However, if you are pursuing new markets in other geographical areas or other industries, there are still plenty of data available—principally from the Bureau of Labor Statistics under the Department of Commerce in Washington, D.C. Other sources of labor rate data are the trade unions, professional and technical societies, and publishers who specialize in printing large handbooks of labor wage data such as Construction Data Services, Inc., of Washington, D.C.

The key to developing a realistic labor estimate is the proper definition and selection of skill categories and skill levels within these skill categories. Examples of skill categories would be engineering manufacturing, quality and reliability assurance, tooling, and testing. Examples of skill levels within, say, the engineering category would be

Engineer level	Title
Engineer I	Engineer-in-training
Engineer II	Junior engineer
Engineer III	Assistant or associate engineer
Engineer IV	Engineer
Engineer V	Senior engineer
Engineer VI	Principal engineer
Engineer VII	Chief engineer
Engineer VIII	Engineering manager or director
Engineer IX	Vice president, engineering

If your organization is flexibly organized, it is wise to observe and adjust the skill level mix carefully to provide the lowest-cost crew at any point in the schedule. A skill mix with a higher percentage of more experienced (and higher paid) personnel may be appropriate at the beginning of a complex project; but as the work progresses, lower-paid skills can be placed on the job as the bugs get ironed out and the work becomes more routine and less demanding.

Labor unit prices for your own company can be obtained from your accounting or finance department. Estimators have a need to know about labor unit prices or labor rates because there are often resource constraints stated in terms of dollars, and for reasons mentioned earlier, the estimator may want to time-phase and balance skill levels to fit within a given funding profile. Since most of the microcomputer cost estimating programs that are available have a quick turnaround capability and can produce estimates very rapidly, there is ample opportunity to run an estimate several times with different labor rate profiles before final estimate publication.

Material Unit Quantities

Material unit quantities (or material usage factors) like labor unit quantities, can be obtained from past estimates, handbooks, or mathematical calculations based on the dimensions of the material units and finished product units (for example, the number of bricks or blocks per foot or yard of an 8-foot-high wall). Materials can be estimated at the lowest possible level (i.e., amount of solder required per solder joint), but it is often more practical to estimate materials on a per-job basis (i.e., amount of solder required for a printed circuit board assembly or an electronic component assembly).

Material Prices

Material unit prices are best obtained from direct quotes for specific quantities needed for the job at hand or to replenish material stocks. Often a price break can be obtained if quantities are sufficient. The capabilities of microcomputers will also permit the entry, storage, and update of a complete price and quantity structure for often-used materials. Then the estimating program can select the right price for the quantity desired through the use of "lookup" tables or database access programs. Some vertical market microcomputer systems have the feature of automatic on-line price updating through communications links. As the use of this type of data access procedure for material or part prices increases, cost estimates will become more timely, accurate, and competitive. If your business requires a rapid turnover of goods, materials, parts, or supplies, look for this capability in a microcomputer system.

Costs of Subcontracts and Purchased Parts

The very best type of data input from a subcontractor or part supplier is a written, firm price bid or quote. Since the supplier will have to develop a detailed cost estimate, the supplier's firm quote will be highly credible and can be relied upon as a verifiable cost number. The next best approach is to obtain a rough quote by telephone or to use data from past subcontracts of a similar nature with the same supplier. The same approach should be taken for large quantities of purchased parts, subsystems, components, tooling, or equipment.

Labor Overhead Percentage

The labor overhead percentage is obtained by dividing all labor-related indirect or overhead expenses by the company's total directly related costs in a given calendar period (and multiplying the result by 100 to convert to percentage). The total indirect or overhead expenses for the given calendar period (say, fiscal year) include the following cost elements:

1. Labor burden
   Bonuses
   Social security
   Supervisor's salary
   Pensions

   Health insurance
   Paid holidays
   Paid vacations

2. Other overhead
   Amortization
   Bid and proposal costs
   Claims
   Communications
   Custodial
   Depreciation
   Heating and cooling
   Independent research and development
   Industrial relations

   Insurance
   Lighting
   Maintenance
   Operating supplies
   Power
   Rental of buildings
   Waste disposal
   Water

Travel and Other Direct Costs

This cost category is included in most estimates because these costs do not normally fit well under the categories of labor, materials, subcontracts, and purchased parts. But these costs are easily allocable to a specific job, task, or work element. Travel costs include per diem (food and lodging), transportation (air, rental car, taxi fares), other on-site living expenses, and communications. Some other costs included in this category are directly related computer services, reproduction services, and directly related training costs. Cost data in these categories are obtained from direct quotes or past history of similar jobs.

G&A Percentage

The percentage of G&A expenses is obtained by dividing the total G&A costs incurred in a calendar period by the total plant or business costs

(labor, overhead, materials, and material burden) for that calendar period and multiplying by 100 to convert to percentage. General and administrative expenses are usually segregated from overhead expenses if the
company has a home office or corporate function above the on-site division that is proposing on the work. G&A costs include overall corporate
costs that are incurred for all divisions and typically include the following elements:

Administration	Finance
Advanced design	Marketing
Advertising	Personnel department
Corporate expenses	Research
Corporate taxes	Training department
Executive salaries	

Profit or Fee Percentage

Profit or fee is the reward for doing business; therefore, it is established
by the company at a level that will permit a reasonable return on the
investment required to do the work. Profit or fee is usually used to: (1)
provide the required return to company stockholders for investing in the
company; (2) reinvest funds into the company to ensure continued
growth; and (3) purchase important facilities, capital equipment, and
tooling required to assure a competitive posture and continued growth.
The profit or fee percentage is obtained by dividing the required profit or
fee dollar amounts for a calendar period by the total company income,
exclusive of fees, for a calendar period. This number may then be adjusted
by company management to account for: (1) increased or decreased demand for the product or service; (2) market analysis results that may
show that a different fee is warranted or achievable; or (3) company long-
term goals and objectives relative to profitability.

The Availability of Cost Estimating Data

One area that is of continuing concern to the cost estimator is the availability of estimating data. This is no problem to the estimator whose
company has kept complete, organized records of resource expenditures—
both estimated and actual—for all past jobs and whose jobs tend to be
rather standardized or routine. It is our observation, however, that there
are more companies who do not keep good, detailed, organized records of
past performance than who do; and with rapidly advancing technology,
continued product improvement, and changing product lines, the estimator is continually looking for outside sources of information. In this

regard there is good news for the estimator. There is a wealth of data available on labor unit quantities, material unit quantities, labor rates, and material prices if the estimator knows where to look for it. In an area or discipline that is normally thought to be highly competitive, there is, in fact, an abundance of estimating information available from outside sources.

Construction

By far the greatest wealth of data available in the cost estimating profession is in the construction industry. Many of these data can be immediately accessed by your own personal or office microcomputer through a modem and on-line data service from one of several companies. The largest suppliers of construction cost estimating data are the R. S. Means Company of Duxbury, Massachusetts; Sweet's Division of McGraw-Hill (the Dodge construction cost manuals and databases); and Richardson Engineering Services, Inc., of Solana Beach, California. Other sources are the Craftsman Book Company, of Solana Beach, California, and the United States Army Corps of Engineers at Huntsville, Alabama, and other locations. Some examples of the types of data available from these sources are shown later in this chapter.

Electronics and Manufacturing

The electronics and manufacturing industries have not been as free with their information as has the construction industry, but with some digging your can get reliable productivity data. The industry associations—such as the Electronics Industries Association, the Institute of Electrical and Electronic Engineers, and one of the 350 or so manufacturer associations, institutes, and societies ranging from the Adhesives Manufacturers Association of America to the Writing Instrument Manufacturers Association, Inc. (addresses of these can be obtained from a compilation published by Columbia Books, Washington, D.C.)—are excellent sources of productivity as well as wage rate data for jobs in their specific industries. The Defense Logistics Agency in Alexandria, Virginia, and Corporate-Tech Planning, Inc., of Waltham, Massachusetts, have put together a comprehensive compilation of electronics industry cost estimating data that can be obtained by special permission from the U.S. government and the publisher. This compilation includes mechanical and metalworking productivity as well as electronics manufacturing productivity data. Selected data on aerospace weapons systems and high technology productivity can be obtained from unclassified publications of Department of Defense (DOD) and National Aeronautics and Space Administration (NASA) that are available under the Freedom of Information Act.

Chemical and Process Engineering

The chemical and process industries have pioneered in the use of factors and indexes for estimating capital and utility costs for the processes, products, and services offered by those industries. Excellent data are available from the American Association of Cost Engineers, Morgantown, West Virginia; from *Chemical Engineering* magazine (published by McGraw-Hill); and from some excellent textbooks listed in the bibliography. Factors are updated periodically and are empirically fit to actual cost data from real-life projects—so these factors are highly reliable methods of getting realistic cost estimates.

Industrial Engineering Productivity Information

Overall industrial productivity as well as individual worker productivity figures can be obtained from the U.S. Department of Commerce, Bureau of Labor Statistics, and other government and nonprofit agencies. A good source of information about where to get industrial productivity factors is the Institute of Industrial Engineers at Norcross, Georgia.

Computer Software Development

In the rapidly growing and changing field of computer software, it is difficult to find good historical resource data. One good model, however, is described in the book *Software Engineering Economics* by Barry W. Boehm. This book defines a model named COCOMO (COnstructive COst MOdel). The book has information, methods, and factors for estimating software management, software systems engineering, software programming, software testing and validation, software documentation, software implementation, and software maintenance. The estimating factors and relationships were based on 63 actual software projects ranging from business systems applications to scientific and control applications; and the data include scheduling as well as costing relationships for computer software. Two other excellent references are: (1) *Handbook of Software Engineering* (articles starting on pages 469 and 494) (1984), and (2) *Software Engineering* (Chapter 6) (1983).

Labor Rates, Wages, and Salaries

The U.S. Bureau of Labor Statistics conducts the largest existing monthly sampling operation in the field of social statistics. An outfall of its mammoth data gathering and organization activity is a marvelous collection of labor rate, salary, and wage data. This collection of data is made available to the public at a nominal charge in the form of nine different publication titles, many of which are published periodically (monthly, quarterly, or yearly). These documents provide information on the geographic influences on wages and salaries, the comparison of incomes among various demographic groups, and the escalation and inflation factors for a large number of trades and professions. More general, summarized labor rate data can be obtained from *The American Almanac of Jobs and Salaries* (1984) and other similar commercially available publications. Trade unions are a good source of statistical, minimum, and recommended wage rates for various skill levels within given specialized trades. Updated wages and benefits for the construction trades are compiled periodically by Construction Data Services, Inc., of Washington, D.C., in its *Handbook of Wages and Benefits for Construction Unions.*

Material Prices

The descriptions and prices of materials, parts, supplies, and equipment can be obtained from the handbooks, catalogs, and supply manuals of individual suppliers or from any one of a number of compiled catalog series, *The Thomas Register* being one of the better-known ones. Material prices are also available from the same sources that provide labor unit price and labor productivity data.

Format and Content of Cost Estimating Data

Because of traditional accounting, cost-tracking, and pricing practices in various industries, there is very little uniformity in the format of cost estimating data. To illustrate what is possible, however, we will present here some ways that cost estimating data are formatted, displayed, and used in the discipline of construction. The displays are extracted from the computer-aided cost estimating system (CACES) that was developed and is maintained by the U.S. Army Corps of Engineers. Although the CACES is a mainframe computer system, many of the techniques of coding, organizing, displaying, and computing cost estimate data are applicable for microcomputer use. The data are also used to provide the reader with an idea of the typical scope and content of cost estimating data available. The Corps of Engineers' national cost estimating database is updated annually (every June). Regional databases (the United States is subdivided into 10 regions) are updated in July of each year, and location-specific databases are updated each August. The system uses labor rates for 41 different skills; contains 150 material adjustment indicators (used to update material costs for time and geographic location); has 150 types or pieces of equipment; lists crew costs for about 500 different construction crews (units consisting of different equipment skill categories and skill levels required to do a specific task); and contains labor, material, and equipment unit costs for about 25,000 items or tasks. The computer system will produce cost estimates containing work elements down to level 5 of the work breakdown structure. Because of the need to handle this mammoth amount of data, the corps has developed a highly structured coding and identification system. Since microcomputers are growing rapidly in memory and storage capability microcomputer users can take a page out of the corps' book and start to organize databases to handle larger amounts of data.

Reliability of Cost Estimating Data

If the work to be done is defined in detail at the outset of the project through an excellent "statement of work," and if the producer's own experience is used to derive the number of production units and unit costs, the estimate can be relied upon by management to be a true prediction of the most probable cost of the project or work activity. As more outside data are used, the reliability of the estimate will decrease, but not inordinately so if a careful matchup is made between the work being estimated and the historical data being used for the estimate. The various sources of data mentioned above have proved to be reliable for preliminary cost estimates and, where profit margins are sufficient to allow for some cost fluctuations, even for certain contract bidding situations. But, as Barry Boehm says in his book *Software Engineering Economics, "The only reliable data base for software cost estimating is that which has been developed by the organization that is going to do the work."* The same statement may tend to hold true for other services and products as well.

Geographic Variation of Costs

In 1983 the average labor rate for carpenters and electricians for Akron, Ohio, was just about equal to the national average wage rate for each of these skills or crafts. But in Anchorage, Alaska, the average rates for these skills was approximately 50 percent higher than the national average. In the meantime, the average labor rates in Nashville, Tennessee, for the same two skills was about 75 percent of the national average. What influences or causes this wide disparity in labor rates between different geographic locations? The case of Anchorage, Alaska, is easy to see because of the obvious added costs of transportation, energy consumption, and dislocation premiums for workers in Alaska. Actually, the variation in wages and salaries, and prices in general, is due to a number of factors.

Union disagreements; weather conditions that affect the actual available work hours; energy, labor force, and food availability; and even the community's traditions can have a bearing on wage and salary rates. The wages in large cities and metropolitan areas tend to be higher than those in the suburbs or rural areas. Wages in the north tend to be greater than those in the south, and so on. Most handbooks of labor and material unit quantities and rates or prices contain adjustment tables for each skill or trade for each geographic area. These wage modification factors are multiplied by the national average rate for the skill at hand to derive the local wage rate.

Effects of Inflation and Escalation

Inflation causes increases in labor rates and material prices, while escalation results in the need for more labor hours or materials to perform the same task (or the production of less work output with the same amount of labor hours or materials). *Inflation* is caused by the government spending more than its income, while *escalation* is caused by the following factors, generally in decreasing order:

1. Inaccuracies in the original resource estimates

2. Incomplete design or changes in design, production quantity, or schedule

3. Increases in overhead and fringe benefits

4. Unexpected or unplanned customer involvement

5. Increased government regulation and control

6. Inability to acquire or adapt personnel to the job (results in decreased productivity)

There is little we can do to control inflation, but at least we can allow for it and adjust estimates as inflation indexes change. Through perceptive planning and tight management, some of the factors that cause escalation can be controlled.

Accurate cost estimating using the most advanced planning and estimating methods and tools and subsequent aggressive management cost control of the project can do a lot to sizably reduce escalation. The impact of an incomplete design at the start of the project can be included in the cost estimate at the outset by a rule of thumb. If the design of the project is N percent complete, divide the cost estimate by $N/100$. The rationale for this rule of thumb is that if you have estimated a cost of $85,000 and the design is 85 percent complete, you have not estimated the other 15 percent. The remaining cost is likely to be at least equal to the remaining 15 percent, or $15,000, making the total probable cost at least $100,000.

Undue customer involvement can be avoided or at least predicted by good planning and contracting practices, as well as good management. Government regulation and control, union actions, and unexpected disasters cannot always be foreseen or predicted, so an additional cost growth allowance must be added for these eventualities. The important thing to remember is that an underestimate is caused by poor estimating and an overrun is caused by poor management. Defining which is which is difficult, but the estimator, using the best possible tools and techniques, can give management an estimate that is achievable.

Cost Indexes and Cost Models

Prior to the debut of the microcomputer, the cost estimator in smaller firms was limited to simple cost relationships and rules of thumb like the "six-tenths" rule below:

> When the cost of a particular item at one capacity is known, and the cost of that particular item at another capacity of X times the known is desired, divide the known capacity into the desired capacity, raise to the power of 0.6, and multiply by the known hours to obtain the hours for the second capacity.
>
> For example, if a pump with a capacity of 3 gallons per minute costs $45, how much does a pump with a capacity of 9 gallons per minute cost?

$$\text{Calculation:} \quad \frac{\text{Desired capacity}}{\text{Known capacity}} = \frac{9}{3} = 3$$

$$\text{Cost of larger pump} = 3^{0.6} \times \$45.00 = \$87.00$$

But now we have the microcomputer and we can deal quickly with a large number of variables that affect cost. In later chapters we will show how more complex cost estimating relationships can be derived with ease using modern computer spreadsheet, database, or integrated software packages. Cost may be a function of delivery schedule, weight, gallons-per-minute capacity, and revolutions per minute. Empirical equations can be developed to take into account all of these variables. The six-tenths factor has become a series of exponents that vary with the product, service, or industry involved and can be derived from historical data for each unique work activity.

Microestimating Symbols and Notations

Since this is a book about cost estimating with microcomputers, throughout the remainder of the book, we will use computer notation rather than conventional mathematical notation in equations, formulas, and mathematical relationships. This practice will permit the reader to adapt more readily to the input needs of programs written in the high order computer languages (FORTRAN, COBOL, BASIC), spreadsheet software packages, and computer database programs.

Conventional notation	Computer notation
Addition, $+$	$+$
Subtraction, $-$	$-$
Division, $\div$	/
Multiplication, $\times$	*
Exponentiation, N^2	N^2

Parentheses are used extensively in computer language formulas to separate the mathematical operations and to ensure that the computer knows in which sequence to perform the operation. Although the precedence of operations is relatively standard, it is always safe to use parentheses when in doubt. Be sure that there are the same number of right parentheses as there are left parentheses.

So much for the estimating fundamentals. Now, how do we compute an estimate using the various modern microcomputer tools?

3

BASIC
COST ESTIMATING PROGRAMS

Even though there are many handy spreadsheet programs, database systems, scheduling packages, and vertical market systems (see Chapters 4 to 7) available to assist in the job of cost estimating, a practicing professional, a small company, or small estimating group may want to start out with programs written in the BASIC computer language to perform routine analysis and estimating functions that are time-consuming and expensive if done by hand.

A Nucleus for Your Estimating Software

In this chapter, we provide a selected set of simple cost analysis and estimating computer programs that can be run with little or no modification on any computer that operates in the BASIC language. The programs are driven by a master menu called DATACOST and include several tools that are commonly used by estimators to solve problems related to developing cost estimating relationships, solving learning curve problems, and estimating interest expenses. To use these programs on your existing microcomputer, you merely have to type in the accompanying program listings, making any modifications necessary to conform to your

particular version of BASIC computer language (the programs given are
written in Microsoft BASIC for the Texas Instruments Professional Computer). All will run virtually unmodified on the IBM Personal Computer
or any computer that is compatible with the IBM Personal Computer.
(Since the authors hold the copyright on these programs, you are au-
thorized to reproduce them in hardcopy or software form for your own use
but not to sell or distribute them.)

Using the main menu (Figure 3-1) and the 7 programs provided, you
can add general- or special-purpose programs of your own choosing as
your knowledge of your computer system and the BASIC language increases. Even those who have had little or no experience with the BASIC
language can see from Figure 3-2 how easy it would be to add additional
items to the main menu, reference the corresponding file names, and add
the proper statement numbers in the GOTO statement on line 260. Of
course, any new program or file would have to be added to the same
diskette containing the menu and the seven BASIC programs that follow:

CER.ALS	CURVEL.ALS
BFIT.ALS	AMORT.ALS
TFU.ALS	MANYCOST.ALS
LCURVE.ALS	

Notice that the current time and date automatically appear on the
computer screen and printouts to help identify the latest version of a cost

```
                    D A T A C O S T (TM)

        (Copyright 1984 by MOBILE DATA SERVICES,Huntsville,AL)
        ----------------------------------------------
            DATE:07-29-1985                TIME:10:59:32

        NAME                    FUNCTION
    ******************************************************************
                    |
        1  CER      | Produces a linear cost estimating relationship
        2  BFIT     | Produces a least-squares best-fit learning curve
        3  TFU      | Calculates the theoretical first unit cost or hours
        4  LCURVE   | Computes costs or hours for N'th unit, large numbers
        5  CURVEL   | Computes costs or hours for N'th unit, small numbers
        6  AMORT    | Calculates monthly payment, interest,loan balance
        7  MANYCOST | Cost determination using multiple linear regression
        8  RESERVED |
        9  RESERVED |
       10 RESERVED |
       11 ******************* RETURN TO BASIC ****************************


    TO RUN ONE OF ABOVE, TYPE IN YOUR SELECTION NUMBER AND PRESS RETURN.WHICH SELECT
    ION WOULD YOU PREFER?
```

Figure 3-1 DATACOST menu.

analysis output. If your computer or BASIC language version does not support this feature you may omit statement 80 from the listing shown on Figure 3-2 and corresponding statements containing date and time on the listings provided later in this chapter for the other programs. To make the programs easy to operate, you can add your operating system files and BASIC language files to the same diskette. Then all that is required to bring up the main menu is to turn on the system, allow it to "boot," and type in BASIC DATACOST after the prompt "A:" or "A>" that appears on the video screen after the startup procedure is completed.

```
10 CLS ' THIS PROGRAM IS CALLED "DATACOST.BAS"
20 COLOR 7
30 PRINT TAB(24)"D  A  T  A  C  O  S  T  (TM)"
40 PRINT
50 COLOR 5
60 PRINT TAB(12) "(Copyright 1984 by MOBILE DATA SERVICES,Huntsville,AL)"
70 PRINT TAB(15) "---------------------------------------------"
75 COLOR 7
80 PRINT TAB(15) " DATE:";DATE$,"    TIME:";TIME$
82 PRINT
85 COLOR 5
90 PRINT TAB(5) "  NAME                    FUNCTION"
100 PRINT TAB(5) "**********************************************************
****"
110 PRINT TAB(17) "|"
120 PRINT TAB(5) "1  CER      | Produces a linear cost estimating relationship"
130 PRINT TAB(5) "2  BFIT     | Produces a least-squares best-fit learning curve
"
140 PRINT TAB(5) "3  TFU      | Calculates the theoretical first unit cost or ho
urs"
150 PRINT TAB(5 "4  LCURVE   | Computes costs or hours for N'th unit, large numb
ers"
160 PRINT TAB(5)"5  CURVEL   | Computes costs or hours for N'th unit, small numb
ers"
170 PRINT TAB(5) "6  AMORT    | Calculates monthly payment, interest,loan balanc
e"
180 PRINT TAB(5) "7  MANYCOST | Cost determination using multiple linear regress
ion"
190 PRINT TAB(5) "8  RESERVED |
200 PRINT TAB(5) "9  RESERVED |
210 PRINT TAB(5) "10 RESERVED |
220 PRINT TAB(5) "11 ****************** RETURN TO BASIC ***********************
*****"
230 PRINT
240 PRINT
250 INPUT "TO RUN ONE OF ABOVE, TYPE IN YOUR SELECTION NUMBER AND PRESS RETURN.W
HICH SELECTION WOULD YOU PREFER";S
260 ON S GOTO 290,300,310,320,330,340,350,360,370,380,390
270 COLOR 7
280 END
290 RUN "CER.ALS"
300 RUN "BFIT.ALS"
310 RUN "TFU.ALS"
320 RUN "LCURVE.ALS"
330 RUN "CURVEL.ALS"
340 RUN "AMORT.ALS"
350 RUN "MANYCOST.ALS"
360 RUN "LCPLOT.ALS"
370 RUN "LCOMP.ALS"
380 RUN "BARPLOT.ALS"
390 COLOR 7
400 CLS
410 END
```

Figure 3-2 Listing for DATACOST.BAS.

Linear Cost Estimating Relationships

The menu selection number 1 in Figure 3-1, which is called CER (cost estimating relationship) performs a least-squares best fit of a straight line to a set of cost or time data points. This program is used to develop the equation for a straight line that best represents the accumulated historical data represented by pairs of data points of cost or time (dependent variable) and some other factor like weight, speed, power, revolutions per minute, etc. (independent variable). This linear relationship is modeled by the equation:

$$Y = M*X + B \qquad\qquad (3\text{-}1)$$

where Y = the cost or time (dependent variable)
     M = the slope of the straight line
     X = the independent variable
     B = the intercept on the Y (cost or time) axis of the straight line

The least-squares best-fit method minimizes the sum of the squares of the vertical distances of each of the data points to the resulting best-fit straight line. The linear cost estimating relationship is the single most commonly used method of correlating data, but curved lines can also be fit to data points using power, exponential, or logarithmic relationships as follows:

POWER

$$Y = B*X^M \qquad\qquad (3\text{-}2)$$

where Y = the cost or time (dependent variable)
     B = the intercept at X = 1
     X = the independent variable
     M = the slope on a logarithmic plot

EXPONENTIAL

$$Y = A*e^{(B*X)} \qquad\qquad (3\text{-}3)$$

where   Y = the cost or time (dependent variable)
  A and B = derived constants
        e = 2.71828
        X = the dependent variable

LOGARITHMIC

$$Y = A + (B*\ln(X)) \qquad\qquad (3\text{-}4)$$

where   Y = the cost or time (dependent variable)
  A and B = derived constants
    ln(X) = the natural logarithm of the independent variable

The two general simultaneous equations used to obtain a linear cost estimating relationship are

1. $SUM(Y(I)) = (N*B) + (M*SUMX(I))$ $\qquad$ (3-5)

2. $SUM(Y(I)) * X(I) = B*SUM(X(I)) + (M*(SUM(X(I)))^2)$ $\qquad$ (3-6)

where $Y(I)$ = each value of the cost or time (dependent variable)
$\qquad X(I)$ = each value of the independent variable
$\qquad N$ = the number of data points
$\qquad B$ = the intercept on the cost or time (Y) axis (X = 0)
$\qquad M$ = the slope of the straight line

These two simultaneous equations can be solved for M to make it easy to use the equations in a BASIC program:

$$M = (((SUM(X(I)*Y(I))*N)/SUM(X(I)))) - SUM(Y(I)))/$$
$$(((SUM(X(I)^2)*N/(SUM\ X(I))) - SUM(X(I)))) \qquad (3-7)$$

You will notice in the program listing for "CER" on line 320 that the equation uses X1, X3, Y1 and Y3 to designate:

$X1 = SUM(X(I))$
$X3 = SUM(X(I)^2)$
$Y1 = SUM(Y(I))$
$Y3 = SUM(X(I)*Y(I))$

The B value or Y intercept for the line can then be determined by the equation:

$$B = (SUM(Y(I)) - (M*SUM(X(I))))/N \qquad (3-8)$$

To run the linear cost estimating relationship program, choose selection number 1 on the main menu. Then enter the number of pairs of data values to be evaluated and the values themselves as shown on Figure 3-3. On pressing ENTER or RETURN after the last data pair entry, the display shown on Figure 3-4 will appear. If you want a printout of the cost estimating relationship calculations, which repeats your inputs and the principal values used in the calculations, you can select Y or YES in answer to the question *Do you want this to be printed on the printer?*, and the resulting printout will appear as shown on Figure 3-5 (p. 43).

Armed with the slope and Y intercept point, you can then easily plot a straight line through plotted data points on cartesian coordinate graph paper and derive the cost or time for other points within the range of the plotted line. When you become more familiar with BASIC programming, you can then add a few program statements that will make the computer derive cost or time for this estimating relationship for any input value of

```
                    COST ESTIMATING RELATIONSHIP CALCULATIONS


        DATE:           10-16-1985
        TIME:           09:37:36

        ENTER THE NUMBER OF PAIRS OF POINTS TO BE EVALUATED  ? 10

        ENTER THE NEXT PAIR OF X AND Y VALUES ? 20,3.5
        ENTER THE NEXT PAIR OF X AND Y VALUES ? 30,7.4
        ENTER THE NEXT PAIR OF X AND Y VALUES ? 40,7.1
        ENTER THE NEXT PAIR OF X AND Y VALUES ? 60,15.6
        ENTER THE NEXT PAIR OF X AND Y VALUES ? 70,11.1
        ENTER THE NEXT PAIR OF X AND Y VALUES ? 90,14.9
        ENTER THE NEXT PAIR OF X AND Y VALUES ? 100,23.5
        ENTER THE NEXT PAIR OF X AND Y VALUES ? 120,27.1
        ENTER THE NEXT PAIR OF X AND Y VALUES ? 150,22.1
        ENTER THE NEXT PAIR OF X AND Y VALUES ? 180,32.9
```

Figure 3-3   Input screen for cost estimating relationship calculations.

```
        ENTER THE NEXT PAIR OF X AND Y VALUES ? 30,7.4
        ENTER THE NEXT PAIR OF X AND Y VALUES ? 40,7.1
        ENTER THE NEXT PAIR OF X AND Y VALUES ? 60,15.6
        ENTER THE NEXT PAIR OF X AND Y VALUES ? 70,11.1
        ENTER THE NEXT PAIR OF X AND Y VALUES ? 90,14.9
        ENTER THE NEXT PAIR OF X AND Y VALUES ? 100,23.5
        ENTER THE NEXT PAIR OF X AND Y VALUES ? 120,27.1
        ENTER THE NEXT PAIR OF X AND Y VALUES ? 150,22.1
        ENTER THE NEXT PAIR OF X AND Y VALUES ? 180,32.9
            WT        COST       CUM.WT    CUM CST    WT.SQ      CUM.SQ     CUM.PRD
          20.00       3.50       20.00      3.50     400.00     400.00       70.00
          30.00       7.40       50.00     10.90     900.00    1300.00      292.00
          40.00       7.10       90.00     18.00    1600.00    2900.00      576.00
          60.00      15.60      150.00     33.60    3600.00    6500.00     1512.00
          70.00      11.10      220.00     44.70    4900.00   11400.00     2289.00
          90.00      14.90      310.00     59.60    8100.00   19500.00     3630.00
         100.00      23.50      410.00     83.10   10000.00   29500.00     5980.00
         120.00      27.10      530.00    110.20   14400.00   43900.00     9232.00
         150.00      22.10      680.00    132.30   22500.00   66400.00    12547.00
         180.00      32.90      860.00    165.20   32400.00   98800.00    18469.00
        THE SLOPE OF THE ESTIMATING RELATIONSHIP IS:    .17157
        THE INTERCEPT ON THE COST AXIS IS:$ 1.764978
        DO YOU WANT THIS TO BE PRINTED ON THE PRINTER?(YES/NO)? N
        PROCESS ANOTHER CER (YES/NO) ?
```

Figure 3-4   Input and output screen for cost estimating relationship.

the independent variable. (Notice that the independent variable is named WEIGHT in this program and the dependent variable is called COST.) Further additions to this program can also be made to add the capability of power, exponential, and logarithmic equations as well as the linear relationship.

Figure 3-6 (p. 44) is a program listing of the program file called CER.ALS and can be put into your computer by typing in each program line statement exactly as shown in this figure. Be sure to proofread this and other programs before running them to minimize or eliminate any required debugging. This program can be amended or modified as desired to compute specific points on the CER line as in the MANYCOST example that appears later in this chapter or to plot the data points and the derived CER.

Learning Curves (Progress Functions)

The learning curve or progress function is an approximation of a geometric progression that forecasts the cost or labor-hour reduction from one unit of production to its succeeding unit. The units of production are assumed to be essentially identical from one production unit to the other, and the operation will be repetitive. The job content of the operation varies over a wide range of activities, with the job varying from a pure hands-on operation to jobs which are primarily mental exercises. A learning curve as plotted will forecast the cost or labor-hour reduction from one article to the next successive article. The amount of decrease will be less with each successive unit. The slope of the curve as plotted on logarithmic graph paper is used as the principle parameter in gauging

COST ESTIMATING RELATIONSHIP CALCULATIONS

10-16-1985   10:07:20

WT	COST	CUM.WT	CUM CST	WT.SQ	CUM.SQ	CUM.PRD
20.00	3.50	20.00	3.50	400.00	400.00	70.00
30.00	7.40	50.00	10.90	900.00	1300.00	292.00
40.00	7.10	90.00	18.00	1600.00	2900.00	576.00
60.00	15.60	150.00	33.60	3600.00	6500.00	1512.00
70.00	11.10	220.00	44.70	4900.00	11400.00	2289.00
90.00	14.90	310.00	59.60	8100.00	19500.00	3630.00
100.00	23.50	410.00	83.10	10000.00	29500.00	5980.00
120.00	27.10	530.00	110.20	14400.00	43900.00	9232.00
150.00	22.10	680.00	132.30	22500.00	66400.00	12547.00
180.00	32.90	860.00	165.20	32400.00	98800.00	18469.00

THE SLOPE OF THE ESTIMATING RELATIONSHIP IS: .17157
THE INTERCEPT ON THE COST AXIS IS:$ 1.764978

Figure 3-5 Output screen cost estimating relationship.

the effectiveness of a particular learning curve. The slope is usually expressed in percent, i.e., 80 percent, 85 percent, 90 percent. The slope is steeper as the percentage decreases. This slope can be used to express the ratio of the cost of any unit to the cost of double that unit value. For example, if the cost of the initial unit value of 90 percent curve is 100

```
10 CLS
20 COLOR 7
30 REM THIS PROGRAM IS NAMED "CER"
40 PRINT
50 PRINT TAB(15)"COST ESTIMATING RELATIONSHIP CALCULATIONS"
60 REM     X IS THE WEIGHT OR INDEPENDENT VARIABLE
70 REM     Y IS THE COST OR DEPENDENT VARIABLE
80 REM     X1 IS THE CUMULATIVE VALUES OF WEIGHT OF ALL POINTS
90 REM     Y1 IS THE CUMULATIVE VALUE OF THE COST OF ALL POINTS
100 REM    X2 IS THE WEIGHT SQUARED
110 REM    X3 IS THE CUMULATIVE VALUE OF THE WEIGHT SQUARED
120 REM    Y2 IS THE PRODUCT OF WEIGHT AND COST
130 REM    Y3 IS THE CUMULATIVE PRODUCT OF WEIGHT AND COST
140 REM    B IS THE INTERCEPT ON THE Y (COST) AXIS OF THE BEST FIT LINE
150 REM    M IS THE SLOPE OF THE BEST-FIT LINE
160 PRINT
170 PRINT "DATE:",DATE$
180 PRINT "TIME:",TIME$
190 PRINT
200 INPUT "ENTER THE NUMBER OF PAIRS OF POINTS TO BE EVALUATED   ";N
210 PRINT
220 X1=0:Y1=0:X3=0:Y3=0
230 FOR I=1 TO N
240 INPUT "ENTER THE NEXT PAIR OF X AND Y VALUES ";X(I),Y(I)
250 NEXT I
260 PRINT "       WT"; "       COST";"       CUM.WT   ";"CUM CST    ";"WT.SQ
    ";"CUM.SQ       ";"CUM.PRD    "
270 FOR I = 1 TO N
280 X1=X1+X(I):Y1=Y1+Y(I):X2=X(I)^2:X3=X3+X2:Y2=X(I)*Y(I)
290 Y3=Y3+Y2
300 PRINT USING "########.##"; X(I);Y(I);X1;Y1;X2;X3;Y3
310 NEXT I
320 M=(((Y3*N)/(X1))-Y1)/(((X3*N)/(X1))-X1)
330 PRINT "THE SLOPE OF THE ESTIMATING RELATIONSHIP IS: ";M
340 B=(Y1-(M*X1))/N
350 PRINT "THE INTERCEPT ON THE COST AXIS IS:$";B
360 INPUT "DO YOU WANT THIS TO BE PRINTED ON THE PRINTER?(YES/NO)";P$
370 IF P$ = "NO" THEN GOTO 550
380 IF P$ = "N" THEN GOTO 550
390 LPRINT
400 LPRINT TAB(15)"COST ESTIMATING RELATIONSHIP CALCULATIONS"
410 LPRINT
420 LPRINT DATE$,TIME$
430 LPRINT
440 X1=0:Y1=0:X3=0:Y3=0
450 LPRINT "       WT"; "       COST";"       CUM.WT   ";"CUM CST    ";"WT.SQ
    ";"CUM.SQ       ";"CUM.PRD    "
460 FOR I = 1 TO N
470 X1=X1+X(I):Y1=Y1+Y(I):X2=X(I)^2:X3=X3+X2:Y2=X(I)*Y(I)
480 Y3=Y3+Y2
490 LPRINT USING "########.##"; X(I);Y(I);X1;Y1;X2;X3;Y3
500 NEXT I
510 M=(((Y3*N)/(X1))-Y1)/(((X3*N)/(X1))-X1)
520 LPRINT "THE SLOPE OF THE ESTIMATING RELATIONSHIP IS: ";M
530 B=(Y1-(M*X1))/N
540 LPRINT "THE INTERCEPT ON THE COST AXIS IS:$";B
550 INPUT "PROCESS ANOTHER CER (YES/NO) ";A$
560 IF A$="YES" THEN GOTO 10
570 IF A$="Y" THEN GOTO 10
580 COLOR 7
590 RUN "DATACOST.BAS"
600 END
```

Figure 3-6 Listing for CER.

hours, the curve will predict that the second unit will take 90 hours, and the cost for the fourth unit will take 81 hours.

Another way of looking at the situation is to express the cost reduction in terms of a percentage of reduction, i.e., for an 80 percent learning curve the reduction will be 20 percent of the direct labor or direct cost. Each time the number of articles is doubled the reduction in direct labor or cost for the doubled unit will be 20 percent, and for a 90 percent curve it would be a reduction of 10 percent each time the quantity is doubled.

This "unit" learning curve scheme is called the "Crawford" system and is based on the following equation:

$$Y = B*X^M \tag{3-9}$$

where Y = the cost or labor hours required to produce the Xth unit
      B = the cost or labor hours to produce the first unit
      X = the number of units being evaluated
      M = the slope on a logarithmic plot and equals $\ln(P)/\ln(2)$, where P is the learning curve percentage expressed in positive hundredths (e.g., 0.80 for an 80 percent learning curve)

Notice that Equation (3-9) above is essentially the same as the power equation [Equation (3-2)]. If any three of the four values Y, B, X, or P are known, then the fourth value can be determined.

An approximate equation for the cumulative average labor hours or cost for X number of units if X is a large number (greater than 100) is

$$V = B*[((X*(1+M))/(((X+0.5)^{\wedge}(1+M)) - ((0.5)^{\wedge}(1+M))))^{\wedge}(1/M)]^{\wedge}M \tag{3-10}$$

where V = the cumulative average labor hours or costs required to produce X units
      B = the cost or labor hours required to produce the first unit
      X = the number of units being evaluated
      M = $\ln(P)/\ln(2)$, where P is the learning curve percentage expressed in positive hundredths (e.g., 0.80 for an 80 percent learning curve)

Various forms of the above equations are used in the learning curve programs BFIT, TFU, LCURVE, and CURVEL. Unfortunately, because of the need for special and unique symbols in computer programming, all of the above variables may not be immediately recognizable in the computer program listings provided. With some digging, however, and an understanding of the BASIC computer software programming language, you can relate the equations in the program listings to Equations (3-9) and (3-10) above.

Determining Learning Curve Percentage (Slope)

Menu selection 2, BFIT, uses the least-squares linear regression technique to find the resulting estimated learning curve percentage if two or more values on the learning curve are known. This program uses Equation (3-9) in conjunction with Equations (3-5) to (3-8) to solve for learning curve percentage and theoretical first unit (TFU) hours or dollars. The only difference between the technique used here and that used in the CER program is that the B and M values in Equation (3-9) are transformed into natural logarithmic form prior to manipulation by Equations (3-5) through (3-8).

To compute a best-fit learning curve, select menu option 2. The display shown on Figure 3-7 will appear on your monitor, and the program will ask you for the number of data sets and the X and Y values for each data set. The X value is the number of the unit for which the cost or hours are known, and the Y value is the labor hours or cost of that Xth unit.

When the last data pair is entered, press ENTER or RETURN to display the information shown in Figure 3-8. The TFU cost or hours and the learning curve percentage can now be used in one or more of the subsequent learning curve programs as required to solve specific problems associated with the derived learning curve percentage. Figure 3-9 (p. 48) is a program listing of BFIT, which can be keyed into your computer to serve as part of your overall estimating software package or be subsequently added to or modified to suit your own needs.

```
                    BEST FIT LEARNING CURVE PROGRAM



  DATE:           10-16-1985
  TIME:           08:51:36

  HOW MANY PAIRS OF DATA POINTS ARE YOU GOING TO ENTER? 5
  ******************************************************************************
   'X' is the NUMBER of the unit for which the cost or hours are known.
   'Y' is the COST or HOURS for that 'X'th unit.
  ******************************************************************************
  INPUT DATA IN THE FORM X,Y
  INPUT DATA PAIR #  1
  ? 8,700
  INPUT DATA PAIR #  2
  ? 20,900
  INPUT DATA PAIR #  3
  ? 10,500
  INPUT DATA PAIR #  4
  ? 100,600
  INPUT DATA PAIR #  5
  ? 100,350
```

Figure 3-7   Input screen for best-fit learning curve program.

The Theoretical First Unit (TFU)

Occasionally in learning curve problems it is desirable to compute the labor hours or costs *theoretically* needed to produce the very first unit of production when one point on the learning curve and the learning curve percentage are known. This computation is sometimes desirable as a check of the reasonableness of the assumed learning curve percentage. If an unrealistically high or low theoretical first unit value is derived, then the learning curve percentage assumption may be subject to question. Figure 3-10 (p. 49) shows how the input screen appears for this program and Figure 3-11 (p. 49) displays the screen display after computation of the results. (Notice that in the programs contained in this chapter, the user can exercise the option to print out the results of the computation so it can be available in hard-copy form for later reference and ease of use. Also notice that these programs permit optimal multiple runs without returning to the main menu.) The program listing for TFU is shown in Figure 3-12 (p. 50).

Learning in Large Production Lots

Menu selection number 4, LCURVE, is a program that computes the unit and cumulative average labor hours or costs for unit numbers over 100. The program will work for lower numbers of units, say 10 to 100, but will not yield as accurate results as the CURVEL program that follows be-

```
THIS IS DATA YOU INPUT :
PAIR          X                Y
 1            8               700
 2            20              900
 3            10              500
 4            100             600
 5            100             350
HERE ARE TRANSFORMED DATA POINTS TO BE FIT :
PAIR          LN X            LN Y
 1            2.079442         6.55108
 2            2.995732         6.802395
 3            2.302585         6.214608
 4            4.60517          6.39693
 5            4.60517          5.857933
SUMMATION OF X VALUES IS      16.5881
SUMMATION OF Y VALUES IS      31.82295
SUMMATION OF X*Y VALUES IS    104.7461
SUMMATION OF X^2 VALUES IS    61.01557
S=            -.1387885
B=            6.825036
THE THEORETICAL FIRST UNIT COST OR HOURS ARE: 920.6092
THE LEARNING CURVE PERCENTAGE IS: % 90.82816
DO YOU WANT THIS TO BE PRINTED ON THE PRINTER?(YES/NO)? N
DO YOU WANT TO RUN ANOTHER BEST FIT LEARNING CURVE?(YES/NO)?
```

Figure 3-8   Output screen for best-fit learning curve program.

```
10 CLS
20 COLOR 6
30 PRINT TAB(20) "BEST FIT LEARNING CURVE PROGRAM"
40 PRINT:PRINT:PRINT
45 PRINT "DATE:",DATE$
46 PRINT "TIME:",TIME$
47 PRINT
50 REM PROGRAM FITS "BEST" LEARNING CURVE TO DATA POINTS
60 REM USES LINEAR LEAST SQUARES ON TRANSFORMED (LOGARITHM) DATA VALUES
70 INPUT "HOW MANY PAIRS OF DATA POINTS ARE YOU GOING TO ENTER";N
75 PRINT "*************************************************************"
80 PRINT " 'X' is the NUMBER of the unit for which the cost or hours are known.
90 PRINT " 'Y' is the COST or HOURS for that 'X'th unit.
95 PRINT "*************************************************************"
100 PRINT "INPUT DATA IN THE FORM X,Y"
110 FOR I=1 TO N
120 PRINT "INPUT DATA PAIR # ";I
130 INPUT X(I),Y(I)
140 NEXT I
150 PRINT "THIS IS DATA YOU INPUT :"
160 PRINT "PAIR","X","Y"
170 FOR I=1 TO N
180 PRINT I,X(I),Y(I)
190 NEXT I
200 FOR I=1 TO N
210 LNX(I)=LOG(X(I))
220 LNY(I)=LOG(Y(I))
230 NEXT I
240 PRINT "HERE ARE TRANSFORMED DATA POINTS TO BE FIT :"
250 PRINT "PAIR","LN X","LN Y"
260 FOR I=1 TO N
270 PRINT I,LNX(I),LNY(I)
280 NEXT I
290 SX=0
300 FOR I=1 TO N
310 SX=SX+LNX(I)
320 NEXT I
330 PRINT "SUMMATION OF X VALUES IS ",SX
340 SY=0
350 FOR I=1 TO N
360 SY=SY+LNY(I)
370 NEXT I
380 PRINT "SUMMATION OF Y VALUES IS ",SY
390 SXY=0:SXSQ=0
400 FOR I=1 TO N
410 SXY=SXY+(LNX(I)*LNY(I))
420 SXSQ=SXSQ+(LNX(I)*LNX(I))
430 NEXT I
440 PRINT "SUMMATION OF X*Y VALUES IS ",SXY
450 PRINT "SUMMATION OF X^2 VALUES IS ",SXSQ
460 S=(N*SXY-(SX*SY))/(N*SXSQ-(SX*SX))
470 B=(SY/N)-(S*SX/N)
480 PRINT "S=",S
490 PRINT "B=",B
500 LC=100*2^S
510 K=EXP(B)
520 PRINT "THE THEORETICAL FIRST UNIT COST OR HOURS ARE:";K
530 PRINT "THE LEARNING CURVE PERCENTAGE IS: %";LC
540 INPUT "DO YOU WANT THIS TO BE PRINTED ON THE PRINTER?(YES/NO)";P$
550 IF P$ = "NO" THEN GOTO 640
560 IF P$ = "N" THEN GOTO 640
570 LPRINT "DATA POINTS ARE"
580 LPRINT:LPRINT "X","Y"
590 FOR I=1 TO N
600 LPRINT X(I),Y(I)
610 NEXT I
620 LPRINT:LPRINT "THE THEORETICAL FIRST UNIT COST OR HOURS ARE:";K
630 LPRINT:LPRINT "THE LEARNING CURVE PERCENTAGE IS: %";LC
640 INPUT "DO YOU WANT TO RUN ANOTHER BEST FIT LEARNING CURVE?(YES/NO)";R$
650 IF R$ = "YES" THEN GOTO 10
660 IF R$ = "Y" THEN GOTO 10
670 COLOR 7
680 RUN "DATACOST.BAS"
```

Figure 3-9 Listing for BFIT.

cause of the approximation formula that is used. The principal formulas used in this program are based on Equations (3-9) and (3-10). Figure 3-13 (p. 50) shows the input screen and Figure 3-14 (p. 51) shows the inputs and outputs after the computations are completed. The *algebraic midpoint* of the quantity is the unit number that has exactly the cumulative average value. In this case, the cumulative average value of labor hours or dollars falls between the 3280th and 3281st units. The program listing for LCURVE is shown in Figure 3-15 (p. 52).

Learning in Small Production Lots

Menu selection 5, CURVEL, is based on exact computations of Xth unit values. Because it is based on exact equations, it takes longer to compute

```
                    THEORETICAL FIRST UNIT PROGRAM (TFU)

      DATE:           10-16-1985
      TIME:           09:14:54

      ENTER THE LEARNING CURVE PERCENTAGE ? 85

      ENTER THE UNIT NUMBER FOR WHICH THE HOURS ARE KNOWN ? 100

      ENTER THE HOURS REQUIRED TO PRODUCE THAT UNIT ? 1250
```

Figure 3-10   Input screen for theoretical first unit program.

```
                    THEORETICAL FIRST UNIT PROGRAM (TFU)


      DATE:           10-16-1985
      TIME:           09:14:54

      ENTER THE LEARNING CURVE PERCENTAGE ? 85

      ENTER THE UNIT NUMBER FOR WHICH THE HOURS ARE KNOWN ? 100

      ENTER THE HOURS REQUIRED TO PRODUCE THAT UNIT ? 1250

      FOR A LEARNING CURVE OF   85 PERCENT AND A 100 TH UNIT
      MAN-HOURS OF 1250 :
      THE MAN-HOURS THEORETICALLY REQUIRED TO PRODUCE THE FIRST
      UNIT ARE 3679.939 HOURS.
      DO YOU WANT THIS TO BE PRINTED ON THE PRINTER?(YES/NO)? N
      PROCESS ANOTHER TFU (YES/NO) ?
```

Figure 3-11   Output screen for theoretical first unit program.

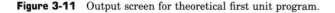

than LCURVE and, therefore, it is recommended for fewer numbers of units (say less than 100). If the value 1.00 is used for the first unit hours, a learning curve factor table will result. This feature is handy because it eliminates the necessity of running the program every time a new unit number must be found and replaces the need for large, voluminous handbooks of learning curve factors because you need only print out values for

```
10 CLS
20 COLOR 7
30  PRINT TAB(20) "THEORETICAL FIRST UNIT PROGRAM (TFU)"
40  PRINT
50 PRINT "DATE:",DATE$
60 PRINT "TIME:",TIME$
70 PRINT
80 REM  THIS PROGRAM IS DESIGNED TO COMPUTE THE MAN-HOURS THEORETICALLY
90 REM  REQUIRED TO PRODUCE THE FIRST UNIT WHEN THE HOURS 'Y' REQUIRED
100 REM  TO PRODUCE THE X1TH UNIT AND THE LEARNING CURVE PERCENTAGE 'N'
110 REM ARE KNOWN.
120 REM
130 REM   "THIS PROGRAM APPLIES TO THE CRAWFORD SYSTEM ONLY"
140 REM
150 INPUT "ENTER THE LEARNING CURVE PERCENTAGE ";N:PRINT
160 INPUT "ENTER THE UNIT NUMBER FOR WHICH THE HOURS ARE KNOWN ";X1
170 PRINT
180 INPUT "ENTER THE HOURS REQUIRED TO PRODUCE THAT UNIT ";Y1:PRINT
190 B = (LOG(N/100)/LOG(2))
200 K = (Y1)/(X1^B)
210 PRINT "FOR A LEARNING CURVE OF "; N; "PERCENT AND A";X1;"TH UNIT"
220 PRINT "MAN-HOURS OF";Y1;":"
230 PRINT "THE MAN-HOURS THEORETICALLY REQUIRED TO PRODUCE THE FIRST"
240 PRINT "UNIT ARE";K; "HOURS."
250 INPUT "DO YOU WANT THIS TO BE PRINTED ON THE PRINTER?(YES/NO)";P$
260 IF P$ = "NO" THEN GOTO 370
270 IF P$ = "N" THEN GOTO 370
280 LPRINT TAB(10) "MOBILE DATA SERVICES THEORETICAL FIRST UNIT PROGRAM (TFU)"
290 LPRINT
300 LPRINT DATE$,TIME$
310 B = (LOG(N/100)/LOG(2))
320 K = (Y1)/(X1^B)
330 LPRINT "FOR A LEARNING CURVE OF "; N; "PERCENT AND A";X1;"TH UNIT"
340 LPRINT "MAN-HOURS OF";Y1;":"
350 LPRINT "THE MAN-HOURS THEORETICALLY REQUIRED TO PRODUCE THE FIRST"
360 LPRINT "UNIT ARE";K; "HOURS."
370 INPUT "PROCESS ANOTHER TFU (YES/NO) ";A$
380 IF A$ = "YES" THEN GOTO 10
390 IF A$ = "Y" THEN GOTO 10
400 RUN "DATACOST.BAS"
```

Figure 3-12 Listing for theoretical first unit program.

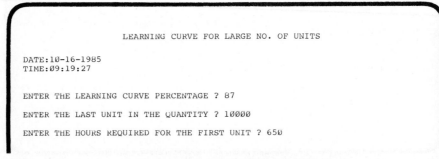

```
           LEARNING CURVE FOR LARGE NO. OF UNITS

  DATE:10-16-1985
  TIME:09:19:27


  ENTER THE LEARNING CURVE PERCENTAGE ? 87

  ENTER THE LAST UNIT IN THE QUANTITY ? 10000

  ENTER THE HOURS REQUIRED FOR THE FIRST UNIT ? 650
```

Figure 3-13 Input screen for learning curve for large number of units.

the specific learning curve percentage you are using at the time. This program also eliminates the need for interpolation between learning curve percentage or unit numbers because the unique percentage and unit numbers desired can be subject to analysis. Figure 3-16 (p. 53) shows an input example based on a TFU value of 650 hours, and the results are shown in Figure 3-17 (p. 53). Figure 3-18 (p. 54) shows the instances where a learning curve factor table is desired for an 82.75 percent learning curve, and Figure 3-19 (p. 55) shows the resulting learning curve factor table. Using this table, the estimator merely needs to multiply the theoretical first unit labor hours or dollars by the factor(s) shown in columns 2 and/or 4 to derive the unit labor hours or dollars and/or cumulative average labor hours or dollars, respectively. The computer program statement listing for this program, called CURVEL.ALS, was shown earlier in Chapter 1 as Figure 1-1.

Estimating Interest Expenses

Menu selection 6 will run a program called AMORT.ALS, which computes the monthly payment, interest and principal amounts in each payment, balance remaining, and total interest to be paid on a loan. Figure 3-20 (p. 56) shows how the three inputs: loan amount, interest rate percentage, and loan term in years are entered. Figure 3-21 (p. 56) shows a

```
                   LEARNING CURVE FOR LARGE NO. OF UNITS


   DATE:10-16-1985
   TIME:09:19:27


  ENTER THE LEARNING CURVE PERCENTAGE ? 87

  ENTER THE LAST UNIT IN THE QUANTITY ? 10000

  ENTER THE HOURS REQUIRED FOR THE FIRST UNIT ? 650

     THE FOLLOWING VALUES HAVE BEEN COMPUTED FOR A 87
     PERCENT LEARNING CURVE WHEN THE FIRST UNIT TAKES 650
   HOURS

  THE ALGEBRAIC MIDPOINT OF THE QUANTITY IS 3280.116
  THE TOTAL MAN-HOURS REQUIRED FOR THIS QUANTITY IS: 1277988
  THE MAN-HOURS OF THE LAST UNIT IN THE LOT IS 102.1537 HOURS.
  THE CUMULATIVE AVERAGE MAN-HOURS FOR THIS QUANTITY IS 127.7988
  DO YOU WANT THIS PRINTED ON THE PRINTER? (YES/NO)?
```

Figure 3-14   Output screen for learning curve for large number of units.

printout of the amortization schedule for a $10,000 loan at 13.5 percent for 4 years. The program listing in BASIC is shown in Figure 3-22 (p. 57).

Cost or Time Determination Using Multiple Linear Regression

In some instances the cost estimator would like to express or find labor hours or cost in terms of two or more independent variables. For example,

```
10 CLS
20 COLOR 7
30 REM THIS PROGRAM IS NAMED "LCURVE"
40 PRINT TAB(20) "LEARNING CURVE FOR LARGE NO. OF UNITS"
50 PRINT
60   PRINT "DATE:";DATE$
70   PRINT "TIME:";TIME$
80   PRINT
90 REM   THIS PROGRAM IS FILED UNDER "LCURVE.ALS"
100 PRINT
110 REM   LCURVE WILL COMPUTE THE HOURS REQUIRED TO PRODUCE THE Q1'TH UNIT
120 REM   OF A PRODUCT AND THE TOTAL AND CUMULATIVE MAN-HOURS REQUIRED TO
130 REM   PRODUCE A PRODUCTION LOT STARTING AT S1 AND ENDING WITH Q1
140 REM   OTHER INPUTS ARE THE LEARNING CURVE PERCENTAGE (L1) AND THE FIRST
150 REM   UNIT HOURS (H1).  SINCE THIS PROGRAM IS BASED ON APPROXIMATE
160 REM   FORMULAS, IT WILL NOT GIVE EXACT ANSWERS:  USE IF FOR QUANTITIES
170 REM   OF TEN OR MORE.  FOR QUANTITIES OF UP TO 100, USE THE PROGRAM
180 REM   ENTITLED "CURVEL."
190 INPUT "ENTER THE LEARNING CURVE PERCENTAGE ";L1:PRINT
200 INPUT "ENTER THE LAST UNIT IN THE QUANTITY ";Q1:PRINT
210 INPUT "ENTER THE HOURS REQUIRED FOR THE FIRST UNIT ";H1:PRINT
220 B1=(LOG(L1/100)/LOG(2)):F1=Q1
230 PRINT "    THE FOLLOWING VALUES HAVE BEEN COMPUTED FOR A";L1
240 PRINT "    PERCENT LEARNING CURVE WHEN THE FIRST UNIT TAKES";H1
250 PRINT "  HOURS"
260 PRINT
270 Q2 = ((Q1*(1+B1))/(((F1+.5)^(1+B1))-((.5)^(1+B1))))^-(1/B1)
280 PRINT "THE ALGEBRAIC MIDPOINT OF THE QUANTITY IS";Q2
290 H3 = H1*Q2^B1:H4=Q1*H3
300 PRINT "THE TOTAL MAN-HOURS REQUIRED FOR THIS QUANTITY IS:";H4
310 H5 = H1*(F1+1)^B1
320 PRINT "THE MAN-HOURS OF THE LAST UNIT IN THE LOT IS";H5;"HOURS."
330 PRINT "THE CUMULATIVE AVERAGE MAN-HOURS FOR THIS QUANTITY IS";H3
340 INPUT "DO YOU WANT THIS PRINTED ON THE PRINTER? (YES/NO)"; P$
350 IF P$ = "NO" THEN GOTO 530
360 IF P$ = "N" THEN GOTO 530
370 LPRINT TAB(20) "LEARNING CURVE FOR LARGE NO. OF UNITS"
380 LPRINT
390 LPRINT DATE$,TIME$
400 LPRINT "AVERAGE IS DESIRED)":PRINT
410 B1=(LOG(L1/100)/LOG(2)):F1=Q1
420 LPRINT "    THE FOLLOWING VALUES HAVE BEEN COMPUTED FOR A";L1
430 LPRINT "    PERCENT LEARNING CURVE WHEN THE FIRST UNIT TAKES";H1
440 LPRINT "  HOURS"
450 LPRINT
460 Q2 = ((Q1*(1+B1))/(((F1+.5)^(1+B1))-((.5)^(1+B1))))^-(1/B1)
470 LPRINT "THE ALGEBRAIC MIDPOINT OF THE QUANTITY IS";Q2
480 H3 = H1*Q2^B1:H4=Q1*H3
490 LPRINT "THE TOTAL MAN-HOURS REQUIRED FOR THIS QUANTITY IS:";H4
500 H5 = H1*(F1+1)^B1
510 LPRINT "THE MAN-HOURS OF THE LAST UNIT IN THE LOT IS";H5;"HOURS."
520 LPRINT "THE CUMULATIVE AVERAGE MAN-HOURS FOR THIS QUANTITY IS";H3
530 INPUT "PROCESS ANOTHER LCURVE (YES/NO) ";A$
540 IF A$="YES" THEN GOTO 10
550 IF A$ = "Y" THEN GOTO 10
560 COLOR 7
570 RUN "DATACOST.BAS"
580 END
```

Figure 3-15 Listing for LCURVE.

```
                    LEARNING CURVE FOR SMALL NO. OF UNITS

DATE:10-16-1985
TIME:09:27:47

PUT IN THE LEARNING CURVE PERCENTAGE ? 87

IF ONE (1) IS USED FOR THE FIRST UNIT HOURS, A LEARNING CURVE
FACTOR TABLE WILL RESULT

PUT IN THE HOURS REQUIRED FOR THE FIRST UNIT ? 650

PUT IN THE NUMBER OF UNITS ? 10
```

Figure 3-16   Input screen for learning curve for small number of units.

```
PUT IN THE LEARNING CURVE PERCENTAGE ? 87

IF ONE (1) IS USED FOR THE FIRST UNIT HOURS, A LEARNING CURVE
FACTOR TABLE WILL RESULT

PUT IN THE HOURS REQUIRED FOR THE FIRST UNIT ? 650

PUT IN THE NUMBER OF UNITS ? 10

UNIT, CUM, & CUM AVG HRS FOR A L.C. OF 87 % & TFU HRS OF 650 :

UNIT NO.   XTH UNIT HRS.    CUM TOTAL      CUM AVERAGE
  1          650            650            650
  2          565.5          1215.5         607.75
  3          521.2591       1736.759       578.9197
  4          491.985        2228.744       557.1861
  5          470.4153       2699.16        539.832
  6          453.4955       3152.655       525.4425
  7          439.6656       3592.32        513.1886
  8          428.027        4020.347       502.5434
  9          418.017        4438.365       493.1516
 10          409.2613       4847.626       484.7626
DO YOU WANT THIS PRINTED ON THE PRINTER?(YES/NO)? N
```

Figure 3-17   Output screen for learning curve for small number of units.

the cost of an airplane may be correlated to its speed, weight, range, and payload; the cost of a milling machine may be expressed in terms of its cutting speed, depth of cut, and maximum workpiece size; or the labor hours required to produce a pump may be expressed in terms of weight and gallons-per-minute capacity. To develop these relationships, it is necessary to have several sets of data from previously made detailed estimates or from actual experience in manufacturing and selling the product. The more data sets that are available, the more representative the resulting estimate. The cost estimator may also want to know how well the data fit together or correlate. Measures of this fit are the coefficient of determination, the coefficient of multiple correlation, and the standard error. These values indicate how well the data points fit the derived estimating relationship. The standard error measures the average amount that the data points deviate from those which would be calculated from the derived equation. Naturally, the smaller the standard error, the better. The coefficient of multiple correlation also measures the closeness of fit of the regression equation to the sample data. The better the fit, the closer the coefficient of multiple correlation will be to 1. The coefficient of multiple correlation is the ratio of the explained deviation to the total deviation, where the total deviation is the sum of the explained and unexplained deviations defined below:

Explained deviation.   The difference between calculated values of the dependent variable and the mean value of the dependent variable (cost or labor hours).

```
                         LEARNING CURVE FOR SMALL NO. OF UNITS


    DATE:10-16-1985
    TIME:09:33:36

    PUT IN THE LEARNING CURVE PERCENTAGE ? 82.75

    IF ONE (1) IS USED FOR THE FIRST UNIT HOURS, A LEARNING CURVE
    FACTOR TABLE WILL RESULT

    PUT IN THE HOURS REQUIRED FOR THE FIRST UNIT ? 1

    PUT IN THE NUMBER OF UNITS ? 50
```

Figure 3-18   Input screen for learning curve for small number of units.

Unexplained deviation. The difference between actual measured data points (the input values) of the dependent variable (cost or labor hours) and the value that would be calculated from the derived equation.

Another way of expressing the degree of closeness of fit of the data points to the derived equation is through the use of the coefficient of determination. The coefficient of determination is merely the coefficient of multiple correlation squared.

```
                   LEARNING CURVE FOR SMALL NO. OF UNITS

10-16-1985      09:35:09

LEARNING CURVE FACTORS FOR A CURVE OF 82.75 PERCENT ARE:
UNIT, CUM, & CUM AVG HRS FOR A L.C. OF 82.75 % & TFU HRS OF 1 :

UNIT NO.    XTH UNIT HRS.    CUM TOTAL      CUM AVERAGE
  1         1                1              1
  2          .8275           1.8275          .91375
  3          .7407392        2.568239        .8560798
  4          .6847562        3.252996        .8132489
  5          .644263         3.897259        .7794518
  6          .6129616        4.51022         .7517033
  7          .5876862        5.097906        .7282723
  8          .5666357        5.664542        .7080677
  9          .5486946        6.213237        .6903596
 10          .5331276        6.746364        .6746364
 11          .5194263        7.26579         .6605263
 12          .5072257        7.773016        .6477513
 13          .4962555        8.269271        .6360978
 14          .4863103        8.755581        .6253986
 15          .4772308        9.232812        .6155208
 16          .468891         9.701703        .6063565
 17          .4611898        10.16289        .5978173
 18          .4540448        10.61694        .5898299
 19          .447388         11.06433        .582333
 20          .441163         11.50549        .5752745
 21          .4353223        11.94081        .56861
 22          .4298252        12.37064        .5623016
 23          .4246376        12.79527        .5563162
 24          .4197293        13.215          .5506251
 25          .4150747        13.63008        .545203
 26          .4106514        14.04073        .540028
 27          .4064396        14.44717        .5350803
 28          .4024218        14.84959        .5303425
 29          .3985826        15.24817        .5257991
 30          .3949085        15.64308        .5214361
 31          .3913871        16.03447        .5172409
 32          .3880073        16.42248        .5132024
 33          .3847594        16.80724        .5093102
 34          .3816345        17.18887        .505555
 35          .3786245        17.56749        .5019284
 36          .375722         17.94322        .4984227
 37          .3729204        18.31614        .4950308
 38          .3702135        18.68635        .4917461
 39          .3675959        19.05395        .4885627
 40          .3650624        19.41901        .4854752
 41          .3626082        19.78162        .4824785
 42          .3602291        20.14185        .4795678
 43          .357921         20.49977        .4767388
 44          .3556804        20.85545        .4739875
 45          .3535036        21.20895        .4713101
 46          .3513875        21.56034        .4687031
 47          .3493292        21.90967        .4661632
 48          .3473259        22.257          .4636874
 49          .3453751        22.60237        .4612729
 50          .3434743        22.94584        .4589169
```

Figure 3-19 Printout for learning curve for small number of units.

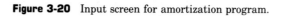

```
                          AMORTIZATION PROGRAM

     DATE:10-16-1985
     TIME:09:43:59

     ENTER THE AMOUNT OF THE LOAN? 10000
     WHAT IS THE INTEREST RATE PERCENTAGE? 13.5
     ENTER THE TERM IN YEARS? 4
```

Figure 3-20 Input screen for amortization program.

```
DATE:10-16-1985          TIME:09:49:13
FOR A LOAN OF $ 10000 AT AN INTEREST RATE OF 13.5 %,
FOR 4 YEARS:
THE MONTHLY PAYMENT IS $ 270.76
```

PMT	INTEREST	PRINCIPAL	BALANCE	TOTAL INTEREST
1	112.5	158.26	9841.74	112.5
2	110.72	160.04	9681.7	223.22
3	108.92	161.84	9519.86	332.14
4	107.1	163.66	9356.2	439.24
5	105.26	165.5	9190.7	544.5
6	103.4	167.36	9023.34	647.9
7	101.51	169.25	8854.09	749.41
8	99.61	171.15	8682.94	849.02
9	97.68	173.08	8509.86	946.7
10	95.74	175.02	8334.84	1042.44
11	93.76	176.99	8157.85	1136.21
12	91.78	178.98	7978.87	1227.99
13	89.76	181	7797.87	1317.75
14	87.73	183.03	7614.84	1405.48
15	85.67	185.09	7429.75	1491.15
16	83.58	187.18	7242.57	1574.73
17	81.48	189.28	7053.29	1656.21
18	79.35	191.41	6861.88	1735.56
19	77.2	193.56	6668.32	1812.76
20	75.02	195.74	6472.58	1887.78
21	72.82	197.94	6274.64	1960.6
22	70.59	200.17	6074.47	2031.19
23	68.34	202.42	5872.05	2099.53
24	66.06	204.7	5667.35	2165.59
25	63.76	207	5460.35	2229.35
26	61.43	209.33	5251.02	2290.78
27	59.07	211.69	5039.33	2349.85
28	56.69	214.07	4825.26	2406.54
29	54.28	216.48	4608.78	2460.82
30	51.85	218.91	4389.87	2512.67
31	49.39	221.37	4168.5	2562.06
32	46.9	223.86	3944.64	2608.96
33	44.38	226.38	3718.26	2653.34
34	41.83	228.93	3489.33	2695.17
35	39.25	231.51	3257.82	2734.42
36	36.65	234.11	3023.71	2771.07
37	34.02	236.74	2786.97	2805.09
38	31.35	239.41	2547.56	2836.44
39	28.66	242.1	2305.46	2865.1
40	25.94	244.82	2060.64	2891.04
41	23.18	247.58	1813.06	2914.22
42	20.4	250.36	1562.7	2934.62
43	17.58	253.18	1309.52	2952.2
44	14.73	256.03	1053.49	2966.93
45	11.85	258.91	794.58	2978.78
46	8.93	261.82	532.76	2987.72
47	5.99	264.77	267.99	2993.71
48	3.01	267.99	0	2996.72

Figure 3-21 Printout for amortization program.

```
10 COLOR 5,0,0,0
20 CLS
30 PRINT TAB(30)"AMORTIZATION PROGRAM":PRINT :PRINT
40 PRINT "DATE:";DATE$
50 PRINT "TIME:";TIME$
60 PRINT
70 INPUT "ENTER THE AMOUNT OF THE LOAN";L
80 INPUT "WHAT IS THE INTEREST RATE PERCENTAGE";R
90 INPUT "ENTER THE TERM IN YEARS";Y
100 I = R/1200
110 M= Y*12
120 A=(I*L)/((1-(1+I)^-M))
130 X=A
140 GOSUB 750
150 A=X
160 PRINT "THE MONTHLY PAYMENT IS $";A
170 B=L
180 T=0
190 PRINT "PMT               INTEREST    PRINCIPAL     BALANCE    TOTAL INTEREST"
200 FOR J=1 TO M
210 I1=B*I
220 X=I1
230 GOSUB 750
240 I1=X
250 P=A-I1
260 X=P
270 GOSUB 750
280 P=X
290 IF J=M THEN LET P=B
300 B=B-P
310 X=B
320 GOSUB 750
330 B=X
340 T=T+I1
350 X=T
360 GOSUB 750
370 T=X
380 PRINT J,I1,P,B,T
390 NEXT J
400 INPUT "DO YOU WANT THIS TO BE PRINTED ON THE PRINTER?(YES/NO)";P$
410 IF P$ ="NO"THEN GOTO 690
420 IF P$="N" THEN GOTO 690
425 LPRINT "DATE:";DATE$;"          TIME:";TIME$
430 LPRINT "FOR A LOAN OF $";L;"AT AN INTEREST RATE OF";(R);"%,"
440 LPRINT "FOR";Y;"YEARS:"
450 LPRINT "THE MONTHLY PAYMENT IS $";A
460 B=L
470 T=0
480 LPRINT "PMT               INTEREST    PRINCIPAL     BALANCE    TOTAL INTEREST"
490 FOR J=1 TO M
500 I1=B*I
510 X=I1
520 GOSUB 750
530 I1=X
540 P=A-I1
550 X=P
560 GOSUB 750
570 P=X
580 IF J=M THEN LET P=B
590 B=B-P
600 X=B
610 GOSUB 750
620 B=X
630 T=T+I1
640 X=T
650 GOSUB 750
660 T=X
670 LPRINT J,I1,P,B,T
680 NEXT J
690 INPUT "PROCESS ANOTHER LOAN ? (YES/NO)";A$
700 IF A$="YES" THEN GOTO 70
710 IF A$ = "Y" THEN GOTO 70
720 IF A$ = "NO" THEN GOTO 770
730 IF A$ = "N" THEN GOTO 770
740 GOTO 450
750 X=(INT(100*(X+.005)))/100
760 RETURN
770 COLOR 7,0,0,0
780 RUN "DATACOST.BAS"
```

Figure 3-22 Listing for AMORT.

The formula for the multiple regression calculations takes the following form:

$$Y = C + (A1*X1) + (A2*X2) + \ldots + (AN*XN) \qquad (3\text{-}11)$$

where
$$Y = \text{the dependent variable (cost or labor hours)}$$
$$C = \text{a constant derived by the program}$$
$$A1, A2, \ldots, AN = \text{constants or coefficients for each independent variable derived by the program}$$
$$X1, X2, \ldots, XN = \text{the independent variables}$$

To show how the multiple linear regression program works, we have provided a sample problem as follows:

A company has manufactured eight different models of a centrifugal pump, each with a different weight and gallons-per-minute capacity. An average cost for each of the first 100 units was recorded from production records. The estimating department wants to develop an equation and a computer program to determine the cost of other pumps of different weights and different capacities but in the same general size range. The following is a table of the actual recorded data:

	Pump model no.							
	1	2	3	4	5	6	7	8
Independent variables								
Weight, pounds	80	90	60	100	80	90	90	70
Gallons per minute	480	490	440	590	550	510	550	500
Dependent variable cost, dollars	590	550	500	800	610	750	670	580

Figure 3-23 (in two parts) shows the input screens that appear after menu selection 7 (MANYCOST) is chosen. The operator enters the name of the dependent variable, the number of sets of data available (8), the number of independent variables (2), and the names of the independent variables (pounds and gallons per minute), and the data for each pump model. On entering the last data set, the display in Figure 3-24 (p. 60) appears, which shows, first, the equation coefficients. Using the coefficients provided, you can write an equation that matches your data as follows by substituting into Equation (3-11):

$$\text{Cost(\$)} = -157.02 + (3.7*\text{pounds}) + (0.943*\text{gallons per minute}) \qquad (3\text{-}12)$$

or

$$\text{Cost(\$)} = (3.7*\text{pounds}) + (0.943*\text{gallons per minute}) - 157.02 \qquad (3\text{-}13)$$

```
              COST OR TIME DETERMINATION USING MULTIPLE LINEAR REGRESSION


    DATE:10-16-1985
    TIME:10:34:44

    WHAT IS THE NAME OF THE DEPENDENT VARIABLE(COST,HOURS,ETC.)? COST ($)

    HOW MANY DATA SETS DO YOU HAVE? 8

    NUMBER OF INDEPENDENT VARIABLES IN EACH DATA SET? 2

    INPUT THE NAMES OF THE INDEPENDENT VARIABLES:
    WHAT IS THE NAME OF INDEPENDENT VARIABLE # 1 ? POUNDS
    WHAT IS THE NAME OF INDEPENDENT VARIABLE # 2 ? GALLONS PER MINUTE
    DATA SET # 1
         POUNDS? 80
         GALLONS PER MINUTE? 480
           COST ($)? 590
    DATA SET # 2
         POUNDS? 90
         GALLONS PER MINUTE? 490
           COST ($)? 550
```

```
    DATA SET # 3
         POUNDS? 60
         GALLONS PER MINUTE? 440
           COST? 500
    DATA SET # 4
         POUNDS? 100
         GALLONS PER MINUTE? 590
           COST? 800
    DATA SET # 5
         POUNDS? 80
         GALLONS PER MINUTE? 550
           COST? 610
    DATA SET # 6
         POUNDS? 90
         GALLONS PER MINUTE? 510
           COST? 750
    DATA SET # 7
         POUNDS? 90
         GALLONS PER MINUTE? 550
           COST? 670
    DATA SET # 8
         POUNDS? 70
         GALLONS PER MINUTE? 500
           COST? 580
```

Figure 3-23 Input screens for cost or time determination using multiple linear regression.

Notice that the coefficient of determination, coefficient of multiple correlation, and standard error of the estimate are also provided on the output display. In solving a problem, you may want to select various sets of independent variables until the coefficients are closest to 1 and the standard error is the least. When these outputs have been recorded, you can then solve for specific points on the equation by using the interpolation feature provided in the program. Figure 3-25 shows the calculated cost value for pumps weighing 50, 82.5, and 200 pounds and producing 300, 485, and 1000 gallons per minute, respectively. When running the program, you may encounter the message NO UNIQUE SOLUTION. This message appears when you have not provided enough data points to provide a meaningful correlation or when your data points are too widely scattered to develop a single equation that fits all points.

The program listing for MANYCOST is shown in Figure 3-26 (p. 62). If entered exactly as shown (or with appropriate modifications for your form of BASIC) it provides you with a handy and easily used program for developing estimating relationships from existing or historical data.

Sample Problem Using DATACOST

The following is a sample cost estimating problem that you can solve with your computer once you have input and tested the programs given in this chapter.

```
      POUNDS? 90
      GALLONS PER MINUTE? 510
        COST($)? 750
DATA SET # 7
      POUNDS? 90
      GALLONS PER MINUTE? 550
        COST($)? 670
DATA SET # 8
      POUNDS? 70
      GALLONS PER MINUTE? 500
        COST($)? 580

EQUATION COEFFICIENTS:
      CONSTANT:-157.0213
VARIABLE( 1  ): 3.680851
VARIABLE( 2  ): .9432624

COEFFICIENT OF DETERMINATION (R^2) = .7156974
COFFICIENT OF MULTIPLE CORRELATION = .845989
STANDARD ERROR OF ESTIMATE  64.2888

INTERPOLATION:  (ENTER 0 TO END PROGRAM)
DETERMINING COST($) FROM ENTERED INDEPENDENT VARIABLES
POUNDS?
```

Figure 3-24 Output screen for cost or time determination using multiple linear regression.

SAMPLE COST ESTIMATING PROBLEM

Inputs:

1. Manufacturing hours for the Xth item for a particular production run are as follows:

X	No. of hours
10	150
20	120
30	95

Find:

1. The learning curve slope and TFU for the best fit to the above points.

2. The hours required for the 100th unit.

3. The TFU if the learning curve is increased by 10 percent (same 100th unit hours).

4. Plot the two curves and read off the value of the 200th unit for each curve.

5. Plot the original curve and its cumulative average curve. What is the unit cost and cumulative average cost of 50 units?

6. Determine the unit, cumulative average, and total costs for the original curve for the first 10 units. Record the cumulative average costs for the first 10 units.

7. Assume that we are purchasing one of the first 10 units at $25 per hour and a down payment of $1000; develop an amortization schedule for 1 year at a 12.5 percent loan. How much is your loan payment?

```
VARIABLE( 1  ): 3.680851
VARIABLE( 2  ): .9432624

COEFFICIENT OF DETERMINATION (R^2) = .7156974
COFFICIENT OF MULTIPLE CORRELATION = .845989
STANDARD ERROR OF ESTIMATE  64.2888

INTERPOLATION:  (ENTER 0 TO END PROGRAM)
DETERMINING COST($) FROM ENTERED INDEPENDENT VARIABLES
POUNDS? 50
GALLONS PER MINUTE? 300
COST($)= 310

POUNDS? 82.5
GALLONS PER MINUTE? 485
COST($)= 604.1313

POUNDS? 200
GALLONS PER MINUTE? 1000
COST($)= 1522.411

POUNDS? 0
Ok
```

Figure 3-25 Output screen for cost or time determination using multiple linear regression.

```
10 CLS
20  PRINT "           COST OR TIME DETERMINATION USING MULTIPLE LINEAR REGRESSION"
30  PRINT
40 PRINT "DATE:";DATE$
50 PRINT "TIME:";TIME$
60 PRINT
70 INPUT "WHAT IS THE NAME OF THE DEPENDENT VARIABLE(COST,HOURS,ETC.)";D$
80 PRINT
90  REM - SET ARRAY LIMITS TO X(N+1),S(N+1),T(N+1),A(N+1,N+2)
100  DIM X(9),S(9),T(9),A(9,10)
110  PRINT "HOW MANY DATA SETS DO YOU HAVE";
120  INPUT N
130 PRINT
140  PRINT "NUMBER OF INDEPENDENT VARIABLES IN EACH DATA SET";
150  INPUT V
160 PRINT
170 PRINT "INPUT THE NAMES OF THE INDEPENDENT VARIABLES:"
180 FOR J=1 TO V
190 PRINT "WHAT IS THE NAME OF INDEPENDENT VARIABLE #";J;
200 INPUT I$(J)
210 NEXT J
220  X(1)=1
230  FOR I=1 TO N
240  PRINT "DATA SET #";I
250  FOR J=1 TO V
260  REM - ENTER INDEPENDENT VARIABLES FOR EACH POINT
270  PRINT "        ";I$(J);
280  INPUT X(J+1)
290  NEXT J
300  REM - ENTER DEPENDENT VARIABLE FOR EACH POINT
310  PRINT "        ";D$;
320  INPUT X(V+2)
330  REM - POPULATE A MATRIX TO BE USED IN CURVE FITTING
340  FOR K=1 TO V+1
350  FOR L=1 TO V+2
360  A(K,L)=A(K,L)+X(K)*X(L)
370  S(K)=A(K,V+2)
380  NEXT L
390  NEXT K
400  S(V+2)=S(V+2)+X(V+2)^2
410  NEXT I
420  REM - STATEMENTS 250 TO 500 FIT CURVE BY SOLVING THE SYSTEM OF
430  REM - LINEAR EQUATIONS IN MATRIX A()
440  FOR I=2 TO V+1
450  T(I)=A(1,I)
460  NEXT I
470  FOR I=1 TO V+1
480  J=I
490  IF A(J,I)<>0 THEN 540
500  J=J+1
510  IF J<=V+1 THEN 490
520  PRINT "NO UNIQUE SOLUTION"
530  GOTO 1040
540  FOR K=1 TO V+2
550  B=A(I,K)
560  A(I,K)=A(J,K)
570  A(J,K)=B
580  NEXT K
590  Z=1/A(I,I)
600  FOR K=1 TO V+2
610  A(I,K)=Z*A(I,K)
620  NEXT K
630  FOR J=1 TO V+1
640  IF J=I THEN 690
650  Z=-A(J,I)
660  FOR K=1 TO V+2
670  A(J,K)=A(J,K)+Z*A(I,K)
680  NEXT K
690  NEXT J
700  NEXT I
710  PRINT
720  PRINT "EQUATION COEFFICIENTS:"
730  PRINT "    CONSTANT:";A(1,V+2)
740  FOR I=2 TO V+1
750  PRINT "VARIABLE(";I-1;" ):";A(I,V+2)
```

Figure 3-26 Listing for MANYCOST. *(Courtesy of Osborne/McGraw-Hill, from Poole and Borchers, SOME COMMON BASIC PROGRAMS, 3d ed., 1979.)*

```
760   NEXT I
770   P=Ø
780   FOR I=2 TO V+1
790   P=P+A(I,V+2)*(S(I)-T(I)*S(1)/N)
800   NEXT I
810   R=S(V+2)-S(1)^2/N
820   Z=R-P
830   L=N-V-1
840   PRINT
850   I=P/R
860   PRINT "COEFFICIENT OF DETERMINATION (R^2) =";I
870   PRINT "COFFICIENT OF MULTIPLE CORRELATION =";SQR(I)
880   PRINT "STANDARD ERROR OF ESTIMATE ";SQR(ABS(Z/L))
890   PRINT
900   REM - ESTIMATE DEPENDENT VARIABLE FROM ENTERED INDEPENDENT VARIABLES
910   PRINT "INTERPOLATION:  (ENTER Ø TO END PROGRAM)"
920   PRINT "DETERMINING ";D$;" FROM ENTERED INDEPENDENT VARIABLES"
930   P=A(1,V+2)
940   FOR J=1 TO V
950   PRINT I$(J);
960   INPUT X
970   REM - TEST FOR END OF PROGRAM
980   IF X=Ø THEN 1040
990   P=P+A(J+1,V+2)*X
1000  NEXT J
1010  PRINT D$"=";P
1020  PRINT
1030  GOTO 930
1040  INPUT "DO YOU WANT TO RUN ANOTHER LINEAR MULTIPLE REGRESSION?(YES/NO)";R$
1050  IF R$="YES" THEN GOTO 10
1060  IF R$="Y" THEN GOTO 10
1070  CLS
1080  LOCATE 12,35:PRINT "THANK YOU"
1090  RUN "DATACOST.BAS"
```

Figure 3-26   Listing for MANYCOST. *(Courtesy of Osborne/McGraw-Hill, from Poole and Borchers, SOME COMMON BASIC PROGRAMS, 3d ed., 1979.)* (Continued)

8. The cost of this item varies with weight. We have three items that have been built in quantity at the following weights and costs:

Item no.	Weight, pounds	Cost, dollars
1	75	3500.00
2	100	5484.50
3	150	7500.00

Find the slope and cost intercept of the cost estimating relationship.

9. With a piece of graph paper, construct this CER and find the cost of units weighing 130 pounds.

Hints:
1. Use the BFIT to perform step 1 above.
2. Use LCURVE or CURVEL to perform step 2.
3. Use TFU to answer step 3.
4. Use LCCOMP to plot the two curves in step 4.
5. Use LCPLOT to plot unit and cumulative average curves.
6. Use CURVEL to answer step 6.
7. Use AMORT to find the loan payment in step 7.
8. Use CER for step 8.
9. Plot the resulting curve manually.

4

SPREADSHEET ESTIMATING

A *spreadsheet* is a large group of interrelated numbers that are usually arranged in columns and rows in a matrix format with appropriate titles along the horizontal and vertical axes. An *estimating spreadsheet* is a group of resource values, arranged in columns (vertically) and rows (horizontally) that depict the labor hours, materials, and other costs required to do a job. The columns or rows can represent time elements (hours, days, weeks, months, quarters, years, etc.), cost elements (labor, materials, other direct costs, overhead, G&A expenses, and fee or profit), work elements, or schedule elements. Spreadsheets are used as a convenient means of organizing data, computing them, and reporting them in an easily readable and understandable format. The microcomputer spreadsheet (or electronic spreadsheet) is an ideal tool for the cost estimator because: (1) the microcomputer spreadsheet itself can be larger than that which could be printed on a single page; (2) calculations can be made rapidly and accurately, eliminating a large amount of cross-checking of horizontal and vertical totals; (3) any part of the spreadsheet can be easily viewed on the video screen; and (4) spreadsheets can be linked together to permit input, display, and computation of a complex multilevel estimate.

There are several dozen good electronic spreadsheet programs on the market. The variety in these programs is sufficient to fit just about any brand of computer. Some of the spreadsheet programs work in conjunction with graphics software products, word processing, and database management systems. Several of the spreadsheet software packages have evolved into third- or fourth-generation programs that contain enhancements designed to improve the ease of use, visibility, and flexibility of the program. The numbers of columns, or vertical subdivisions, and rows, or horizontal subdivisions, vary considerably. Virtually all spreadsheet software packages have a sufficient number of row and column subdivisions for the average estimating job. Some of the more commonly available spreadsheet software packages are: Lotus 1-2-3 from Lotus Systems, Inc.; Multiplan from Microsoft Corporation; Super-Calc 3 from Sorcim Corporation; Visi-Calc IV from VisiCorp; The Financial Planner from Ashton Tate; Peachcalc from Peachtree Software, Inc.; CalcStar from MicroPro International Corporation; EasyPlanner from Information Unlimited Software, Inc.; and Microplan from Digital Research. For the examples shown in this chapter we use Multiplan from Microsoft Corporation.

All of the spreadsheet programs can display and print a large matrix of numbers in the column and row structure format, compute new values from values already in the spreadsheet, place them at designated row-column intersections, and handle both alphabetical and numerical inputs. Some spreadsheet programs can link spreadsheets together, look up numbers from another spreadsheet, and plot spreadsheet results in graphic form. In this chapter we will explore the alphanumeric capabilities of the spreadsheet and how these capabilities can help the cost estimator.

Useful Characteristics of Spreadsheets

Figure 4-1, which is a printout of a simple electronically produced cost estimating spreadsheet, demonstrates some of the useful characteristics of a spreadsheet program for cost estimating. Note that 15 columns and 31 rows are displayed in this example printout. (Multiplan can display up to 64 columns and 255 rows.) Up to 165 characters in width can be printed horizontally on one sheet of wide paper (11 by 14 inches) if a compressed print mode is used in the printer. (The printer will display all columns used up to the maximum of 64 on multiple sheets.)

The Row and Column Structure

For cost estimating, a row and column structure like that shown on Figure 4-1 is typical. Columns in the example are used for a monthly breakout of resources with a final column (column 15) for totals of each of

```
MICROESTIMATING(TM) SYSTEM (Copyright 1984, MOBILE DATA SERVICES
EST.TITLE:COSTPLAN   NES TITLE:TOP   ORIGINATOR ARS   START YR.: 1986
EST.NMBR: .004       NES NMBR: A-O   DATE: 10/16/85
```

NES NO.	TITLE	JAN 1986	FEB 1986	MAR 1986	APR 1986	MAY 1986	JUN 1986	JUL 1986	AUG 1986	SEP 1986	OCT 1986	NOV 1986	DEC 1986	TOTAL 1986
A-0	COSTFORM	$16849.98	$15715.84	$14581.71	$15505.22	$15505.22	$19806.82	$19442.28	$19928.34	$15229.79	$17692.47	$15262.19	$14047.05	$199366.90
A-1	PROGRMMING	$16849.98	$15715.84	$14581.71	$10531.24	$10531.24	$0.00	$0.00	$0.00	$0.00	$0.00	$0.00	$0.00	$68210.00
A-1-1	INPUTS	$5735.47	$1360.96	$1360.96	$777.69	$777.69	$0.00	$0.00	$0.00	$0.00	$0.00	$0.00	$0.00	$10012.77
A-1-2	EDITS	$1360.96	$5735.47	$1360.96	$777.69	$777.69	$0.00	$0.00	$0.00	$0.00	$0.00	$0.00	$0.00	$10012.77
A-1-3	ERROR MSGS	$1360.96	$1360.96	$5735.47	$777.69	$777.69	$0.00	$0.00	$0.00	$0.00	$0.00	$0.00	$0.00	$10012.77
A-1-4	REPT GEN	$1360.96	$1360.96	$1360.96	$5152.20	$777.69	$0.00	$0.00	$0.00	$0.00	$0.00	$0.00	$0.00	$10012.77
A-1-5	USER INTER	$7031.62	$5897.49	$4763.36	$3045.96	$7420.47	$0.00	$0.00	$0.00	$0.00	$0.00	$0.00	$0.00	$28158.90
A-2	TESTING	$0.00	$0.00	$0.00	$4973.98	$4973.98	$7566.29	$8052.34	$8538.40	$0.00	$0.00	$0.00	$0.00	$34105.00
A-2-1	IN-HOUSE	$0.00	$0.00	$0.00	$3710.24	$3710.24	$2252.06	$2252.06	$2252.06	$0.00	$0.00	$0.00	$0.00	$14176.66
A-2-2	MKT USE	$0.00	$0.00	$0.00	$631.87	$631.87	$3629.23	$3629.23	$2171.05	$0.00	$0.00	$0.00	$0.00	$10693.25
A-2-3	UPDATES	$0.00	$0.00	$0.00	$631.87	$631.87	$1685.00	$2171.05	$4115.28	$0.00	$0.00	$0.00	$0.00	$9235.08
A-3	DOCMTATION	$0.00	$0.00	$0.00	$0.00	$0.00	$12240.54	$11389.94	$11389.94	$15229.79	$0.00	$0.00	$0.00	$50250.19
A-3-1	BASICS	$0.00	$0.00	$0.00	$0.00	$0.00	$1053.12	$769.59	$769.59	$1620.19	$0.00	$0.00	$0.00	$4212.49
A-3-2	OP. MANUAL	$0.00	$0.00	$0.00	$0.00	$0.00	$4066.68	$3977.57	$4171.99	$5800.28	$0.00	$0.00	$0.00	$18016.51
A-3-3	SAMPLE EX.	$0.00	$0.00	$0.00	$0.00	$0.00	$5233.21	$4755.26	$4560.83	$5217.01	$0.00	$0.00	$0.00	$19766.32
A-3-4	UPDATES	$0.00	$0.00	$0.00	$0.00	$0.00	$1887.52	$1887.52	$1887.52	$2592.30	$0.00	$0.00	$0.00	$8254.87
A-4	SUPPORT	$0.00	$0.00	$0.00	$0.00	$0.00	$0.00	$0.00	$0.00	$0.00	$17692.47	$15262.19	$14047.05	$47001.71
A-4-1	INSTALLATN	$0.00	$0.00	$0.00	$0.00	$0.00	$0.00	$0.00	$0.00	$0.00	$8668.02	$6237.73	$5022.59	$19928.34
A-4-2	TRAINING	$0.00	$0.00	$0.00	$0.00	$0.00	$0.00	$0.00	$0.00	$0.00	$3288.99	$3288.99	$3288.99	$9866.96
A-4-3	UPDATES	$0.00	$0.00	$0.00	$0.00	$0.00	$0.00	$0.00	$0.00	$0.00	$4860.57	$4860.57	$4860.57	$14581.71
A-4-4	FLD SVC	$0.00	$0.00	$0.00	$0.00	$0.00	$0.00	$0.00	$0.00	$0.00	$874.90	$874.90	$874.90	$2624.71

Figure 4-1 Sample spreadsheet.

several cost elements. Rows are labeled vertically along the left axis to depict resource elements (labor rates, labor hours, labor dollars, labor overhead, material dollars, other direct dollars, G&A costs, cost of money, and fee or profit), along with appropriately interspersed subtotals and a grand total.

Notice in the heading that this spreadsheet printout is for one work element structure titled programming of inputs (PROG INPT) and is numbered A-1-1. Other arrangements of the spreadsheet could include a column structure containing different calendar units (hours, days, weeks, quarters, or years), different work elements (A-1-1, A-1-2, A-1-3, etc.), or different departments within a company. The time-oriented horizontal spread is one of the most convenient to the estimator, however, because this arrangement can be tied to a calendar schedule of the work as described in Chapter 6. In structuring the spreadsheet by defining the columns and rows, the estimator places information into identifiable blocks that will fit onto a printout sheet, as shown in the example on Figure 4-1. How this is done will be covered later in this chapter.

Cell Content and Formulas

For the purpose of this discussion, a spreadsheet *cell* is described as the space where a row and a column intersect. Spreadsheet cells have the capability of containing alphabetical information such as words or titles, or numerical information such as work hours (unit quantities) or dollars (unit prices or costs). In the example shown in Figure 4-1 (notice the column numbering and row numbering system on this figure), the cells containing headings, column titles, and row titles consist of both alphabetical and numerical information. The interior section of the spreadsheet contains only numerical resource information. Most spreadsheets allow the information in each cell to be right-justified, left-justified, or centered; dollar signs, positive or negative values, and a fixed number of decimal spaces can be established if desired. In the example estimating spreadsheet shown, which is an estimate of part of the work required for a software development project, four labor categories have been established, each with its own labor rate per hour. For simplicity, the labor rate per hour was held constant throughout the time period covered by the spreadsheet, although the rate could just as easily have been varied by month. Rates can easily be changed at a later date because the labor rate is built into a formula that enters into the computation of labor costs and then total costs. The rate per hour for each skill and the labor hours required that month for each skill are inputs to the cost estimate: these values are obtained from databases of unit price, and unit quantity values for the type of skills and the type of work being estimated. Typical formulas for this type of spreadsheet program are shown on Figure 4-2, which shows the alphabetical, numerical, and formula inputs used for the first three columns of the spreadsheet.

The formula for labor dollars for the program manager in column 3 is as follows:

$$R[-1]C*R[-2]C \tag{4-1}$$

The R means *row* and the C means *column*. The asterisk is the symbol for multiplication. Therefore, the above formula would read (in plain English): The value in this cell equals the value in the cell in the above row (-1) in the same column times (*) the value in the cell two rows above (-2) in the same column.

This formula is a "relative" formula since it refers to cells in relation to its own position on the spreadsheet. Notice that this type of formula permits the use of exactly the same formula for labor dollars for all skills and for all months. It is handy to use relative references instead of absolute references in building spreadsheet formulas because formulas can then be easily copied and used in other rows and columns. (Absolute references would refer to specific cell locations on the spreadsheet such as:

$$R10C3*R9C3 \tag{4-2}$$

or: The value in row 11, column 3 equals the value in row 10, column 3 times the value in row 9, column 3.)

```
                  1                    2                      3
 8  "LABOR"
 9  "Prg Mgr"            "Rate/Hr"            35
10                       "Hours"              0
11                       "Dollars"            R[-1]C*R[-2]C
12  "Sr Prgmr"           "Rate/Hr"            30
13                       "Hours"              100
14                       "Dollars"            R[-1]C*R[-2]C
15  "Tech Wtr"           "Rate/Hr"            18
16                       "Hours"              10
17                       "Dollars"            R[-1]C*R[-2]C
18  "Data Anl"           "Rate/Hr"            12
19                       "Hours"              30
20                       "Dollars"            R[-1]C*R[-2]C
21  "Tot Lbr."           "Hours"              R[-11]C+R[-8]C+R[-5
                                              ]C+R[-2]C
22                       "Dollars"            R[-11]C+R[-8]C+R[-5
                                              ]C+R[-2]C
23  "LBR OHD"       43%                        R23C2*R[-1]C
24  "MATERIALS"                                0
25  "OTHER DIR."                               0
26  "SUBTOTAL"                                 R[-4]C+R[-3]C+R[-2]
                                              C+R[-1]C
27  "G&A"          2.5%                        R27C2*R[-1]C
28  "COST OF $"    0.5%                        R28C2*R[-2]C
29  "SUBTOTAL"                                 R[-3]C+R[-2]C+R[-1]
                                              C
30  "FEE"          10%                         R30C2*R[-1]C
31  "GND TOTAL"                                R[-2]C+R[-1]C
```

Figure 4-2 Sample spreadsheet formulas.

Notice that the total labor hours formula is

$$R[-11]C + R[-8]C + R[-5]C + R[-2]C \qquad (4\text{-}3)$$

This formula adds the labor hours for each skill in the same column to derive a labor-hour total for January 1984.

The same logic is used in summing resources across the spreadsheet except that the row is kept constant and the column is changed.

The grand total costs for the year would thus be:

$$RC[-12] + RC[-11] + RC[-10] + RC[-9] + RC[-8] + \ldots + RC[-1] \qquad (4\text{-}4)$$

Mathematical Functions

Most spreadsheets have enough mathematical functions or *operators* to meet the needs of almost any estimating situation. All computerized spreadsheets have addition, subtraction, multiplication, division, exponentiation, and percent. Many spreadsheets also have *logical operators,* such as < (less than); <= (less than or equal to); = (equal to); > (greater than); >= (greater than or equal to); and <> (not equal), which are used occasionally in cost estimating situations.

Linking of Spreadsheets

Spreadsheet software programs other than the most primitive ones provide the feature of linking spreadsheets together. This feature can be of great value because it offers the assurance that every time this part is changed, the resulting total estimate that is linked to this part will be changed accordingly. The two example spreadsheet cost estimates used in this chapter incorporate linking of spreadsheets. Linking, using an external copy command on the dependent worksheet, has many uses—one such use which will be demonstrated is the accumulation of resources from lower-level worksheets in the work element structure to a higher-level worksheet or worksheets.

The Lookup Function

Most advanced electronic spreadsheets have a lookup function that allows the estimator to import a value from a table on the same or supporting worksheet. This function can be valuable for inputting labor rates from a table that is updated separately, for computing employee benefits based on salary level or length of service, and in computing taxes or health insurance rates. The lookup function can be used in a formula, with multiple occurrences if necessary, to derive a value based on the value in the lookup table.

Building a Multiple-Spreadsheet Estimate

If multiple spreadsheets are to be used to accumulate the estimated costs of various parts of a job, it is desirable to make these sheets either identical or very similar, even if some of the cells are void of input data. The reason for striving for maximum spreadsheet uniformity is that it is much easier to copy a spreadsheet to a different file (give it a new file name) than to rebuild the worksheet from scratch, entering all titles, headings, formulas, and fixed or semifixed values. In both of the examples presented in this chapter, extensive use was made of copying spreadsheets prior to performing the modifications required to make each spreadsheet unique. Ideally, each spreadsheet would be identical with the exception of its title, a code or file number, and the principal input or variable values in the columns or rows. An example of a multiple spreadsheet estimate for a typical project is shown below on Figure 4-3. The estimate is for the development of a computer software package called COSTPLAN and assumes the use of four basic skills: a program manager, a senior programmer, a technical writer, and a systems data analyst. The work will be performed in a 1-year period (1986) and is subdivided into the work elements shown in Figure 4-3. The work will be performed in accordance with the schedule shown in Figure 4-4.

Development of Input Spreadsheet

The first step in the development of the microestimating spreadsheet is to construct a form that will be used to input labor rates; labor hours; material dollars; other direct dollars; and overhead, G&A, cost of money, and fee percentages at the lowest input level. This form will be used for all three-character work element codes (A-1-1, A-1-2, . . . , A-4-3, etc.), will cover the months of January through December and a total for column headings, and will be subdivided into cost element titles for each row. Labor cost elements for each skill are:

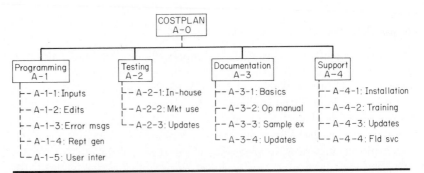

Figure 4-3 Work element structure for example.

Rate per hour (dollar labor rate)

Hours (estimated labor hours)

Dollars (computed labor dollars)

Row titles are provided for total labor hours and total labor dollars for each month and for each total year. Space is provided to insert material dollars; other direct dollars; percentage factors for overhead, G&A, cost of money, and fee; and appropriate subtotals and grand totals. The row titles selected for this specific estimate, then, appear as follows:

LABOR

Prg Mgr   Rate per hour
                      Hours
                      Dollars

Sr Prgmr   Rate per hour
                      Hours
                      Dollars

Tech Wtr   Rate per hour
                      Hours
                      Dollars

Data Anl   Rate per hour
                      Hours
                      Dollars

Tot Lbr   Hours
                      Dollars

LBR OHD

MATERIALS

OTHER DIR

SUBTOTAL

G&A

COST OF $

SUBTOTAL

FEE

GND TOTAL

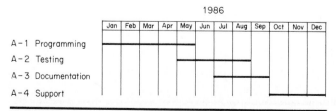

Figure 4-4 Schedule for example.

Of course, there are many other possible arrangements that would depend on the number of skills to be used in the work, the possible need to break out materials or other direct costs to a lower level of detail, and the company's specific method of computing overhead, G&A, cost of money, and fee or profit. This method of grouping cost elements is useful because it includes all source and input data used in computation of the cost estimate on the spreadsheet. Notice that even though all skills are not to be used for all work elements for all months, we are building spreadsheet column and row titles that will be consistent throughout the entire estimate. Again, the authors have found that it is easier to design a form that may leave many cells blank (at the possible risk of using more computer paper) than it is to configure a system that varies among lower-level work elements. (You will discover more about this subject later when we go into an example that varies somewhat in format from this one.)

Figure 4-5 shows how the blank input spreadsheet will appear on your computer video screen. Notice the column numbers across the top and the row numbers along the left-hand margin. This computer screen shows seven columns that are each 10 characters wide. Other microcomputers may display more or less than seven 10-character columns of a spreadsheet at a time, depending on the character dimensions of the video screen and whether windows or bordered windows are used to display the data. Twenty rows are displayed on this monitor. Likewise, the number of rows displayed at one time will vary from one computer to another, depending on the windowing techniques used in the specific spreadsheet software package and on the number of rows that are reserved at the top

```
#1      1            2          3         4          5          6           7
   2  EST.TITLE:            WES TITLE:         ORIGINATOR           START YR.:
   3  EST.NMBR:             WES NMBR:          DATE:
   4  *********************************************************************
   5  MONTH-------------->       JAN      FEB       MAR        APR        MAY
   6  YEAR--------------->       1986     1986      1986       1986       1986
   7  *********************************************************************
   8  LABOR
   9  Prg Mgr    Rate/Hr
  10             Hours
  11             Dollars
  12  Sr Prgmr   Rate/Hr
  13             Hours
  14             Dollars
  15  Tech Wtr   Rate/Hr
  16             Hours
  17             Dollars
  18  Data Anl   Rate/Hr
  19             Hours
  20             Dollars
```

Figure 4-5 Spreadsheet headings and titles.

and bottom of the screen for commands, status information, and error messages. Virtually every microcomputer spreadsheet software package has a scrolling feature that will permit scanning or stepping across and down the spreadsheet to allow the viewing of all cells on the spreadsheet in all rows and columns.

Note in Figure 4-5 that space is provided in the heading for estimate title, estimate number, work element structure title, work element structure number, originator, data, and starting year of the estimate schedule. These headings allow the estimator to keep track of which spreadsheet is being used, displayed, or modified; who originated the information; and the date of origination or last update. Since there will be multiple worksheets for most estimates, it will be important for the estimator to enter the date of last revision of each worksheet as it is produced or updated. This dating helps keep track of the version of the estimate that is being viewed.

Constructing Spreadsheet Formulas

Because the specific formula techniques, as well as column and row identification techniques, vary between the various commercially available spreadsheet software packages, we provide here only very generic instructions on how to build the formulas. Some of the more advanced of the computer spreadsheet products have a capability of building the formulas merely by positioning the cursor over the active variable to be placed in the formula and pressing the correct mathematical function key or keys. This technique is very user friendly and does not require detailed thought by the operator concerning exactly which columns, rows, and cells of the spreadsheet are involved in the calculations.

Regardless of the exact naming conventions used, the resulting built-in spreadsheet formulas will look something like those shown on Figure 4-2. Fortunately, in most situations using spreadsheet estimating, multiplication and addition are about the most complex functions used. You should be able to master rapidly the formula-building process by referring to the software instruction manual or by participating in the tutorial exercise if one is provided with your estimating software package. A review of the earlier paragraph in this chapter which describes Figure 4-2 and a study of this figure will give you an idea of the general technique used by all spreadsheet software programs in generating mathematical formulas.

Formatting Cells to Improve Appearance and Readability

Most spreadsheet programs permit the formatting of cells to improve appearance and readability. The cell contents can either be left-justified, right-justified, or centered; a dollar format can be chosen to include a dollar sign and two-digit decimal accuracy for dollar amounts; and a "continuous" format can be chosen to include long titles or dividing lines that go across several cells. Columns can also be widened if necessary to accommodate larger numbers if the input or computed values represent more digits than the default column character width (usually 10 characters).

Preliminary Testing of Base Input Spreadsheet

Once the basic input spreadsheet has been developed using instructions in the spreadsheet software documentation, some simple testing of this spreadsheet is recommended before making the multiple copies that may be needed for a large estimate. Inputting a row of labor rates and hours in one or more of the skill categories and adding the percentages for overhead and other factors will show if the spreadsheet is working properly. This step is usually not required for development of a single spreadsheet because corrections can be made so easily. If multiple copies are to be made, however, it is much easier to correct any small errors in format or formula content now than to have to correct every copied sheet.

Building Other Parallel Supporting Worksheets

Spreadsheet programs usually give each spreadsheet a name or title containing up to eight digits or characters. The name can also contain an *extender,* which is the three characters (letters or numbers) following the period in the format

XXXXXXXX.XXX

We like to use a file name or designation such as

A-2-3-4.XXX

which would represent a fourth-level element in an estimate designated as A. The A represents the first level, A-2 represents the second level, A-2-3 represents the third level, and A-2-3-4 represents the fourth-level elements. Hence, the number of letters or numbers in the initial portion of the file name represents the level of the estimate. An *alpha* character is used first because some spreadsheets immediately assume that any numerical value typed in is to be considered as a value rather than as a part of an alphanumeric string. The dashes are used merely to denote separate levels. This work element identification system permits the use of up to nine elements under any dependent element. The use of all element designators up to

A-9-9-9.XXX

would permit 26 estimates or estimate revisions (A through Z), and 9 ×
9 × 9 or 729 work elements or tasks in each. This coding also has an
advantage in that work element designators can be alphabetically sorted
on most spreadsheet programs to develop a hierarchical list of work
elements.

The three-digit extender can be used as an estimate number to designate an overall project or a family of estimates. For example, the work
element designator

A-4-1-3.006

would be a fourth-level element in estimate series number 006.

Using this numbering system, then, for the three-level work element
structure we are using as an example, we can fill in the headings in our
initial input spreadsheet as shown in Figure 4-6.

Once the headings are filled in the first spreadsheet in the example,
A-1-1 should be saved under the filename A-1-1.004 since .004 is the
estimate number. (This worksheet can be saved with all labor rates or
rate per hour cells filled in and the percentages filled in if these values
are going to be the same throughout the estimate.) When this step is
completed, the work element structure (WES) title and WES number for
the next work element can be typed over the respective inputs for the
previous worksheet, and the worksheet saved under the new designator
or filename of

A-1-2.004

```
#1      1           2          3          4          5          6          7
 2  EST.TITLE:COSTFORM   WES TITLE:PROG INPT ORIGINATOR    ARS    START YR.:
 3  EST.NMBR: .004       WES NMBR: A-1-1    DATE:      7/15/85
 4  ********************************************************************
 5  MONTH-------------->     JAN       FEB       MAR       APR       MAY
 6  YEAR--------------->    1986      1986      1986      1986      1986
 7  ********************************************************************
 8  LABOR
 9  Prg Mgr    Rate/Hr
10             Hours
11             Dollars
12  Sr Prgmr   Rate/Hr
13             Hours
14             Dollars
15  Tech Wtr   Rate/Hr
16             Hours
17             Dollars
18  Data Anl   Rate/Hr
19             Hours
20             Dollars
```

Figure 4-6   Filled-in headings.

In the same manner, worksheets can be made for all of the 16 lower-level or input-level work elements shown in Figure 4-3.

Filling in the Worksheets

As mentioned above, the labor rates and percentages for overhead and other factors can be copied to all spreadsheets if these values are going to be consistent throughout the entire estimate. If they have not been inserted, now is the time to do it. The results will appear as shown in Figure 4-7. Then, the labor hour estimates are inserted as shown in Figure 4-8.

To be able to fill in the remainder of the worksheet, it is convenient and helpful to use the windowing feature available in most spreadsheet software packages. Figure 4-9 shows the same spreadsheet segmented into four windows. Horizontal scrolling of window #3 is automatically accompanied by simultaneous horizontal scrolling of the column headings in window #2. Vertical scrolling of window #3 will be automatically accompanied by simultaneous vertical scrolling of the row titles in window #4. This feature allows you to see the proper column headings and row titles for all cells on the spreadsheet and prevents errors caused by uncertainties as to column or row designations. If window #3 is scrolled to the right to the end of the worksheet (actually, the *text in the window* is scrolled to the *left*), the result is shown in Figure 4-10. Scrolling window #3

```
#1      1        2         3         4         5         6          7
 1 COSTPLAN---MOBILE DATA SERVICES COST ESTIMATING SYSTEM
 2 EST.TITLE:COSTFORM  WES TITLE:PROG INPT ORIGINATOR   ARS     START YR.:
 3 EST.NMBR: .004      WES NMBR: A-1-1     DATE:     7/15/85
 4 ***************************************************************************
 5 MONTH-------------->      JAN      FEB       MAR       APR       MAY
 6 YEAR--------------->     1986     1986      1986      1986      1986
 7 ***************************************************************************
 8 LABOR
 9 Prg Mgr    Rate/Hr    $35.00   $35.00    $35.00    $35.00    $35.00
10            Hours           0        0         0         0         0
11            Dollars     $0.00    $0.00     $0.00     $0.00     $0.00
12 Sr Prgmr   Rate/Hr    $30.00   $30.00    $30.00    $30.00    $30.00
13            Hours           0        0         0         0         0
14            Dollars     $0.00    $0.00     $0.00     $0.00     $0.00
15 Tech Wtr   Rate/Hr    $18.00   $18.00    $18.00    $18.00    $18.00
16            Hours           0        0         0         0         0
17            Dollars     $0.00    $0.00     $0.00     $0.00     $0.00
18 Data Anl   Rate/Hr    $12.00   $12.00    $12.00    $12.00    $12.00
19            Hours           0        0         0         0         0
20            Dollars     $0.00    $0.00     $0.00     $0.00     $0.00
```

Figure 4-7 Labor rate entries.

```
#1        1           2           3           4           5           6           7
 1 COSTPLAN---MOBILE DATA SERVICES COST ESTIMATING SYSTEM
 2 EST.TITLE:COSTFORM   WES TITLE:PROG INPT ORIGINATOR     ARS     START YR.:
 3 EST.NMBR: .004       WES NMBR: A-1-1      DATE:      7/15/85
 4 ***********************************************************************
 5 MONTH-------------->    JAN       FEB       MAR       APR       MAY
 6 YEAR--------------->    1986      1986      1986      1986      1986
 7 ***********************************************************************
 8 LABOR
 9 Prg Mgr   Rate/Hr     $35.00    $35.00    $35.00    $35.00    $35.00
10           Hours           0         0         0         0         0
11           Dollars      $0.00     $0.00     $0.00     $0.00     $0.00
12 Sr Prgmr  Rate/Hr     $30.00    $30.00    $30.00    $30.00    $30.00
13           Hours         100        10        10        10        10
14           Dollars   $3000.00   $300.00   $300.00   $300.00   $300.00
15 Tech Wtr  Rate/Hr     $18.00    $18.00    $18.00    $18.00    $18.00
16           Hours          10        10        10        10        10
17           Dollars    $180.00   $180.00   $180.00   $180.00   $180.00
18 Data Anl  Rate/Hr     $12.00    $12.00    $12.00    $12.00    $12.00
19           Hours          30        30        30         0         0
20           Dollars    $360.00   $360.00   $360.00     $0.00     $0.00
```

Figure 4-8 Work-hour entries.

```
#1        1           2      #2   3          4          5          6          7
 1 COSTPLAN---MOBILE DA       TA SERVICES COST ESTIMATING SYSTEM
 2 EST.TITLE:COSTFORM         WES TITLE:PROG INPT ORIGINATOR    ARS     START YR.:
 3 EST.NMBR: .004             WES NMBR: A-1-1      DATE:      7/15/85
 4 ********************        **************************************************
 5 MONTH-------------->          JAN       FEB       MAR       APR       MAY
 6 YEAR--------------->          1986      1986      1986      1986      1986
 7 ********************        **************************************************
 8 LABOR
#4                        #3
 9 Prg Mgr   Rate/Hr         $35.00    $35.00    $35.00    $35.00    $35.00
10           Hours               0         0         0         0         0
11           Dollars          $0.00     $0.00     $0.00     $0.00     $0.00
12 Sr Prgmr  Rate/Hr         $30.00    $30.00    $30.00    $30.00    $30.00
13           Hours             100        10        10        10        10
14           Dollars       $3000.00   $300.00   $300.00   $300.00   $300.00
15 Tech Wtr  Rate/Hr         $18.00    $18.00    $18.00    $18.00    $18.00
16           Hours              10        10        10        10        10
17           Dollars        $180.00   $180.00   $180.00   $180.00   $180.00
18 Data Anl  Rate/Hr         $12.00    $12.00    $12.00    $12.00    $12.00
19           Hours              30        30        30         0         0
```

Figure 4-9 Screen windowing.

down (actually, the *text in the window* is scrolled *up*), results in a screen display that looks like the one shown in Figure 4-11.

All labor rates, labor hours, and percentages are entered, the spreadsheet is calculated—most spreadsheets calculate results as new inputs are made unless the calculate function is turned off—and saved. The total spreadsheet as it would be seen on a printout is shown in Figure 4-12. (Figure 4-12 is the same as the example shown on Figure 4-1 except that the row and column numbers are omitted.) The next worksheet (A-1-2.004) is then loaded into the computer's memory, inputs are made in the same manner, and the spreadsheet is saved under its file name. Likewise, spreadsheets designated A-1-3 through A-1-5 are loaded, provided with input values, and saved. The last thing we do is select a name for the group of cells at the bottom which is the grand total of the worksheet. We have selected the name Grandtotal. Figure 4-13 shows how sheet A-1-2.004 will appear on a printout, and Figure 4-14 shows how the last input-level spreadsheet in the estimate (for work element A-4-4) appears on the estimate printout report.

Constructing the Top-Level Estimate Summary

The headings of the top-level estimate summary are the same as those of the supporting worksheets for all columns down to row 7. Therefore, the top summary sheet can be copied from one of the other worksheets and all rows after row 7 deleted (of course, the WES title and WES number must

Figure 4-10 Horizontally scrolled window.

be changed accordingly to indicate that this is the top-level worksheet). Then the WES designators and titles are used for row titles as shown in Figure 4-15.

In constructing the worksheet, we place the subtotals at the top of each third-level group and the grand totals at the very *top* of the worksheet rather than at the *bottom* where they would normally appear in a hand-calculated worksheet. This is done for two reasons. First, it permits the addition of other level 3 or level 4 work elements within the spreadsheet or at the bottom of the spreadsheet without having to relocate the grand total row. This is a convenient feature in spreadsheet estimating because additional rows can be formatted, and, if desired, formulas can be built for the possible future addition of more work elements. This assures that the grand total figures will always appear in the same rows and columns: a feature that may be needed if this top-level worksheet were to be linked to other even higher-level worksheets. Even if other parallel top-level summary sheets had different numbers of work elements, the totals would always appear in the same place, making it easier for both computer and visual correlation of companion worksheets.

Formulas and external linking   Figures 4-16 through 4-20 show the cell formulas and linking instructions that bring data in from the lower-level input worksheets. Notice first the "formula" in column 3, row 13 in Figure 4-16: [A-1-1.004 Grandtotal]. This formula tells the computer to go to

```
#1       1         2    #2      11         12         13         14          15
   1 COSTPLAN---MOBILE DA
   2 EST.TITLE:COSTFORM
   3 EST.NMBR:  .004
   4 ********************  ***********************************************************
   5 MONTH------------->            SEP        OCT        NOV        DEC       TOTAL
   6 YEAR-------------->           1986       1986       1986       1986        1986
   7 ********************  ***********************************************************
   8 LABOR
#4                        #3
  21 Tot Lbr.   Hours             0          0          0          0         280
  22            Dollars       $0.00      $0.00      $0.00      $0.00    $6180.00
  23 LBR OHD    43.00%        $0.00      $0.00      $0.00      $0.00    $2657.40
  24 MATERIALS                $0.00      $0.00      $0.00      $0.00       $0.00
  25 OTHER DIR.               $0.00      $0.00      $0.00      $0.00       $0.00
  26 SUBTOTAL                 $0.00      $0.00      $0.00      $0.00    $8837.40
  27 G&A        2.50%         $0.00      $0.00      $0.00      $0.00     $220.94
  28 COST OF $  0.50%         $0.00      $0.00      $0.00      $0.00      $44.19
  29 SUBTOTAL                 $0.00      $0.00      $0.00      $0.00    $9102.52
  30 FEE        10.00%        $0.00      $0.00      $0.00      $0.00     $910.25
  31 GND TOTAL                $0.00      $0.00      $0.00      $0.00   $10012.77
```

Figure 4-11   Vertically scrolled window.

MICROESTIMATING(TM) SYSTEM :Copyright 1984, MOBILE DATA SERVICES
EST.TITLE:COSTPLAN   WBS TITLE:PROG INPT ORIGIN: ARS   START YR.: 1986
EST.NMBR: .004   WBS NMBR: A-1-1   DATE: 10/16/85

MONTH		JAN 1986	FEB 1986	MAR 1986	APR 1986	MAY 1986	JUN 1986	JUL 1986	AUG 1986	SEP 1986	OCT 1986	NOV 1986	DEC 1986	TOTAL 1986
LABOR														
Prg Mgr	Rate/Hr	$35.00	$35.00	$35.00	$35.00	$35.00	$35.00	$35.00	$35.00	$35.00	$35.00	$35.00	$35.00	$35.00
	Hours	0	0	0	0	0	0	0	0	0	0	0	0	0
	Dollars	$0.00	$0.00	$0.00	$0.00	$0.00	$0.00	$0.00	$0.00	$0.00	$0.00	$0.00	$0.00	$0.00
Sr Prgmr	Rate/Hr	$30.00	$30.00	$30.00	$30.00	$30.00	$30.00	$30.00	$30.00	$30.00	$30.00	$30.00	$30.00	$30.00
	Hours	100	10	10	10	10	0	0	0	0	0	0	0	140
	Dollars	$3000.00	$300.00	$300.00	$300.00	$300.00	$0.00	$0.00	$0.00	$0.00	$0.00	$0.00	$0.00	$4200.00
Tech Wtr	Rate/Hr	$18.00	$18.00	$18.00	$18.00	$18.00	$18.00	$18.00	$18.00	$18.00	$18.00	$18.00	$18.00	$18.00
	Hours	10	10	10	10	10	0	0	0	0	0	0	0	50
	Dollars	$180.00	$180.00	$180.00	$180.00	$180.00	$0.00	$0.00	$0.00	$0.00	$0.00	$0.00	$0.00	$900.00
Data Anl	Rate/Hr	$12.00	$12.00	$12.00	$12.00	$12.00	$12.00	$12.00	$12.00	$12.00	$12.00	$12.00	$12.00	$12.00
	Hours	30	30	30	0	0	0	0	0	0	0	0	0	90
	Dollars	$360.00	$360.00	$360.00	$0.00	$0.00	$0.00	$0.00	$0.00	$0.00	$0.00	$0.00	$0.00	$1080.00
Tot Lbr.	Hours	140	50	50	20	20	0	0	0	0	0	0	0	280
	Dollars	$3540.00	$840.00	$840.00	$480.00	$480.00	$0.00	$0.00	$0.00	$0.00	$0.00	$0.00	$0.00	$6180.00
LBR OHD 43.00%		$1522.20	$361.20	$361.20	$206.40	$206.40	$0.00	$0.00	$0.00	$0.00	$0.00	$0.00	$0.00	$2657.40
MATERIALS		$0.00	$0.00	$0.00	$0.00	$0.00	$0.00	$0.00	$0.00	$0.00	$0.00	$0.00	$0.00	$0.00
OTHER DIR.		$0.00	$0.00	$0.00	$0.00	$0.00	$0.00	$0.00	$0.00	$0.00	$0.00	$0.00	$0.00	$0.00
SUBTOTAL		$5062.20	$1201.20	$1201.20	$686.40	$686.40	$0.00	$0.00	$0.00	$0.00	$0.00	$0.00	$0.00	$8837.40
G&A 2.50%		$126.56	$30.03	$30.03	$17.16	$17.16	$0.00	$0.00	$0.00	$0.00	$0.00	$0.00	$0.00	$220.94
COST OF $ 0.50%		$25.31	$6.01	$6.01	$3.43	$3.43	$0.00	$0.00	$0.00	$0.00	$0.00	$0.00	$0.00	$44.19
SUBTOTAL		$5214.07	$1237.24	$1237.24	$706.99	$706.99	$0.00	$0.00	$0.00	$0.00	$0.00	$0.00	$0.00	$9102.52
FEE 10.00%		$521.41	$123.72	$123.72	$70.70	$70.70	$0.00	$0.00	$0.00	$0.00	$0.00	$0.00	$0.00	$910.25
GND TOTAL		$5735.47	$1360.96	$1360.96	$777.69	$777.69	$0.00	$0.00	$0.00	$0.00	$0.00	$0.00	$0.00	$10012.77

Figure 4-12 Completed spreadsheet A-1-1.

EST.TITLE: WBS TITLE:EDITS   ORIGINATOR ARB START YR.: 1986
EST.NMBR: .004   WBS NMBR: A-1-2   DATE: 10/16/85

LABOR		JAN 1986	FEB 1986	MAR 1986	APR 1986	MAY 1986	JUN 1986	JUL 1986	AUG 1986	SEP 1986	OCT 1986	NOV 1986	DEC 1986	TOTAL 1986
Prg Mgr	Rate/Hr	$35.00	$35.00	$35.00	$35.00	$35.00	$35.00	$35.00	$35.00	$35.00	$35.00	$35.00	$35.00	$35.00
	Hours	0	0	0	0	0	0	0	0	0	0	0	0	0
	Dollars	$0.00	$0.00	$0.00	$0.00	$0.00	$0.00	$0.00	$0.00	$0.00	$0.00	$0.00	$0.00	$0.00
Sr Prgmr	Rate/Hr	$30.00	$30.00	$30.00	$30.00	$30.00	$30.00	$30.00	$30.00	$30.00	$30.00	$30.00	$30.00	$30.00
	Hours	10	100	10	10	10	0	0	0	0	0	0	0	140
	Dollars	$300.00	$3000.00	$300.00	$300.00	$300.00	$0.00	$0.00	$0.00	$0.00	$0.00	$0.00	$0.00	$4200.00
Tech Wtr	Rate/Hr	$18.00	$18.00	$18.00	$18.00	$18.00	$18.00	$18.00	$18.00	$18.00	$18.00	$18.00	$18.00	$18.00
	Hours	10	10	10	10	10	0	0	0	0	0	0	0	50
	Dollars	$180.00	$180.00	$180.00	$180.00	$180.00	$0.00	$0.00	$0.00	$0.00	$0.00	$0.00	$0.00	$900.00
Data Anl	Rate/Hr	$12.00	$12.00	$12.00	$12.00	$12.00	$12.00	$12.00	$12.00	$12.00	$12.00	$12.00	$12.00	$12.00
	Hours	30	30	30	0	0	0	0	0	0	0	0	0	90
	Dollars	$360.00	$360.00	$360.00	$0.00	$0.00	$0.00	$0.00	$0.00	$0.00	$0.00	$0.00	$0.00	$1080.00
Tot Lbr.	Hours	50	140	50	20	20	0	0	0	0	0	0	0	280
	Dollars	$840.00	$3540.00	$840.00	$480.00	$480.00	$0.00	$0.00	$0.00	$0.00	$0.00	$0.00	$0.00	$6180.00
LBR OHD	43.00%	$361.20	$1522.20	$361.20	$206.40	$206.40	$0.00	$0.00	$0.00	$0.00	$0.00	$0.00	$0.00	$2657.40
MATERIALS		$0.00	$0.00	$0.00	$0.00	$0.00	$0.00	$0.00	$0.00	$0.00	$0.00	$0.00	$0.00	$0.00
OTHER DIR.		$0.00	$0.00	$0.00	$0.00	$0.00	$0.00	$0.00	$0.00	$0.00	$0.00	$0.00	$0.00	$0.00
SUBTOTAL		$1201.20	$5062.20	$1201.20	$686.40	$686.40	$0.00	$0.00	$0.00	$0.00	$0.00	$0.00	$0.00	$8837.40
G&A	2.50%	$30.03	$126.56	$30.03	$17.16	$17.16	$0.00	$0.00	$0.00	$0.00	$0.00	$0.00	$0.00	$220.94
COST OF $	0.50%	$6.01	$25.31	$6.01	$3.43	$3.43	$0.00	$0.00	$0.00	$0.00	$0.00	$0.00	$0.00	$44.19
SUBTOTAL		$1237.24	$5214.07	$1237.24	$706.99	$706.99	$0.00	$0.00	$0.00	$0.00	$0.00	$0.00	$0.00	$9102.52
FEE	10.00%	$123.72	$521.41	$123.72	$70.70	$70.70	$0.00	$0.00	$0.00	$0.00	$0.00	$0.00	$0.00	$910.25
GND TOTAL		$1360.96	$5735.47	$1360.96	$777.69	$777.69	$0.00	$0.00	$0.00	$0.00	$0.00	$0.00	$0.00	$10012.77

Figure 4-13 Completed spreadsheet A-1-2.

MICROESTIMATING(TM) SYSTEM (Copyright 1984, MOBILE DATA SERVICES

EST.TITLE:COSTPLAN   WES TITLE:FLD SERVICORIGINATOR   ARS   START YR.: 1986

EST.NMBR: .004   WES NMBR: A-4-4   DATE: 10/16/85

MONTH		JAN 1986	FEB 1986	MAR 1986	APR 1986	MAY 1986	JUN 1986	JUL 1986	AUG 1986	SEP 1986	OCT 1986	NOV 1986	DEC 1986	TOTAL 1986
LABOR														
Prg Mgr	Rate/Hr	$35.00	$35.00	$35.00	$35.00	$35.00	$35.00	$35.00	$35.00	$35.00	$35.00	$35.00	$35.00	$35.00
	Hours	0	0	0	0	0	0	0	0	0	0	0	0	0
	Dollars	$0.00	$0.00	$0.00	$0.00	$0.00	$0.00	$0.00	$0.00	$0.00	$0.00	$0.00	$0.00	$0.00
Sr Prgmr	Rate/Hr	$30.00	$30.00	$30.00	$30.00	$30.00	$30.00	$30.00	$30.00	$30.00	$30.00	$30.00	$30.00	$30.00
	Hours	0	0	0	0	0	0	0	0	0	10	10	10	30
	Dollars	$0.00	$0.00	$0.00	$0.00	$0.00	$0.00	$0.00	$0.00	$0.00	$300.00	$300.00	$300.00	$900.00
Tech Wtr	Rate/Hr	$18.00	$18.00	$18.00	$18.00	$18.00	$18.00	$18.00	$18.00	$18.00	$18.00	$18.00	$18.00	$18.00
	Hours	0	0	0	0	0	0	0	0	0	0	0	0	0
	Dollars	$0.00	$0.00	$0.00	$0.00	$0.00	$0.00	$0.00	$0.00	$0.00	$0.00	$0.00	$0.00	$0.00
Data Anl	Rate/Hr	$12.00	$12.00	$12.00	$12.00	$12.00	$12.00	$12.00	$12.00	$12.00	$12.00	$12.00	$12.00	$12.00
	Hours	0	0	0	0	0	0	0	0	0	20	20	20	60
	Dollars	$0.00	$0.00	$0.00	$0.00	$0.00	$0.00	$0.00	$0.00	$0.00	$240.00	$240.00	$240.00	$720.00
Tot Lbr.	Hours	0	0	0	0	0	0	0	0	0	30	30	30	90
	Dollars	$0.00	$0.00	$0.00	$0.00	$0.00	$0.00	$0.00	$0.00	$0.00	$540.00	$540.00	$540.00	$1620.00
LBR OHD 43.00%		$0.00	$0.00	$0.00	$0.00	$0.00	$0.00	$0.00	$0.00	$0.00	$232.20	$232.20	$232.20	$696.60
MATERIALS		$0.00	$0.00	$0.00	$0.00	$0.00	$0.00	$0.00	$0.00	$0.00	$0.00	$0.00	$0.00	$0.00
OTHER DIR.		$0.00	$0.00	$0.00	$0.00	$0.00	$0.00	$0.00	$0.00	$0.00	$0.00	$0.00	$0.00	$0.00
SUBTOTAL		$0.00	$0.00	$0.00	$0.00	$0.00	$0.00	$0.00	$0.00	$0.00	$772.20	$772.20	$772.20	$2316.60
G&A 2.50%		$0.00	$0.00	$0.00	$0.00	$0.00	$0.00	$0.00	$0.00	$0.00	$19.31	$19.31	$19.31	$57.92
COST OF $ 0.50%		$0.00	$0.00	$0.00	$0.00	$0.00	$0.00	$0.00	$0.00	$0.00	$3.86	$3.86	$3.86	$11.58
SUBTOTAL		$0.00	$0.00	$0.00	$0.00	$0.00	$0.00	$0.00	$0.00	$0.00	$795.37	$795.37	$795.37	$2386.10
FEE 10.00%		$0.00	$0.00	$0.00	$0.00	$0.00	$0.00	$0.00	$0.00	$0.00	$79.54	$79.54	$79.54	$238.61
GND TOTAL		$0.00	$0.00	$0.00	$0.00	$0.00	$0.00	$0.00	$0.00	$0.00	$874.90	$874.90	$874.90	$2624.71

Figure 4-14 Completed spreadsheet A-4-4.

```
MICROESTIMATING(TM) SYSTEM (Copyright 1984, MOBILE DATA SERVICES
EST.TITLE:COSTPLAN    WBS TITLE:TOP    ORIGINATOR  WBS  START VR.:  :986
EST.NMBR:.004        WBS NMBR: 1-0    DATE:  10/16/85
==========================================================================================
MONTH----------:    JAN    FEB    MAR    APR    MAY    JUN    JUL    AUG    SEP    OCT    NOV    DEC   TOTAL
YEAR-----------:   :986   :986   :986   :986   :986   :986   :986   :986   :986   :986   :986   :986   :986
==========================================================================================
WBS NO.    TITLE
1-0        COSTFORM

1-1        PROGRAMMING

1-1-1      INPUTS
1-1-2      EDITS
1-1-3      ERROR MSG
1-1-4      REPT GEN
1-1-5      USER INTER

1-2        TESTING

1-2-1      IN-HOUSE
1-2-2      MKT USE
1-2-3      UPDATES

1-3        DOCMTATION

1-3-1      BASICS
1-3-2      OP. MANUAL
1-3-3      SAMPLE EX.
1-3-4      UPDATES

1-4        SUPPORT

1-4-1      INSTALLATN
1-4-2      TRAINING
1-4-3      UPDATES
1-4-4      FLD SVC
```

Figure 4-15 Summary sheet headings and titles.

the sheet with the file designation A-1-1.004 and look for a number or group of numbers named Grandtotal. (It so happens that we have named the row at the bottom of each input level worksheet as Grandtotal.) If your spreadsheet software package does not have the capability to name cells or groups of cells, the appropriate coordinate designations will replace the name Grandtotal. Scanning across the monthly inputs to this

	1	2	3
1	"MICROESTIMATING(TM) SYSTEM :Copyright 1984, MOBILE DATA SERVICES"		
2	"EST.TITLE:"	"COSTPLAN"	"WES TITLE:"
3	"EST.NMBR:"	".004"	"WES NMBR:"
4	"*****************"	"*****************"	"*****************"
5	"MONTH----->"	"--------->"	"JAN"
6	"YEAR------>"	"--------->"	R2C8
7	"*****************"	"*****************"	"*****************"
8	"WES NO."	"TITLE"	
9	"A-Ø"	"TOTAL COST"	R[+23]C+R[+16]C+R[+ 10]C+R[+2]C
10			
11	"A-1"	"PROGRMMING"	R[+6]C+R[+5]C+R[+4] C+R[+3]C+R[+2]C
12	"----------"	"----------"	"----------"
13	"A-1-1"	"INPUTS"	[A-1-1.004 Grandtot al]
14	"A-1-2"	"EDITS"	[A-1-2.004 Grandtot al]
15	"A-1-3"	"ERROR MSGS"	[A-1-3.004 Grandtot al]
16	"A-1-4"	"REPT GEN"	[A-1-4.004 Grandtot al]
17	"A-1-5"	"USER INTER."	[A-1-5.004 Grandtot al]
18			
19	"A-2"	"TESTING"	R[+4]C+R[+3]C+R[+2] C
20	"----------"	"----------"	"----------"
21	"A-2-1"	"IN-HOUSE"	[A-2-1.004 Grandtot al]
22	"A-2-2"	"MKT USE"	[A-2-2.004 Grandtot al]
23	"A-2-3"	"UPDATES"	[A-2-3.004 Grandtot al]
24			
25	"A-3"	"DOCMTATION"	R[+5]C+R[+4]C+R[+3] C+R[+2]C
26	"----------"	"----------"	"----------"
27	"A-3-1"	"BASICS"	[A-3-1.004 Grandtot al]
28	"A-3-2"	"OP. MANUAL"	[A-3-2.004 Grandtot al]
29	"A-3-3"	"SAMPLE EX."	[A-3-3.004 Grandtot al]
30	"A-3-4"	"UPDATES"	[A-3-4.004 Grandtot al]
31			
32	"A-4"	"SUPPORT"	R[+5]C+R[+4]C+R[+3] C+R[+2]C
33	"----------"	"----------"	"----------"
34	"A-4-1"	"INSTALLATN"	[A-4-1.004 Grandtot al]
35	"A-4-2"	"TRAINING"	[A-4-2.004 Grandtot al]
36	"A-4-3"	"UPDATES"	[A-4-3.004 Grandtot al]
37	"A-4-4"	"FLD SVC"	[A-4-4.004 Grandtot al]

Figure 4-16 Importing of data.

top-level spreadsheet formula matrix (Figures 4-16 through 4-20), you will notice that the cell formulas are identical for each month horizontally and change only by the work element designator vertically. This feature permits extensive use of the copy and edit functions of the spreadsheet rather than having to put in every formula.

Now notice the four boxed-in formulas on Figure 4-17. These are the

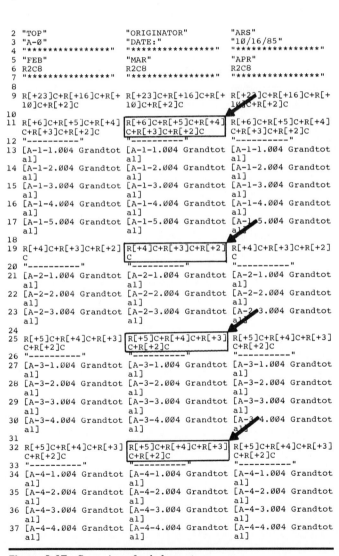

```
                  4                 5                 6
 1

 2 "TOP"              "ORIGINATOR"      "ARS"
 3 "A-Ø"              "DATE:"           "1Ø/16/85"
 4 "****************" "****************" "****************"
 5 "FEB"              "MAR"             "APR"
 6 R2C8               R2C8              R2C8
 7 "****************" "****************" "****************"
 8
 9 R[+23]C+R[+16]C+R[+ R[+23]C+R[+16]C+R[+ R[+23]C+R[+16]C+R[+
   1Ø]C+R[+2]C        1Ø]C+R[+2]C        1Ø]C+R[+2]C
1Ø
11 R[+6]C+R[+5]C+R[+4] R[+6]C+R[+5]C+R[+4] R[+6]C+R[+5]C+R[+4]
   C+R[+3]C+R[+2]C    C+R[+3]C+R[+2]C    C+R[+3]C+R[+2]C
12 "----------"       "----------"       "----------"
13 [A-1-1.ØØ4 Grandtot [A-1-1.ØØ4 Grandtot [A-1-1.ØØ4 Grandtot
   al]                al]                al]
14 [A-1-2.ØØ4 Grandtot [A-1-2.ØØ4 Grandtot [A-1-2.ØØ4 Grandtot
   al]                al]                al]
15 [A-1-3.ØØ4 Grandtot [A-1-3.ØØ4 Grandtot [A-1-3.ØØ4 Grandtot
   al]                al]                al]
16 [A-1-4.ØØ4 Grandtot [A-1-4.ØØ4 Grandtot [A-1-4.ØØ4 Grandtot
   al]                al]                al]
17 [A-1-5.ØØ4 Grandtot [A-1-5.ØØ4 Grandtot [A-1-5.ØØ4 Grandtot
   al]                al]                al]
18
19 R[+4]C+R[+3]C+R[+2] R[+4]C+R[+3]C+R[+2] R[+4]C+R[+3]C+R[+2]
   C                  C                  C
2Ø "----------"       "----------"       "----------"
21 [A-2-1.ØØ4 Grandtot [A-2-1.ØØ4 Grandtot [A-2-1.ØØ4 Grandtot
   al]                al]                al]
22 [A-2-2.ØØ4 Grandtot [A-2-2.ØØ4 Grandtot [A-2-2.ØØ4 Grandtot
   al]                al]                al]
23 [A-2-3.ØØ4 Grandtot [A-2-3.ØØ4 Grandtot [A-2-3.ØØ4 Grandtot
   al]                al]                al]
24
25 R[+5]C+R[+4]C+R[+3] R[+5]C+R[+4]C+R[+3] R[+5]C+R[+4]C+R[+3]
   C+R[+2]C           C+R[+2]C           C+R[+2]C
26 "----------"       "----------"       "----------"
27 [A-3-1.ØØ4 Grandtot [A-3-1.ØØ4 Grandtot [A-3-1.ØØ4 Grandtot
   al]                al]                al]
28 [A-3-2.ØØ4 Grandtot [A-3-2.ØØ4 Grandtot [A-3-2.ØØ4 Grandtot
   al]                al]                al]
29 [A-3-3.ØØ4 Grandtot [A-3-3.ØØ4 Grandtot [A-3-3.ØØ4 Grandtot
   al]                al]                al]
3Ø [A-3-4.ØØ4 Grandtot [A-3-4.ØØ4 Grandtot [A-3-4.ØØ4 Grandtot
   al]                al]                al]
31
32 R[+5]C+R[+4]C+R[+3] R[+5]C+R[+4]C+R[+3] R[+5]C+R[+4]C+R[+3]
   C+R[+2]C           C+R[+2]C           C+R[+2]C
33 "----------"       "----------"       "----------"
34 [A-4-1.ØØ4 Grandtot [A-4-1.ØØ4 Grandtot [A-4-1.ØØ4 Grandtot
   al]                al]                al]
35 [A-4-2.ØØ4 Grandtot [A-4-2.ØØ4 Grandtot [A-4-2.ØØ4 Grandtot
   al]                al]                al]
36 [A-4-3.ØØ4 Grandtot [A-4-3.ØØ4 Grandtot [A-4-3.ØØ4 Grandtot
   al]                al]                al]
37 [A-4-4.ØØ4 Grandtot [A-4-4.ØØ4 Grandtot [A-4-4.ØØ4 Grandtot
   al]                al]                al]
```

Figure 4-17 Summing of subelements.

formulas that sum the inputs from level 3 to level 2. Notice also that the respective formulas in the same rows for all months are identical. This feature, too, permits extensive use of the spreadsheet's copy function instead of entering each formula individually. Likewise, the formula in row 9 of column 8 in Figure 4-18 is the formula that sums the level 2 estimates into the top-level estimate for each month. This formula is

```
              7                    8                    9
 1

 2 "START YR.:"         1986
 3
 4 "****************"    "****************"    "****************"
 5 "MAY"                 "JUN"                 "JUL"
 6 R2C8                  R2C8                  R2C8
 7 "****************"    "****************"    "****************"
 8
 9 R[+23]C+R[+16]C+R[+  R[+23]C+R[+16]C+R[+  R[+23]C+R[+16]C+R[+
   10]C+R[+2]C           10]C+R[+2]C          10]C+R[+2]C
10
11 R[+6]C+R[+5]C+R[+4]  R[+6]C+R[+5]C+R[+4]  R[+6]C+R[+5]C+R[+4]
   C+R[+3]C+R[+2]C       C+R[+3]C+R[+2]C      C+R[+3]C+R[+2]C
12 "----------"         "----------"         "----------"
13 [A-1-1.004 Grandtot  [A-1-1.004 Grandtot  [A-1-1.004 Grandtot
   al]                   al]                  al]
14 [A-1-2.004 Grandtot  [A-1-2.004 Grandtot  [A-1-2.004 Grandtot
   al]                   al]                  al]
15 [A-1-3.004 Grandtot  [A-1-3.004 Grandtot  [A-1-3.004 Grandtot
   al]                   al]                  al]
16 [A-1-4.004 Grandtot  [A-1-4.004 Grandtot  [A-1-4.004 Grandtot
   al]                   al]                  al]
17 [A-1-5.004 Grandtot  [A-1-5.004 Grandtot  [A-1-5.004 Grandtot
   al]                   al]                  al]
18
19 R[+4]C+R[+3]C+R[+2]  R[+4]C+R[+3]C+R[+2]  R[+4]C+R[+3]C+R[+2]
   C                     C                    C
20 "----------"         "----------"         "----------"
21 [A-2-1.004 Grandtot  [A-2-1.004 Grandtot  [A-2-1.004 Grandtot
   al]                   al]                  al]
22 [A-2-2.004 Grandtot  [A-2-2.004 Grandtot  [A-2-2.004 Grandtot
   al]                   al]                  al]
23 [A-2-3.004 Grandtot  [A-2-3.004 Grandtot  [A-2-3.004 Grandtot
   al]                   al]                  al]
24
25 R[+5]C+R[+4]C+R[+3]  R[+5]C+R[+4]C+R[+3]  R[+5]C+R[+4]C+R[+3]
   C+R[+2]C              C+R[+2]C             C+R[+2]C
26 "----------"         "----------"         "----------"
27 [A-3-1.004 Grandtot  [A-3-1.004 Grandtot  [A-3-1.004 Grandtot
   al]                   al]                  al]
28 [A-3-2.004 Grandtot  [A-3-2.004 Grandtot  [A-3-2.004 Grandtot
   al]                   al]                  al]
29 [A-3-3.004 Grandtot  [A-3-3.004 Grandtot  [A-3-3.004 Grandtot
   al]                   al]                  al]
30 [A-3-4.004 Grandtot  [A-3-4.004 Grandtot  [A-3-4.004 Grandtot
   al]                   al]                  al]
31
32 R[+5]C+R[+4]C+R[+3]  R[+5]C+R[+4]C+R[+3]  R[+5]C+R[+4]C+R[+3]
   C+R[+2]C              C+R[+2]C             C+R[+2]C
33 "----------"         "----------"         "----------"
34 [A-4-1.004 Grandtot  [A-4-1.004 Grandtot  [A-4-1.004 Grandtot
   al]                   al]                  al]
35 [A-4-2.004 Grandtot  [A-4-2.004 Grandtot  [A-4-2.004 Grandtot
   al]                   al]                  al]
36 [A-4-3.004 Grandtot  [A-4-3.004 Grandtot  [A-4-3.004 Grandtot
   al]                   al]                  al]
37 [A-4-4.004 Grandtot  [A-4-4.004 Grandtot  [A-4-4.004 Grandtot
   al]                   al]                  al]
```

Figure 4-18 Summing of monthly costs.

identical for all months. Since *relative* formulas are used, the formulas can again be copied to the other top-level cells for each month.

In Figure 4-19, the R2C8 located in row 6 of column 11 puts the start year into the column heading. The same value is used for all column headings on this spreadsheet. For multiyear estimates, a formula:

$$[R2C8] + 1 \qquad\qquad (4\text{-}5)$$

can be used to designate the next year, and

$$[R2C8] + 2 \qquad\qquad (4\text{-}6)$$

the following year, and so on.

Column 15, as seen on Figure 4-20, imports the row grand totals from the previous input sheets and sums the level 2 and top-level costs horizontally. The total estimate at the top level is computed by the relative formula in row 9 of column 15.

Computing the top level summary   Now that the top-level worksheet and its formulas are built, the top sheet can be calculated. When the top sheet (A-0) is loaded from the file COSTPLAN.004, inputs are automatically provided from the supporting worksheets, and the top level summary is calculated and displayed on the video screen. A printout of the final, consolidated, and computed estimate is shown on Figure 4-21.

On comparing Figure 4-22 with 4-4, it is seen that schedule elements coincide with work elements at level 2 of the estimate (A-1, A-2, A-3, and A-4). Therefore, we see that resources for level 3 elements under each of these level 2 elements occur in the months shown on the project schedule.

The spread of costs during the project at level 2 of the estimate can be observed in the boxed-in rows on Figure 4-23. The total program costs for all elements and the grand total are automatically printed in the last column of the spreadsheet (Figure 4-24).

Typical Construction Estimating Spreadsheet Template

Not only can a detailed estimate be built for a specific project as shown above, but spreadsheet templates can be constructed to cover an entire discipline within one of the four major categories of work activities and work outputs (process, product, project, and service). For some specific applications such as home construction, the estimator may wish to ignore, for cost estimating purposes, the *time-based* or *schedule* dimension of estimating. The following represents such a template. More detailed help is provided to the estimator in providing factors that can be used over and over again in subsequent estimates once the initial estimate spreadsheet or *template* is built.

Figure 4-25 shows a WES that is configured for a typical home construction contractor who usually subcontracts the labor for the major elements of work and who may or may not buy the materials for each part of the home construction project.

```
                  10                      11                      12
 1

 2
 3
 4  "****************"  "**************"  "****************"
 5  "AUG"              "SEP"             "OCT"
 6  R2C8               R2C8              R2C8
 7  "****************"  "**************"  "****************"
 8
 9  R[+23]C+R[+16]C+R[+  R[+23]C+R[+16]C+R[+  R[+23]C+R[+16]C+R[+
    10]C+R[+2]C          10]C+R[+2]C          10]C+R[+2]C
10
11  R[+6]C+R[+5]C+R[+4]  R[+6]C+R[+5]C+R[+4]  R[+6]C+R[+5]C+R[+4]
    C+R[+3]C+R[+2]C      C+R[+3]C+R[+2]C      C+R[+3]C+R[+2]C
12  "----------"        "----------"        "----------"
13  [A-1-1.004 Grandtot  [A-1-1.004 Grandtot  [A-1-1.004 Grandtot
    al]                  al]                  al]
14  [A-1-2.004 Grandtot  [A-1-2.004 Grandtot  [A-1-2.004 Grandtot
    al]                  al]                  al]
15  [A-1-3.004 Grandtot  [A-1-3.004 Grandtot  [A-1-3.004 Grandtot
    al]                  al]                  al]
16  [A-1-4.004 Grandtot  [A-1-4.004 Grandtot  [A-1-4.004 Grandtot
    al]                  al]                  al]
17  [A-1-5.004 Grandtot  [A-1-5.004 Grandtot  [A-1-5.004 Grandtot
    al]                  al]                  al]
18
19  R[+4]C+R[+3]C+R[+2]  R[+4]C+R[+3]C+R[+2]  R[+4]C+R[+3]C+R[+2]
    C                    C                    C
20  "----------"        "----------"        "----------"
21  [A-2-1.004 Grandtot  [A-2-1.004 Grandtot  [A-2-1.004 Grandtot
    al]                  al]                  al]
22  [A-2-2.004 Grandtot  [A-2-2.004 Grandtot  [A-2-2.004 Grandtot
    al]                  al]                  al]
23  [A-2-3.004 Grandtot  [A-2-3.004 Grandtot  [A-2-3.004 Grandtot
    al]                  al]                  al]
24
25  R[+5]C+R[+4]C+R[+3]  R[+5]C+R[+4]C+R[+3]  R[+5]C+R[+4]C+R[+3]
    C+R[+2]C             C+R[+2]C             C+R[+2]C
26  "----------"        "----------"        "----------"
27  [A-3-1.004 Grandtot  [A-3-1.004 Grandtot  [A-3-1.004 Grandtot
    al]                  al]                  al]
28  [A-3-2.004 Grandtot  [A-3-2.004 Grandtot  [A-3-2.004 Grandtot
    al]                  al]                  al]
29  [A-3-3.004 Grandtot  [A-3-3.004 Grandtot  [A-3-3.004 Grandtot
    al]                  al]                  al]
30  [A-3-4.004 Grandtot  [A-3-4.004 Grandtot  [A-3-4.004 Grandtot
    al]                  al]                  al]
31
32  R[+5]C+R[+4]C+R[+3]  R[+5]C+R[+4]C+R[+3]  R[+5]C+R[+4]C+R[+3]
    C+R[+2]C             C+R[+2]C             C+R[+2]C
33  "----------"        "----------"        "----------"
34  [A-4-1.004 Grandtot  [A-4-1.004 Grandtot  [A-4-1.004 Grandtot
    al]                  al]                  al]
35  [A-4-2.004 Grandtot  [A-4-2.004 Grandtot  [A-4-2.004 Grandtot
    al]                  al]                  al]
36  [A-4-3.004 Grandtot  [A-4-3.004 Grandtot  [A-4-3.004 Grandtot
    al]                  al]                  al]
37  [A-4-4.004 Grandtot  [A-4-4.004 Grandtot  [A-4-4.004 Grandtot
    al]                  al]                  al]
```

Figure 4-19 Treatment of year designator.

```
 1            13                14                      15

 2
 3
 4   "****************"  "****************"   "****************"
 5   "NOV"              "DEC"                "TOTAL"
 6   R2C8              R2C8                  R2C8
 7   "****************"  "****************"   "****************"
 8
 9   R[+23]C+R[+16]C+R[+   R[+23]C+R[+16]C+R[+   R[+23]C+R[+16]C+R[+10]C+R[+
10   10]C+R[+2]C          10]C+R[+2]C          2]C
11   R[+6]C+R[+5]C+R[+4]   R[+6]C+R[+5]C+R[+4]   R[+6]C+R[+5]C+R[+4]C+R[+3]C
     C+R[+3]C+R[+2]C      C+R[+3]C+R[+2]C      +R[+2]C
12   "----------"        "----------"         "----------"
13   [A-1-1.004 Grandtot  [A-1-1.004 Grandtot  [A-1-1.004 Grandtotal]
     al]                  al]
14   [A-1-2.004 Grandtot  [A-1-2.004 Grandtot  [A-1-2.004 Grandtotal]
     al]                  al]
15   [A-1-3.004 Grandtot  [A-1-3.004 Grandtot  [A-1-3.004 Grandtotal]
     al]                  al]
16   [A-1-4.004 Grandtot  [A-1-4.004 Grandtot  [A-1-4.004 Grandtotal]
     al]                  al]
17   [A-1-5.004 Grandtot  [A-1-5.004 Grandtot  [A-1-5.004 Grandtotal]
     al]                  al]
18
19   R[+4]C+R[+3]C+R[+2]   R[+4]C+R[+3]C+R[+2]   R[+4]C+R[+3]C+R[+2]C
     C                    C
20   "----------"        "----------"         "----------"
21   [A-2-1.004 Grandtot  [A-2-1.004 Grandtot  [A-2-1.004 Grandtotal]
     al]                  al]
22   [A-2-2.004 Grandtot  [A-2-2.004 Grandtot  [A-2-2.004 Grandtotal]
     al]                  al]
23   [A-2-3.004 Grandtot  [A-2-3.004 Grandtot  [A-2-3.004 Grandtotal]
     al]                  al]
24
25   R[+5]C+R[+4]C+R[+3]   R[+5]C+R[+4]C+R[+3]   R[+5]C+R[+4]C+R[+3]C+R[+2]C
     C+R[+2]C             C+R[+2]C
26   "----------"        "----------"         "----------"
27   [A-3-1.004 Grandtot  [A-3-1.004 Grandtot  [A-3-1.004 Grandtotal]
     al]                  al]
28   [A-3-2.004 Grandtot  [A-3-2.004 Grandtot  [A-3-2.004 Grandtotal]
     al]                  al]
29   [A-3-3.004 Grandtot  [A-3-3.004 Grandtot  [A-3-3.004 Grandtotal]
     al]                  al]
30   [A-3-4.004 Grandtot  [A-3-4.004 Grandtot  [A-3-4.004 Grandtotal]
     al]                  al]
31
32   R[+5]C+R[+4]C+R[+3]   R[+5]C+R[+4]C+R[+3]   R[+5]C+R[+4]C+R[+3]C+R[+2]C
     C+R[+2]C             C+R[+2]C
33   "----------"        "----------"         "----------"
34   [A-4-1.004 Grandtot  [A-4-1.004 Grandtot  [A-4-1.004 Grandtotal]
     al]                  al]
35   [A-4-2.004 Grandtot  [A-4-2.004 Grandtot  [A-4-2.004 Grandtotal]
     al]                  al]
36   [A-4-3.004 Grandtot  [A-4-3.004 Grandtot  [A-4-3.004 Grandtotal]
     al]                  al]
37   [A-4-4.004 Grandtot  [A-4-4.004 Grandtot  [A-4-4.004 Grandtotal]
     al]                  al]
```

Figure 4-20 Summing of total costs.

MICROESTIMATING(TM) SYSTEM (Copyright 1984, MOBILE DATA SERVICES
EST.TITLE:COSTPLAN   WES TITLE:TOP   ORIGINATOR WES   START YR.: 1986
EST.NMBR: .004   WES NMBR: A-0   DATE: 10/16/85

WES NO.	TITLE	JAN 1986	FEB 1986	MAR 1986	APR 1986	MAY 1986	JUN 1986	JUL 1986	AUG 1986	SEP 1986	OCT 1986	NOV 1986	DEC 1986	TOTAL 1986
A-0	TOTAL COST	$16849.98	$15715.84	$14581.71	$15505.22	$15505.22	$19806.82	$19442.28	$19928.34	$15229.79	$17692.47	$15262.19	$14047.05	$199566.90
A-1	PROGRAMMING	$16849.98	$15715.84	$14581.71	$10531.24	$10531.24	$0.00	$0.00	$0.00	$0.00	$0.00	$0.00	$0.00	$68210.00
A-1-1	INPUTS	$5735.47	$1360.96	$1360.96	$777.69	$777.69	$0.00	$0.00	$0.00	$0.00	$0.00	$0.00	$0.00	$10012.77
A-1-2	EDITS	$1360.96	$5735.47	$1360.96	$777.69	$777.69	$0.00	$0.00	$0.00	$0.00	$0.00	$0.00	$0.00	$10012.77
A-1-3	ERROR MSGS	$1360.96	$1360.96	$5735.47	$777.69	$777.69	$0.00	$0.00	$0.00	$0.00	$0.00	$0.00	$0.00	$10012.77
A-1-4	REPT GEN	$1360.96	$1360.96	$1360.96	$5152.20	$777.69	$0.00	$0.00	$0.00	$0.00	$0.00	$0.00	$0.00	$10012.77
A-1-5	USER INTER	$7031.62	$5897.49	$4763.36	$3045.96	$7420.47	$0.00	$0.00	$0.00	$0.00	$0.00	$0.00	$0.00	$28158.90
A-2	TESTING	$0.00	$0.00	$0.00	$4973.98	$4973.98	$7566.29	$8052.34	$8538.40	$0.00	$0.00	$0.00	$0.00	$34105.00
A-2-1	IN-HOUSE	$0.00	$0.00	$0.00	$3710.24	$3710.24	$2252.06	$2252.06	$2252.06	$0.00	$0.00	$0.00	$0.00	$14176.66
A-2-2	MKT USE	$0.00	$0.00	$0.00	$631.87	$631.87	$3629.23	$3629.23	$2171.05	$0.00	$0.00	$0.00	$0.00	$10693.25
A-2-3	UPDATES	$0.00	$0.00	$0.00	$631.87	$631.87	$1685.00	$2171.05	$4115.28	$0.00	$0.00	$0.00	$0.00	$9235.08
A-3	DOCMTATION	$0.00	$0.00	$0.00	$0.00	$0.00	$12240.54	$11389.74	$11389.74	$15229.79	$0.00	$0.00	$0.00	$50250.19
A-3-1	BASICS	$0.00	$0.00	$0.00	$0.00	$0.00	$1053.12	$769.59	$769.59	$1620.19	$0.00	$0.00	$0.00	$4212.49
A-3-2	OP. MANUAL	$0.00	$0.00	$0.00	$0.00	$0.00	$4066.68	$3977.57	$4171.99	$5800.28	$0.00	$0.00	$0.00	$18016.51
A-3-3	SAMPLE EX.	$0.00	$0.00	$0.00	$0.00	$0.00	$5233.21	$4755.26	$4560.83	$5217.01	$0.00	$0.00	$0.00	$19766.32
A-3-4	UPDATES	$0.00	$0.00	$0.00	$0.00	$0.00	$1887.52	$1887.52	$1887.52	$2592.30	$0.00	$0.00	$0.00	$8254.87
A-4	SUPPORT	$0.00	$0.00	$0.00	$0.00	$0.00	$0.00	$0.00	$0.00	$0.00	$17692.47	$15262.19	$14047.05	$47001.71
A-4-1	INSTALLA'N	$0.00	$0.00	$0.00	$0.00	$0.00	$0.00	$0.00	$0.00	$0.00	$8668.02	$6237.73	$5022.59	$19928.34
A-4-2	TRAINING	$0.00	$0.00	$0.00	$0.00	$0.00	$0.00	$0.00	$0.00	$0.00	$3288.99	$3288.99	$3288.99	$9866.96
A-4-3	UPDATES	$0.00	$0.00	$0.00	$0.00	$0.00	$0.00	$0.00	$0.00	$0.00	$4860.57	$4860.57	$4860.57	$14581.71
A-4-4	FLD SVC	$0.00	$0.00	$0.00	$0.00	$0.00	$0.00	$0.00	$0.00	$0.00	$874.90	$874.90	$874.90	$2624.71

Figure 4-21 Completed summary worksheet.

```
MICROESTIMATING(TM) SYSTEM :Copyright 1984, MOBILE DATA SERVICES
EST.TITLE:COSTPLAN   WES TITLE:TOP      ORIGINATOR ARS   START YR.: 1986
EST.NMBR: .004       WES NMBR: A-0      DATE: 10/16/85
```

MONTH YEAR	JAN 1986	FEB 1986	MAR 1986	APR 1986	MAY 1986	JUN 1986	JUL 1986	AUG 1986	SEP 1986	OCT 1986	NOV 1986	DEC 1986	TOTAL 1986
WES NO. TITLE													
A-0 TOTAL COST	$16849.98	$15715.84	$14581.71	$15505.22	$15505.22	$19806.82	$19442.28	$19928.34	$15229.79	$17692.47	$15262.19	$14047.05	$199566.90
A-1 PROGRAMMING	$16849.98	$15715.84	$14581.71	$10531.24	$10531.24	$0.00	$0.00	$0.00	$0.00	$0.00	$0.00	$0.00	$68210.00
A-1-1 INPUTS	$5735.47	$1360.96	$1360.96	$777.69	$777.69	$0.00	$0.00	$0.00	$0.00	$0.00	$0.00	$0.00	$10012.77
A-1-2 EDITS	$1360.96	$5735.47	$1360.96	$777.69	$777.69	$0.00	$0.00	$0.00	$0.00	$0.00	$0.00	$0.00	$10012.77
A-1-3 ERROR MSG	$1360.96	$1360.96	$5735.47	$777.69	$777.69	$0.00	$0.00	$0.00	$0.00	$0.00	$0.00	$0.00	$10012.77
A-1-4 REPT GEN	$1360.96	$1360.96	$1360.96	$5152.20	$777.69	$0.00	$0.00	$0.00	$0.00	$0.00	$0.00	$0.00	$10012.77
A-1-5 USER INTER	$7031.62	$5897.49	$4763.36	$3045.96	$7420.47	$0.00	$0.00	$0.00	$0.00	$0.00	$0.00	$0.00	$28158.90
A-2 TESTING	$0.00	$0.00	$0.00	$4973.98	$4973.98	$7566.29	$9052.34	$8538.40	$0.00	$0.00	$0.00	$0.00	$34105.00
A-2-1 IN-HOUSE	$0.00	$0.00	$0.00	$3710.24	$3710.24	$2252.06	$2252.06	$2252.06	$0.00	$0.00	$0.00	$0.00	$14176.66
A-2-2 MKT USE	$0.00	$0.00	$0.00	$631.87	$631.87	$3629.23	$3629.23	$2171.05	$0.00	$0.00	$0.00	$0.00	$10693.25
A-2-3 UPDATES	$0.00	$0.00	$0.00	$631.87	$631.87	$1685.00	$2171.05	$4115.28	$0.00	$0.00	$0.00	$0.00	$9235.08
A-3 DOCMTATION	$0.00	$0.00	$0.00	$0.00	$0.00	$12240.54	$11389.94	$11389.94	$15229.79	$0.00	$0.00	$0.00	$50250.19
A-3-1 BASICS	$0.00	$0.00	$0.00	$0.00	$0.00	$1053.12	$769.59	$769.59	$1620.19	$0.00	$0.00	$0.00	$4212.49
A-3-2 OP. MANUAL	$0.00	$0.00	$0.00	$0.00	$0.00	$4066.68	$3977.57	$4171.99	$5800.28	$0.00	$0.00	$0.00	$18016.51
A-3-3 SAMPLE EX.	$0.00	$0.00	$0.00	$0.00	$0.00	$5233.21	$4755.26	$4560.83	$5217.01	$0.00	$0.00	$0.00	$19766.32
A-3-4 UPDATES	$0.00	$0.00	$0.00	$0.00	$0.00	$1887.52	$1887.52	$1887.52	$2592.30	$0.00	$0.00	$0.00	$8254.87
A-4 SUPPORT	$0.00	$0.00	$0.00	$0.00	$0.00	$0.00	$0.00	$0.00	$0.00	$17692.47	$15262.19	$14047.05	$47001.71
A-4-1 INSTALLATN	$0.00	$0.00	$0.00	$0.00	$0.00	$0.00	$0.00	$0.00	$0.00	$8668.02	$6237.73	$5022.59	$19928.34
A-4-2 TRAINING	$0.00	$0.00	$0.00	$0.00	$0.00	$0.00	$0.00	$0.00	$0.00	$3288.99	$3288.99	$3288.99	$9866.96
A-4-3 UPDATES	$0.00	$0.00	$0.00	$0.00	$0.00	$0.00	$0.00	$0.00	$0.00	$4860.57	$4860.57	$4860.57	$14581.71
A-4-4 FLD SVC	$0.00	$0.00	$0.00	$0.00	$0.00	$0.00	$0.00	$0.00	$0.00	$874.90	$874.90	$874.90	$2624.71

Figure 4-22 Correlation of inputs with schedule.

MICROESTIMATING(TM) SYSTEM :Copyright 1984, MOBILE DATA SERVICES

EST.TITLE:COSTPLAN   WBS TITLE:TOP   ORIGINATOR ARS   START YR.: 1986
EST.NMBR: .004   WBS NMBR: A-0   DATE: 10/16/85

WBS NO.	TITLE	JAN 1986	FEB 1986	MAR 1986	APR 1986	MAY 1986	JUN 1986	JUL 1986	AUG 1986	SEP 1986	OCT 1986	NOV 1986	DEC 1986	TOTAL 1986
A-0	TOTAL COST	$16849.98	$15715.84	$14581.71	$15505.22	$15305.22	$19806.82	$19442.48	$19928.34	$15229.79	$17692.47	$15262.19	$14047.05	$199566.90
A-1	PROGRMMING	$16849.98	$15715.84	$14581.71	$10531.24	$10531.24	$0.00	$0.00	$0.00	$0.00	$0.00	$0.00	$0.00	$68210.00
A-1-1	INPUTS	$5735.47	$1360.96	$1360.96	$777.69	$777.69	$0.00	$0.00	$0.00	$0.00	$0.00	$0.00	$0.00	$10012.77
A-1-2	EDITS	$1360.96	$5735.47	$1360.96	$777.69	$777.69	$0.00	$0.00	$0.00	$0.00	$0.00	$0.00	$0.00	$10012.77
A-1-3	ERROR MSGS	$1360.96	$1360.96	$5735.47	$777.69	$777.69	$0.00	$0.00	$0.00	$0.00	$0.00	$0.00	$0.00	$10012.77
A-1-4	REPT GEN	$1360.96	$1360.96	$1360.96	$5152.20	$777.69	$0.00	$0.00	$0.00	$0.00	$0.00	$0.00	$0.00	$10012.77
A-1-5	USER INTER	$7031.62	$5897.49	$4763.36	$3045.96	$7420.47	$0.00	$0.00	$0.00	$0.00	$0.00	$0.00	$0.00	$28158.90
A-2	TESTING	$0.00	$0.00	$0.00	$4973.98	$4973.98	$7566.29	$8052.34	$8538.40	$0.00	$0.00	$0.00	$0.00	$34105.00
A-2-1	IN-HOUSE	$0.00	$0.00	$0.00	$3710.24	$3710.24	$2252.06	$2252.06	$2252.06	$0.00	$0.00	$0.00	$0.00	$14176.66
A-2-2	MKT USE	$0.00	$0.00	$0.00	$631.87	$631.87	$3629.23	$3629.23	$2171.05	$0.00	$0.00	$0.00	$0.00	$10693.25
A-2-3	UPDATES	$0.00	$0.00	$0.00	$631.87	$631.87	$1685.00	$2171.06	$4115.28	$0.00	$0.00	$0.00	$0.00	$9235.08
A-3	DOCMTATION	$0.00	$0.00	$0.00	$0.00	$0.00	$12240.54	$11389.94	$11389.94	$15229.79	$0.00	$0.00	$0.00	$50250.19
A-3-1	BASICS	$0.00	$0.00	$0.00	$0.00	$0.00	$1053.12	$769.59	$769.59	$1620.19	$0.00	$0.00	$0.00	$4212.49
A-3-2	OP. MANUAL	$0.00	$0.00	$0.00	$0.00	$0.00	$4066.88	$3977.57	$4171.99	$5800.28	$0.00	$0.00	$0.00	$18016.51
A-3-3	SAMPLE EX.	$0.00	$0.00	$0.00	$0.00	$0.00	$5233.21	$4785.26	$4560.83	$5217.01	$0.00	$0.00	$0.00	$19766.32
A-3-4	UPDATES	$0.00	$0.00	$0.00	$0.00	$0.00	$1887.52	$1887.52	$1887.52	$2592.30	$0.00	$0.00	$0.00	$8254.87
A-4	SUPPORT	$0.00	$0.00	$0.00	$0.00	$0.00	$0.00	$0.00	$0.00	$0.00	$17692.47	$15262.19	$14047.05	$47001.71
A-4-1	INSTALLATN	$0.00	$0.00	$0.00	$0.00	$0.00	$0.00	$0.00	$0.00	$0.00	$8668.02	$6237.73	$5022.59	$19928.34
A-4-2	TRAINING	$0.00	$0.00	$0.00	$0.00	$0.00	$0.00	$0.00	$0.00	$0.00	$3288.99	$3288.99	$3288.99	$9866.96
A-4-3	UPDATES	$0.00	$0.00	$0.00	$0.00	$0.00	$0.00	$0.00	$0.00	$0.00	$4860.57	$4860.57	$4860.57	$14581.71
A-4-4	FLD SVC	$0.00	$0.00	$0.00	$0.00	$0.00	$0.00	$0.00	$0.00	$0.00	$874.90	$874.90	$874.90	$2624.71

Figure 4-23 Level 2 summaries identified.

MICROESTIMATING(TM) SYSTEM :Copyright 1984, MOBILE DATA SERVICES

EST.TITLE:COSTPLAN   WBS TITLE:TOP   ORIGINATOR ARS   START YR.:   1986
EST.NMBR: .004   WBS NMBR: A-0   DATE: 10/16/85

WBS NO.	TITLE	JAN 1986	FEB 1986	MAR 1986	APR 1986	MAY 1986	JUN 1986	JUL 1986	AUG 1986	SEP 1986	OCT 1986	NOV 1986	DEC 1986	TOTAL 1986
A-0	TOTAL COST	$16849.98	$15715.84	$14581.71	$15505.22	$15505.22	$19806.82	$19442.28	$19928.34	$15229.79	$17692.47	$15262.19	$14047.05	$1995566.90
A-1	PROGRMMING	$16849.98	$15715.84	$14581.71	$10531.24	$10531.24	$0.00	$0.00	$0.00	$0.00	$0.00	$0.00	$0.00	$68210.00
A-1-1	INPUTS	$5735.47	$1360.96	$1360.96	$777.69	$777.69	$0.00	$0.00	$0.00	$0.00	$0.00	$0.00	$0.00	$10012.77
A-1-2	EDITS	$1360.96	$5735.47	$1360.96	$777.69	$777.69	$0.00	$0.00	$0.00	$0.00	$0.00	$0.00	$0.00	$10012.77
A-1-3	ERROR MSGS	$1360.96	$1360.96	$5735.47	$777.69	$777.69	$0.00	$0.00	$0.00	$0.00	$0.00	$0.00	$0.00	$10012.77
A-1-4	REPT GEN	$1360.96	$1360.96	$1360.96	$5152.20	$777.69	$0.00	$0.00	$0.00	$0.00	$0.00	$0.00	$0.00	$10012.77
A-1-5	USER INTER	$7031.62	$5897.49	$4763.36	$3045.96	$7420.47	$0.00	$0.00	$0.00	$0.00	$0.00	$0.00	$0.00	$28158.90
A-2	TESTING	$0.00	$0.00	$0.00	$4973.98	$4973.98	$7566.29	$8052.34	$8538.40	$0.00	$0.00	$0.00	$0.00	$34105.00
A-2-1	IN-HOUSE	$0.00	$0.00	$0.00	$3710.24	$3710.24	$2252.06	$2252.06	$2252.06	$0.00	$0.00	$0.00	$0.00	$14176.66
A-2-2	MKT USE	$0.00	$0.00	$0.00	$631.87	$631.87	$3629.23	$3629.23	$2171.05	$0.00	$0.00	$0.00	$0.00	$10693.25
A-2-3	UPDATES	$0.00	$0.00	$0.00	$631.87	$631.87	$1685.00	$2171.05	$4115.28	$0.00	$0.00	$0.00	$0.00	$9235.08
A-3	DOCMTATION	$0.00	$0.00	$0.00	$0.00	$0.00	$12240.54	$11389.94	$11389.94	$15229.79	$0.00	$0.00	$0.00	$50250.19
A-3-1	BASICS	$0.00	$0.00	$0.00	$0.00	$0.00	$1053.12	$769.59	$769.59	$1620.19	$0.00	$0.00	$0.00	$4212.49
A-3-2	OP. MANUAL	$0.00	$0.00	$0.00	$0.00	$0.00	$4066.68	$3977.57	$4171.99	$5800.28	$0.00	$0.00	$0.00	$18016.51
A-3-3	SAMPLE EX.	$0.00	$0.00	$0.00	$0.00	$0.00	$5233.21	$4755.26	$4560.83	$5217.01	$0.00	$0.00	$0.00	$19786.32
A-3-4	UPDATES	$0.00	$0.00	$0.00	$0.00	$0.00	$1887.52	$1887.52	$1887.52	$2592.30	$0.00	$0.00	$0.00	$8254.87
A-4	SUPPORT	$0.00	$0.00	$0.00	$0.00	$0.00	$0.00	$0.00	$0.00	$0.00	$17692.47	$15262.19	$14047.05	$47001.71
A-4-1	INSTALLATN	$0.00	$0.00	$0.00	$0.00	$0.00	$0.00	$0.00	$0.00	$0.00	$8668.02	$6237.73	$5022.59	$19928.34
A-4-2	TRAINING	$0.00	$0.00	$0.00	$0.00	$0.00	$0.00	$0.00	$0.00	$0.00	$3288.99	$3288.99	$3288.99	$9866.96
A-4-3	UPDATES	$0.00	$0.00	$0.00	$0.00	$0.00	$0.00	$0.00	$0.00	$0.00	$4860.57	$4860.57	$4860.57	$14581.71
A-4-4	FLD SVC	$0.00	$0.00	$0.00	$0.00	$0.00	$0.00	$0.00	$0.00	$0.00	$874.90	$874.90	$874.90	$2624.71

Figure 4-24 Total year costs identified.

The home-building project is subdivided into 10 major subdivisions of work, or categories, under which all materials, labor, and other costs are estimated. Those items that may be considered as overhead by a larger contractor or industrial firm are lumped as a direct cost under legal and general. The 10 subdivisions of work are

1. Legal and general
2. Site preparation
3. Framing
4. Plumbing

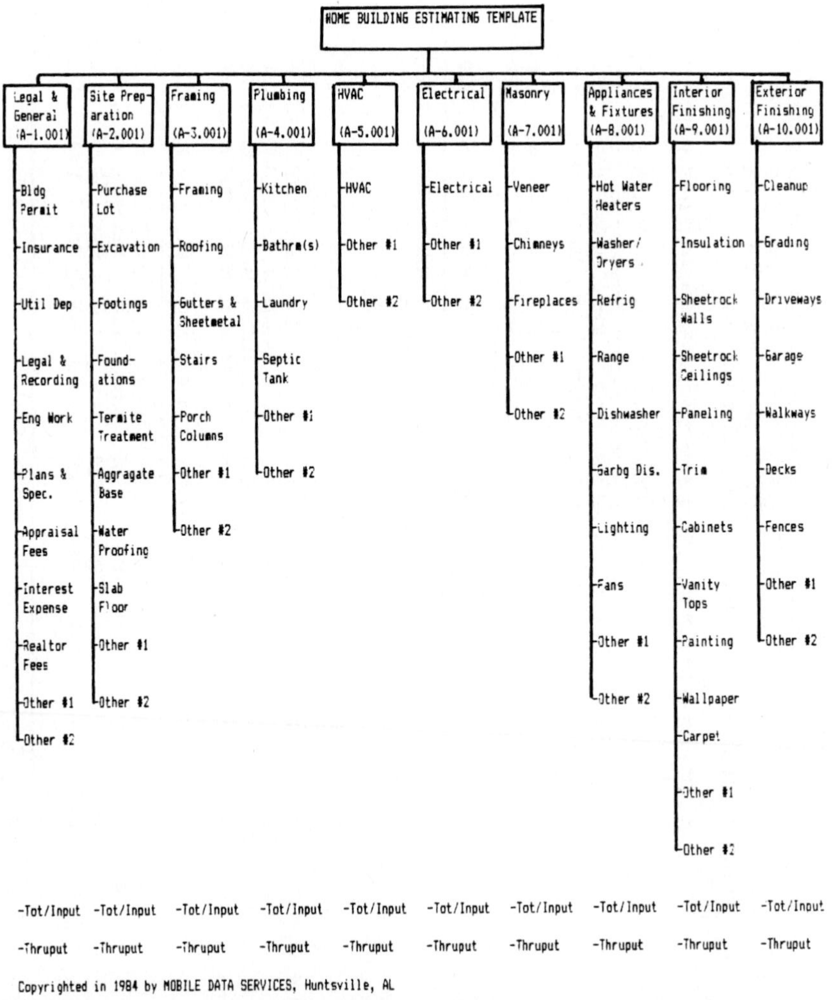

Figure 4-25 Construction work element structure.

5. Heating, ventilating, and air conditioning (HVAC)

6. Electrical

7. Masonry

8. Appliances and fixtures

9. Interior finishing

10. Exterior finishing

The basic WES and the estimating worksheets are built to easily permit a further detailed breakout of the subcontracted work, say, in the heating, ventilating, and air conditioning (HVAC), plumbing, electrical, framing, or masonry work.

Then, each of the 10 major subdivisions is subdivided to meet the needs of the specific home-building contractor. Notice that two other categories are added to each major category to allow easy expansion of the WES. The spreadsheet, however, will not be limited to two additional level 3 elements because the spreadsheet row capacity usually equals or exceeds 255 rows. We constructed a WES for this example that would fit on one page to give an "at-a-glance" look at the total work element estimate. Considerably more detail can be added without exceeding the memory and storage capacities of most microcomputers.

Notice also that two entries have been provided in each major subdivision of work: one for a total-input and one for a thruput. These two entries are provided for all cost elements in each supporting worksheet to permit: (1) the direct estimating of a lump sum of labor, materials, or total costs; and (2) the addition of a contingency or estimate adjustment to that computed within the worksheet which can either be positive or negative. Hence, the spreadsheet formats will hold considerable flexibility for the estimator while still providing a framework, structure, computation, and reporting capability for a fairly detailed estimate.

Building the Supporting Input Worksheets

As in the case of the previous estimate example, a heading is constructed that will be of the same format for each supporting or input worksheet. The outlined section on Figure 4-26 shows that this heading contains a job title, company information, estimating sheet number (which is also the spreadsheet's computer file name), name of the estimator, data, and category title. The heading is arranged to provide a place for subtotals for subcontract and/or labor, materials, and other costs. A category subtotal is shown that sums the previous three subtotals. Major column headings are: (1) description of the work; (2) subcontract or labor estimates; (3) materials estimates; (4) "other dollars" estimates; (5) material quantity estimates; and (6) totals.

Subcontract and labor estimates   The subcontract and labor category is subdivided into four columns:

Price

Units

Quantity

Dollars

This set of columns is provided to allow the estimator to input either subcontracted labor, total subcontract costs, or in-house labor costs. The price can be a percentage, as is the case of realtor fees (with the quantity being estimated total home price); or a dollar value per unit of work. The units field is an alphabetical field in each spreadsheet row that reminds the estimator of what units he or she is dealing with in that row under the subcontract-labor set of columns. Formulas are built, in the manner shown in the previous example, to multiply the price cell by the quantity cell in each row to derive the dollars amount in each row.

```
        1       2       3       4       5       6       7       8       9      10      11   12   13
 1 HOME BUILDING ESTIMATING TEMPLATE        JOB TITLE:
 2 ##############################################################################################
 3 Copyright 1984 by MOBILE DATA SERVICES, P.O. Box 5042, Huntsville, AL
 4 --------------------------------------------------------------------------------------------
 5   SHEET #:A-1.001                 NAME:              SUBCON TOT   $0.00 MTL SUBTOT   $0.00         OTHER:
 6 --------------------------------------------------------------------------------------------
 7             DATE:            CATEGORY: LEGAL & GENERAL COSTS                      CATEGORY SUBTOTAL:
 8 ##############################################################################################
 9 DESCRIPT !------SUBCONTRACT/LABOR------------!    !----------MATERIALS----------!  OTHER   MATERIAL QUANTITIES
10           PRICE/UNITS QUANTITY   DOLLARS      PRICE/UNITS   QUANTITY DOLLARS  DOLLARS  DEPTH WIDTH VOLUME
11 ##############################################################################################
12 Bldg
13 Permit
14
15 Insurance
16
17 Utility
18 Deposit
19
20 Legal &
21 Recording
22
23 Engrng.
24 Work
25
26 Plans &
27 Spec.
28
29 Appraisal
30 Fees
31
32 Interest
33 Expense
34
35 Realtor
36 Fees
37
38 Disct Pts
39
40 Closing
```

Figure 4-26   Input sheet headings.

Material estimates   The material estimating column headings and formulas are identical to the subcontract-labor column headings. This set of columns is provided in the event the contractors are to supply materials for either their own use or for a subcontractor's use in the project. The quantity value in this column can be imported from the volume column under material quantities (columns 11, 12, and 13).

Other dollars   The other dollars column is provided to give the estimator even further flexibility in that a capability exists to add costs that are unforeseen at the time the WES is developed. This column can also include travel costs, computer costs, reproduction costs, or other costs directly associated with the row of costs being estimated.

Material quantities   The material quantities set of columns can be used to compute material volumes such as cubic feet of concrete, topsoil, gravel, fill dirt, sand, aggregate, etc. Since wall, footing, walkway, and driveway *lengths* are usually provided to compute labor or materials in the other columns, only depth and width are added to compute total volume of material. If the labor or material quantities are given in square feet, then depth is the only parameter needed to compute total volume.

Total dollars   The total dollars column is merely the sum of the subcontract/labor dollars, material dollars, and other dollars. This column is added vertically (including any entries in the total-input and thruput categories) to develop the category subtotal cost in the heading block. The other three dollars columns are also totaled, and the totals will appear in the SUBCON TOT, MTL SUBTOT, and OTHER blocks in the heading.

Building Work Elements Within Each Major Work Category

Figure 4-27 shows the first worksheet (sheet #A-1.001) of the home construction estimate. It can be readily seen that all columns on the worksheet will not be used for all subelements of work. Indeed, some columns may not even be appropriate for estimating some subelements. In most subelements in this category, the quantity will be 1, but, in the event of a multifamily dwelling, some items such as utility deposits, could occur in multiple units. Again, as in the previous example, the advantages of standardization of at least the column and formula structure far outweigh the risk of having some columns that are not applicable to some subelements. Since computer power and computer paper are cheaper than spreadsheet programming time, we recommend standardization wherever possible. Notice one other feature of the spreadsheet A-1.001 shown on Figure 4-27: a special formula has been built in for realtor fees as mentioned above. The realtor fee percentage is multiplied by an "order-of-magnitude" estimate of the structure costs to produce the realtor fee dollar amount. This dollar amount is structured to appear in the other dollars column since it is not subcontract-labor or materials.

Copying of Worksheets and Formulas

Because the names of the subelements are different for each work category, the descriptive names must be blanked prior to copying the worksheet and its formulas. The formulas and cell formatting can continue down through a low enough row on the spreadsheet to accommodate the longest spreadsheet (the spreadsheet with the greatest number of rows) or even beyond if it is anticipated that additional subelements may be added at a future date. Once the worksheet and formulas are copied onto to a new file (say A-2.001), the appropriate subelement titles can be

Figure 4-27 Special built-in formulas.

added to the new worksheet. Figure 4-28 shows how the second work-sheet may look when completed and sample values added.

Special Built-in Formulas for Specific Worksheets

As shown on Figure 4-27, there are two places where special formulas have been built into the worksheet. The cost of materials (concrete) for the footings was calculated at $39.00 per cubic yard. The volume of concrete in the footings was derived from a special formula built into the materials quantities columns. The footing depth and width (8 by 18 inches) were first converted to feet (0.67 by 1.5 feet), and then the depth, width, and linear feet from the subcontract-labor quantity column were multiplied by each other and divided by 27 (cubic feet per cubic yard) to produce cubic yards. The resulting cubic yard figure was transposed (by the spreadsheet) to the material quantity column where it is used to derive material costs.

Figure 4-28 Use of material quantity information.

In a like manner, the cubic yards of concrete needed in the slab floor was computed by a built-in formula. The 2000 square feet in the subcontract-labor quantity column was multiplied by the slab thickness in feet (0.33) and divided by 27 (cubic feet per cubic yard) to arrive at 24.69 cubic yards of concrete. This number was then automatically transferred by the spreadsheet to the materials quantity column to develop material dollar costs.

Completion of Remaining Input Worksheets

Figures 4-29 through 4-36 show the remaining worksheets for the sample home construction estimating template. Relationships such as framing costs per wall, heat pump costs per ton, and brick veneer labor and materials per brick and per thousand bricks, respectively, are used in these worksheets. Where the total job is done by a subcontractor, the thruput is used in several instances to inject the bidding subcontractor's price. The thruput feature is also used to add a contingency, allowance for cost growth, or to adjust the estimate to meet the costs actually to be expected on the job in the judgment of the estimator.

```
HOME BUILDING ESTIMATING TEMPLATE      JOB TITLE:
::::::::::::::::::::::::::::::::::::::::::::::::::::::::::::::::::::::::::::::::::::::::::::::::::::::::::::::::
Copyright 1984 by MOBILE DATA SERVICES, P.O. Box 5042, Huntsville, AL  35805, Phone: 205-536-2628
-----------------------------------------------------------------------------------------------------------
SHEET #:  A-3.001          NAME:            SUBCON TOT  3000 MTL SUBTOT  2700          OTHER:  $175.00
-----------------------------------------------------------------------------------------------------------
         DATE:                CATEGORY: FRAMING                              CATEGORY SUBTOTAL:  $10875.00
::::::::::::::::::::::::::::::::::::::::::::::::::::::::::::::::::::::::::::::::::::::::::::::::::::::::::::::::
DESCRIPT :------SUBCONTRACT/LABOR-----------;    ;----------MATERIALS----------;   OTHER   MATERIAL QUANTITIES    TOTAL
         PRICE/UNITS   QUANTITY DOLLARS   PRICE   /UNITS  QUANTITY DOLLARS  DOLLARS  DEPTH WIDTH VOLUME  DOLLARS
::::::::::::::::::::::::::::::::::::::::::::::::::::::::::::::::::::::::::::::::::::::::::::::::::::::::::::::::
Framing  $200.00 /WALL      10  $2000.00   250 /WALL       10     2500                                    $4500.00

Siding                          $0.00                             0       75                              $75.00

Roofing                         $0.00                             0      100                              $100.00

Gutters &
Sheetmetal $500.00           2  $1000.00   200              1     200                                     $1200.00

Stairs                          $0.00                             0                                       $0.00

Porch
Columns                         $0.00                             0                                       $0.00

Other #1                        $0.00                             0                                       $0.00

Other #2                        $0.00                             0                                       $0.00


TOT/INPUT                                                                                                 $0.00

THRUPUT                                                                                                   $5000.00
```

Figure 4-29 Construction estimate input sheet—framing.

Linking Spreadsheets to the Top Cost Summary

The cost estimates for various cost elements on the input worksheets are imported to the top-level worksheet shown on Figure 4-37. The column headings show the work element designator; the work category description; subcontract, materials, other, and thruput costs; total cost for each category; percentage of total job costs represented by that category, and a bar chart that shows this percentage plotted against a linear scale to show the relative sizes of the various cost category estimates.

The linking method is similar to that used in the previous example

```
HOME BUILDING ESTIMATING TEMPLATE     JOB TITLE:
::::::::::::::::::::::::::::::::::::::::::::::::::::::::::::::::::::::::::::::::::::::::::::::::::::::::::
Copyright 1984 by MOBILE DATA SERVICES, P.O. Box 5042, Huntsville, AL  35805, Phone: 205-536-2628
------------------------------------------------------------------------------------------------------
  SHEET #:  A-4.001          NAME:              SUBCON TOT $1500.00 MTL SUBTOT $2100.00          OTHER: $500.00

        DATE:              CATEGORY: PLUMBING                              CATEGORY SUBTOTAL:  $8100.00
::::::::::::::::::::::::::::::::::::::::::::::::::::::::::::::::::::::::::::::::::::::::::::::::::::::::::
DESCRIPT :------SUBCONTRACT/LABOR-----------:   :---------MATERIALS----------:   OTHER   MATERIAL QUANTITIES   TOTAL
         PRICE/UNITS   QUANTITY DOLLARS      PRICE/UNITS   QUANTITY DOLLARS   DOLLARS   DEPTH WIDTH VOLUME  DOLLARS
::::::::::::::::::::::::::::::::::::::::::::::::::::::::::::::::::::::::::::::::::::::::::::::::::::::::::
Kitchen  $500.00           1   $500.00  $2000.00            1  $2000.00                                     $2500.00

Bathrooms $1000.00          1  $1000.00  $50.00             2  $100.00                                      $1100.00

Laundry                        $0.00                           $0.00   $500.00                              $500.00

Septic
Tank                           $0.00                           $0.00                                        $0.00

Other #1                       $0.00                           $0.00                                        $0.00

Other #2                       $0.00                           $0.00                                        $0.00

TOT/INPUT                                                                                                   $0.00

THRUPUT                                                                                                     $4000.00
```

Figure 4-30 Construction estimate input sheet—plumbing.

```
HOME BUILDING ESTIMATING TEMPLATE     JOB TITLE:
::::::::::::::::::::::::::::::::::::::::::::::::::::::::::::::::::::::::::::::::::::::::::::::::::::::::::
Copyright 1984 by MOBILE DATA SERVICES, P.O. Box 5042, Huntsville, AL  35805, Phone: 205-536-2628
------------------------------------------------------------------------------------------------------
  SHEET #:  A-5.001          NAME:              SUBCON TOT $2500.00 MTL SUBTOT $400.00          OTHER: $75.00

        DATE:              CATEGORY: HVAC                                CATEGORY SUBTOTAL:  $3175.00
::::::::::::::::::::::::::::::::::::::::::::::::::::::::::::::::::::::::::::::::::::::::::::::::::::::::::
DESCRIPT :------SUBCONTRACT/LABOR-----------:   :---------MATERIALS----------:   OTHER   MATERIAL QUANTITIES   TOTAL
         PRICE/UNITS   QUANTITY DOLLARS      PRICE/UNITS   QUANTITY DOLLARS   DOLLARS   DEPTH WIDTH VOLUME  DOLLARS
::::::::::::::::::::::::::::::::::::::::::::::::::::::::::::::::::::::::::::::::::::::::::::::::::::::::::
HVAC  $1250.00 /TON        2  $2500.00  $200.00             2  $400.00                                      $2900.00

Other #1                       $0.00                           $0.00   $75.00                               $75.00

Other #2                       $0.00                           $0.00                                        $0.00

TOT/INPUT                                                                                                   $0.00

THRUPUT                                                                                                     $200.00
```

Figure 4-31 Construction estimate input sheet—HVAC.

except that individual cost elements, subtotals, and totals are imported to the top estimate sheet individually rather than "a line at a time." Subtotals for each cost element are computed at the bottom of this top worksheet and a grand total is shown in the heading at the right side of the worksheet.

Printing and Print Instructions

Both this example and the previous one use compressed print on a dot matrix printer to allow more columns on a sheet than would be permitted by conventional letter-quality or typewriter-style inputs at 10 or 12

```
HOME BUILDING ESTIMATING TEMPLATE      JOB TITLE:
::::::::::::::::::::::::::::::::::::::::::::::::::::::::::::::::::::::::::::::::::::::::::::::::::::::::
Copyright 1984 by MOBILE DATA SERVICES, P.O. Box 5042, Huntsville, AL  35805, Phone: 205-536-2628
----------------------------------------------------------------------------------------------------
  SHEET #:   A-6.001          NAME:                   SUBCON TOT  $400.00 MTL SUBTOT  $300.00        OTHER:   $50.00
----------------------------------------------------------------------------------------------------
          DATE:                     CATEGORY: ELECTRICAL                       CATEGORY SUBTOTAL:  $6750.00
::::::::::::::::::::::::::::::::::::::::::::::::::::::::::::::::::::::::::::::::::::::::::::::::::::::::
DESCRIPT :------SUBCONTRACT/LABOR------------:    :---------MATERIALS----------:   OTHER    MATERIAL QUANTITIES   TOTAL
          PRICE/UNITS    QUANTITY  DOLLARS        PRICE/UNITS   QUANTITY  DOLLARS   DOLLARS  DEPTH WIDTH VOLUME  DOLLARS
::::::::::::::::::::::::::::::::::::::::::::::::::::::::::::::::::::::::::::::::::::::::::::::::::::::::
Electrical  $200.00               2  $400.00                             $0.00                                $400.00

Other #1                             $0.00       $300.00        1  $300.00  $50.00                            $350.00

Other #2                             $0.00                             $0.00                                  $0.00

TOT/INPUT                                                                                                     $0.00

THRUPUT                                                                                                       $6000.00
```

Figure 4-32 Construction estimate input sheet—electrical.

```
HOME BUILDING ESTIMATING TEMPLATE      JOB TITLE:
::::::::::::::::::::::::::::::::::::::::::::::::::::::::::::::::::::::::::::::::::::::::.:::::::::::::::::::::::::::::
Copyright 1984 by MOBILE DATA SERVICES, P.O. Box 5042, Huntsville, AL  35805, Phone: 205-536-2628
----------------------------------------------------------------------------------------------------
  SHEET #:   A-7.001          NAME:                   SUBCON TOT  $4000.00 MTL SUBTOT  $1250.00       OTHER:   $50.00
----------------------------------------------------------------------------------------------------
          DATE:                     CATEGORY: MASONRY                         CATEGORY SUBTOTAL:  $12300.00
::::::::::::::::::::::::::::::::::::::::::::::::::::::::::::::::::::::::::::::::::::::::::::::::::::::::
DESCRIPT :------SUBCONTRACT/LABOR------------:    :---------MATERIALS----------:   OTHER    MATERIAL QUANTITIES   TOTAL
          PRICE/UNITS    QUANTITY  DOLLARS        PRICE/UNITS   QUANTITY  DOLLARS   DOLLARS  DEPTH WIDTH VOLUME  DOLLARS
::::::::::::::::::::::::::::::::::::::::::::::::::::::::::::::::::::::::::::::::::::::::::::::::::::::::
Veneer    $0.80 /brick       5000  $4000.00  $250.00 /1000        5  $1250.00                                $5250.00

Chimneys                             $0.00                             $0.00  $50.00                          $50.00

Fireplaces                           $0.00                             $0.00                                  $0.00

Other #1                             $0.00                             $0.00                                  $0.00

Other #2                             $0.00                             $0.00                                  $0.00

TOT/INPUT                                                                                                     $0.00

THRUPUT                                                                                                       $7000.00
```

Figure 4-33 Construction estimate input sheet—masonry.

characters per inch. The dot matrix printer is far more versatile and flexible for printing cost estimating spreadsheets because it has the compressed print feature which prints approximately 17 characters per inch. This latter example permits the printout of each estimate sheet on standard 8½ by 11 inch paper and permits the use of a narrow carriage printer. If your existing printer does not have a wide carriage, you should consider the use of compressed print as shown in this example to permit viewing of the entire spreadsheet on one page.

Other Uses of Spreadsheets for Estimating

Because of the flexibility and adaptability of microcomputer spreadsheet software programs, the possible applications in estimating are virtually limitless. The above are only two of the endless possibilities available to the estimator in displaying, computing, reporting, tracking, and updating cost estimates. One convenient feature is the sorting capability available on most spreadsheets, which permits a list of cost elements, work elements, or schedule elements and their attendant resource values to be sorted in ascending or descending order (either alphabetically or numeri-

```
HOME BUILDING ESTIMATING TEMPLATE      JOB TITLE:
::::::::::::::::::::::::::::::::::::::::::::::::::::::::::::::::::::::::::::::::::::::::::::::::::::
Copyright 1984 by MOBILE DATA SERVICES, P.O. Box 5042, Huntsville, AL  35805, Phone: 205-536-2628
------------------------------------------------------------------------------------------------
 SHEET #:  A-8.001       NAME:                  SUBCON TOT  $150.00 MTL SUBTOT  $750.00        OTHER:   $50.00
------------------------------------------------------------------------------------------------
             DATE:           CATEGORY: APPLIANCES & FIXTURES            CATEGORY SUBTOTAL:  $8950.00
:::::::::::::::::::::::::::::::::::::::::::::::::::::::::::::::::::::::::::::::::::::::::::::::::::::
 DESCRIPT :------SUBCONTRACT/LABOR-----------:  :----------MATERIALS----------:  OTHER   MATERIAL QUANTITIES   TOTAL
           PRICE/UNITS   QUANTITY DOLLARS         PRICE/UNITS   QUANTITY DOLLARS  DOLLARS DEPTH WIDTH VOLUME   DOLLARS
:::::::::::::::::::::::::::::::::::::::::::::::::::::::::::::::::::::::::::::::::::::::::::::::::::::
Hot Water
Heaters    $50.00            1   $50.00  $150.00           1  $150.00  $50.00                            $250.00

Washer/
Dryers     $50.00 /UNIT      2  $100.00  $300.00 /UNIT     2  $600.00                                   $700.00

Refridg                          $0.00                        $0.00                                     $0.00

Range                            $0.00                        $0.00                                     $0.00

Dishwasher                       $0.00                        $0.00                                     $0.00

Garbg Dis.                       $0.00                        $0.00                                     $0.00

Lighting                         $0.00                        $0.00                                     $0.00

Fans                             $0.00                        $0.00                                     $0.00

Other #1                         $0.00                        $0.00                                     $0.00

Other #2                         $0.00                        $0.00                                     $0.00

TOT/INPUT                                                                                               $0.00

THRUPUT                                                                                                 $8000.00
```

Figure 4-34 Construction estimate input sheet—appliances & fixtures.

cally) by work element number, work element name, subelement cost, or total cost. This feature can be used for a variety of purposes: one being the descending-order sorting of a row of information based on one column of information, say, subcontract costs. In particularly long estimates, this feature would be useful in identifying the largest subcontract values, the largest material cost items, the largest labor hour items, the largest other cost items, or the largest categories from a total cost standpoint.

Most spreadsheets have a MIN, MAX, and AVERAGE function. The MIN function could be used, for example, to automatically identify and flag the lowest bidder in a long list of bidders, to identify the lowest-cost alternative among a large number of ways of doing a job, or to identify which job takes the least work hours. Other statistical functions such as standard deviations are available on some spreadsheet software packages and are useful in performing a built-in, automatic *analysis* of the costs

```
HOME BUILDING ESTIMATING TEMPLATE      JOB TITLE:
$$$$$$$$$$$$$$$$$$$$$$$$$$$$$$$$$$$$$$$$$$$$$$$$$$$$$$$$$$$$$$$$$$$$$$$$$$$$$$$$$$$$$$$$$$$$$$
Copyright 1984 by MOBILE DATA SERVICES, P.O. Box 5042, Huntsville, AL  35805, Phone: 205-536-2628
------------------------------------------------------------------------------------------
  SHEET #:  A-9.001      NAME:              SUBCON TOT $750.00 MTL SUBTOT $3000.00     OTHER:  $10.00

       DATE:             CATEGORY: INTERIOR FINISHING              CATEGORY SUBTOTAL: $12760.00
$$$$$$$$$$$$$$$$$$$$$$$$$$$$$$$$$$$$$$$$$$$$$$$$$$$$$$$$$$$$$$$$$$$$$$$$$$$$$$$$$$$$$$$$$$$$$$
 DESCRIPT :------SUBCONTRACT/LABOR------------:  :----------MATERIALS----------:  OTHER    MATERIAL QUANTITIES  TOTAL
          PRICE/UNITS   QUANTITY  DOLLARS       PRICE/UNITS   QUANTITY  DOLLARS   DOLLARS  DEPTH WIDTH VOLUME  DOLLARS
$$$$$$$$$$$$$$$$$$$$$$$$$$$$$$$$$$$$$$$$$$$$$$$$$$$$$$$$$$$$$$$$$$$$$$$$$$$$$$$$$$$$$$$$$$$$$$
Flooring  $0.50 /SQ FT     1500   $750.00       $2.00 /SQ FT     1500  $3000.00   $10.00                        $3760.00

Insulation                        $0.00                               $0.00                                    $0.00

Sheetrock
Walls                             $0.00                               $0.00                                    $0.00

Sheetrock
Ceilings                          $0.00                               $0.00                                    $0.00

Paneling                          $0.00                               $0.00                                    $0.00

Trim                              $0.00                               $0.00                                    $0.00

Cabinets                          $0.00                               $0.00                                    $0.00

Vanity
Tops                              $0.00                               $0.00                                    $0.00

Painting                          $0.00                               $0.00                                    $0.00

Wallpaper                         $0.00                               $0.00                                    $0.00

Carpet                            $0.00                               $0.00                                    $0.00

Other #1                          $0.00                               $0.00                                    $0.00

Other #2                          $0.00                               $0.00                                    $0.00


TOT/INPUT                                                                                                      $0.00

THRUPUT                                                                                                        $9000.00
```

Figure 4-35 Construction estimate input sheet—interior finishing.

```
HOME BUILDING ESTIMATING TEMPLATE      JOB TITLE:
##################################################################################
Copyright 1984 by MOBILE DATA SERVICES, P.O. Box 5042, Huntsville, AL  35805, Phone: 205-536-2628
--------------------------------------------------------------------------------
  SHEET #:  A-10.001          NAME:           SUBCON TOT  $0.00 MTL SUBTOT  $0.00           OTHER:   $0.00
--------------------------------------------------------------------------------
           DATE:            CATEGORY: EXTERIOR FINISHING                CATEGORY SUBTOTAL:  $10000.00
##################################################################################
  DESCRIPT :------SUBCONTRACT/LABOR-----------:    :----------MATERIALS-----------:   OTHER    MATERIAL QUANTITIES    TOTAL
             PRICE/UNITS    QUANTITY  DOLLARS       PRICE/UNITS    QUANTITY  DOLLARS   DOLLARS  DEPTH WIDTH VOLUME   DOLLARS
##################################################################################
Cleanup                          $0.00                             $0.00                                               $0.00

Grading                          $0.00                             $0.00                                               $0.00

Driveway                         $0.00                             $0.00                                               $0.00

Garage                           $0.00                             $0.00                                               $0.00

Walkways                         $0.00                             $0.00                                               $0.00

Decks                            $0.00                             $0.00                                               $0.00

Fences                           $0.00                             $0.00                                               $0.00

Other #1                         $0.00                             $0.00                                               $0.00

Other #2                         $0.00                             $0.00                                               $0.00

TOT/INPUT                                                                                                              $0.00

THRUPUT                                                                                                           $10000.00
```

Figure 4-36 Construction estimate input sheet—exterior finishing.

```
HOME BUILDING ESTIMATING TEMPLATE  JOB TITLE:SAMPLE ESTIMATE
##################################################################################
Copyright 1984 by MOBILE DATA SERVICES, P.O. Box 5042, Huntsville, AL  35805, Phone: 205-536-2628
--------------------------------------------------------------------------------
        MULTIPLAN FILE #:                  NAME:
--------------------------------------------------------------------------------
DATE:01/06/84                    TOP COST SUMMARY                      GND TOTAL: $109059.30
##################################################################################
ELEMT        DESCRIPTION      SUBCON   MATERIALS   OTHER    THRUPUT     COST     PERCENT      BARCHART
##################################################################################
A-1  Legal and General Costs     $0.00      $0.00 $17550.00           $17550.00   16.09%  ################################

A-2  Site/Foundation Preparation $1771.00 $1328.30 $15500.00          $18599.30   17.05%  #################################

A-3  Framing and Related Costs   $3000.00 $2700.00   $175.00 $5000.00 $10875.00    9.97%  ###################

A-4  Plumbing and Related Costs  $1500.00 $2100.00   $500.00 $4000.00  $8100.00    7.43%  ##############

A-5  HVAC and Related Costs      $2500.00  $400.00    $75.00  $200.00  $3175.00    2.91%  #####

A-6  Electrical and Related Costs $400.00  $300.00    $50.00 $6000.00  $6750.00    6.19%  ###########

A-7  Masonry and Related Costs   $4000.00 $1250.00    $50.00 $7000.00 $12300.00   11.28%  #####################

A-8  Appliances and Fixtures      $150.00  $750.00    $50.00 $8000.00  $8950.00    8.21%  ###############

A-9  Interior Finishing           $750.00 $3000.00    $10.00 $9000.00 $12760.00   11.70%  ######################

A-10 Exterior Finishing           $0.00     $0.00     $0.00 $10000.00 $10000.00    9.17%  #################

             SUBTOTALS $14071.00 $11828.30 $33960.00 $49200.00 $109059.30
```

Figure 4-37 Summary of home construction estimate.

once the costs have been estimated. The division function can be used to compute estimating relationships such as cost per pound, cost per board foot, etc., and the average, or mean, and standard deviation functions can be used to develop cost estimating relationships.

In conclusion, estimating personnel with little or no computer training can learn the simple spreadsheet commands in a very short time. Once spreadsheet models or templates have been created by the engineering or estimating professional, estimate revisions and alternate case investigations can be performed by technician-level personnel. The use of these templates can also serve as a training tool for persons unfamiliar with the firm's estimating procedures. Construction contractors have found spreadsheets useful for inserting last-minute subcontract or mate-

TABLE 4-1   Checklist of Spreadsheet Characteristics

Maximum rows per spreadsheet?
Maximum columns per spreadsheet?
Allows nonuniform column widths?
Automatic label spillover?
Automatic cell advance?
Status area position?
Viewing through a desired window?
Border suppression if desired?
Printing of desired cells' values?
Dump of all information about desired
 cells?
Cell definitions—constants:
  Character?
  Logical?
  Numeric?
  Numeric precision (digits)?
Cell definitions—formulas:
  Maximum formula length (characters)?
  Allows macros in formula?
  Assignment statements?
  IF statements?
  IF-THEN-ELSE statements?
  WHILE-DO iteration?
  TEST-CASE statements?
Insert rows and columns?
Delete rows and columns?
Replication of cell definitions:
  Absolute?
  Relative?
  Absolute-relative mixture?
Temporary cell value override?
Combine portions of different spread-
 sheets:
  Absolute combination?
  Relative combination?
  Absolute-relative mixture?

Cell definition protection:
  Individual cell?
  Block of cells?
  With write access codes?
  Unconcealment subject to security
   clearance?
Cell value presentation style:
  For individual cell?
  For block of cells?
  Indivisible value?
  Cell background color?
  Value foreground color?
  PERFORM procedures?
  Data management commands?
  Ad hoc inquiry and statistics?
  Nested cell references?
  Indefinite cell references?
  Numeric column references allowed?
  User-controlled cell names?
  Can be specified from outside of the
   spreadsheet?
Undefine a cell?
Undefine a block of cells?
Edit a cell's definition?
  Intensity control?
  Bell sounding?
  Blinking cell?
  Reverse video cell?
  Conditional activation?
  Conditional deactivation?
User controls when spreadsheet recalcu-
 lation occurs:
  Row-by-row order?
  Column-by-column?

rial quotations into their bids. Portable microcomputers, which are all compatible with at least one spreadsheet software product, are often transported to the work site or to the bid location for this purpose.

The principal advantage of using a microcomputer spreadsheet for estimating as opposed to a prewritten computer program is user flexibility. The user is not constrained by predefined procedures or units that have been written into a computer program. Although some effort is required to learn how to use a spreadsheet system and to establish initial templates, the time and effort savings in making revisions, as well as the use of the template for identical or similar projects, is well worth the effort expended, particularly for a small or medium-sized business that cannot afford a custom-tailored microcomputer cost estimating software package.

Table 4-1 is a checklist you can use to evaluate some of the important characteristics of spreadsheet programs. As is the case with other software packages, however, acquisition of a good spreadsheet program for cost estimating should be based on a thorough comparison of all available systems and a detailed demonstration and hands-on working session with the one you are about to purchase.

5

ESTIMATING WITH DATABASE SYSTEMS

Modern microcomputer database software applications packages are in-dispensable tools for cost estimators, particularly those cost estimators who produce multiple estimates based on some or all of the same data elements. The characteristics of (1) organized and methodical data stor-age and (2) speed, flexibility, and ease of data selection and retrieval make the microcomputer database system ideal for estimates containing multiple work elements and estimates containing multiple cost (skill and material) elements. So far, the most common usage of database systems in general has been for the storage and retrieval of information and records rather than the storage, retrieval, and computation of numerical resource information for cost estimates. We predict an explosive growth in the use of database systems for handling mostly numeric information (as in cost estimates) as opposed to mostly alphanumeric information (as in employee records, client or customer records, and inventory control systems).

Microcomputer database systems use five subdivisions or breakdowns of information. These subdivisions are named below along with a rough equivalent of their counterparts in a conventional file system:

Disk   equivalent to a file cabinet
File   equivalent to a file drawer
Record   equivalent to a file folder

Field   equivalent to the name of an employee

Character   equivalent to a letter or number

The developers of microcomputer database systems have used available computer memory, computation, and storage abilities in many different ways to develop applications packages that vary widely in numbers of characters per field, numbers of fields per record, and number of records per file. The minimum characters per field is about 32; the minimum fields per record is about 15; and the minimum records per file is about 100 in currently available microcomputer database applications programs. Most packages permit sizes of these minimums, and many have maximum field, record, and file sizes which are established by the computer's memory or storage capacity.

Microcomputer database systems have four basic attributes or capabilities:

1. The ability to define the characteristics of the data to be manipulated [alphabetic, numeric, alphanumeric, dollars($), or Julian date]

2. Acquisition of data from keyboard inputs, files generated by other programs, or communications links, and storage of the data in the correct records and fields

3. Updating of the data when changes are required

4. The ability to update the data in a predefined format and/or sequence and to display it on the computer's video screen, print it as a report, store it in a file for use by another program, or transmit it over a communications link

While the above attributes represent a minimum requirement for microcomputer database systems, there are also useful optional features available on database applications programs that include the following:

1. The ability to recover from errors

2. Facilities to protect data from use by unauthorized persons (password systems)

3. Database file maintenance utilities

4. A variety of arithmetic and logical functions

5. A programming language to automate operation (keyboard "macros" and menus)

Components of a Database

Disks

In the conventional microcomputer database system that is most commonly used in business and industry today, the file cabinet has been replaced by the flexible (diskette, or floppy disk) or rigid magnetic storage disk.

Files

A microcomputer database system will usually involve the storage of one or more *files* of information on the magnetic disk. These files can be thought of as equivalent to the conventional file drawer found in the file cabinet. A small company may keep its employee records in one file folder or in one drawer of the file cabinet. The group of employee files, then, can be considered as equivalent to a database *file*.

Records

Within each database file are *records* or folders that contain information on each employee, customer or client, or piece of equipment. A record on Joe Smith will contain all of the pertinent data on this specific employee.

Fields

A data *field* within a record is the name of the employee, hiring data, salary, or other piece of pertinent information about that employee.

Characters

The *characters* in a database are the alphabetical or numeric symbols that make up the data fields.

Cost Estimating Databases

A cost estimating microcomputer database will contain the same five basic subdivisions of data but will contain principally numeric or resource data rather than alphabetical or alphanumeric data. A disk could contain cost estimate files for one or more projects just as a file cabinet could contain several drawers containing cost estimates for several projects. A cost estimate file could be equated to a complete cost estimate on a given project, work activity, or work output. A record in a microcomputer-based cost estimate is the record of resources for one work element, while a field is the name of a skill or resource, or the unit quantity or unit price of that resource for a given calendar period. The characters are the alphabetical or numeric symbols that make up the cost estimate inputs.

Cost estimate databases fall into five general categories: (1) the free-form index card or forms-oriented system, (2) the file manager, (3) the relational database, (4) the hierarchical database, and (5) the network database. Because there is considerable overlap in the structure, makeup, and nomenclature for these five types of database systems, we will not try to describe them, but we will provide example cost estimates developed on two of the generic types: the forms-oriented database and the file manager. We will also discuss the characteristics and merits of a third type of microcomputer database system, the relational database. Each of these types of database systems has its own advantages and limitations when applied to various cost estimating situations.

The Work Element as a Database Record

In Chapter 2 we described the WES and promoted the concept that any work activity or work output consists of a buildup of tasks or subdivisions of work. These subdivisions of work can be as large or small as the estimator chooses, but each should represent an identifiable piece of the job that can be described as an entity and that can be loaded with labor or material resources to develop a resource estimate for that work element. Because there is often commonality of work elements between two or more work activities or work outputs (and even *within* a work activity or work output), it is desirable to use the work element as the key segment of a cost estimate. In a microcomputer database system, the logical identity for a work element is as a database record. Since one of the principal benefits of a microcomputer database system is to rapidly and accurately select specific data records based on a given set of criteria, the work element's form as a data record will permit its use in different estimates or even within the same estimate.

Figure 5-1 shows a work element data input record built on a forms-oriented database (PFS File by Software Publishing, Inc.). As in many other forms-oriented database systems, the software package allows you to design your own form so that data can be conveniently added to the various fields in the record. Keep in mind that there will be a number of records in the total cost estimate file—one for each work element at the input level. This particular form in Figure 5-1 was constructed for a three-level estimate, so the record includes fields for both a level 2 designator and a work element structure number. Why this was done will become apparent as we later discuss the generation of the output report of the total cost estimate. Also provided on the record blank form are names of other fields such as WES name, skill name, labor rate in dollars per hour, material name, material unit cost, unit labor hours for each month, and unit material quantities for each month.

Numbering of Work Elements in a Database System

The numbering or naming of the work element records in a database system must be done with care because the computer will be used to sort the resources into their proper slots when the final cost report is generated. The scheme shown in Chapter 2 in Figure 2-5 is a convenient one because the computer can do an alphanumeric sort on characters starting with a letter and separated by dashes. Notice that the top level of the estimate is A-0 (or simply A), that level 2 elements have two characters separated by a dash (A-1), and that level 3 elements have three characters separated by a dash (A-1-1). This is a handy system to use because the number of characters separated by dashes is equal to the level of the work element. One can easily tell by its designator, then, the level of the element.

Alphanumeric rather than numerical designations are used because a computer only recognizes one decimal point. The very common numerical paragraph numbering in specifications, work breakdown structures, and other documents of 1.2.8.6.4, etc., is simply not feasible using conventional numeric data handling techniques.

If it is likely that there will be more than two digits per level in any work element number (for example, A-12-6-10), a zero should be placed in front of any single digit number to validate the sort (for example, A-12-06-10 or A-01-03-02).

```
Lvl 2 WES:              WES No:              WES Name:

Skill Name:               Rate ($/Hr):        Mtl Name:

                                            Unit Cost:

Jan86/Hrs:    Feb86/Hrs:    Mar86/Hrs:    Apr86/Hrs:    May86/Hrs:
Jun86/Hrs:    Jul86/Hrs:    Aug86/Hrs:    Sep86/Hrs:    Oct86/Hrs:
Nov86/Hrs:    Dec86/Hrs:    Jan87/Hrs:    Feb87/Hrs:    Mar87/Hrs:
Apr87/Hrs:    May87/Hrs:    Jun87/Hrs:    Jul87/Hrs:    Aug87/Hrs:
Sep87/Hrs:    Oct87/Hrs:    Nov87/Hrs:    Dec87/Hrs:

Jan86/Mtl:    Feb86/Mtl:    Mar86/Mtl:    Apr86/Mtl:    May86/Mtl:
Jun86/Mtl:    Jul86/Mtl:    Aug86/Mtl:    Sep86/Mtl:    Oct86/Mtl:
Nov86/Mtl:    Dec86/Mtl:    Jan87/Mtl:    Feb87/Mtl:    Mar87/Mtl:
Apr87/Mtl:    May87/Mtl:    Jun87/Mtl:    Jul87/Mtl:    Aug87/Mtl:
Sep87/Mtl:    Oct87/Mtl:    Nov87/Mtl:    Dec87/Mtl:


---------------------------------------------------------------------
File: A:COSTWARE.PFS            DESIGN                     Page 1

F5-Date     F6-Time                                    F10-Continue
```

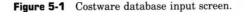

Figure 5-1 Costware database input screen.

Cost Estimating with a Low-Cost
Forms-Oriented Database

PFS File is a low-cost forms-oriented database system that is likely to be already on the software shelf of your business or firm. Since it is definitely on the low end of the database market in price and capability (although it is very user friendly and easy to operate), we thought it would be profitable to see if we could develop cost estimates using this software package. In doing this, we also wanted to convey to you, the reader, how easy it is to use a database system for cost estimating and to illustrate some of the principles used in building a cost estimating system from a database microcomputer software applications package. We found that we could easily develop a data record for a three-level estimate that would contain labor or materials resources and rates. We found that the computer would sort all work elements into their proper slots; produce total direct labor hours or material quantities, and direct labor dollars or material dollars for each of several skill or material categories; provide subtotals for each level 2 work element and grand totals of direct costs for the estimate. As a sample, we prepared an estimate of a Costware software development project using four skills:

Program manager

Senior programmer

Technical writer

Systems data analyst

(The database system could easily have accommodated more skill categories or skill levels.)

The input form developed for the sample estimate record contained the following fields:

Level 2 Designator:	Total Hours
WES number:	Name of material:
Name of skill:	Material unit price:
Labor rate:	Material quantity:

We performed a direct labor cost estimate using entries in all but the last three fields. Both the level 2 designator and the level 3 WES number were entered because we wanted to have level 2 subtotals printed in the report and we wanted to have each level 3 work element resource listed, in order, under its respective level 2 designator. Since PFS File will sort on two fields, this was no problem. Figure 5-2 shows the output cost estimate report with total direct costs of $123,175. Notice that the database system printed the subtotals for each level 2 work element. Also notice that column 3 did not sort identically in all level 2 elements.

TOTAL COSTWARE ESTIMATE

Level 2 Des	WES No	Name of Skill	LbrRt	Total Hrs	TOTAL $
D-1	D-1-1	PROGRAM MGR	35.00	0	0.00
		SR PROGRAMMER	30.00	140	4,200.00
		TECH WRTR	18.00	50	900.00
		SYS DAT ANAL	12.00	90	1,080.00
	D-1-2	PROGRAM MGR	35.00	0	0.00
		SR PROGRAMMER	30.00	140	4,200.00
		TECH WRTR	18.00	50	900.00
		SYS DAT ANAL	12.00	90	1,080.00
	D-1-3	PROGRAM MGR	35.00	0	0.00
		SR PROGRAMMER	30.00	140	4,200.00
		TECH WRTR	18.00	50	900.00
		SYS DAT ANAL	12.00	90	1,080.00
	D-1-4	PROGRAM MGR	35.00	0	0.00
		SR PROGRAMMER	30.00	140	4,200.00
		TECH WRTR	18.00	50	900.00
		SYS DAT ANAL	12.00	90	1,080.00
	D-1-5	PROGRAM MGR	35.00	320	11,200.00
		SR PROGRAMMER	30.00	140	4,200.00
		TECH WRTR	18.00	50	900.00
		SYS DAT ANAL	12.00	90	1,080.00
			Total:	1,720	42,100.00
D-2	D-2-1	PROGRAM MGR	35.00	100	3,500.00
		SR PROGRAMMER	30.00	50	1,500.00
		TECH WRTR	18.00	25	450.00
		SYS DAT ANAL	12.00	275	3,300.00
	D-2-2	PROGRAM MGR	35.00	30	1,050.00
		SR PROGRAMMER	30.00	60	1,800.00
		TECH WRTR	18.00	25	450.00
		SYS DAT ANAL	12.00	275	3,300.00
	D-2-3	PROGRAM MGR	35.00	30	1,050.00
		SR PROGRAMMER	30.00	60	1,800.00
		TECH WRTR	18.00	25	450.00
		SYS DAT ANAL	12.00	200	2,400.00
			Total:	1,155	21,050.00
D-3	D-3-1	SYS DAT ANAL	12.00	40	480.00
		TECH WRTR	18.00	40	720.00
		SR PROGRAMMER	30.00	0	0.00
		PROGRAM MGR	35.00	40	1,400.00
	D-3-2	SYS DAT ANAL	12.00	100	1,200.00
		TECH WRTR	18.00	340	6,120.00
		SR PROGRAMMER	30.00	80	2,400.00
		PROGRAM MGR	35.00	40	1,400.00
	D-3-3	SYS DAT ANAL	12.00	460	5,520.00
		TECH WRTR	18.00	160	2,880.00
		SR PROGRAMMER	30.00	80	2,400.00
		PROGRAM MGR	35.00	40	1,400.00
	D-3-4	SYS DAT ANAL	12.00	40	480.00
		TECH WRTR	18.00	55	990.00
		SR PROGRAMMER	30.00	80	2,400.00
		PROGRAM MGR	35.00	35	1,225.00
			Total:	1,630	31,015.00
D-4	D-4-1	SYS DAT ANAL	12.00	150	1,800.00
		TECH WRTR	18.00	0	0.00
		SR PROGRAMMER	30.00	175	5,250.00
		PROGRAM MGR	35.00	150	5,250.00
	D-4-2	SYS DAT ANAL	12.00	120	1,440.00
		TECH WRTR	18.00	0	0.00
		SR PROGRAMMER	30.00	120	3,600.00
		PROGRAM MGR	35.00	30	1,050.00
	D-4-3	SYS DAT ANAL	12.00	150	1,800.00
		TECH WRTR	18.00	150	2,700.00
		SR PROGRAMMER	30.00	150	4,500.00
		PROGRAM MGR	35.00	0	0.00
	D-4-4	SYS DAT ANAL	12.00	60	720.00
		TECH WRTR	18.00	0	0.00
		SR PROGRAMMER	30.00	30	900.00
		PROGRAM MGR	35.00	0	0.00
			Total:	1,285	29,010.00
			Total:	5,790	123,175.00

Figure 5-2 Total Costware estimate.

This is one reason why you may want to look for a database system that sorts on more than two key fields. Many larger database systems will sort on any or all fields.

Figure 5-3 shows how one can select specific records for reporting or display. We selected all of the systems data analyst entries under work element D-1 to determine how many hours and direct dollars were needed to support the systems data analyst during the first phase (programming) of the project. We could just as well have extracted any other skill (or material) category for all or part of the estimate; or we could have asked for the number of hours and dollars to be expended by employees receiving more than $18.00 per hour salary. By specifying the exact record selection criteria we are interested in, we can single out data records with unique characteristics and lump them into a group for reporting purposes.

In another cut at the same estimate, we developed two 6-month or semiannual estimates of the project using the data input form shown in Figure 5-1. Figures 5-4 and 5-5 show the printouts of all the data records in the database for each of two 6-month periods: January to June 1986 and July to December 1986. The above two examples show that considerable flexibility of output can be gained from even the most rudimentary database system, one which is available and on-hand already in many organizations. For only a little more investment, one can now purchase database systems that have few limitations regarding number of derived columns, number of columns that can be printed out in a single report, and number of fields on which a sort can be performed prior to printing out the results.

Combining Databases with Spreadsheets (Integrated Software)

There are a number of integrated software packages that combine the functions of a database applications program with spreadsheets and other

```
                  D-1 SYSTEM DATA ANALYST LABOR REPORT

Level 2 Des   WES No    Name of Skill   LbrRt   Total Hrs   TOTAL $
-----------   ------    -------------   -----   ---------   --------
D-1           D-1-1     SYS DAT ANAL    12.00          90   1,080.00
              D-1-2     SYS DAT ANAL    12.00          90   1,080.00
              D-1-3     SYS DAT ANAL    12.00          90   1,080.00
              D-1-4     SYS DAT ANAL    12.00          90   1,080.00
              D-1-5     SYS DAT ANAL    12.00          90   1,080.00

                                        Total:        450   5,400.00


                                        -------------------------
                                        Total:        450   5,400.00
                                        -------------------------
```

Figure 5-3   Example labor report for Costware.

Lvl 2 WBS	WBS No	Skill Name	Rate ($/Hr)	Jan86/Hrs	Feb86/Hrs	Mar86/Hrs	Apr86/Hrs	May86/Hrs	Jun86/Hrs	TOT LBR HRS	TOT LBR $
A-01	A-01-01	PROGRAM MGR	35.00								
		SR PROGRAMMER	30.00	100	10	10	10	10		140	4,200.00
		TECH WRTR	18.00	10	10	10	10	10		50	900.00
		SYS DAT ANAL	12.00	30	30	30				90	1,080.00
		SYS DAT ANAL	12.00	30	30	30				90	1,080.00
	A-01-02	PROGRAM MGR	35.00								
		SR PROGRAMMER	30.00	10	100	10	10	10		140	4,200.00
		TECH WRTR	18.00	10	10	10	10	10		50	900.00
	A-01-03	PROGRAM MGR	35.00								
		SR PROGRAMMER	30.00	10	10	100	10	10		140	4,200.00
		TECH WRTR	18.00	10	10	10	10	10		50	900.00
		SYS DAT ANAL	12.00	30	30	30				90	1,080.00
	A-01-04	PROGRAM MGR	35.00								
		SR PROGRAMMER	30.00	10	10	10	100	10		140	4,200.00
		TECH WRTR	18.00	10	10	10	10	10		50	900.00
		SYS DAT ANAL	12.00	30	30	30				90	1,080.00
	A-01-05	PROGRAM MGR	35.00	100	80	60	40	40		320	11,200.00
		SR PROGRAMMER	30.00	10	10	10	10	100		140	4,200.00
		TECH WRTR	18.00	10	10	10	10	10		50	900.00
		SYS DAT ANAL	12.00	30	30	30				90	1,080.00
		Total:		440	420	400	230	230		1,720	42,100.00
A-02	A-02-01	PROGRAM MGR	35.00				20	20	20	60	2,100.00
		SR PROGRAMMER	30.00				10	10	10	30	900.00
		TECH WRTR	18.00				5	5	5	15	270.00
		SYS DAT ANAL	12.00				100	100	25	225	2,700.00
	A-02-02	PROGRAM MGR	35.00						10	10	350.00
		SR PROGRAMMER	30.00						20	20	600.00
		TECH WRTR	18.00				5	5	5	15	270.00
		SYS DAT ANAL	12.00				25	25	100	150	1,800.00
	A-02-03	PROGRAM MGR	35.00						10	10	350.00
		SR PROGRAMMER	30.00						10	10	300.00
		TECH WRTR	18.00				5	5	5	15	270.00
		SYS DAT ANAL	12.00				25	25	25	75	900.00
		Total:		0	0	0	195	195	245	635	10,810.00
A-03	A-03-01	PROGRAM MGR	35.00						10	10	350.00
		SR PROGRAMMER	30.00								
		TECH WRTR	18.00						10	10	180.00
		SYS DAT ANAL	12.00						10	10	120.00
	A-03-02	PROGRAM MGR	35.00						10	10	350.00
		SR PROGRAMMER	30.00						20	20	600.00
		TECH WRTR	18.00						80	80	1,440.00
		SYS DAT ANAL	12.00						10	10	120.00
	A-03-03	PROGRAM MGR	35.00						10	10	350.00
		SR PROGRAMMER	30.00						20	20	600.00
		TECH WRTR	18.00						40	40	720.00
		SYS DAT ANAL	12.00						130	130	1,560.00
	A-03-04	PROGRAM MGR	35.00						5	5	175.00
		SR PROGRAMMER	30.00						20	20	600.00
		TECH WRTR	18.00						15	15	270.00
		SYS DAT ANAL	12.00						10	10	120.00
		Total:		0	0	0	0	0	400	400	7,555.00
A-04	A-04-01	PROGRAM MGR	35.00								
		SR PROGRAMMER	30.00								
		TECH WRTR	18.00								
		SYS DAT ANAL	12.00								
	A-04-02	PROGRAM MGR	35.00								
		SR PROGRAMMER	30.00								
		TECH WRTR	18.00								
		SYS DAT ANAL	12.00								
	A-04-03	PROGRAM MGR	35.00								
		SR PROGRAMMER	30.00								
		TECH WRTR	18.00								
		SYS DAT ANAL	12.00								
	A-04-04	PROGRAM MGR	35.00								
		SR PROGRAMMER	30.00								
		TECH WRTR	18.00								
		SYS DAT ANAL	12.00								
		Total:		0	0	0	0	0	0	0	0.00
		Total:		440	420	400	425	425	645	2,755	60,465.00

Figure 5-4 Costware cost estimate for January to June.

COSTWARE COST ESTIMATE

Lvl Z WBS	WBS No	Skill Name	Rate ($/Hr)	Jul86/Hrs	Aug86/Hrs	Sep86/Hrs	Oct86/Hrs	Nov86/Hrs	Dec86/Hrs	TOT LBR HRS	TOT LBR $
A-01	A-01-01	PROGRAM MGR	35.00								
		SR PROGRAMMER	30.00								
		TECH WRTR	18.00								
		SYS DAT ANAL	12.00								
		SYS DAT ANAL	12.00								
	A-01-02	PROGRAM MGR	35.00								
		SR PROGRAMMER	30.00								
		TECH WRTR	18.00								
	A-01-03	PROGRAM MGR	35.00								
		SR PROGRAMMER	30.00								
		TECH WRTR	18.00								
		SYS DAT ANAL	12.00								
	A-01-04	PROGRAM MGR	35.00								
		SR PROGRAMMER	30.00								
		TECH WRTR	18.00								
		SYS DAT ANAL	12.00								
	A-01-05	PROGRAM MGR	35.00								
		SR PROGRAMMER	30.00								
		TECH WRTR	18.00								
		SYS DAT ANAL	12.00								
		Total:									
A-02	A-02-01	PROGRAM MGR	35.00	20	20					40	1,400.00
		SR PROGRAMMER	30.00	10	10					20	600.00
		TECH WRTR	18.00	5	5					10	180.00
		SYS DAT ANAL	12.00	25	25					50	600.00
	A-02-02	PROGRAM MGR	35.00	10	10					20	700.00
		SR PROGRAMMER	30.00	20	20					40	1,200.00
		TECH WRTR	18.00	5	5					10	180.00
		SYS DAT ANAL	12.00	100	25					125	1,500.00
	A-02-03	PROGRAM MGR	35.00	10	10					20	700.00
		SR PROGRAMMER	30.00	20	30					50	1,500.00
		TECH WRTR	18.00	5	5					10	180.00
		SYS DAT ANAL	12.00	25	100					125	1,500.00
		Total:		255	265	0	0	0	0	520	10,240.00
A-03	A-03-01	PROGRAM MGR	35.00	5	5	20				30	1,050.00
		SR PROGRAMMER	30.00								
		TECH WRTR	18.00	10	10	10				30	540.00
		SYS DAT ANAL	12.00	10	10	10				30	360.00
	A-03-02	PROGRAM MGR	35.00	5	5	20				30	1,050.00
		SR PROGRAMMER	30.00	20	20	20				60	1,800.00
		TECH WRTR	18.00	80	80	100				260	4,680.00
		SYS DAT ANAL	12.00	20	30	40				90	1,080.00
	A-03-03	PROGRAM MGR	35.00	5	5	20				30	1,050.00
		SR PROGRAMMER	30.00	20	20	20				60	1,800.00
		TECH WRTR	18.00	40	40	40				120	2,160.00
		SYS DAT ANAL	12.00	120	110	100				330	3,960.00
	A-03-04	PROGRAM MGR	35.00	5	5	20				30	1,050.00
		SR PROGRAMMER	30.00	20	20	20				60	1,800.00
		TECH WRTR	18.00	15	15	10				40	720.00
		SYS DAT ANAL	12.00	10	10	10				30	360.00
		Total:		385	385	460	0	0	0	1,230	23,460.00
A-04	A-04-01	PROGRAM MGR	35.00				50	50	50	150	5,250.00
		SR PROGRAMMER	30.00				100	50	25	175	5,250.00
		TECH WRTR	18.00								
		SYS DAT ANAL	12.00				50	50	50	150	1,800.00
	A-04-02	PROGRAM MGR	35.00				10	10	10	30	1,050.00
		SR PROGRAMMER	30.00				40	40	40	120	3,600.00
		TECH WRTR	18.00								
		SYS DAT ANAL	12.00				40	40	40	120	1,440.00
	A-04-03	PROGRAM MGR	35.00								
		SR PROGRAMMER	30.00				50	50	50	150	4,500.00
		TECH WRTR	18.00				50	50	50	150	2,700.00
		SYS DAT ANAL	12.00				50	50	50	150	1,800.00
	A-04-04	PROGRAM MGR	35.00								
		SR PROGRAMMER	30.00				10	10	10	30	900.00
		TECH WRTR	18.00								
		SYS DAT ANAL	12.00				20	20	20	60	720.00
		Total:		0	0	0	470	420	395	1,285	29,010.00
		Total:		640	650	460	470	420	395	3,035	62,710.00

Figure 5-5 Costware cost estimate for July to December.

functions. We have chosen one of these integrated packages, Lotus 1-2-3, to develop another version of the COSTWARE estimate. The database is a file manager type of system normally associated with business record keeping, one that is normally used to keep track of sales, personnel, addresses, parts, telephone numbers, etc. But the file manager type of database system, particularly when combined with the functions of a spreadsheet, is particularly useful as a cost estimating tool. As was the case in the previous estimate, each input-level work element is a database record. In the Lotus 1-2-3 system, the field names are placed across a row of the spreadsheet, and each record is placed below this row of field names, with the entries for each field falling directly below their respective field names. Figure 5-6 shows the database entries that include the level 3 WES designator (A-01-01), the skill or material name, the title of the work element, and the labor hours (or material unit quantities) estimated for each calendar period. With the exceptions of the headings, titles, and dates, the Total Hrs column at the right-hand margin of these two figures, and the Total Labor Hours row at the bottom of the second sheet (Figure 5-6), these two figures represent the cost estimate work-hour database.

Using the COPY function provided in the spreadsheet commands, the headings and first two columns can be copied to a virtually identical work space to the right of this original database. By changing the headings slightly (we put the $ symbol in front of each field name or column heading), each data record can be extended to include a labor dollars portion of the database or spreadsheet. A $$/Hr or labor rate field is added as column 3 of this new spreadsheet section, and, using the spreadsheet formulas to multiply each labor hour entry by this labor rate, a labor dollar spreadsheet can be generated. What we have really generated is another spreadsheet consisting of rows of database records or *work elements* records. The monthly totals and work element totals are computed using spreadsheet formulas and are shown in the bottom row and the rightmost column of Figure 5-7. Notice that the WES numbers are placed in perfect sequence along the leftmost column. We could have entered the database records (rows) in any sequence and then have sorted the records in ascending order using the first column as the primary sorting basis and the second column as the secondary sorting basis to arrive at a display or printout exactly as that shown on Figures 5-6 and 5-7.

So far, we have not really used the database features of the software package to help us develop the cost estimate. The database features really come into play when we want to sort the database in some specific way or when we want to select a specific set of records, say those within one level 2 work element or those containing one skill. Figure 5-8 shows the results if we were to sort out each skill name and place them in

```
**************DATABASE FOR 'COSTWARE' COST ESTIMATE**************************************************************************
      (A work element structure based labor/materials estimate
*********************************************************************************************************************
DATE:    16-Oct-85                      CALENDAR--------------------)
*********************************************************************************************************************
                                        LABOR HOURS
W.E.S.#  Skill/mtl.      WES Title      Jan86 Feb86 Mar86 Apr86 May86 Jun86 Jul86 Aug86 Sep86 Oct86 Nov86 Dec86 Total Hrs
```

```
**************DATABASE FOR 'COSTWARE' COST ESTIMATE**************************************************************************
      (A work element structure based labor/materials estimate)
*********************************************************************************************************************
DATE:    16-Oct-85                      CALENDAR--------------------)
*********************************************************************************************************************
                                        LABOR HOURS
```

W.E.S.#	Skill/mtl.	WES Title	Jan86	Feb86	Mar86	Apr86	May86	Jun86	Jul86	Aug86	Sep86	Oct86	Nov86	Dec86	Total Hrs
A-01-01	Program Manager	Programming Inputs	0	0	0	0	0	0	0	0	0	0	0	0	0
A-01-01	Senior Programmer	Programming Inputs	100	10	10	10	10	0	0	0	0	0	0	0	140
A-01-01	Systems Analyst	Programming Inputs	30	30	30	0	0	0	0	0	0	0	0	0	90
A-01-01	Technical Writer	Programming Inputs	10	10	10	10	10	0	0	0	0	0	0	0	50
A-01-02	Program Manager	Programming Edits	0	0	0	0	0	0	0	0	0	0	0	0	0
A-01-02	Senior Programmer	Programming Edits	10	100	10	10	10	0	0	0	0	0	0	0	140
A-01-02	Systems Analyst	Programming Edits	30	30	30	0	0	0	0	0	0	0	0	0	90
A-01-02	Technical Writer	Programming Edits	10	10	10	10	10	0	0	0	0	0	0	0	50
A-01-03	Program Manager	Prgm Error Messages	0	0	0	0	0	0	0	0	0	0	0	0	0
A-01-03	Senior Programmer	Prgm Error Messages	10	10	100	10	10	0	0	0	0	0	0	0	140
A-01-03	Systems Analyst	Prgm Error Messages	30	30	30	0	0	0	0	0	0	0	0	0	90
A-01-03	Technical Writer	Prgm Error Messages	10	10	10	10	10	0	0	0	0	0	0	0	50
A-01-04	Program Manager	Prgm Rept Generator	0	0	0	0	0	0	0	0	0	0	0	0	0
A-01-04	Senior Programmer	Prgm Rept Generator	10	10	10	100	10	0	0	0	0	0	0	0	140
A-01-04	Systems Analyst	Prgm Rept Generator	30	30	30	0	0	0	0	0	0	0	0	0	90
A-01-04	Technical Writer	Prgm Rept Generator	10	10	10	10	10	0	0	0	0	0	0	0	50
A-01-05	Program Manager	Prgm User Inputs	100	80	60	40	40	0	0	0	0	0	0	0	320
A-01-05	Senior Programmer	Prgm User Inputs	10	10	10	10	100	0	0	0	0	0	0	0	140
A-01-05	Systems Analyst	Prgm User Inputs	30	30	30	0	0	0	0	0	0	0	0	0	90
A-01-05	Technical Writer	Prgm User Inputs	10	10	10	10	10	0	0	0	0	0	0	0	50
A-02-01	Program Manager	In-House Testing	0	0	0	20	20	20	20	20	0	0	0	0	100
A-02-01	Senior Programmer	In-House Testing	0	0	0	10	10	10	10	10	0	0	0	0	50
A-02-01	Systems Analyst	In-House Testing	0	0	0	100	100	25	25	25	0	0	0	0	275
A-02-01	Technical Writer	In-House Testing	0	0	0	5	5	5	5	5	0	0	0	0	25
A-02-02	Program Manager	Market Testing	0	0	0	0	0	10	10	10	0	0	0	0	30
A-02-02	Senior Programmer	Market Testing	0	0	0	0	0	20	20	20	0	0	0	0	60
A-02-02	Systems Analyst	Market Testing	0	0	0	25	25	100	100	25	0	0	0	0	275
A-02-02	Technical Writer	Market Testing	0	0	0	5	5	5	5	5	0	0	0	0	25
A-02-03	Program Manager	Testing Feedback	0	0	0	0	0	10	10	10	0	0	0	0	30
A-02-03	Senior Programmer	Testing Feedback	0	0	0	0	0	10	20	30	0	0	0	0	60
A-02-03	Systems Analyst	Testing Feedback	0	0	0	25	25	25	25	100	0	0	0	0	200
A-02-03	Technical Writer	Testing Feedback	0	0	0	5	5	5	5	5	0	0	0	0	25
A-03-01	Program Manager	Basic Documentation	0	0	0	0	0	0	5	5	20	0	0	0	40
A-03-01	Senior Programmer	Basic Documentation	0	0	0	0	0	0	0	0	0	0	0	0	0
A-03-01	Systems Analyst	Basic Documentation	0	0	0	0	0	10	10	10	10	0	0	0	40
A-03-01	Technical Writer	Basic Documentation	0	0	0	0	0	10	10	10	10	0	0	0	40
A-03-02	Program Manager	Operator's Manual	0	0	0	0	0	10	5	5	20	0	0	0	40
A-03-02	Senior Programmer	Operator's Manual	0	0	0	0	0	20	20	20	20	0	0	0	80
A-03-02	Systems Analyst	Operator's Manual	0	0	0	0	0	10	20	30	40	0	0	0	100
A-03-02	Technical Writer	Operator's Manual	0	0	0	0	0	80	80	80	100	0	0	0	340
A-03-03	Program Manager	Sample Problems	0	0	0	0	0	10	5	5	20	0	0	0	40
A-03-03	Senior Programmer	Sample Problems	0	0	0	0	0	20	20	20	20	0	0	0	80
A-03-03	Systems Analyst	Sample Problems	0	0	0	0	0	130	120	110	100	0	0	0	460
A-03-03	Technical Writer	Sample Problems	0	0	0	0	0	40	40	40	40	0	0	0	160
A-03-04	Program Manager	Documenting Updates	0	0	0	0	0	5	5	5	20	0	0	0	35
A-03-04	Senior Programmer	Documenting Updates	0	0	0	0	0	20	20	20	20	0	0	0	80
A-03-04	Systems Analyst	Documenting Updates	0	0	0	0	0	10	10	10	10	0	0	0	40
A-03-04	Technical Writer	Documenting Updates	0	0	0	0	0	15	15	15	10	0	0	0	55
A-04-01	Program Manager	Installation Support	0	0	0	0	0	0	0	0	0	50	50	50	150
A-04-01	Senior Programmer	Installation Support	0	0	0	0	0	0	0	0	0	100	50	25	175
A-04-01	Systems Analyst	Installation Support	0	0	0	0	0	0	0	0	0	50	50	50	150
A-04-01	Technical Writer	Installation Support	0	0	0	0	0	0	0	0	0	0	0	0	0
A-04-02	Program Manager	Training Support	0	0	0	0	0	0	0	0	0	10	10	10	30
A-04-02	Senior Programmer	Training Support	0	0	0	0	0	0	0	0	0	40	40	40	120
A-04-02	Systems Analyst	Training Support	0	0	0	0	0	0	0	0	0	40	40	40	120
A-04-02	Technical Writer	Training Support	0	0	0	0	0	0	0	0	0	0	0	0	0
A-04-03	Program Manager	Support of Updates	0	0	0	0	0	0	0	0	0	0	0	0	0
A-04-03	Senior Programmer	Support of Updates	0	0	0	0	0	0	0	0	0	50	50	50	150
A-04-03	Systems Analyst	Support of Updates	0	0	0	0	0	0	0	0	0	50	50	50	150
A-04-03	Technical Writer	Support of Updates	0	0	0	0	0	0	0	0	0	50	50	50	150
A-04-04	Program Manager	Field Svc Support	0	0	0	0	0	0	0	0	0	0	0	0	0
A-04-04	Senior Programmer	Field Svc Support	0	0	0	0	0	0	0	0	0	10	10	10	30
A-04-04	Systems Analyst	Field Svc Support	0	0	0	0	0	0	0	0	0	20	20	20	60
A-04-04	Technical Writer	Field Svc Support	0	0	0	0	0	0	0	0	0	0	0	0	0
	TOTAL LABOR HOURS		440	420	400	425	425	645	640	650	460	470	420	395	5790

Figure 5-6 Costware estimate labor-hour database.

LABOR DOLLARS

W.E.S.#	Skill/mtl.	$$/hr	$Jan86	$Feb86	$Mar86	$Apr86	$May86	$Jun86	$Jul86	$Aug86	$Sep86	$Oct86	$Nov86	$Dec86	Total $
A-01-01	Program Manager	$35.00	$0	$0	$0	$0	$0	$0	$0	$0	$0	$0	$0	$0	$0
A-01-01	Senior Programmer	$30.00	$3,000	$300	$300	$300	$300	$0	$0	$0	$0	$0	$0	$0	$4,200
A-01-01	Systems Analyst	$12.00	$360	$360	$360	$0	$0	$0	$0	$0	$0	$0	$0	$0	$1,080
A-01-01	Technical Writer	$18.00	$180	$180	$180	$180	$180	$0	$0	$0	$0	$0	$0	$0	$900
A-01-02	Program Manager	$35.00	$0	$0	$0	$0	$0	$0	$0	$0	$0	$0	$0	$0	$0
A-01-02	Senior Programmer	$30.00	$300	$3,000	$300	$300	$300	$0	$0	$0	$0	$0	$0	$0	$4,200
A-01-02	Systems Analyst	$12.00	$360	$360	$360	$0	$0	$0	$0	$0	$0	$0	$0	$0	$1,080
A-01-02	Technical Writer	$18.00	$180	$180	$180	$180	$180	$0	$0	$0	$0	$0	$0	$0	$900
A-01-03	Program Manager	$35.00	$0	$0	$0	$0	$0	$0	$0	$0	$0	$0	$0	$0	$0
A-01-03	Senior Programmer	$30.00	$300	$300	$3,000	$300	$300	$0	$0	$0	$0	$0	$0	$0	$4,200
A-01-03	Systems Analyst	$12.00	$360	$360	$360	$0	$0	$0	$0	$0	$0	$0	$0	$0	$1,080
A-01-03	Technical Writer	$18.00	$180	$180	$180	$180	$180	$0	$0	$0	$0	$0	$0	$0	$900
A-01-04	Program Manager	$35.00	$0	$0	$0	$0	$0	$0	$0	$0	$0	$0	$0	$0	$0
A-01-04	Senior Programmer	$30.00	$300	$300	$300	$3,000	$300	$0	$0	$0	$0	$0	$0	$0	$4,200
A-01-04	Systems Analyst	$12.00	$360	$360	$360	$0	$0	$0	$0	$0	$0	$0	$0	$0	$1,080
A-01-04	Technical Writer	$18.00	$180	$180	$180	$180	$180	$0	$0	$0	$0	$0	$0	$0	$900
A-01-05	Program Manager	$35.00	$3,500	$2,800	$2,100	$1,400	$1,400	$0	$0	$0	$0	$0	$0	$0	$11,200
A-01-05	Senior Programmer	$30.00	$300	$300	$300	$300	$3,000	$0	$0	$0	$0	$0	$0	$0	$4,200
A-01-05	Systems Analyst	$12.00	$360	$360	$360	$0	$0	$0	$0	$0	$0	$0	$0	$0	$1,080
A-01-05	Technical Writer	$18.00	$180	$180	$180	$180	$180	$0	$0	$0	$0	$0	$0	$0	$900
A-02-01	Program Manager	$35.00	$0	$0	$0	$700	$700	$700	$700	$700	$0	$0	$0	$0	$3,500
A-02-01	Senior Programmer	$30.00	$0	$0	$0	$300	$300	$300	$300	$300	$0	$0	$0	$0	$1,500
A-02-01	Systems Analyst	$12.00	$0	$0	$0	$1,200	$1,200	$300	$300	$300	$0	$0	$0	$0	$3,300
A-02-01	Technical Writer	$18.00	$0	$0	$0	$90	$90	$90	$90	$90	$0	$0	$0	$0	$450
A-02-02	Program Manager	$35.00	$0	$0	$0	$0	$0	$350	$350	$350	$0	$0	$0	$0	$1,050
A-02-02	Senior Programmer	$30.00	$0	$0	$0	$0	$0	$600	$600	$600	$0	$0	$0	$0	$1,800
A-02-02	Systems Analyst	$12.00	$0	$0	$0	$300	$300	$1,200	$1,200	$300	$0	$0	$0	$0	$3,300
A-02-02	Technical Writer	$18.00	$0	$0	$0	$90	$90	$90	$90	$90	$0	$0	$0	$0	$450
A-02-03	Program Manager	$35.00	$0	$0	$0	$0	$0	$350	$350	$350	$0	$0	$0	$0	$1,050
A-02-03	Senior Programmer	$30.00	$0	$0	$0	$0	$0	$300	$600	$900	$0	$0	$0	$0	$1,800
A-02-03	Systems Analyst	$12.00	$0	$0	$0	$300	$300	$300	$300	$1,200	$0	$0	$0	$0	$2,400
A-02-03	Technical Writer	$18.00	$0	$0	$0	$90	$90	$90	$90	$90	$0	$0	$0	$0	$450
A-03-01	Program Manager	$35.00	$0	$0	$0	$0	$0	$350	$175	$175	$700	$0	$0	$0	$1,400
A-03-01	Senior Programmer	$30.00	$0	$0	$0	$0	$0	$0	$0	$0	$0	$0	$0	$0	$0
A-03-01	Systems Analyst	$12.00	$0	$0	$0	$0	$0	$120	$120	$120	$120	$0	$0	$0	$480
A-03-01	Technical Writer	$18.00	$0	$0	$0	$0	$0	$180	$180	$180	$180	$0	$0	$0	$720
A-03-02	Program Manager	$35.00	$0	$0	$0	$0	$0	$350	$175	$175	$700	$0	$0	$0	$1,400
A-03-02	Senior Programmer	$30.00	$0	$0	$0	$0	$0	$600	$600	$600	$600	$0	$0	$0	$2,400
A-03-02	Systems Analyst	$12.00	$0	$0	$0	$0	$0	$120	$240	$360	$480	$0	$0	$0	$1,200
A-03-02	Technical Writer	$18.00	$0	$0	$0	$0	$0	$1,440	$1,440	$1,440	$1,800	$0	$0	$0	$6,120
A-03-03	Program Manager	$35.00	$0	$0	$0	$0	$0	$350	$175	$175	$700	$0	$0	$0	$1,400
A-03-03	Senior Programmer	$30.00	$0	$0	$0	$0	$0	$600	$600	$600	$600	$0	$0	$0	$2,400
A-03-03	Systems Analyst	$12.00	$0	$0	$0	$0	$0	$1,560	$1,440	$1,320	$1,200	$0	$0	$0	$5,520
A-03-03	Technical Writer	$18.00	$0	$0	$0	$0	$0	$720	$720	$720	$720	$0	$0	$0	$2,880
A-03-04	Program Manager	$35.00	$0	$0	$0	$0	$0	$175	$175	$175	$700	$0	$0	$0	$1,225
A-03-04	Senior Programmer	$30.00	$0	$0	$0	$0	$0	$600	$600	$600	$600	$0	$0	$0	$2,400
A-03-04	Systems Analyst	$12.00	$0	$0	$0	$0	$0	$120	$120	$120	$120	$0	$0	$0	$480
A-03-04	Technical Writer	$18.00	$0	$0	$0	$0	$0	$270	$270	$270	$180	$0	$0	$0	$990
A-04-01	Program Manager	$35.00	$0	$0	$0	$0	$0	$0	$0	$0	$0	$1,750	$1,750	$1,750	$5,250
A-04-01	Senior Programmer	$30.00	$0	$0	$0	$0	$0	$0	$0	$0	$0	$3,000	$1,500	$750	$5,250
A-04-01	Systems Analyst	$12.00	$0	$0	$0	$0	$0	$0	$0	$0	$0	$600	$600	$600	$1,800
A-04-01	Technical Writer	$18.00	$0	$0	$0	$0	$0	$0	$0	$0	$0	$0	$0	$0	$0
A-04-02	Program Manager	$35.00	$0	$0	$0	$0	$0	$0	$0	$0	$0	$350	$350	$350	$1,050
A-04-02	Senior Programmer	$30.00	$0	$0	$0	$0	$0	$0	$0	$0	$0	$1,200	$1,200	$1,200	$3,600
A-04-02	Systems Analyst	$12.00	$0	$0	$0	$0	$0	$0	$0	$0	$0	$480	$480	$480	$1,440
A-04-02	Technical Writer	$18.00	$0	$0	$0	$0	$0	$0	$0	$0	$0	$0	$0	$0	$0
A-04-03	Program Manager	$35.00	$0	$0	$0	$0	$0	$0	$0	$0	$0	$0	$0	$0	$0
A-04-03	Senior Programmer	$30.00	$0	$0	$0	$0	$0	$0	$0	$0	$0	$1,500	$1,500	$1,500	$4,500
A-04-03	Systems Analyst	$12.00	$0	$0	$0	$0	$0	$0	$0	$0	$0	$600	$600	$600	$1,800
A-04-03	Technical Writer	$18.00	$0	$0	$0	$0	$0	$0	$0	$0	$0	$900	$900	$900	$2,700
A-04-04	Program Manager	$35.00	$0	$0	$0	$0	$0	$0	$0	$0	$0	$0	$0	$0	$0
A-04-04	Senior Programmer	$30.00	$0	$0	$0	$0	$0	$0	$0	$0	$0	$300	$300	$300	$900
A-04-04	Systems Analyst	$12.00	$0	$0	$0	$0	$0	$0	$0	$0	$0	$240	$240	$240	$720
A-04-04	Technical Writer	$18.00	$0	$0	$0	$0	$0	$0	$0	$0	$0	$0	$0	$0	$0
Total Hrs			$10,400	$9,700	$9,000	$9,570	$9,570	$12,225	$12,000	$12,300	$9,400	$10,920	$9,420	$8,670	$123,175
GRAND TOTAL ESTIMATE			$16,853	$15,719	$14,585	$15,508	$15,508	$19,811	$19,446	$19,932	$15,233	$17,696	$15,265	$14,050	$199,607

Figure 5-7   Labor dollars output for Costware estimate.

LABOR DOLLARS FOR "COSTWARE" COST ESTIMATE

LABOR DOLLARS

$W.E.S.#	$Skill/ntl.	$$/hr	$Jan86	$Feb86	$Mar86	$Apr86	$May86	$Jun86	$Jul86	$Aug86	$Sep86	$Oct86	$Nov86	$Dec86	$Total $
A-01-01	Program Manager	$35.00	$0	$0	$0	$0	$0	$0	$0	$0	$0	$0	$0	$0	$0
A-01-02	Program Manager	$35.00	$0	$0	$0	$0	$0	$0	$0	$0	$0	$0	$0	$0	$0
A-01-03	Program Manager	$35.00	$0	$0	$0	$0	$0	$0	$0	$0	$0	$0	$0	$0	$0
A-01-04	Program Manager	$35.00	$0	$0	$0	$0	$0	$0	$0	$0	$0	$0	$0	$0	$0
A-01-05	Program Manager	$35.00	$3,500	$2,800	$2,100	$1,400	$1,400	$0	$0	$0	$0	$0	$0	$0	$11,200
A-02-01	Program Manager	$35.00	$0	$0	$0	$700	$700	$700	$700	$700	$0	$0	$0	$0	$3,500
A-02-02	Program Manager	$35.00	$0	$0	$0	$0	$0	$350	$350	$350	$0	$0	$0	$0	$1,050
A-02-03	Program Manager	$35.00	$0	$0	$0	$0	$0	$350	$350	$350	$0	$0	$0	$0	$1,050
A-03-01	Program Manager	$35.00	$0	$0	$0	$0	$0	$350	$175	$175	$700	$0	$0	$0	$1,400
A-03-02	Program Manager	$35.00	$0	$0	$0	$0	$0	$350	$175	$175	$700	$0	$0	$0	$1,400
A-03-03	Program Manager	$35.00	$0	$0	$0	$0	$0	$350	$175	$175	$700	$0	$0	$0	$1,400
A-03-04	Program Manager	$35.00	$0	$0	$0	$0	$0	$175	$175	$175	$700	$0	$0	$0	$1,225
A-04-01	Program Manager	$35.00	$0	$0	$0	$0	$0	$0	$0	$0	$0	$1,750	$1,750	$1,750	$5,250
A-04-02	Program Manager	$35.00	$0	$0	$0	$0	$0	$0	$0	$0	$0	$350	$350	$350	$1,050
A-04-03	Program Manager	$35.00	$0	$0	$0	$0	$0	$0	$0	$0	$0	$0	$0	$0	$0
A-04-04	Program Manager	$35.00	$0	$0	$0	$0	$0	$0	$0	$0	$0	$0	$0	$0	$0
A-01-01	Senior Programmer	$30.00	$3,000	$300	$300	$300	$300	$0	$0	$0	$0	$0	$0	$0	$4,200
A-01-02	Senior Programmer	$30.00	$300	$3,000	$300	$300	$300	$0	$0	$0	$0	$0	$0	$0	$4,200
A-01-03	Senior Programmer	$30.00	$300	$300	$3,000	$300	$300	$0	$0	$0	$0	$0	$0	$0	$4,200
A-01-04	Senior Programmer	$30.00	$300	$300	$300	$3,000	$300	$0	$0	$0	$0	$0	$0	$0	$4,200
A-01-05	Senior Programmer	$30.00	$300	$300	$300	$300	$3,000	$0	$0	$0	$0	$0	$0	$0	$4,200
A-02-01	Senior Programmer	$30.00	$0	$0	$0	$0	$300	$300	$300	$300	$0	$0	$0	$0	$1,500
A-02-02	Senior Programmer	$30.00	$0	$0	$0	$0	$0	$600	$600	$600	$0	$0	$0	$0	$1,800
A-02-03	Senior Programmer	$30.00	$0	$0	$0	$0	$0	$300	$600	$900	$0	$0	$0	$0	$1,800
A-03-01	Senior Programmer	$30.00	$0	$0	$0	$0	$0	$0	$0	$0	$0	$0	$0	$0	$0
A-03-02	Senior Programmer	$30.00	$0	$0	$0	$0	$0	$600	$600	$600	$600	$0	$0	$0	$2,400
A-03-03	Senior Programmer	$30.00	$0	$0	$0	$0	$0	$600	$600	$600	$600	$0	$0	$0	$2,400
A-03-04	Senior Programmer	$30.00	$0	$0	$0	$0	$0	$600	$600	$600	$600	$0	$0	$0	$2,400
A-04-01	Senior Programmer	$30.00	$0	$0	$0	$0	$0	$0	$0	$0	$0	$3,000	$1,500	$750	$5,250
A-04-02	Senior Programmer	$30.00	$0	$0	$0	$0	$0	$0	$0	$0	$0	$1,200	$1,200	$1,200	$3,600
A-04-03	Senior Programmer	$30.00	$0	$0	$0	$0	$0	$0	$0	$0	$0	$1,500	$1,500	$1,500	$4,500
A-04-04	Senior Programmer	$30.00	$0	$0	$0	$0	$0	$0	$0	$0	$0	$300	$300	$300	$900
A-01-01	Systems Analyst	$12.00	$360	$360	$360	$0	$0	$0	$0	$0	$0	$0	$0	$0	$1,080
A-01-02	Systems Analyst	$12.00	$360	$360	$360	$0	$0	$0	$0	$0	$0	$0	$0	$0	$1,080
A-01-03	Systems Analyst	$12.00	$360	$360	$360	$0	$0	$0	$0	$0	$0	$0	$0	$0	$1,080
A-01-04	Systems Analyst	$12.00	$360	$360	$360	$0	$0	$0	$0	$0	$0	$0	$0	$0	$1,080
A-01-05	Systems Analyst	$12.00	$360	$360	$360	$0	$0	$0	$0	$0	$0	$0	$0	$0	$1,080
A-02-01	Systems Analyst	$12.00	$0	$0	$0	$1,200	$1,200	$300	$300	$300	$0	$0	$0	$0	$3,300
A-02-02	Systems Analyst	$12.00	$0	$0	$0	$300	$300	$1,200	$1,200	$300	$0	$0	$0	$0	$3,300
A-02-03	Systems Analyst	$12.00	$0	$0	$0	$300	$300	$300	$300	$1,200	$0	$0	$0	$0	$2,400
A-03-01	Systems Analyst	$12.00	$0	$0	$0	$0	$0	$120	$120	$120	$120	$0	$0	$0	$480
A-03-02	Systems Analyst	$12.00	$0	$0	$0	$0	$0	$120	$240	$360	$480	$0	$0	$0	$1,200
A-03-03	Systems Analyst	$12.00	$0	$0	$0	$0	$0	$1,560	$1,440	$1,320	$1,200	$0	$0	$0	$5,520
A-03-04	Systems Analyst	$12.00	$0	$0	$0	$0	$0	$120	$120	$120	$120	$0	$0	$0	$480
A-04-01	Systems Analyst	$12.00	$0	$0	$0	$0	$0	$0	$0	$0	$0	$600	$600	$600	$1,800
A-04-02	Systems Analyst	$12.00	$0	$0	$0	$0	$0	$0	$0	$0	$0	$480	$480	$480	$1,440
A-04-03	Systems Analyst	$12.00	$0	$0	$0	$0	$0	$0	$0	$0	$0	$600	$600	$600	$1,800
A-04-04	Systems Analyst	$12.00	$0	$0	$0	$0	$0	$0	$0	$0	$0	$240	$240	$240	$720
A-01-01	Technical Writer	$18.00	$180	$180	$180	$180	$180	$0	$0	$0	$0	$0	$0	$0	$900
A-01-02	Technical Writer	$18.00	$180	$180	$180	$180	$180	$0	$0	$0	$0	$0	$0	$0	$900
A-01-03	Technical Writer	$18.00	$180	$180	$180	$180	$180	$0	$0	$0	$0	$0	$0	$0	$900
A-01-04	Technical Writer	$18.00	$180	$180	$180	$180	$180	$0	$0	$0	$0	$0	$0	$0	$900
A-01-05	Technical Writer	$18.00	$180	$180	$180	$180	$180	$0	$0	$0	$0	$0	$0	$0	$900
A-02-01	Technical Writer	$18.00	$0	$0	$0	$90	$90	$90	$90	$90	$0	$0	$0	$0	$450
A-02-02	Technical Writer	$18.00	$0	$0	$0	$90	$90	$90	$90	$90	$0	$0	$0	$0	$450
A-02-03	Technical Writer	$18.00	$0	$0	$0	$90	$90	$90	$90	$90	$0	$0	$0	$0	$450
A-03-01	Technical Writer	$18.00	$0	$0	$0	$0	$0	$180	$180	$180	$180	$0	$0	$0	$720
A-03-02	Technical Writer	$18.00	$0	$0	$0	$0	$0	$1,440	$1,440	$1,440	$1,800	$0	$0	$0	$6,120
A-03-03	Technical Writer	$18.00	$0	$0	$0	$0	$0	$720	$720	$720	$720	$0	$0	$0	$2,880
A-03-04	Technical Writer	$18.00	$0	$0	$0	$0	$0	$270	$270	$270	$180	$0	$0	$0	$990
A-04-01	Technical Writer	$18.00	$0	$0	$0	$0	$0	$0	$0	$0	$0	$0	$0	$0	$0
A-04-02	Technical Writer	$18.00	$0	$0	$0	$0	$0	$0	$0	$0	$0	$0	$0	$0	$0
A-04-03	Technical Writer	$18.00	$0	$0	$0	$0	$0	$0	$0	$0	$0	$900	$900	$900	$2,700
A-04-04	Technical Writer	$18.00	$0	$0	$0	$0	$0	$0	$0	$0	$0	$0	$0	$0	$0
	Total Hrs		$10,400	$9,700	$9,000	$9,570	$9,570	$12,225	$12,000	$12,300	$9,400	$10,920	$9,420	$8,670	$123,175
	GRAND TOTAL ESTIMATE		$16,853	$15,719	$14,585	$15,508	$15,508	$19,811	$19,446	$19,932	$15,233	$17,696	$15,265	$14,050	$199,607

Figure 5-8 Costware estimate sorted by labor category.

alphabetical order. Notice that the entire row of fields or record of information is repositioned in the spreadsheet in keeping with the alphabetical sorting sequence of the skill title. The total rows and columns still add up because we have not changed the number of records in the spreadsheet but merely resorted them.

A better place to position totals in relation to an output range of a database is at the top or *above* the output data range as shown in Figures 5-9 and 5-10. If you want to select records meeting selected criteria and you are not sure how many records will be chosen, placing the totals at the top will prevent the total formulas from being obliterated by selected database records. (The selected data records are always listed below the row of field names in this applications package.) The criterion used to select the set of data records shown on Figure 5-9 was "the #W.E.S.# field contents equals A-03-??." This criterion caused the computer to select all work elements under the level 2 designator of A-03.

The criterion used to generate Figure 5-10 from the input database was "the $Skill/mtl field equals Technical Writer." Hence, it is easy to select records from any work element grouping, skill or skills, or even labor rate or labor dollar value or range of values. This feature would be useful for determining all individuals in a department who are estimated to spend over 40 hours on the job, all those who are not scheduled to work on the project in July 1986 (as evidenced by a zero dollar labor cost), and other arrangements. The most common use of this database selection feature would be to develop a complete WES-related cost breakout by sequentially selecting and printing each work element grouping.

Using Multiple Criteria in a Cost Estimate Database

As shown in the above example, multiple criteria can be used to select work element resource records. A record can be selected only if it meets *all* of the criteria (the AND function), or a record can be selected if it fits *any one* of the criteria (the OR function). For example, we may wish to choose all records containing the technical writer skill AND labor costs greater than $100 in any month; or we may choose all records containing the project manager skill OR any resource value greater than $1000 in any month. The use of multiple criteria is valuable for performing a cost analysis of the estimate to determine the highest-cost work elements, the skills with the biggest labor costs, or the months with the highest labor hour estimates. The use of these criteria, along with the database statistical functions described below, can help you thoroughly analyze a cost estimate.

```
*************************************************************************************
            LABOR DOLLARS FOR "COSTWARE" COST ESTIMATE
*************************************************************************************
                           LABOR DOLLARS
```

$W.E.S.# $Skill/mtl.	$Jan86	$Feb86	$Mar86	$Apr86	$May86	$Jun86	$Jul86	$Aug86	$Sep86	$Oct86	$Nov86	$Dec86	$Total $
TOTALS FOR SELECTED DATA RECORDS	DATE: 16-Oct												

```
*************************************************************************************
```

| TOTAL DOLLARS V | $0 | $0 | $0 | $0 | $0 | $7,555 | $7,030 | $7,030 | $7,400 | $0 | $0 | $0 | $31,015 |

$W.E.S.# $Skill/mtl.	$Jan86	$Feb86	$Mar86	$Apr86	$May86	$Jun86	$Jul86	$Aug86	$Sep86	$Oct86	$Nov86	$Dec86	$Total $
A-03-01 Program Manager	$0	$0	$0	$0	$0	$350	$175	$175	$700	$0	$0	$0	$1,400
A-03-01 Senior Programmer	$0	$0	$0	$0	$0	$0	$0	$0	$0	$0	$0	$0	$0
A-03-01 Systems Analyst	$0	$0	$0	$0	$0	$120	$120	$120	$120	$0	$0	$0	$480
A-03-01 Technical Writer	$0	$0	$0	$0	$0	$180	$180	$180	$180	$0	$0	$0	$720
A-03-02 Program Manager	$0	$0	$0	$0	$0	$350	$175	$175	$700	$0	$0	$0	$1,400
A-03-02 Senior Programmer	$0	$0	$0	$0	$0	$600	$600	$600	$600	$0	$0	$0	$2,400
A-03-02 Systems Analyst	$0	$0	$0	$0	$0	$120	$240	$360	$480	$0	$0	$0	$1,200
A-03-02 Technical Writer	$0	$0	$0	$0	$0	$1,440	$1,440	$1,440	$1,800	$0	$0	$0	$6,120
A-03-03 Program Manager	$0	$0	$0	$0	$0	$350	$175	$175	$700	$0	$0	$0	$1,400
A-03-03 Senior Programmer	$0	$0	$0	$0	$0	$600	$600	$600	$600	$0	$0	$0	$2,400
A-03-03 Systems Analyst	$0	$0	$0	$0	$0	$1,560	$1,440	$1,320	$1,200	$0	$0	$0	$5,520
A-03-03 Technical Writer	$0	$0	$0	$0	$0	$720	$720	$720	$720	$0	$0	$0	$2,880
A-03-04 Program Manager	$0	$0	$0	$0	$0	$175	$175	$175	$700	$0	$0	$0	$1,225
A-03-04 Senior Programmer	$0	$0	$0	$0	$0	$600	$600	$600	$600	$0	$0	$0	$2,400
A-03-04 Systems Analyst	$0	$0	$0	$0	$0	$120	$120	$120	$120	$0	$0	$0	$480
A-03-04 Technical Writer	$0	$0	$0	$0	$0	$270	$270	$270	$180	$0	$0	$0	$990

Figure 5-9 Costware estimate sorted by work element (A-03).

```
**************************************************************************************
     LABOR DOLLARS FOR "COSTWARE" COST ESTIMATE
**************************************************************************************
```

LABOR DOLLARS

$W.E.S.#	$Skill/mtl.	$$/hr	$Jan86	$Feb86	$Mar86	$Apr86	$May86	$Jun86	$Jul86	$Aug86	$Sep86	$Oct86	$Nov86	$Dec86	$Total $
TOTALS FOR SELECTED DATA RECORDS	DATE: 16-Oct														
TOTAL DOLLARS ∨			$900	$900	$900	$1,170	$1,170	$2,880	$2,880	$2,880	$2,880	$900	$900	$900	$19,260

$W.E.S.#	$Skill/mtl.	$$/hr/uni	$Jan86	$Feb86	$Mar86	$Apr86	$May86	$Jun86	$Jul86	$Aug86	$Sep86	$Oct86	$Nov86	$Dec86	$Total $
A-01-01	Technical Writer		$180	$180	$180	$180	$180	$0	$0	$0	$0	$0	$0	$0	$900
A-01-02	Technical Writer		$180	$180	$180	$180	$180	$0	$0	$0	$0	$0	$0	$0	$900
A-01-03	Technical Writer		$180	$180	$180	$180	$180	$0	$0	$0	$0	$0	$0	$0	$900
A-01-04	Technical Writer		$180	$180	$180	$180	$180	$0	$0	$0	$0	$0	$0	$0	$900
A-01-05	Technical Writer		$180	$180	$180	$180	$180	$0	$0	$0	$0	$0	$0	$0	$900
A-02-01	Technical Writer		$0	$0	$0	$90	$90	$90	$90	$90	$0	$0	$0	$0	$450
A-02-02	Technical Writer		$0	$0	$0	$70	$90	$90	$90	$90	$0	$0	$0	$0	$450
A-02-03	Technical Writer		$0	$0	$0	$90	$90	$90	$90	$90	$0	$0	$0	$0	$450
A-03-01	Technical Writer		$0	$0	$0	$0	$0	$180	$180	$180	$180	$0	$0	$0	$720
A-03-02	Technical Writer		$0	$0	$0	$0	$0	$1,440	$1,440	$1,440	$1,800	$0	$0	$0	$6,120
A-03-03	Technical Writer		$0	$0	$0	$0	$0	$720	$720	$720	$720	$0	$0	$0	$2,880
A-03-04	Technical Writer		$0	$0	$0	$0	$0	$270	$270	$270	$180	$0	$0	$0	$990
A-04-01	Technical Writer		$0	$0	$0	$0	$0	$0	$0	$0	$0	$0	$0	$0	$0
A-04-02	Technical Writer		$0	$0	$0	$0	$0	$0	$0	$0	$0	$0	$0	$0	$0
A-04-03	Technical Writer		$0	$0	$0	$0	$0	$0	$0	$0	$0	$900	$900	$900	$2,700
A-04-04	Technical Writer		$0	$0	$0	$0	$0	$0	$0	$0	$0	$0	$0	$0	$0

Figure 5-10 Costware estimate for technical writer.

Using Database Statistical Functions

Most microcomputer database systems contain statistical functions that will scan designated fields to determine their sum, average, variance, standard deviation, maximum, or minimum values. For example, if we wanted to determine the average hours spent per month by the technical writer for the first 6 months, we could specify the range of data, the field or fields to be searched, and the criterion. The average hours would be quickly and automatically computed. One can also use a function to count the number of data entries in a given field. For example, note that there are a lot of zero or blank months in the previous examples where labor hours are not expended and dollar resources are not allocated. The number of months containing nonzero labor-hour entries could be counted. Using these functions, almost an unlimited amount of analysis can be done on a cost database. The average, variance, and standard deviation values of work element resource records could be automatically calculated using the database statistical functions to help develop cost estimating relationships for specific task areas.

Resource Leveling and Skill Mix Adjustment

One of the handy features of the Lotus 1-2-3 combined database and spreadsheet software package and some other similar integrated software systems is that the data extraction feature can be combined with a MOVE command to check the effect of changing the time relationship between two jobs or within a single job on the people and skills required. Figure 5-11 shows a 20-week project of four scheduled tasks (A, B, C, and D) in which the peak staffing is 10 people. The asterisks at the far right of the chart adjacent to tasks B and C are indications that these two tasks can be moved downstream without affecting the completion date of the project. Tasks A and D are on the critical path (see Chapter 6 for definitions and scheduling techniques). If we slip task B downstream 5 weeks and, at the same time, move task C downstream 10 weeks, the staffing profile is reconfigured as shown on Figure 5-12. Note that the maximum staffing of the job is now only six persons. Such a rescheduling could prevent hiring more people for just the initial 5 weeks of the project or using expensive overtime to take care of the peak workload. The microcomputer database system, particularly one that contains or is coupled with a graphics package, is ideal for performing this type of exercise because innumerable what-if exercises can be done with little expense once the database is entered. Such an exercise—again performed on the Lotus 1-2-3 database—is shown on Figures 5-13 through 5-17. Starting with two 6-month jobs, job A and job B, we want to determine the effects on skill mix and overall staffing resulting from overlapping these jobs by 2, 4, and 6 months. Figure 5-13 shows the original time base for time-phasing of jobs A and B, and the values for each skill for each month in labor-months. The data for jobs A and B are input into an *input range*, and all records are extracted as is into an output range and subsequently totaled by skill as shown on Figure 5-13. The totals are charted as shown on Figure 5-14. Note that the maximum staffing is a little over 300 persons and that the skill mix varies drastically from one month to the next. The chart shown in Figure 5-15 is a result of accelerating the start of job B by 2 months. This was done by moving the job B input resources 2

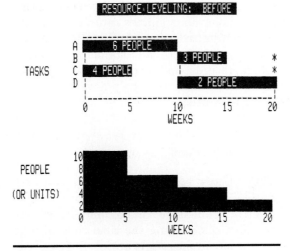

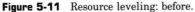

Figure 5-11 Resource leveling: before.

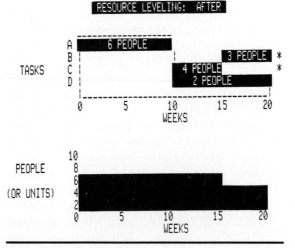

Figure 5-12 Resource leveling: after.

months to the left (easily done with the MOVE command), extracting the new data records, and plotting the results. Similarly, moving job B to the left two more months results in the chart shown in Figure 5-16. The final resource distribution in numerical format is shown in Figure 5-17. Notice that the resulting staffing for 1986 is still only a little over 300 and the skill mix, although it changes some, does not go through the wild fluctuations encountered when the two jobs were time-phased originally.

This example shows only one of the many possibilities of using data-

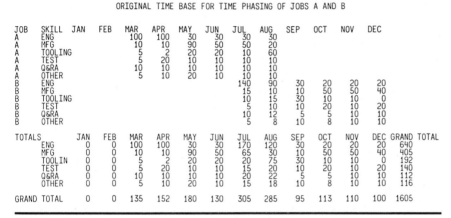

```
                    ORIGINAL TIME BASE FOR TIME PHASING OF JOBS A AND B

JOB  SKILL   JAN  FEB  MAR  APR  MAY  JUN  JUL  AUG  SEP  OCT  NOV  DEC
A    ENG                100  100   30   30   30   30
A    MFG                 10   10   90   50   50   20
A    TOOLING             5    2    20   20   10   60
A    TEST                5   20    10   10   10   10
A    Q&RA               10   10    10   10   10   10
A    OTHER               5   10    20   10   10   10
B    ENG                               140   90   30   20   20   20
B    MFG                                15   10   10   50   50   40
B    TOOLING                            10   15   30   10   10    0
B    TEST                                5   10   20   10   20
B    Q&RA                               10   12    5    5   10   10
B    OTHER                               5    8   10    8   10   10

TOTALS   JAN  FEB  MAR  APR  MAY  JUN  JUL  AUG  SEP  OCT  NOV  DEC  GRAND TOTAL
ENG       0    0   100  100   30   30  170  120   30   20   20   20     640
MFG       0    0    10   10   90   50   65   30   10   50   50   40     405
TOOLIN    0    0     5    2   20   20   20   75   30   10   10    0     192
TEST      0    0     5   20   10   10   15   20   10   20   10   20     140
Q&RA      0    0    10   10   10   10   20   22    5    5   10   10     112
OTHER     0    0     5   10   20   10   15   18   10    8   10   10     116

GRAND TOTAL 0   0   135  152  180  130  305  285   95  113  110  100    1605
```

Figure 5-13   Original resource loading of jobs A and B.

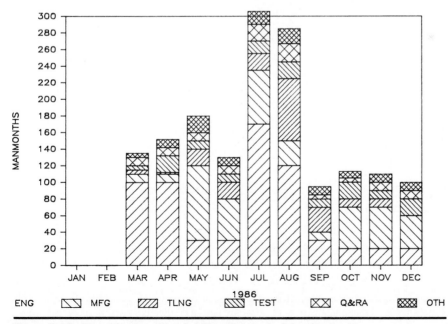

Figure 5-14   Time phasing of total skills prior to schedule adjustment.

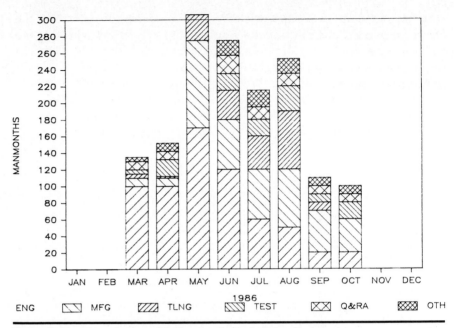

Figure 5-15 Time phasing of skills after first schedule adjustment.

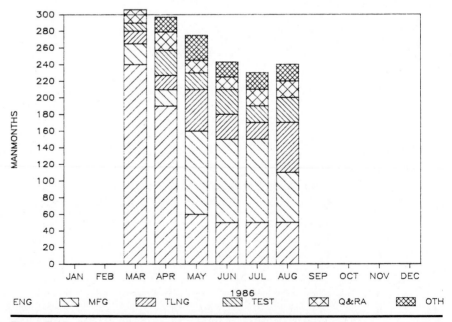

Figure 5-16 Time phasing of skills after second schedule adjustment.

base systems to play what-if games. The graphs can be viewed on the screen without printing until an acceptable arrangement is derived.

Estimating with Other Types of Database Programs

We have demonstrated only two of the many database microcomputer applications software packages that could be used for cost estimating. These two applications programs were chosen because they are likely to be already in the software inventory of your company or organization. The same basic techniques shown could be used for virtually any microcomputer database system. One type of system which holds probably the greatest promise for cost estimators is the relational database. In the relational database, more than one file can be open at any one time.

Central to the operation of *both* the file manager type of database and the relational database is the simple table of rows and columns often referred to as a *flat file*.

Work element #	Skill or material	Rate or unit price, dollars
D-2-4	Architect	24.00
D-6-3	Carpenter	15.00
D-1-2	Plumber	16.50
D-8-6	Supervisor	18.00

Typical operations on this database might include locating all of the work elements that include a certain skill, all of the skills that cost more than $17.00 per hour, or sorting the database in order of work element number or labor rate. Suppose, however, that, like the previous Lotus

ADJUSTED DATA BASE FOR TIME PHASING OF JOBS A AND B

JOB	SKILL	JAN	FEB	MAR	APR	MAY	JUN	JUL	AUG	SEP	OCT	NOV	DEC
A	ENG			100	100	30	30	30	30				
A	MFG			10	10	90	50	50	20				
A	TOOLING			5	2	20	20	10	60				
A	TEST			5	20	10	10	10	10				
A	Q&RA			10	10	10	10	10	10				
A	OTHER			5	10	20	10	10	10				
B	ENG			140	90	30	20	20	20				
B	MFG			15	10	10	50	50	40				
B	TOOLING			10	15	30	10	10	0				
B	TEST			5	10	10	20	10	20				
B	Q&RA			10	12	5	5	10	10				
B	OTHER			5	8	10	8	10	10				

TOTALS		JAN	FEB	MAR	APR	MAY	JUN	JUL	AUG	SEP	OCT	NOV	DEC	GRAND TOTAL
	ENG	0	0	240	190	60	50	50	50	0	0	0	0	640
	MFG	0	0	25	20	100	100	100	60	0	0	0	0	405
	TOOLIN	0	0	15	17	50	30	20	60	0	0	0	0	192
	TEST	0	0	10	30	20	30	20	30	0	0	0	0	140
	Q&RA	0	0	20	22	15	15	20	20	0	0	0	0	112
	OTHER	0	0	10	18	30	18	20	20	0	0	0	0	116
GRAND TOTAL		0	0	320	297	275	243	230	240	0	0	0	0	1605

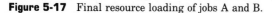

Figure 5-17 Final resource loading of jobs A and B.

1-2-3 example, this database must contain information on the number of hours spent and labor costs for each of these skills. The database may then appear as follows:

WES#	Skill	Rate, dollars	Jan 86 hrs	Feb 86 hrs
D-2-4	Architect	24.00	15.0	20.0
D-2-5	Architect	24.00	35.0	40.0
D-6-3	Carpenter	15.00	80.0	65.0
D-6-4	Carpenter	15.00	60.0	40.0
D-6-5	Carpenter	15.00	20.0	35.0
D-1-2	Plumber	16.50	10.0	20.0
D-1-3	Plumber	16.50	0.0	5.0
D-8-6	Supervisor	18.00	160.0	200.0

As can be seen in this simple example, and as shown in the COST-WARE example worked on the Lotus 1-2-3 file manager system, the problems of duplication of information and wasted space are quite obvious. In a file manager system, even if the duplicate fields were removed, the space they formerly occupied would still be reserved, taking up much needed and valuable disk space. In addition to the obvious wasted space, a file arranged in this manner also causes some difficulty when using logical operators (IF, AND, OR) and in manipulating the data.

A relational database can operate on multiple files at the same time, however, and could accommodate two separate files as follows:

Rate file		
WES#	Skill	Rate, dollars
D-2-4	Architect	24.00
D-6-3	Carpenter	15.00
D-1-2	Plumber	16.50
D-8-6	Supervisor	18.00

Resource file		
WES#	Jan 86 hrs	Feb 86 hrs
D-2-4	15.0	20.0
D-2-5	35.0	40.0
D-6-3	80.0	65.0
D-6-4	60.0	40.0
D-6-5	20.0	35.0
D-1-2	10.0	20.0
D-1-3	0.0	5.0
D-8-6	160.0	200.0

Although the above example has been simplified to assume only one skill per work element, one can readily see how multiple files could be built and referenced to work element number to include all of the resources needed to complete a job. Hence, we could have a rate file and one or more resource files which can be related to each other to build a complete estimate. This feature is provided by the relational database because several files can be open at one time. When more information needs to be added about a work element, a new file can be built rather than having to go into an existing file and modify it. Therefore, when acquiring microcomputer database software to automate your cost estimating, seriously consider the attributes of the fully or partially relational database system.

Factors to Be Considered in Acquiring a Database System

Other factors to consider when acquiring a database system are ease of startup, ease of learning, ease of use, error handling capabilities, performance (speed), versatility, value for the money, memory and storage required, price, and other features such as:

Is it a command- or menu-driven system?

Are formulas permitted or used in data fields?

Are the files protected by passwords?

Is the output format flexible and easily incorporated into a report? (page numbering, headings, etc.)

And, finally, is the database fully relational, partially relational, or not relational? (already mentioned above)

The *Software Digest*, published in Wynnewood, Pennsylvania, provides an excellent summary comparison of more than 20 of the most commonly used microcomputer database systems. Complete information is provided on the supplier, price, hardware requirements, and results of testing of the software packages. Review of an updated version of this or a similar software review publication is desirable before investing in a database applications software package for cost estimating, and a hands-on demonstration by your computer dealer is a must.

A Final Note on Databases for Cost Estimating

Because of the investment of time and resources needed to place even the easiest to use database in an operational status, considerable prepurchase research should be done and the database system should be weighed against the other systems and programs described in the other chapters of this book. Our impression is that the database system is best where you have a lot of historical, actual data that can be assembled and tracked in a systematic manner, where the data can be effectively used for subsequent estimates, and where the work activity or work output being estimated falls into a general discipline, profession, or work category (i.e., home construction, nuclear plant construction, design and manufacture of a specific product line, etc.). If your cost estimating requirements are diverse and unpredictable, a generic cost estimating package may be more practical.

6

COMBINING SCHEDULING WITH ESTIMATING

Because of the time value of money, the necessity of optimum phasing of resource expenditures, the need to control and optimize cash flow, and the importance of scheduling resource allocations, an important microcomputer application is the combination of cost estimating and scheduling techniques. In the October 1984 issue of *Personal Computing* magazine, 50 programs for microcomputers were listed that are available on the commercial market. These programs range from $55,000 for Unix-based systems to $50 for systems requiring memories as small as 48 kilobytes. Their primary function is to manage time and people, i.e., to allocate resources for a project, but many of these systems are also good cost estimating tools.

The Need for Scheduling

Good cost estimating requires the best possible time phasing of the use of equipment, labor, and materials. The estimating plan should have (1) milestones representing goals and objectives of the work activity, (2) a time-phased action plan for supplying the work output, (3) deadline requirements of the delivered product or service, and (4) schedule elements that make up the work activity. There should be little waste, duplication, or overlap. Supplies must arrive "just in time" rather than sit in a warehouse for several months taking up valuable and expensive space. By dovetailing projects, people can be kept busy moving from one project to another as the skills required for the project change, and expensive equipment can be scheduled for optimum use. Combined project scheduling and estimating microcomputer systems will help the estimator significantly in many of these engineering management functions.

The Basic Concept

The basic concept of estimating with scheduling software is relating work activities to resources. Just as in a WES, each project is broken down into jobs or tasks, and the resources needed to accomplish the job are assigned and scheduled on a time basis. When the work elements (or "jobs" in scheduling jargon) and their respective resources are entered into the scheduling software, the program creates graphs that represent the work flow. Each job or task is assigned the proper number of workdays, workweeks, work months, or work years required during each of its calendar increments. For example, if the job requires the expenditure of 12 work months of effort (and you are assigning two engineers), the schedule for that task would be 6 months long. Of course, you could decide to speed up the work and assign four engineers working simultaneously who could complete the job in 3 months time, or you might want to put your engineers on overtime to further speed the project.

Scheduling Methods

The Gantt chart or timeline was one of the first graphic presentations and dates back to 1912 with the publication of *The Bar Chart* by Harry Gantt. Milestone charts appeared during World War II and PERT charts were developed in Sunnyvale, California, to help the United States Navy manage the Polaris missile project. Originally, PERT was used only for scheduling. It did not include costs but did include probabilities for the elapsed time of activities. It has since been modified to include additional factors such as employee staffing and cost. About the same time, Kelley and Walker developed the critical path method (CPM) to expedite projects. The CPM includes costs and defines a chain of activities that must be completed on time in order to meet the overall schedule of the project.

Scheduling Software for Microcomputers

Scheduling software packages today use Gantt, PERT, CPM, or a combination of any of these to produce their graphic presentations, the critical path bar chart being the most common. The horizontal axis represents time, activities are listed down the left side, and horizontal bars for each job begin at start dates and end at completion dates. Each job except the first one(s) have one or more predecessor jobs that must be completed before it can start. If a job depends on an earlier one which is delayed, the dependent job can be linked through the software to slip downstream to a later start and finish date.

The PERT chart is the second most common type of graph used in scheduling software. Events and activities are linked by lines to represent relationships and dependencies. If an activity cannot be finished until several earlier tasks are finished, each of these tasks is linked to that activity. Since PERT charts cannot represent time visually, they are best suited for analysis rather than graphic display. PERT charts are particularly useful for projects with so many interdependent steps that there is a high degree of uncertainty about the total time needed for each step. Where it is not readily apparent what the total time sequence will be, the PERT technique can supply a rapid means of determining the flow of work.

Microcomputer software applications packages differ in the maximun number of resources per activity and in the maximum number of activities per project. A mainframe computer can support 10,000 or more activities while the Harvard Project Manager (Harvard Software) for microcomputers supports 200; MacProject (Apple Computer) and Microsoft Project (Microsoft), 200; Pertmaster (Westminister Software), 1500; and Project Scheduler 5000 (Scitor Corporation), 750 with 256K memory, 1500 with 320K, and 5250 with 640K memory. Some of the many features found in a variety of packages are the ability to compare similar projects, the ability to combine several projects into one major project, and the ability to use both printers and plotters and selectively print sections of a bar chart or resource analysis graphs.

A Scheduling Example

Our estimating examples in this book were done with Project Scheduler 5000 with Graphics by Scitor Corporation. The critical path bar chart (Gantt chart) method is used to develop a time-based schedule, and labor costs and other costs are allocated commensurate with this schedule. The project scheduler permits the use of 96 different labor and/or material resource types so that the resources needed to accomplish each job within the project can be estimated and entered into the program.

Figure 6-1 is a representation of the computer video screen showing the overall schedule of a typical project with jobs or tasks entered and resources assigned to each time period. The name of the project is at the

top of the chart along with a project number. Spread across the sheet are
the months from JAN through DEC with numbers 0 to 11 under them.

Note the differences between the bars: job 10 is partially displayed
with colons; job 20 shows a combination of hyphens and periods; while
jobs 30, 40, 50, 60, and 70 are represented by equal signs (a double line).
Job 65 is an asterisk. If you were to view this chart in color, you would
find that the first 2 months of job 10 would be in green and the last month
would be red along with all the other jobs except 20 which would be
white. Green (and colons) indicate finished work, red (and equal signs)
indicate critical path, and white (and hyphens) indicate noncritical jobs.
The periods (or dots) on the noncritical job indicate slack time. Job 10
shows a + sign after its number and the graph starts with an O indicating that it is the first job in the project. Jobs 20 and 30 have asterisks
after their numbers to indicate that they are the first jobs after the starting one. All bars for jobs with successor jobs end with >; terminator jobs,
those without successor jobs, end with X and milestones (jobs with zero
duration) are shown as asterisks.

The numbers across the top under the months are used to determine
the start times and the lengths of the bars. For instance, the first job, No.
10 Programming1, starts at 0 and lasts for 3 months. The length of the
bar can be input directly if resource or work-month loadings are not going
to be added. Otherwise, the length of the bar is determined by the resources put into that bar. From the cost summary at the bottom of the

```
COSTTIME DEVELOPMT 1986
  (P)roject = 1    JAN  FEB  MAR  APR  MAY  JUN  JUL  AUG  SEP  OCT  NOV  DEC
JOB      NAME      0    1    2    3    4    5    6    7    8    9    10   11
  10+Programming1  O:::::::::::====>.    .    .    .    .    .    .    .
  20*Programming2  .    .    .    >--->....>.   .    .    .    .    .
  30*Testing1      .    .    .    >========>.   .    .    .    .    .
  40 Testing2      .    .    .    .    >=============>.   .    .    .
  50 Documentation1.   .    .    .    >=============>.   .    .    .
  60 Documentation2.   .    .    .    .    .    >===>.   .    .    .
  65 Doc. Completed.   .    .    .    .    .    .    *    .    .    .
  70 Support       .    .    .    .    .    .    .    >=============X.
                   .    .    .    .    .    .    .    .    .    .    .
                   .    .    .    .    .    .    .    .    .    .    .
                   .    .    .    .    .    .    .    .    .    .    .
                   .    .    .    .    .    .    .    .    .    .    .
                   .    .    .    .    .    .    .    .    .    .    .
                   .    .    .    .    .    .    .    .    .    .    .
LABOR UNITS        440  420  400  425  195  645  640  650  460  470  420  395
LABOR COST   $     17K  16K  15K  16K4976   20K  19K  20K  15K  18K  15K  14K
OTHER COST   $     0    0    0    0    0    0    0    0    0    0    0    0

Options >   (A)dd    (I)nsert   (C)hange   (M)ove   (K)ill   (F)inish   (N)umber
Screen commands:  (U)p  (D)own  (L)eft  (R)ight  (H)ome  or  (O)ther   (E)nd
```

Figure 6-1 Bar chart, Costtime development.

screen (a subscreen brought to the standard bar chart from the options menu), we see that 440 labor units at a cost of 17K were entered into January; 420 labor units at 16K in February, and 400 labor units at 15K were entered for March. (In Project Scheduler, the K adds three zeros and represents thousands; M adds six zeros to the number and represents millions.)

HITEK Missile System

To show the versatility and depth of scheduling software available for microcomputers, we are using as our main example a large development project, the HITEK Missile System. This project, nearly 5 years in length, is for the development of a highly sophisticated missile system consisting of a battery of three high-technology antiaircraft or surface-to-air missiles to be mounted on a tracked launching vehicle. The missiles will be guided by the most advanced tracking equipment available and will be designed to shoot down enemy aircraft within 100 miles and at a maximum speed of more than 1600 miles per hour.

Our project, under the direction of Victor McDowell, is scheduled on a monthly basis for a 57-month period starting February 3, 1986. The project is divided and coded into four main areas of activity: missile development (100 series); launcher development (200 series); mobility system #1 (300 series); and mobility system #2 (400 series). Figures 6-2 and 6-3 are input sheets showing overall information on the project, work element numbers, names, resources, and durations, and predecessor relation-

---

INPUT SHEET FOR PROJECT SCHEDULER (PS5000 by Scitor)

PROJECT INFORMATION

    Project Name   : _HITEK Missile System_

    Manager   : _Victor McDowell_

    Project Start Date   : _2/1/86_

CALENDAR INFORMATION

    Overall Start Date   : _2/1/86_

    Work Days(M,Tu,etc.) : _____

    Time Scale (day, wk, month) : _Month_

    Number of Shifts   : _____

    Holidays   : _____

Figure 6-2 Input sheet for Project Scheduler (page 1).

ships. The use of input sheets as shown will save valuable keyboard input and computer time and will also permit someone other than the estimate originator to enter the estimate data.

Preliminary Estimating

This project has not been fully defined, and there was no requirement for a detailed work hour and material estimate. Therefore, composite rates which include work hours, materials, equipment, labor burdens, overhead, G&A expenses, and fee for each work month have been developed.

INPUT SHEET FOR PROJECT SCHEDULER (PS5000 BY SCITOR)   Page 2

Project *HITEK Missile System*   Start Date: *February 1986*

WES #	WES Name	Resources	Duration	Predecessors
101	Missile Delay	none	11	0
102	Missile Development	Composite 100	15	101
103	Missile Delay	none	3	102
104	Missile Verification	Composite 100	2	103
105	Missile Delay	none	7	104
106	Missile Design Test 1	Composite 100	6	105
107	Missile Type Classification	Composite 100	8	106
142	Missile Type Classification	none	0	107
208	Design Launcher Prototypes	Composite 200	8	0
209	Fabricate Launcher Prototypes	Composite 200	12	208
210	Signal	none	0	208
211	Redesign Launcher Prototype	Composite 200	8	209
212	Fabricate New Launcher Prototype	Composite 200	18	211
213	Launcher Type Classification	Composite 200	5	212, 216
243	Launcher Type Classification	none	0	213
214	Launcher Delay	none	8	210
215	Launcher Test	Composite 200	16	214
216	Signal	none	0	215
217	Launcher Initial Production Facility	Composite 200	12	209
218	Signal	none	6	209
219	Signal	none	6	209
220	Hd. Missile Requalification	Composite 200	13	217
221	Signal	none	0	220
322	Mobility System #1 Delay	none	3	0
323	Mobile #1 Eng. Development	Composite 300	25	322
324	Signal	none	0	323
325	Mob #1 Prod. Qual. Test -Contr	Composite 300	5	218
326	Mobile #1 Delay	none	4	325
327	Mob #1 Prod. Qual. Test Govt	Composite 300	9	326
328	Signal	none	0	326
329	Mobile #1 Delay	none	1	328
330	Mob #1 Operational Test	Composite 300	8	329
331	Mob #1 Type Classification	Composite 300	3	327, 330
344	Mob #1 Type Classification	none	0	331
432	Mobility System #2 Delay	none	3	0
433	Mobile #2 Eng. Development	Composite 400	25	432
434	Signal	none	0	433
435	Mob #2 Prod. Qual. Test - Contr	Composite 400	6	218
436	Mobile #2 Delay	none	3	435
437	Mob #2 Prod. Qual. Test - Govt	Composite 400	11	436

Figure 6-3   Input sheet for Project Scheduler (pages 2 and 3).

There are different composite labor rates for missile development, launcher development, and mobility system development. Figure 6-4 shows the Input Sheet for Resource Information for the HITEK Missile System. With the exception of work element 102, Missile Development, all work months have been spread evenly over the estimated time periods. Because of the complexity of missile development, the point estimate of 25,000 hours required over the 15-month period to do the job has been spread using a SPREAD program, with 60 percent of the cost occurring in 50 percent of the time. This program produced a front-loaded labor

INPUT SHEET FOR PROJECT SCHEDULER (PS5000 BY SCITOR)   Page 3

Project _HITE._ _missile System (Con)_ Start Date: _Feb 1986_

WES #	WES Name	Resources	Duration	Predecessors
438	Signal	none	0	436
439	mobile #2 Delay	none	1	438
440	mot#2 Type Classification	Composite 400	10	439
441	mot#2 type Classification	Composite 400	1	437, 440
445	mot#2 type classification	none	0	441
446	Continue Program Time	Composite 400	10	142, 243, 221, 344, 445

Figure 6-3 Input sheet for Project Scheduler (pages 2 and 3). (Continued)

curve (see Figure 6-5) of variable work months over the time period. The Input Sheet for Resources spread over time is shown in Figure 6-6.

Using the Scheduling Software

Now we are ready to estimate our project. The main menu of PS5000 gives us several choices of processing mode: (1) single, (2) multi-independent, and (3) multicombined. This means that we can work with one project, work with several projects independently, or even combine several projects into one large project. This feature is especially useful if, for instance, we want to compare resources used among several projects. Gantt charts, reports, and histograms can all be used in the three processing modes. The default value is the single processing mode. From this menu we can *D*efine a new project; *R*etrieve an existing table and/or project from disk; *S*ave a table and/or project onto disk; *Z*ap (erase) a

INPUT SHEET FOR PROJECT SCHEDULER (PS5000 BY SCITOR)   Page 4

RESOURCE TABLE INFORMATION

Name of resource, unit cost, and whether the resource is Labor or Other Direct Cost. Unit cost may be hourly, weekly, or monthly. If an hourly unit is used in a project reported by month, the number of units listed for a particular month should reflect the number of hours to be expended for that month. ODC, entered as total units, can be travel, direct computer services, subcontracts, etc. Maximum number of resources is 96 total. Enter Labor resources first followed by ODC resources.

No.	Resource	Unit Cost	Category (L or O)	No.	Resource	Unit Cost	Category (L or O)
1	Composite 100	8300	L	25			
2	Composite 200	7900	L	26			
3	Composite 300	7500	L	27			
4	Composite 400	7500	L	28			
5				29			
6				30			
7				31			
8				32			
9				33			
10				34			
11				35			
12				36			
13				37			
14				38			
15				39			
16				40			
17				41			
18				42			
19				43			
20				44			
21				45			
22				46			
23				47			
24				48			

Figure 6-4   Input sheet for Project Scheduler (page 4).

project from memory; *P*roceed to Constants, Tables, and Applications; or *E*nd session and return to operating system. Since we are going to define a new project, we press *D*efine and the Constants, Tables, and Applications Selection Menu appears (see Figure 6-7). Now, starting at the top of the menu and using the input sheets shown on Figures 6-2 and 6-4, we fill in the information as needed. Figures 6-8 through 6-11 show the overall

```
                                                       Page 5
===============================================================
SPREAD TOOLKIT                 DATE:        16-Oct-85
===============================================================
PROJECT :HITEK MISSILE SYSTEM
WBS NAME:MISSILE
WES/WBS#:    102           ITEM/PHASE:MISSILE DEVELOPMENT
===============================================================
Enter Total Dollars To Be Spread         25,000 (Can Be Any Number)
Enter No. Of Months For Spread               15 (Up To 120 Months)
Enter % Cost To Spread In 50% Time           60 (20,40,50,60,70 or 80)
Enter Start Year                           1986
Enter Start Month     \                       2 (1,2,...or 12)

---------------------------------------------------------------
To Get From Base Year* Dollars To 1986 Dollars Use:      1.000
To Get From 1986 Dollars to 1987 Dollars Use:            1.000
To Get From 1987 Dollars to 1988 Dollars Use:            1.000
To Get From 1988 Dollars to 1989 Dollars Use:            1.000
To Get From 1989 Dollars to 1990 Dollars Use:            1.000
To Get From 1990 Dollars to 1991 Dollars Use:            1.000
To Get From 1991 Dollars to 1992 Dollars Use:            1.000
To Get From 1992 Dollars to 1993 Dollars Use:            1.000
To Get From 1993 Dollars to 1994 Dollars Use:            1.000
To Get From 1994 Dollars to 1995 Dollars Use:            1.000
To Get From 1995 Dollars to 1996 Dollars Use:            1.000
===============================================================
```

		Base Year Constant Dollars	Inflated Dollars
Year	Month		
1986	1	0	0
	2	356	356
	3	1,050	1,050
	4	1,680	1,680
	5	2,204	2,204
	6	2,590	2,590
	7	2,820	2,820
	8	2,884	2,884
	9	2,785	2,785
	10	2,537	2,537
	11	2,163	2,163
	12	1,699	1,699
	Year	22,769	22,769
1987	1	1,192	1,192
	2	700	700
	3	292	292
	4	46	46
	5	0	0
	6	0	0
	7	0	0

Figure 6-5   Input sheet for Project Scheduler (page 5).

INPUT SHEET FOR PROJECT SCHEDULER (PS5000 BY SCITOR) Page 6

WORK ELEMENT STRUCTURE INFORMATION

Missile 100..
Launcher 200..
Mobile #1 300..
Mobile #2 400..

Project Name	Start Date	Finish Date
HYTEK Missile Sys	Feb '86	Nov '90

Periods (put in units per period for each resource)

Name of Resource	1	2	3	4	5	6	7	8	9	10	11	12	13	14	15	16	17	18	19	20	21	22	23	24	25
102 Compl 100	356	1050	1680	2201	2526	2839	2884	2785	2537	2163	1699	1193	700	282	76										
104 " 100	240	240																							
106 " 100	602	602	602	602	602	602																			
107 " 100	160	160	160																						
208 " 200	126	126	126	126	126	126	126	126																	
209 " 200	105	105	105	105	105	105	105	105	105	105	105	105													
211 " 200	84	84	84																						
212 " 200	70	70	70	70	70	70	70	70	70	70	70	70	70	70	70	70	70	70							
213 " 200	101	101	101	101	101																				
215 " 200	79	79	79	79	79	79	79	79	79	79	79	79	79	79	79	79									
217 " 200	84	84	84	84	84	84	84	84	84	84	84	84													
220 " 200	97	97	97	97	97	97	97	97	97	97	97	97	97												
323 " 300	155	155	155	155	155	155	155	155	155	155	155	155	155	155	155	155	155	155	155	155	155	155	155	155	155
325 " 300	133	133	133	133	133																				
327 " 300	88	88	88	88	88	88	88	88	88																
330 " 300	33	33	33	33	33	33	33	33																	
331 " 300	88	88	88																						
433 " 400	154	154	154	154	154	154	154	154	154	154	154	154	154	154	154	154	154	154	154	154	154	154	154	154	154
435 " 400	222	222	222	222	222	222																			
437 " 400	72	72	72	72	72	72	72	72	72	72	72														
440 " 400	26	26	26	26	26	26	26	26	26	26															
441 " 400	66																								
446 " 400	133	133	133	133	133	133	133	133	133	133															

Figure 6-6 Input sheet for Project Scheduler (page 6).

```
             CONSTANTS, TABLES, AND APPLICATIONS SELECTION MENU
             ---------------------------------------------------

        Constants and Tables:

             (O)verall constants
             (P)roject constants              Current Project =  1
             (C)alendar for the project
             (T)able for resource classifications and rates

        Applications:

             (G)antt chart scheduling
             (R)eport preparation
             (H)istograms, Bar charts, and Line graphs


        (E)nd and return to main options menu


   Press a letter to select an option >
```

Figure 6-7   Constants, tables, and applications selection menu.

```
                        PROJECT CONSTANTS
                        -----------------


        (N)ame of project          =HITEK MISSILE SYSTEM
         Project number            = 1

        (P)roject manager name     =Victor McDowell

        (S)tarting date of project =2-3-86              {format  mm-dd-yy}




       Option:

          (E)nd changes to project constants

   Press a letter to select an option or to change a field >
```

Figure 6-8   Overall constants.

```
                        OVERALL CONSTANTS
                        -----------------


        Starting date           =2-3-86      {These fields are initialized}
        Day of the week         =MON         {by the Project Constants menu}

        (T)ime scale            =MONTH       {day/week/month}

  Special Display Options:

        (C)ompressed display    =NO          {yes/no}

        (N)umber of shifts      =1           {day time scale only}


  Option:

        (E)nd changes to overall constants


  Press a letter to select an option or to change a field >
```

Figure 6-9 Project constants report.

```
                          PROJECT CALENDAR
                          ----------------

  Work Week:

        (W)orking days of the week =M,TU,W,TH,F            {m,tu,w,th,f,sa,su}

     (H)olidays:                                           {format mm-dd-yy}

        1.            2.            3.            4.            5.
        6.            7.            8.            9.           10.
       11.           12.           13.           14.          15.
       16.           17.           18.           19.          20.
       21.           22.           23.           24.          25.
       26.           27.           28.           29.          30.

  Option:

        (E)nd changes to project calendar


  Press a letter to select an option or change a field >
```

Figure 6-10 Project calendar.

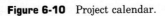

constants and tables for the HITEK Missile System. Notice that, since the project is on a monthly basis, we did not bother to fill in holidays.

Gantt chart scheduling   Now we can begin scheduling each job of our project along with its resources. The software, using the constant information previously entered, has brought up a Gantt chart beginning in February 1986. From the menu at the bottom of the Gantt chart schedule, we select *Add* (to add a new job) and enter our first work element, 101, Missile Delay, duration of 11 months, and no predecessors or resources (see Figure 6-3). Since there are no resources in job 101, the duration is entered directly. The screen representation in Figure 6-12 shows the first job already on the schedule and ready to add the next job. Job code 102 is entered and *C* is pressed to continue the operation. In this case all that is necessary is to type in the name of the job because the predecessor established by the program is correct and it will determine the start time. We do have the opportunity to change or add predecessors or set a start date independently.

Scheduling resources   Project Scheduler also determines the length of a job by its resources, and job 102, unlike 101, has resources (see Figure 6-2e for resource inputs). Remember, for this project our composite labor resources are Composite 100, 200, 300, and 400 and are known to the program as codes 1, 2, 3, and 4. According to the input sheet, Composite

```
             RESOURCE CLASSIFICATIONS AND RATES TABLE
             -----------------------------------------

                         UNIT  LABOR/                      UNIT  LABOR/
      CODE   NAME         COST  OTHER    CODE   NAME        COST  OTHER

         1 COMPOSITE 100  8300.00 L
         2 COMPOSITE 200  7900.00 L
         3 COMPOSITE 300  7500.00 L
         4 COMPOSITE 400  7500.00 L




      (R)esource code, name, cost and L/O :

     (E)nd changes to resources

    Press a letter to select an option >

      Press PgUp or PgDn to review resources
```

Figure 6-11   Resource classifications and rates table.

100 (code 1) is used in job 102; however, the work-month quantities vary with each month. The program takes care of this situation by allowing for the input of each different resource value in sequence. In other words, job 102 has a different number of work months for each month of its existence, and each of these different numbers is called a *sequence* of that particular resource code (in this case code 1 or Composite 100). Sequences do not affect the number of resources available for the job. There can still be up to 96 resources listed for each job. (All jobs draw on one or more of the up to 96 resource types or resource inputs.) The completed resources for job 102 are shown on Figure 6-13 (the fifteenth sequence must be seen by scrolling down). We continue to add jobs according to our input sheet. Resources for the rest of the jobs are entered only once in the sequence since the same resource quantity is used over the total job period. In these cases we have only one resource listing of, say, two periods duration for job 104 or six periods duration for job 106.

Cost summary and schedule   At any time while we are working on the schedule we can superimpose a cost summary at the bottom of the screen as shown on Figure 6-14. This screen displays the totals of the entire project and we can see job numbers 101 through 215. By using the screen commands in the menu we can move down or right to another window to see the job numbers higher than 215 and to see the totals for later months. We can also choose to view labor classifications with corre-

```
HITEK MISSILE SYSTE1986                                                    1987
              FEB  MAR  APR  MAY  JUN  JUL  AUG  SEP  OCT  NOV  DEC  JAN
JOB       NAME  0    1    2    3    4    5    6    7    8    9    10   11
101+MISSILE DELAY O=================================================X. .
               .    .    .    .    .    .    .    .    .    .    .    .
               .    .    .    .    .    .    .    .    .    .    .    .
               .    .    .    .    .    .    .    .    .    .    .    .
               .    .    .    .    .    .    .    .    .    .    .    .
               .    .    .    .    .    .    .    .    .    .    .    .
               .    .    .    .    .    .    .    .    .    .    .    .
               .    .    .    .    .    .    .    .    .    .    .    .
               .    .    .    .    .    .    .    .    .    .    .    .
               .    .    .    .    .    .    .    .    .    .    .    .
               .    .    .    .    .    .    .    .    .    .    .    .
               .    .    .    .    .    .    .    .    .    .    .    .
               .    .    .    .    .    .    .    .    .    .    .    .
               .    .    .    .    .    .    .    .    .    .    .    .
(J)ob Code              (A)FTER or (b)efore   (T)ask 101
Select an Option >      (D)isplay help message   (C)ontinue operation   (E)xit
```

Figure 6-12 Bar chart, HITEK Missile System (first job entered).

```
JOB: 102     JOB NAME: MISSILE DEVELOPMENT
SEQ   RESOURCE CLASS    START  DURATION    END        UNITS           COST
  1   1 COMPOSITE 100      0       1        1        356.00      2954800.00
  2   1 COMPOSITE 100      1       1        2       1050.00      8715000.00
  3   1 COMPOSITE 100      2       1        3       1680.00     13944000.00
  4   1 COMPOSITE 100      3       1        4       2204.00     18293200.00
  5   1 COMPOSITE 100      4       1        5       2590.00     21497000.00
  6   1 COMPOSITE 100      5       1        6       2820.00     23406000.00
  7   1 COMPOSITE 100      6       1        7       2884.00     23937200.00
  8   1 COMPOSITE 100      7       1        8       2785.00     23115500.00
  9   1 COMPOSITE 100      8       1        9       2537.00     21057100.00
 10   1 COMPOSITE 100      9       1       10       2163.00     17952900.00
 11   1 COMPOSITE 100     10       1       11       1699.00     14101700.00
 12   1 COMPOSITE 100     11       1       12       1192.00      9893600.00
 13   1 COMPOSITE 100     12       1       13        700.00      5810000.00
 14   1 COMPOSITE 100     13       1       14        292.00      2423600.00
                          PgUp or PgDn to scroll resources
LABOR TOTALS                                       24998.00            ***
OTHER TOTALS                                           0.00           0.00
TOTAL COSTS   K$                                   24998.00      207483.40

(J)ob Code=102     (N)ame=MISSILE DEVELOPMENT            (S)tart time=0
(P)redecessors=101 0 0 0 0 0 0 0 0                       (D)uration=15
Select a  CHANGE   option >                    (R)esources   (U)se   (E)xit
```

Figure 6-13 Resources for job 102, Missile Development.

```
HITEK MISSILE SYSTE1986                                                1987
   (P)roject = 1    FEB  MAR  APR  MAY  JUN  JUL  AUG  SEP  OCT  NOV  DEC  JAN
JOB      NAME        0    1    2    3    4    5    6    7    8    9   10   11
101+MISSILE DELAY  O=================================================>.    .
102*MISSILE DEVELO.      .    .    .    .    .    .    .    .    .  >======
103 MISSILE DELAY  .     .    .    .    .    .    .    .    .    .    .    .
104 MISSILE VERIFI.      .    .    .    .    .    .    .    .    .    .    .
105 MISSILE DELAY  .     .    .    .    .    .    .    .    .    .    .    .
106 MISSILE DESIGN.      .    .    .    .    .    .    .    .    .    .    .
107 MSLE TYPE CLAS.      .    .    .    .    .    .    .    .    .    .    .
142 MSLE TYPE CLAS.      .    .    .    .    .    .    .    .    .    .    .
208 DSG LAUNCHER PO======================================>.    .    .    .
209 FAB LAUNCHER P.      .    .    .    .    .    .  >====================
210 SIGNAL (MILEST.     .    .    .    .    .    .    *    .    .    .    .
211 REDSG LAUNCHER.      .    .    .    .    .    .    .    .    .    .    .
212 FAB NEW LAUNCH.      .    .    .    .    .    .    .    .    .    .    .
214 LAUNCHER DELAY.      .    .    .    .    .    .  >-------------->......
215 LAUNCHER TEST .      .    .    .    .    .    .    .    .    .    >-----
LABOR UNITS        126  126  126  435  435  435  435  435  414  414  414  849
LABOR COST   $     995K 995K 995K3313K3313K3313K3313K3313K3147K3147K3147K6726K
OTHER COST   $       0    0    0    0    0    0    0    0    0    0    0    0

Options >   (A)dd   (I)nsert   (C)hange   (M)ove   (K)ill   (F)inish   (N)umber
Screen commands:   (U)p  (D)own  (L)eft  (R)ight  (H)ome  or  (O)ther   (E)nd
```

Figure 6-14 Bar chart, HITEK Missile System (jobs and resources).

sponding numbers of units (that is, Composite 100, Composite 200, etc.) across the bottom of the screen by time periods.

Critical path   As the jobs are entered on the schedule, the bars sometimes take on a different configuration. The first ones were made up of equal signs indicating the critical path. Now we see some bars made up of hyphens and periods. Hyphens indicate noncritical jobs and the periods indicate slack time. These jobs can be moved downstream if the need arises (or if the money allocated to the project is insufficient during these time periods) and the project critical path or end date will not be affected. Once all of the jobs have been entered and the project saved on the disk, we can play what-if games with the schedule and note the effects on our cost estimate or resource usage. This is perhaps the most useful feature when using a scheduling software package for estimating. Since the resources assigned to each job move horizontally along the project time scale as the job is moved, job sequencing, predecessors, delays, and start dates can be changed to adjust the total project funding profile.

Report Preparation

Gantt chart report   Before doing some what-if exercises, we will look at some of the reports that can be produced to determine what figures we are working with on our original schedule. Figure 6-15 shows the complete critical path bar chart for the entire 57-month project. We could have elected to include predecessors for all of the jobs or selected only one particular resource code. We could also have selected a particular date range of the project, or, if more projects had been loaded into the computer's memory, the Gantt charts for all of them could be printed.

Constants, calendar, and resource table   The Project Scheduler software provides a project constants report that shows all the information recorded on the input sheet on Figure 6-2. Such a report is valuable to planners and estimators when a daily schedule is used, since a list of holidays appears on this report. The resource table report showing the code, name, and unit cost of all labor and other direct cost resources is especially valuable when the project or projects has the full complement of 96 labor and other direct cost resources.

Resource distribution report   Another very useful report, the Resource Distribution Report, gives the full cost estimate for the project. It shows resource codes, labor and other units and costs, earned values, and cumulatives for each time period. The estimator can select which (or all) costs and units are desired in the report, and a particular time range can

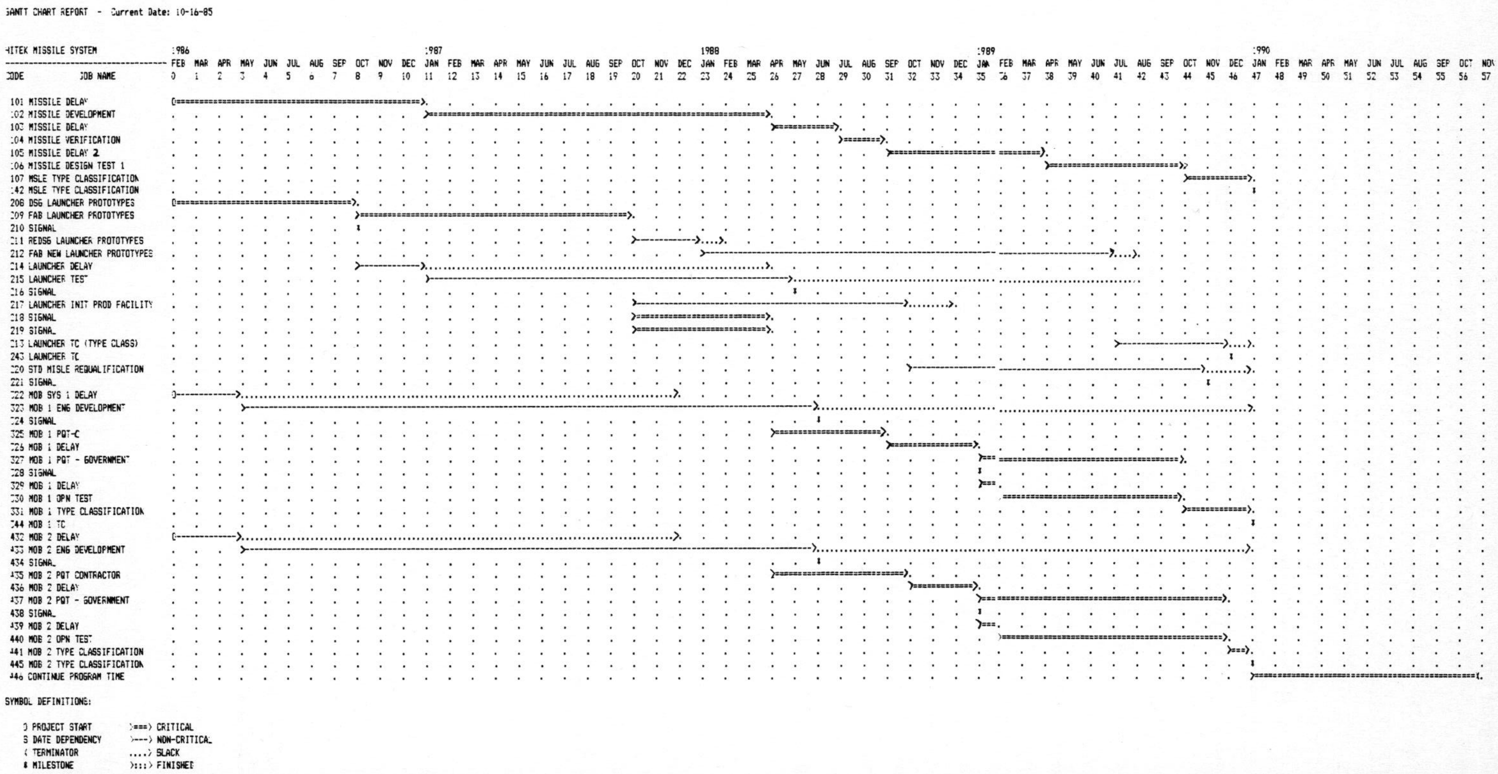

Figure 6-15 Gantt chart report, HITEK Missile System.

also be specified. Figure 6-16 shows the Resource Distribution Report for the HITEK Missile System project. The total cumulative cost of the project is shown in the right-hand corner of the last page.

The value of completed work or *earned value* is of particular interest in that it will indicate the resource units and costs that have been expended as the project moves along toward completion. This feature will be discussed in detail later on in the chapter in another example exercise.

Labor report   The Labor Report for the HITEK Missile System project is shown on Figure 6-17. The information in this report can be used to determine where and when different labor categories are working and if it is feasible to reallocate labor resources to other jobs or projects during slack time. The allocations of the labor resources for the current project or all projects in memory can be printed. The time range for the report can be specified and just one labor resource or all labor resources can be chosen. Such information as the labor code, job number and name, number of units of that particular labor code used in a specific job, to and from dates, critical or noncritical status, and slack time is included.

Job description report   The Job Description Report for job 102, Missile Development, is shown on Figure 6-18. It gives all pertinent information on job 102. It can be produced for each of the work elements of the project giving the dates, predecessors, status, slack, early and late start and finish, listing of each resource class by sequence with respective number of units, cost, and total units and costs for the job. This report can also be configured to give the totals for the entire project (see Figure 6-19 for the Total Job Description for the HITEK Missile System project).

Selectable job report   The Selectable Job Report is what you make it. It is almost limitless—report of critical jobs, report of noncritical jobs, all late jobs, jobs that should be completed within next month, finished and partially finished jobs, etc. Two reports have been selected for our example, a Report of Critical Jobs (Figure 6-20) and a Report of Noncritical Jobs (Figure 6-21).

Graphs and What-If Games with HITEK Missile System Project

A number of graphs are available in our demonstration software package that are useful for the cost estimator. We can graph project resource usage for all resource classifications, both labor and other direct costs; usage for one resource class, period, or job; or compare the resource usage of one class to all classes. Costs by time period can be graphed for labor or other direct costs or both; one plan can be compared to the actual costs, or

HITEK MISSILE SYSTEM		1986 FEB	MAR	APR	MAY	JUN	JUL	AUG	SEP	OCT	NOV	DEC	1987 JAN	FEB	MAR	APR	MAY	JUN	JUL	AUG
CODE RESOURCE NAME	DATA	0	1	2	3	4	5	6	7	8	9	10	11	12	13	14	15	16	17	18
LABOR RESOURCES:																				
1 COMPOSITE 100	UNITS	0.00	0.00	0.00	0.00	0.00	0.00	0.00	0.00	0.00	0.00	0.00	356.00	1050.00	1680.00	2204.00	2590.00	2820.00	2884.00	2785.00
	CUM UNTS	0.00	0.00	0.00	0.00	0.00	0.00	0.00	0.00	0.00	0.00	0.00	356.00	1406.00	3086.00	5290.00	7880.00	10700.00	13584.00	16369.00
	COSTS	0.00	0.00	0.00	0.00	0.00	0.00	0.00	0.00	0.00	0.00	0.00	2954.80K	8715.00K	13944.00K	18293.20K	21497.00K	23406.00K	23937.20K	23115.50K
	CUM CSTS	0.00	0.00	0.00	0.00	0.00	0.00	0.00	0.00	0.00	0.00	0.00	2954.80K	11669.80K	25613.80K	43907.00K	65404.00K	88810.00K	112747.20K	135862.70K
2 COMPOSITE 200	UNITS	126.00	126.00	126.00	126.00	126.00	126.00	126.00	126.00	105.00	105.00	105.00	184.00	184.00	184.00	184.00	184.00	184.00	184.00	184.00
	CUM UNTS	126.00	252.00	378.00	504.00	630.00	756.00	882.00	1008.00	1113.00	1216.00	1323.00	1507.00	1691.00	1875.00	2059.00	2243.00	2427.00	2611.00	2795.00
	COSTS	995400.00	995400.00	995400.00	995400.00	995400.00	995400.00	995400.00	995400.00	829500.00	829500.00	829500.00	1453.60K	1453.60K	1453.60K	1453.60K	1453.60K	1453.60K	1453.60K	1453.60K
	CUM CSTS	995400.00	1990.80K	2986.20K	3981.60K	4977.00K	5972.40K	6967.80K	7963.20K	8792.70K	9622.20K	10451.70K	11905.30K	13358.90K	14812.50K	16266.10K	17719.70K	19173.30K	20626.90K	22080.50K
3 COMPOSITE 300	UNITS	0.00	0.00	0.00	155.00	155.00	155.00	155.00	155.00	155.00	155.00	155.00	155.00	155.00	155.00	155.00	155.00	155.00	155.00	155.00
	CUM UNTS	0.00	0.00	0.00	155.00	310.00	465.00	620.00	775.00	930.00	1085.00	1240.00	1395.00	1550.00	1705.00	1860.00	2015.00	2170.00	2325.00	2480.00
	COSTS	0.00	0.00	0.00	1162.50K	1162.50K	1162.50K	1162.50K	1162.50K	1162.50K	1162.50K	1162.50K	1162.50K	1162.50K	1162.50K	1162.50K	1162.50K	1162.50K	1162.50K	1162.50K
	CUM CSTS	0.00	0.00	0.00	1162.50K	2325.00K	3487.50K	4650.00K	5812.50K	6975.00K	8137.50K	9300.00K	10462.50K	11625.00K	12787.50K	13950.00K	15112.50K	16275.00K	17437.50K	18600.00K
4 COMPOSITE 400	UNITS	0.00	0.00	0.00	154.00	154.00	154.00	154.00	154.00	154.00	154.00	154.00	154.00	154.00	154.00	154.00	154.00	154.00	154.00	154.00
	CUM UNTS	0.00	0.00	0.00	154.00	308.00	462.00	616.00	770.00	924.00	1078.00	1232.00	1386.00	1540.00	1694.00	1848.00	2002.00	2156.00	2310.00	2464.00
	COSTS	0.00	0.00	0.00	1155.00K	1155.00K	1155.00K	1155.00K	1155.00K	1155.00K	1155.00K	1155.00K	1155.00K	1155.00K	1155.00K	1155.00K	1155.00K	1155.00K	1155.00K	1155.00K
	CUM CSTS	0.00	0.00	0.00	1155.00K	2310.00K	3465.00K	4620.00K	5775.00K	6930.00K	8085.00K	9240.00K	10395.00K	11550.00K	12705.00K	13860.00K	15015.00K	16170.00K	17325.00K	18480.00K
TOTAL LABOR UNITS		126.00	126.00	126.00	435.00	435.00	435.00	435.00	435.00	414.00	414.00	414.00	849.00	1543.00	2173.00	2697.00	3083.00	3313.00	3377.00	3278.00
TOTAL CUM LABOR UNITS		126.00	252.00	378.00	813.00	1248.00	1683.00	2118.00	2553.00	2967.00	3381.00	3795.00	4644.00	6187.00	8360.00	11057.00	14140.00	17453.00	20830.00	24108.00
TOTAL LABOR COSTS		995400.00	995400.00	995400.00	3312.90K	3312.90K	3312.90K	3312.90K	3312.90K	3147.00K	3147.00K	3147.00K	6725.90K	12486.10K	17715.10K	22064.30K	25268.10K	27177.10K	27708.30K	26886.60K
TOTAL CUM LABOR COSTS		995400.00	1990.80K	2986.20K	6299.10K	9612.00K	12924.90K	16237.80K	19550.70K	22697.70K	25844.70K	28991.70K	35717.60K	48203.70K	65918.80K	87983.10K	113251.20K	140428.30K	168136.60K	195023.20K

Figure 6-16 Resource distribution report, HITEK Missile System.

151

HITEK MISSILE SYSTEM

CODE RESOURCE NAME	DATA	1987 SEP 19	OCT 20	NOV 21	DEC 22	1988 JAN 23	FEB 24	MAR 25	APR 26	MAY 27	JUN 28	JUL 29	AUG 30	SEP 31	OCT 32	NOV 33	DEC 34	1989 JAN 35	FEB 36	MAR 37
LABOR RESOURCES																				
1 COMPOSITE 100	UNITS	2537.00	2163.00	1699.00	1192.00	700.00	292.00	46.00	0.00	0.00	0.00	0.00	240.00	240.00	0.00	0.00	0.00	0.00	0.00	0.00
	CUM UNITS	18906.00	21069.00	22768.00	23960.00	24660.00	24952.00	24998.00	24998.00	24998.00	24998.00	24998.00	25238.00	25478.00	25478.00	25478.00	25478.00	25478.00	25478.00	25478.00
	COSTS	21057.10K	17952.90K	14101.70K	9893.60K	5810.00K	2423.60K	381800.00	0.00	0.00	0.00	0.00	1992.00K	1992.00K	0.00	0.00	0.00	0.00	0.00	0.00
	CUM CSTS	156919.80K	174872.70K	188974.40K	198868.00K	204678.00K	207101.60K	207483.40K	207483.40K	207483.40K	209475.40K	211467.40K	211467.40K	211467.40K	211467.40K	211467.40K	211467.40K	211467.40K	211467.40K	211467.40K
2 COMPOSITE 200	UNITS	184.00	247.00	247.00	247.00	233.00	233.00	233.00	233.00	154.00	154.00	154.00	154.00	154.00	167.00	167.00	167.00	167.00	167.00	167.00
	CUM UNITS	2979.00	3226.00	3473.00	3720.00	3953.00	4186.00	4419.00	4652.00	4806.00	4960.00	5114.00	5268.00	5422.00	5589.00	5756.00	5923.00	6090.00	6257.00	6424.00
	COSTS	1453.60K	1951.30K	1951.30K	1951.30K	1840.70K	1840.70K	1840.70K	1840.70K	1216.60K	1216.60K	1216.60K	1216.60K	1216.60K	1319.30K	1319.30K	1319.30K	1319.30K	1319.30K	1319.30K
	CUM CSTS	23534.10K	25485.40K	27436.70K	29388.00K	31228.70K	33069.40K	34910.10K	36750.80K	37967.40K	39184.00K	40400.60K	41617.20K	42833.80K	44153.10K	45472.40K	46791.70K	48111.00K	49430.30K	50749.60K
3 COMPOSITE 300	UNITS	155.00	155.00	155.00	155.00	155.00	155.00	155.00	288.00	288.00	133.00	133.00	133.00	0.00	0.00	0.00	0.00	88.00	121.00	121.00
	CUM UNITS	2635.00	2790.00	2945.00	3100.00	3255.00	3410.00	3565.00	3853.00	4141.00	4274.00	4407.00	4540.00	4540.00	4540.00	4540.00	4540.00	4628.00	4749.00	4870.00
	COSTS	1162.50K	1162.50K	1162.50K	1162.50K	1162.50K	1162.50K	1162.50K	2160.00K	2160.00K	997500.00	997500.00	997500.00	0.00	0.00	0.00	0.00	660000.00	907500.00	907500.00
	CUM CSTS	19762.50K	20925.00K	22087.50K	23250.00K	24412.50K	25575.00K	26737.50K	28897.50K	31057.50K	32055.00K	33052.50K	34050.00K	34050.00K	34050.00K	34050.00K	34050.00K	34710.00K	35617.50K	36525.00K
4 COMPOSITE 400	UNITS	154.00	154.00	154.00	154.00	154.00	154.00	154.00	376.00	376.00	222.00	222.00	222.00	222.00	0.00	0.00	0.00	72.00	98.00	98.00
	CUM UNITS	2618.00	2772.00	2926.00	3080.00	3234.00	3388.00	3542.00	3918.00	4294.00	4516.00	4738.00	4960.00	5182.00	5182.00	5182.00	5182.00	5254.00	5352.00	5450.00
	COSTS	1155.00K	1155.00K	1155.00K	1155.00K	1155.00K	1155.00K	1155.00K	2820.00K	2820.00K	1665.00K	1665.00K	1665.00K	1665.00K	0.00	0.00	0.00	540000.00	735000.00	735000.00
	CUM CSTS	19635.00K	20790.00K	21945.00K	23100.00K	24255.00K	25410.00K	26565.00K	29385.00K	32205.00K	33870.00K	35535.00K	37200.00K	38865.00K	38865.00K	38865.00K	38865.00K	39405.00K	40140.00K	40875.00K
TOTAL LABOR UNITS		3030.00	2719.00	2255.00	1748.00	1242.00	834.00	588.00	897.00	818.00	509.00	749.00	749.00	376.00	167.00	167.00	167.00	327.00	386.00	386.00
TOTAL CUM LABOR UNITS		27138.00	29857.00	32112.00	33860.00	35102.00	35936.00	36524.00	37421.00	38239.00	38748.00	39497.00	40246.00	40622.00	40789.00	40956.00	41123.00	41450.00	41836.00	42222.00
TOTAL LABOR COSTS		24828.20K	22221.70K	18370.50K	14162.40K	9968.20K	6581.80K	4540.00K	6820.70K	6196.60K	3879.10K	5871.10K	5871.10K	2881.60K	1319.30K	1319.30K	1319.30K	2519.30K	2961.80K	2961.80K
TOTAL CUM LABOR COSTS		219851.40K	242073.10K	260443.90K	274606.00K	284574.20K	291156.00K	295698.00K	302516.70K	308713.30K	312592.40K	318463.50K	324334.60K	327216.20K	328535.50K	329854.80K	331174.50K	333693.40K	336655.20K	339617.00K

Figure 6-16 Resource distribution report, HITEK Missile System. (Continued)

HITEK MISSILE SYSTEM

LABOR RESOURCES

CODE RESOURCE NAME	DATA	1989 APR 38	MAY 39	JUN 40	JUL 41	AUG 42	SEP 43	OCT 44	NOV 45	DEC 46	1990 JAN 47	FEB 48	MAR 49	APR 50	MAY 51	JUN 52	JUL 53	AUG 54	SEP 55	OCT 56
1 COMPOSITE 100	UNITS	602.00	602.00	602.00	602.00	602.00	602.00	160.00	160.00	160.00	0.00	0.00	0.00	0.00	0.00	0.00	0.00	0.00	0.00	0.00
	CUM UNITS	602.00	1204.00	1806.00	2408.00	3010.00	3612.00	3772.00	3932.00	4092.00	4092.00	4092.00	4092.00	4092.00	4092.00	4092.00	4092.00	4092.00	4092.00	4092.00
	COSTS	4996.60K	4996.60K	4996.60K	4996.60K	4996.60K	4996.60K	1328.00K	1328.00K	1328.00K	0.00	0.00	0.00	0.00	0.00	0.00	0.00	0.00	0.00	0.00
	CUM CSTS	4996.60K	9993.20K	14989.80K	19986.40K	24983.00K	29979.60K	31307.60K	32635.60K	33963.60K	33963.60K	33963.60K	33963.60K	33963.60K	33963.60K	33963.60K	33963.60K	33963.60K	33963.60K	33963.60K
2 COMPOSITE 200	UNITS	167.00	167.00	167.00	198.00	198.00	198.00	198.00	101.00	0.00	0.00	0.00	0.00	0.00	0.00	0.00	0.00	0.00	0.00	0.00
	CUM UNITS	167.00	334.00	501.00	699.00	897.00	1095.00	1293.00	1394.00	1394.00	1394.00	1394.00	1394.00	1394.00	1394.00	1394.00	1394.00	1394.00	1394.00	1394.00
	COSTS	1319.30K	1319.30K	1319.30K	1564.20K	1564.20K	1564.20K	1564.20K	797900.00	0.00	0.00	0.00	0.00	0.00	0.00	0.00	0.00	0.00	0.00	0.00
	CUM CSTS	1319.30K	2638.60K	3957.90K	5522.10K	7086.30K	8650.50K	10214.70K	11012.60K	11012.60K	11012.60K	11012.60K	11012.60K	11012.60K	11012.60K	11012.60K	11012.60K	11012.60K	11012.60K	11012.60K
3 COMPOSITE 300	UNITS	121.00	121.00	121.00	121.00	121.00	121.00	88.00	88.00	88.00	0.00	0.00	0.00	0.00	0.00	0.00	0.00	0.00	0.00	0.00
	CUM UNITS	121.00	242.00	363.00	484.00	605.00	726.00	814.00	902.00	990.00	990.00	990.00	990.00	990.00	990.00	990.00	990.00	990.00	990.00	990.00
	COSTS	907500.00	907500.00	907500.00	907500.00	907500.00	907500.00	660000.00	660000.00	660000.00	0.00	0.00	0.00	0.00	0.00	0.00	0.00	0.00	0.00	0.00
	CUM CSTS	907500.00	1815.00K	2722.50K	3636.00K	4537.50K	5445.00K	6105.00K	6765.00K	7425.00K	7425.00K	7425.00K	7425.00K	7425.00K	7425.00K	7425.00K	7425.00K	7425.00K	7425.00K	7425.00K
4 COMPOSITE 400	UNITS	98.00	98.00	98.00	98.00	98.00	98.00	98.00	98.00	66.00	133.00	133.00	133.00	133.00	133.00	133.00	133.00	133.00	133.00	133.00
	CUM UNITS	98.00	196.00	294.00	392.00	490.00	588.00	686.00	784.00	850.00	983.00	1116.00	1249.00	1382.00	1515.00	1648.00	1781.00	1914.00	2047.00	2180.00
	COSTS	735000.00	735000.00	735000.00	735000.00	735000.00	735000.00	735000.00	735000.00	495000.00	997500.00	997500.00	997500.00	997500.00	997500.00	997500.00	997500.00	997500.00	997500.00	997500.00
	CUM CSTS	735000.00	1470.00K	2205.00K	2940.00K	3675.00K	4410.00K	5145.00K	5880.00K	6375.00K	7372.50K	8370.00K	9367.50K	10365.00K	11362.50K	12360.00K	13357.50K	14355.00K	15352.50K	16350.00K
TOTAL LABOR UNITS		988.00	988.00	988.00	1019.00	1019.00	1019.00	544.00	447.00	314.00	133.00	133.00	133.00	133.00	133.00	133.00	133.00	133.00	133.00	133.00
TOTAL CUM LABOR UNITS		988.00	1976.00	2964.00	3983.00	5002.00	6021.00	6565.00	7012.00	7326.00	7459.00	7592.00	7725.00	7858.00	7991.00	8124.00	8257.00	8390.00	8523.00	8656.00
TOTAL LABOR COSTS		7958.40K	7958.40K	7958.40K	8203.30K	8203.30K	8203.30K	4287.20K	3520.90K	2483.00K	997500.00	997500.00	997500.00	997500.00	997500.00	997500.00	997500.00	997500.00	997500.00	997500.00
TOTAL CUM LABOR COSTS		7958.40K	15916.80K	23875.20K	32078.50K	40281.80K	48485.10K	52772.30K	56293.20K	58776.20K	59773.70K	60771.20K	61768.70K	62766.20K	63763.70K	64761.20K	65758.70K	66756.20K	67753.70K	68751.20K

Figure 6-16 Resource distribution report, HITEK Missile System. (Continued)

153

an initial plan can be compared to a present or updated plan. These costs can also be graphed on a cumulative basis. In addition, a baseline estimate can be compared to the current estimate and the actual cost data either by time period or cumulatively by time period.

Figure 6-22 shows total resources (work months) versus the work months for the Composite 100 labor category. Note that it is the Composite 100 or the missile labor category that produces the bulk of the costs of the project during the peak periods. We have used another graph to illustrate just how great that effect is by selecting period 18 and graphing the use of all skills (see Figure 6-23). Composite 100, the missile skill, accounts for 85 percent of the total resource units used during that period.

Dollars versus time periods for labor costs can give us another picture. Figure 6-24 shows a graph of the HITEK project as it was scheduled on Figure 6-16. Missile Delay, job 101, was reduced to 5 months and all other delays were eliminated to produce the graph on Figure 6-25. Note that the peak costs for the 40 to 45 time period were lowered, the 20 to 30 time period is slightly higher, and the most expensive period has moved from

```
LABOR REPORT   -   Current Date: 10-16-85


PROJECT: HITEK MISSILE SYSTEM
DATE RANGE: 2/1/86 - 11/1/90

CODE           JOB NAME              UNITS        DATES        STATUS      SLACK

LABOR:  1 COMPOSITE 100
  102 MISSILE DEVELOPMENT          24998.00  1/1/87  -4/1/88   Critical       0
  104 MISSILE VERIFICATION           480.00  7/1/88  -9/1/88   Critical       0
  106 MISSILE DESIGN TEST 1         3612.00  4/1/89 -10/1/89   Critical       0
  107 MSLE TYPE CLASSIFICATION       480.00 10/1/89  -1/1/90   Critical       0

LABOR:  2 COMPOSITE 200
  208 DSG LAUNCHER PROTOTYPES       1008.00  2/1/86 -10/1/86   Critical       0
  209 FAB LAUNCHER PROTOTYPES       1260.00 10/1/86 -10/1/87   Critical       0
  211 REDSG LAUNCHER PROTOTYPES      252.00 10/1/87  -1/1/88   NonCritical    1
  212 FAB NEW LAUNCHER PROTOTYPES   1260.00  1/1/88  -7/1/89   NonCritical    1
  215 LAUNCHER TEST                 1264.00  1/1/87  -5/1/88   NonCritical   15
  217 LAUNCHER INIT PROD FACILITY   1008.00 10/1/88 -10/1/88   NonCritical    2
  213 LAUNCHER TC (TYPE CLASS)       505.00  7/1/89 -12/1/89   NonCritical    1
  220 STD MISLE REQUALIFICATION     1261.00 10/1/88 -11/1/89   NonCritical    2

LABOR:  3 COMPOSITE 300
  323 MOB 1 ENG DEVELOPMENT         3875.00  5/1/86  -6/1/88   NonCritical   19
  325 MOB 1 PQT-C                    665.00  4/1/88  -9/1/88   Critical       0
  327 MOB 1 PQT - GOVERNMENT         792.00  1/1/89 -10/1/89   Critical       0
  330 MOB 1 OPN TEST                 264.00  2/1/89 -10/1/89   Critical       0
  331 MOB 1 TYPE CLASSIFICATION      264.00 10/1/89  -1/1/90   Critical       0

LABOR:  4 COMPOSITE 400
  433 MOB 2 ENG DEVELOPMENT         3850.00  5/1/86  -6/1/88   NonCritical   19
  435 MOB 2 PQT CONTRACTOR          1332.00  4/1/88 -10/1/88   Critical       0
  437 MOB 2 PQT - GOVERNMENT         792.00  1/1/89 -12/1/89   Critical       0
  440 MOB 2 OPN TEST                 260.00  2/1/89 -12/1/89   Critical       0
  441 MOB 2 TYPE CLASSIFICATION       66.00 12/1/89  -1/1/90   Critical       0
  446 CONTINUE PROGRAM TIME         1330.00  1/1/90 -11/1/90   Critical       0
```

Figure 6-17 Labor report, HITEK Missile System.

```
                    JOB DESCRIPTION REPORT (Job)

HITEK MISSILE SYSTEM                         Current Date:   10-16-85
                                             Project Start:   2- 1-86

  Job  102    MISSILE DEVELOPMENT
      Predecessors  101    Ø    Ø    Ø    Ø    Ø    Ø    Ø    Ø

        Status        Critical          Early Start    1-87  (    11)
        Duration         15             Early Finish   4-88  (    26)
        Slack          none             Late Start     1-87  (    11)
                                        Late Finish    4-88  (    26)


SEQ    RESOURCE CLASS    START  DUR.  END    UNITS        TOT          COST

LABOR COST

  1    1 COMPOSITE 100      Ø    1    1     356.00       356.00      2954800.00
  2    1 COMPOSITE 100      1    1    2    1050.00      1050.00      8715000.00
  3    1 COMPOSITE 100      2    1    3    1680.00      1680.00     13944000.00
  4    1 COMPOSITE 100      3    1    4    2204.00      2204.00     18293200.00
  5    1 COMPOSITE 100      4    1    5    2590.00      2590.00     21497000.00
  6    1 COMPOSITE 100      5    1    6    2820.00      2820.00     23406000.00
  7    1 COMPOSITE 100      6    1    7    2884.00      2884.00     23937200.00
  8    1 COMPOSITE 100      7    1    8    2785.00      2785.00     23115500.00
  9    1 COMPOSITE 100      8    1    9    2537.00      2537.00     21057100.00
 10    1 COMPOSITE 100      9    1   10    2163.00      2163.00     17952900.00
 11    1 COMPOSITE 100     10    1   11    1699.00      1699.00     14101700.00
 12    1 COMPOSITE 100     11    1   12    1192.00      1192.00      9893600.00
 13    1 COMPOSITE 100     12    1   13     700.00       700.00      5810000.00
 14    1 COMPOSITE 100     13    1   14     292.00       292.00      2423600.00
 15    1 COMPOSITE 100     14    1   15      46.00        46.00       381800.00

LABOR TOTALS                                           24998.00   207483400.00

OTHER COST


OTHER TOTALS                                               0.00          0.00


TOTAL COSTS                                            24998.00   207483400.00
```

Figure 6-18 Job description report (job 102), HITEK Missile System.

```
                    JOB DESCRIPTION REPORT (Total)

HITEK MISSILE SYSTEM                         Current Date:   10-16-85
                                             Project Start:   2- 1-86
                                             Project Finish:    11-90

LABOR CLASSIFICATION        UNIT COST        UNITS             COST

  1 COMPOSITE 100            8300.00       29570.00        245431000.00
  2 COMPOSITE 200            7900.00        7818.00         61762200.00
  3 COMPOSITE 300            7500.00        5860.00         43950000.00
  4 COMPOSITE 400            7500.00        7630.00         57225000.00

Labor Totals:                              50878.00        408368200.00


ODC    CLASSIFICATION       UNIT COST        UNITS             COST


ODC    Totals:                                 0.00              0.00


TOTALS:                                    50878.00        408368200.00
```

Figure 6-19 Job description report (total), HITEK Missile System.

HITEK MISSILE SYSTEM   Current Date: 10-16-85

JOB	NAME	LABOR- UNITS & COST		TOTAL-COST
101	MISSILE DELAY	0.00	0.00	0.00
102	MISSILE DEVELOPMENT	24998.00	207483400.00	207483400.00
103	MISSILE DELAY	0.00	0.00	0.00
104	MISSILE VERIFICATION	480.00	3984000.00	3984000.00
105	MISSILE DELAY 2	0.00	0.00	0.00
106	MISSILE DESIGN TEST 1	3612.00	29979600.00	29979600.00
107	MSLE TYPE CLASSIFICATION	480.00	3984000.00	3984000.00
142	MSLE TYPE CLASSIFICATION	0.00	0.00	0.00
208	DSG LAUNCHER PROTOTYPES	1008.00	7963200.00	7963200.00
209	FAB LAUNCHER PROTOTYPES	1260.00	9954000.00	9954000.00
218	SIGNAL	0.00	0.00	0.00
219	SIGNAL	0.00	0.00	0.00
325	MOB 1 PQT-C	665.00	4987500.00	4987500.00
326	MOB 1 DELAY	0.00	0.00	0.00
327	MOB 1 PQT - GOVERNMENT	792.00	5940000.00	5940000.00
328	SIGNAL	0.00	0.00	0.00
329	MOB 1 DELAY	0.00	0.00	0.00
330	MOB 1 OPN TEST	264.00	1980000.00	1980000.00
331	MOB 1 TYPE CLASSIFICATION	264.00	1980000.00	1980000.00
344	MOB 1 TC	0.00	0.00	0.00
435	MOB 2 PQT CONTRACTOR	1332.00	9990000.00	9990000.00
436	MOB 2 DELAY	0.00	0.00	0.00
437	MOB 2 PQT - GOVERNMENT	792.00	5940000.00	5940000.00
438	SIGNAL	0.00	0.00	0.00
439	MOB 2 DELAY	0.00	0.00	0.00
440	MOB 2 OPN TEST	260.00	1950000.00	1950000.00
441	MOB 2 TYPE CLASSIFICATION	66.00	495000.00	495000.00
445	MOB 2 TYPE CLASSIFICATION	0.00	0.00	0.00
446	CONTINUE PROGRAM TIME	1330.00	9975000.00	9975000.00

37603.00 306585700.00 306585700.00

Figure 6-20   Report of critical jobs, HITEK Missile System.

HITEK MISSILE SYSTEM   Current Date: 10-16-85

JOB	NAME	LABOR- UNITS & COST		TOTAL-COST
210	SIGNAL (MILESTONE)	0.00	0.00	0.00
211	REDSG LAUNCHER PROTOTYPES	252.00	1990800.00	1990800.00
212	FAB NEW LAUNCHER PROTOTYPES	1260.00	9954000.00	9954000.00
214	LAUNCHER DELAY	0.00	0.00	0.00
215	LAUNCHER TEST	1264.00	9985600.00	9985600.00
216	SIGNAL	0.00	0.00	0.00
217	LAUNCHER INIT PROD FACILITY	1008.00	7963200.00	7963200.00
213	LAUNCHER TC (TYPE CLASS)	505.00	3989500.00	3989500.00
243	LAUNCHER TC	0.00	0.00	0.00
220	STD MISLE REQUALIFICATION	1261.00	9961900.00	9961900.00
221	SIGNAL	0.00	0.00	0.00
322	MOB SYS 1 DELAY	0.00	0.00	0.00
323	MOB 1 ENG DEVELOPMENT	3875.00	29062500.00	29062500.00
324	SIGNAL	0.00	0.00	0.00
432	MOB 2 DELAY	0.00	0.00	0.00
433	MOB 2 ENG DEVELOPMENT	3850.00	28875000.00	28875000.00
434	SIGNAL	0.00	0.00	0.00

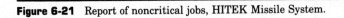

13275.00 101782500.00 101782500.00

Figure 6-21   Report of noncritical jobs, HITEK Missile System.

the 10 to 25 time period (December 1986 through March 1988) to the 5 to 20 period (July 1986 through October 1987).

A change in the schedule will often influence the cost estimate or the use of resources. With scheduling software, we can easily play what-if games to determine the most advantageous use of resources or schedule for the project such as the above example. Some of the methods that can be used are (1) change the start date of the project, (2) reallocate resources among or within jobs, (3) eliminate nonessential jobs, (4) change predecessor relationships, (5) add jobs, (6) build in nonresource carrying delays, or (7) build in milestones.

Assume that available funding for the HITEK Missile System for the first year is $10 million rather than $30 million. We find that if we slip the schedule 6 months (see Figure 6-26), we can reduce the cost for the first year of the project from $25.8 million to $9.6 million which is within the $10 million allocation (see Figure 6-27). Although it was not done in this example, inflation further downstream could be accounted for by increasing the composite labor rates by the amount of rate increase caused by the schedule slippage.

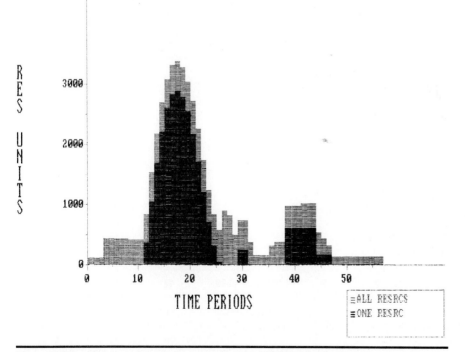

Figure 6-22 All resources versus composite 100, HITEK Missile System.

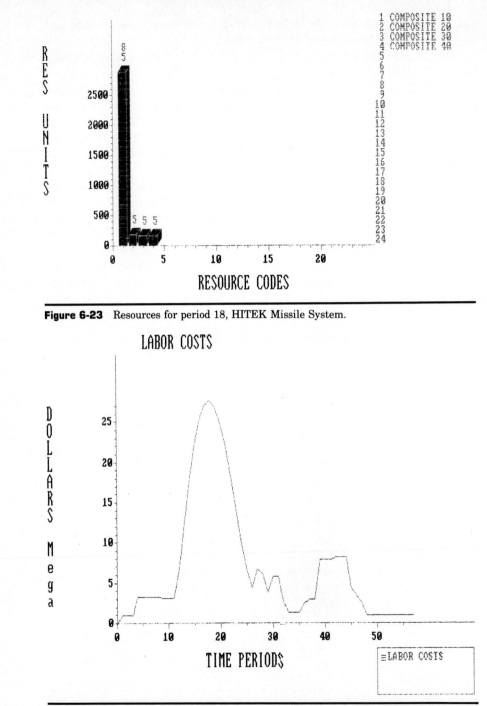

Figure 6-23 Resources for period 18, HITEK Missile System.

Figure 6-24 Labor costs by time periods—project as originally scheduled, HITEK Missile System.

Other Useful Features of Scheduling Software

As mentioned earlier in this chapter, there are a number of other features available on the various scheduling software packages that are useful to the cost estimator. It is often advantageous to be able to compare several projects at once or to compare actual costs against estimates. Project Scheduler 5000 is one of those packages that makes these comparisons. In the next example we have a software development project, SOFTWARE, which was originally estimated on a 12-month basis and was later changed to 15 months. As the project moved ahead, we tracked its progress on our Gantt chart by using the Finish feature. Figure 6-28 shows the finished and partially finished jobs of this project. The finished portions are shown by colons. We go a step further and prepare a Selectable Job Report to show the earned value of the completed or partially completed jobs of the project. Figure 6-29 shows the amounts of the estimate that have been used to date on the project. The next step is to input the total actual costs that have been incurred for each time period for

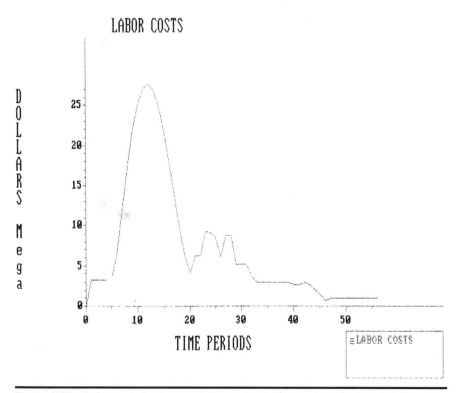

Figure 6-25   Labor costs by time periods—project with schedule changes, HITEK Missile System.

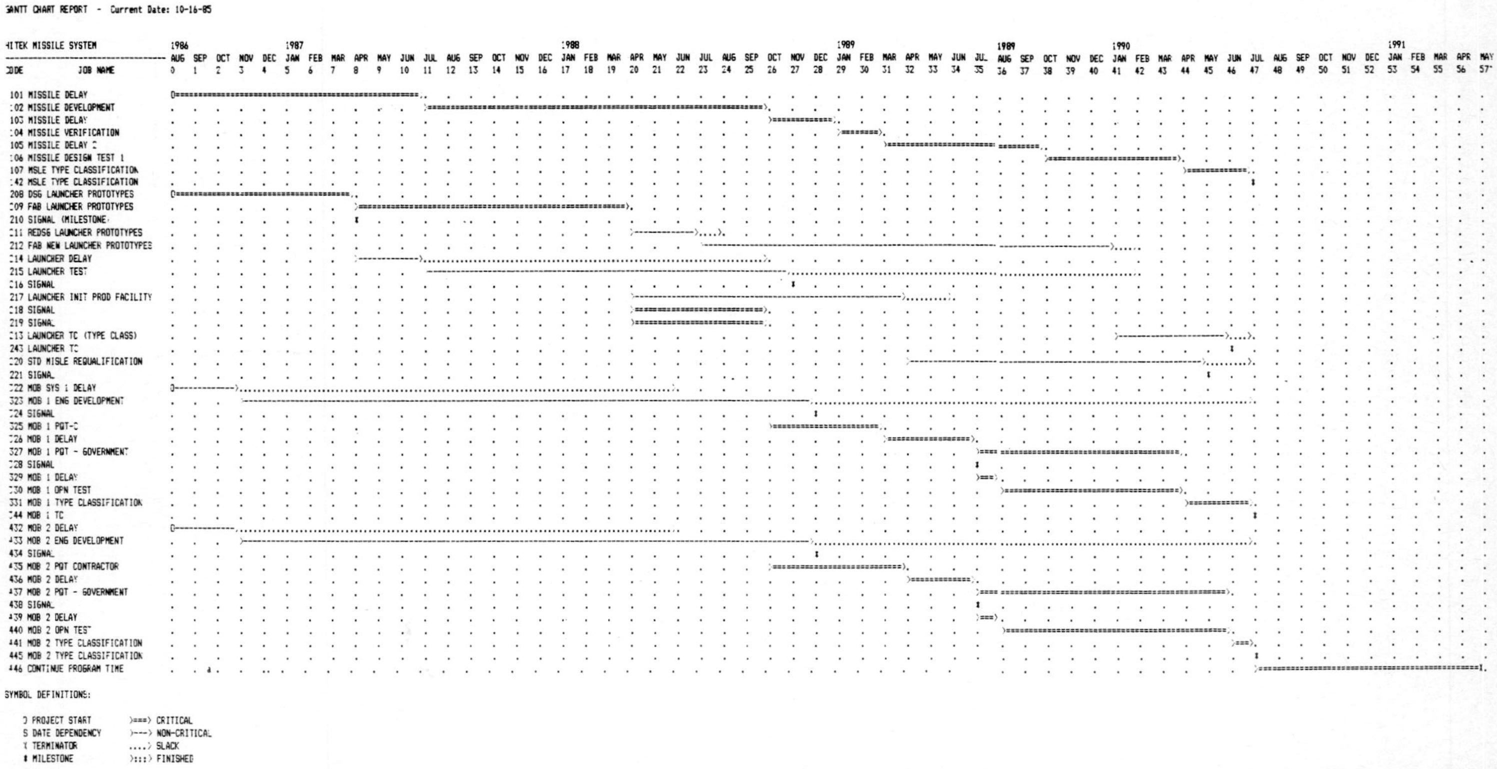

Figure 6-26 Gantt chart report with schedule slipped 6 months, HITEK Missile System.

RESOURCE DISTRIBUTION REPORT - Current Date: 10-16-85

HITEK MISSILE SYSTEM

CODE RESOURCE NAME	DATA	1986 AUG 0	SEP 1	OCT 2	NOV 3	DEC 4	1987 JAN 5	FEB 6	MAR 7	APR 8	MAY 9	JUN 10	JUL 11	AUG 12	SEP 13	OCT 14	NOV 15	DEC 16	1988 JAN 17	FEB 18
LABOR RESOURCES																				
1 COMPOSITE 100	UNITS	0.00	0.00	0.00	0.00	0.00	0.00	0.00	0.00	0.00	0.00	0.00	356.00	1050.00	1680.00	2204.00	2590.00	2820.00	2884.00	2785.00
	CUM UNITS	0.00	0.00	0.00	0.00	0.00	0.00	0.00	0.00	0.00	0.00	0.00	356.00	1406.00	3086.00	5290.00	7880.00	10700.00	13584.00	16369.00
	COSTS	0.00	0.00	0.00	0.00	0.00	0.00	0.00	0.00	0.00	0.00	0.00	2954.80K	8715.00K	13944.00K	18293.20K	21497.00K	23406.00K	23937.20K	23115.50K
	CUM CSTS	0.00	0.00	0.00	0.00	0.00	0.00	0.00	0.00	0.00	0.00	0.00	2954.80K	11669.80K	25613.80K	43907.00K	65404.00K	88810.00K	112747.20K	135862.70K
2 COMPOSITE 200	UNITS	126.00	126.00	126.00	126.00	126.00	126.00	126.00	126.00	105.00	105.00	105.00	184.00	184.00	184.00	184.00	184.00	184.00	184.00	184.00
	CUM UNTS	126.00	252.00	378.00	504.00	630.00	756.00	882.00	1008.00	1113.00	1218.00	1323.00	1507.00	1691.00	1875.00	2059.00	2243.00	2427.00	2611.00	2795.00
	COSTS	995400.00	995400.00	995400.00	995400.00	995400.00	995400.00	995400.00	995400.00	829500.00	829500.00	829500.00	1453.60K	1453.60K	1453.60K	1453.60K	1453.60K	1453.60K	1453.60K	1453.60K
	CUM CSTS	995400.00	1990.80K	2986.20K	3981.60K	4977.00K	5972.40K	6967.80K	7963.20K	8792.70K	9622.20K	10451.70K	11905.30K	13358.90K	14812.50K	16266.10K	17719.70K	19173.30K	20626.90K	22080.50K
3 COMPOSITE 300	UNITS	0.00	0.00	0.00	155.00	155.00	155.00	155.00	155.00	155.00	155.00	155.00	155.00	155.00	155.00	155.00	155.00	155.00	155.00	155.00
	CUM UNTS	0.00	0.00	0.00	155.00	310.00	465.00	620.00	775.00	930.00	1085.00	1240.00	1395.00	1550.00	1705.00	1860.00	2015.00	2170.00	2325.00	2480.00
	COSTS	0.00	0.00	0.00	1162.50K	1162.50K	1162.50K	1162.50K	1162.50K	1162.50K	1162.50K	1162.50K	1162.50K	1162.50K	1162.50K	1162.50K	1162.50K	1162.50K	1162.50K	1162.50K
	CUM CSTS	0.00	0.00	0.00	1162.50K	2325.00K	3487.50K	4650.00K	5812.50K	6975.00K	8137.50K	9300.00K	10462.50K	11625.00K	12787.50K	13950.00K	15112.50K	16275.00K	17437.50K	18600.00K
4 COMPOSITE 400	UNITS	0.00	0.00	0.00	154.00	154.00	154.00	154.00	154.00	154.00	154.00	154.00	154.00	154.00	154.00	154.00	154.00	154.00	154.00	154.00
	CUM UNTS	0.00	0.00	0.00	154.00	308.00	462.00	616.00	770.00	924.00	1078.00	1232.00	1386.00	1540.00	1694.00	1848.00	2002.00	2156.00	2310.00	2464.00
	COSTS	0.00	0.00	0.00	1155.00K	1155.00K	1155.00K	1155.00K	1155.00K	1155.00K	1155.00K	1155.00K	1155.00K	1155.00K	1155.00K	1155.00K	1155.00K	1155.00K	1155.00K	1155.00K
	CUM CSTS	0.00	0.00	0.00	1155.00K	2310.00K	3465.00K	4620.00K	5775.00K	6930.00K	8085.00K	9240.00K	10395.00K	11550.00K	12705.00K	13860.00K	15015.00K	16170.00K	17325.00K	18480.00K
TOTAL LABOR UNITS		126.00	126.00	126.00	435.00	435.00	435.00	435.00	435.00	414.00	414.00	414.00	849.00	1543.00	2173.00	2697.00	3083.00	3313.00	3377.00	3278.00
TOTAL CUM LABOR UNITS		126.00	252.00	378.00	817.00	1248.00	1683.00	2118.00	2553.00	2967.00	3381.00	3795.00	4644.00	6187.00	8360.00	11057.00	14140.00	17453.00	20830.00	24108.00
TOTAL LABOR COSTS		995400.00	995400.00	995400.00	3312.90K	3312.90K	3312.90K	3312.90K	3312.90K	3147.00K	3147.00K	3147.00K	6725.90K	12486.10K	17715.10K	22064.30K	25268.10K	27177.10K	27708.30K	26886.60K
TOTAL CUM LABOR COSTS		995400.00	1990.80K	2986.20K	6299.10K	9612.00K	12924.90K	16237.80K	19550.70K	25844.70K	25844.70K	28991.70K	35717.60K	48205.70K	65918.80K	87983.10K	113251.20K	140428.30K	168136.60K	195023.20K

Figure 6-27 Resource distribution report with schedule slipped 6 months, HITEK Missile System.

161

RESOURCE DISTRIBUTION REPORT - Current Date: 10-16-85

HITEK MISSILE SYSTEM

CODE RESOURCE NAME	DATA	1988 MAR 19	APR 20	MAY 21	JUN 22	JUL 23	AUG 24	SEP 25	OCT 26	NOV 27	DEC 28	1989 JAN 29	FEB 30	MAR 31	APR 32	MAY 33	JUN 34	JUL 35	AUG 36	SEP 37
LABOR RESOURCES:																				
1 COMPOSITE 100	UNITS	2537.00	2163.00	1899.00	1192.00	700.00	292.00	46.00	0.00	0.00	0.00	240.00	240.00	0.00	0.00	0.00	0.00	0.00	0.00	0.00
	CUM UNITS	18906.00	21069.00	22968.00	23960.00	24660.00	24952.00	24998.00	24998.00	24998.00	24998.00	25238.00	25478.00	25478.00	25478.00	25478.00	25478.00	25478.00	25478.00	25478.00
	COSTS	21057.10K	17952.90K	14101.70K	9893.60K	5810.00K	2423.60K	381800.00	0.00	0.00	0.00	1992.00K	1992.00K	0.00	0.00	0.00	0.00	0.00	0.00	0.00
	CUM CSTS	156919.80K	174872.70K	188974.40K	198868.00K	204678.00K	207101.60K	207483.40K	207483.40K	207483.40K	207483.40K	209475.40K	211467.40K	211467.40K	211467.40K	211467.40K	211467.40K	211467.40K	211467.40K	211467.40K
2 COMPOSITE 200	UNITS	184.00	247.00	247.00	247.00	233.00	233.00	233.00	233.00	154.00	154.00	154.00	154.00	154.00	154.00	167.00	167.00	167.00	167.00	167.00
	CUM UNTS	2979.00	3226.00	3473.00	3720.00	3953.00	4186.00	4419.00	4652.00	4806.00	4960.00	5114.00	5268.00	5422.00	5589.00	5756.00	5923.00	6090.00	6257.00	6424.00
	COSTS	1453.60K	1951.30K	1951.30K	1951.30K	1840.70K	1840.70K	1840.70K	1840.70K	1216.60K	1216.60K	1216.60K	1216.60K	1216.60K	1216.60K	1319.30K	1319.30K	1319.30K	1319.30K	1319.30K
	CUM CSTS	23534.10K	25485.40K	27436.70K	29388.00K	31228.70K	33069.40K	34910.10K	36750.80K	37967.40K	39184.00K	40400.60K	41617.20K	42833.80K	44153.10K	45472.40K	46791.70K	48111.00K	49430.30K	50749.60K
3 COMPOSITE 300	UNITS	155.00	155.00	155.00	155.00	155.00	155.00	155.00	288.00	288.00	133.00	133.00	133.00	0.00	0.00	0.00	0.00	88.00	121.00	121.00
	CUM UNTS	2635.00	2790.00	2945.00	3100.00	3255.00	3410.00	3565.00	3853.00	4141.00	4274.00	4407.00	4540.00	4540.00	4540.00	4540.00	4540.00	4628.00	4749.00	4870.00
	COSTS	1162.50K	1162.50K	1162.50K	1162.50K	1162.50K	1162.50K	1162.50K	2160.00K	2160.00K	997500.00	997500.00	997500.00	0.00	0.00	0.00	0.00	660000.00	907500.00	907500.00
	CUM CSTS	19762.50K	20925.00K	22087.50K	23250.00K	24412.50K	25575.00K	26737.50K	28897.50K	31057.50K	32055.00K	33052.50K	34050.00K	34050.00K	34050.00K	34050.00K	34050.00K	34710.00K	35617.50K	36525.00K
4 COMPOSITE 400	UNITS	154.00	154.00	154.00	154.00	154.00	154.00	154.00	376.00	376.00	222.00	222.00	222.00	222.00	0.00	0.00	0.00	72.00	98.00	98.00
	CUM UNTS	2618.00	2772.00	2926.00	3080.00	3234.00	3388.00	3542.00	3918.00	4294.00	4516.00	4738.00	4960.00	5182.00	5182.00	5182.00	5182.00	5254.00	5352.00	5450.00
	COSTS	1155.00K	1155.00K	1155.00K	1155.00K	1155.00K	1155.00K	1155.00K	2820.00K	2820.00K	1665.00K	1665.00K	1665.00K	1665.00K	0.00	0.00	0.00	540000.00	735000.00	735000.00
	CUM CSTS	19635.00K	20790.00K	21945.00K	23100.00K	24255.00K	25410.00K	26565.00K	29385.00K	32205.00K	33870.00K	35535.00K	37200.00K	38865.00K	38865.00K	38865.00K	38865.00K	39405.00K	40140.00K	40875.00K
TOTAL LABOR UNITS		3030.00	2719.00	2255.00	1748.00	1242.00	834.00	588.00	897.00	818.00	509.00	749.00	749.00	376.00	222.00	167.00	167.00	327.00	386.00	386.00
TOTAL CUM LABOR UNITS		27138.00	29857.00	32112.00	33860.00	35102.00	35936.00	36524.00	37421.00	38239.00	38748.00	39497.00	40246.00	40622.00	40789.00	40956.00	41123.00	41450.00	41836.00	42222.00
TOTAL LABOR COSTS		24828.20K	22221.70K	18370.50K	14162.40K	9968.20K	6581.80K	4540.00K	6820.70K	6196.60K	3879.10K	5871.10K	5871.10K	2881.60K	1319.30K	1319.30K	1319.30K	2519.30K	2961.80K	2961.80K
TOTAL CUM LABOR COSTS		219851.40K	242073.10K	260443.60K	274606.00K	284574.20K	291156.00K	295696.00K	302516.70K	308713.30K	312592.40K	318463.50K	324334.60K	327216.20K	328535.50K	329854.80K	331174.10K	333693.40K	336655.20K	339617.00K

Figure 6-27 Resource distribution report with schedule slipped 6 months, HITEK Missile System. (Continued)

HITEK MISSILE SYSTEM

		1989			1990												1991			
CODE / RESOURCE NAME	DATA	OCT 38	NOV 39	DEC 40	JAN 41	FEB 42	MAR 43	APR 44	MAY 45	JUN 46	JUL 47	AUG 48	SEP 49	OCT 50	NOV 51	DEC 52	JAN 53	FEB 54	MAR 55	APR 56

LABOR RESOURCES

CODE / RESOURCE NAME	DATA	OCT 38	NOV 39	DEC 40	JAN 41	FEB 42	MAR 43	APR 44	MAY 45	JUN 46	JUL 47	AUG 48	SEP 49	OCT 50	NOV 51	DEC 52	JAN 53	FEB 54	MAR 55	APR 56
1 COMPOSITE 100	UNITS	602.00	602.00	602.00	602.00	602.00	602.00	160.00	160.00	160.00	0.00	0.00	0.00	0.00	0.00	0.00	0.00	0.00	0.00	0.00
	CUM UNITS	26080.00	26682.00	27284.00	27886.00	28488.00	29090.00	29250.00	29410.00	29570.00	29570.00	29570.00	29570.00	29570.00	29570.00	29570.00	29570.00	29570.00	29570.00	29570.00
	COSTS	4996.60K	4996.60K	4996.60K	4996.60K	4996.60K	4996.60K	1328.00K	1328.00K	1328.00K	0.00	0.00	0.00	0.00	0.00	0.00	0.00	0.00	0.00	0.00
	CUM COSTS	216464.00K	221460.60K	226457.20K	231453.80K	236450.40K	241447.00K	242775.00K	244103.00K	245431.00K	245431.00K	245431.00K	245431.00K	245431.00K	245431.00K	245431.00K	245431.00K	245431.00K	245431.00K	245431.00K
2 COMPOSITE 200	UNITS	167.00	167.00	167.00	198.00	198.00	198.00	198.00	101.00	0.00	0.00	0.00	0.00	0.00	0.00	0.00	0.00	0.00	0.00	0.00
	CUM UNITS	6591.00	6758.00	6925.00	7123.00	7321.00	7519.00	7717.00	7818.00	7818.00	7818.00	7818.00	7818.00	7818.00	7818.00	7818.00	7818.00	7818.00	7818.00	7818.00
	COSTS	1319.30K	1319.30K	1319.30K	1564.20K	1564.20K	1564.20K	1564.20K	797900.00	0.00	0.00	0.00	0.00	0.00	0.00	0.00	0.00	0.00	0.00	0.00
	CUM COSTS	52068.90K	53388.20K	54707.50K	56271.70K	57835.90K	59400.10K	60964.30K	61762.20K	61762.20K	61762.20K	61762.20K	61762.20K	61762.20K	61762.20K	61762.20K	61762.20K	61762.20K	61762.20K	61762.20K
3 COMPOSITE 300	UNITS	121.00	121.00	121.00	121.00	121.00	121.00	88.00	88.00	88.00	0.00	0.00	0.00	0.00	0.00	0.00	0.00	0.00	0.00	0.00
	CUM UNITS	4991.00	5112.00	5233.00	5354.00	5475.00	5596.00	5684.00	5772.00	5860.00	5860.00	5860.00	5860.00	5860.00	5860.00	5860.00	5860.00	5860.00	5860.00	5860.00
	COSTS	907500.00	907500.00	907500.00	907500.00	907500.00	907500.00	660000.00	660000.00	660000.00	0.00	0.00	0.00	0.00	0.00	0.00	0.00	0.00	0.00	0.00
	CUM COSTS	37432.50K	38340.00K	39247.50K	40155.00K	41062.50K	41970.00K	42630.00K	43290.00K	43950.00K	43950.00K	43950.00K	43950.00K	43950.00K	43950.00K	43950.00K	43950.00K	43950.00K	43950.00K	43950.00K
4 COMPOSITE 400	UNITS	98.00	98.00	98.00	98.00	98.00	98.00	98.00	98.00	66.00	133.00	133.00	133.00	133.00	133.00	133.00	133.00	133.00	133.00	133.00
	CUM UNITS	5548.00	5646.00	5744.00	5842.00	5940.00	6038.00	6136.00	6234.00	6300.00	6433.00	6566.00	6699.00	6832.00	6965.00	7098.00	7231.00	7364.00	7497.00	7630.00
	COSTS	735000.00	735000.00	735000.00	735000.00	735000.00	735000.00	735000.00	735000.00	495000.00	997500.00	997500.00	997500.00	997500.00	997500.00	997500.00	997500.00	997500.00	997500.00	997500.00
	CUM COSTS	41610.00K	42345.00K	43080.00K	43815.00K	44550.00K	45285.00K	46020.00K	46755.00K	47250.00K	48247.50K	49245.00K	50242.50K	51240.00K	52237.50K	53235.00K	54232.50K	55230.00K	56227.50K	57225.00K
TOTAL LABOR UNITS		988.00	988.00	988.00	1019.00	1019.00	1019.00	544.00	447.00	314.00	133.00	133.00	133.00	133.00	133.00	133.00	133.00	133.00	133.00	133.00
TOTAL CUM LABOR UNITS		43210.00	44198.00	45186.00	46205.00	47224.00	48243.00	48787.00	49234.00	49548.00	49681.00	49814.00	49947.00	50080.00	50213.00	50346.00	50479.00	50612.00	50745.00	50878.00
TOTAL LABOR COSTS		7958.40K	7958.40K	7958.40K	8203.30K	8203.30K	8203.30K	4287.20K	3520.90K	2483.00K	997500.00	997500.00	997500.00	997500.00	997500.00	997500.00	997500.00	997500.00	997500.00	997500.00
TOTAL CUM LABOR COSTS		347575.40K	355533.80K	363492.20K	371695.50K	379898.80K	388102.10K	392389.30K	395910.20K	398393.20K	399390.70K	400388.20K	401385.70K	402383.20K	403380.70K	404378.20K	405375.70K	406373.20K	407370.70K	408368.20K

Figure 6-27 Resource distribution report with schedule slipped 6 months, HITEK Missile System. (Continued)

```
GANTT CHART REPORT  -  Current Date: 10-16-85


SOFTWARE1                                  1986                                              1987
---------------------------------------    JAN FEB MAR APR MAY JUN JUL AUG SEP OCT NOV DEC JAN FEB MAR APR
CODE        JOB NAME                        0   1   2   3   4   5   6   7   8   9   10  11  12  13  14  15


   10  INPUTS PROGRAMMING                  0:::::::::::::::::::====X.   .   .   .   .   .   .   .   .   .
   20  EDITS PROGRAMMING                   0:::::::::::::::::::====X.   .   .   .   .   .   .   .   .   .
   30  ERROR MSG PROGRAMMING               0:::::::::::::::=========X.   .   .   .   .   .   .   .   .   .
   40  REPT GEN PROGRAMMING                0:::::::::=========X.   .   .   .   .   .   .   .   .   .   .
   50  USER INPUTS PROGRAMMING             0:::::::::=========X.   .   .   .   .   .   .   .   .   .   .
   60  START TESTING                       0:::::::::::::).   .   .   .   .   .   .   .   .   .   .   .
   70  IN-HOUSE TESTING                    .   .   .   ):::::::::::::::=========X.   .   .   .   .   .   .
   80  MARKET TESTING                      .   .   .   ):::::=========X.   .   .   .   .   .   .   .   .
   90  FEEDBACK TESTING                    .   .   .   )=================X.   .   .   .   .   .   .   .   .
  100  START DOCUMENTATION                 .   .   .   ):::::::::::::::=========).   .   .   .   .   .   .
  110  BASIC DOCUMENTATION                 .   .   .   .   .   .   .   .   )=================).   .   .   .
  120  MANUAL                              .   .   .   .   .   .   .   .   )=================).   .   .   .
  130  SAMPLE PROBLEMS DOCUMENTATION       .   .   .   .   .   .   .   .   )=================).   .   .   .
  140  UPDATES DOCUMENTATION               .   .   .   .   .   .   .   .   )=================).   .   .   .
  150  INSTALLATION SUPPORT                .   .   .   .   .   .   .   .   .   .   .   .   )=============X.
  160  TRAINING SUPPORT                    .   .   .   .   .   .   .   .   .   .   .   .   )=============X.
  170  UPDATE SUPPORT                      .   .   .   .   .   .   .   .   .   .   .   .   )=============X.
  180  FIELD SVC SUPPORT                   .   .   .   .   .   .   .   .   .   .   .   .   )=============X.


SYMBOL DEFINITIONS:

   0 PROJECT START          )===) CRITICAL
   S DATE DEPENDENCY        )---) NON-CRITICAL
   X TERMINATOR             ....) SLACK
   * MILESTONE              ):::) FINISHED
```

Figure 6-28   Gantt chart report, Software.

                              EARNED VALUE REPORT
SOFTWARE1   Current Date: 07-10-86

JOB	NAME	STATUS	CompDura	EARN-VALUE
10	INPUTS PROGRAMMING	Critical	4	9236.20
20	EDITS PROGRAMMING	Critical	4	9236.20
30	ERROR MSG PROGRAMMING	Critical	3	8458.50
40	REPT GEN PROGRAMMING	Critical	2	2722.40
50	USER INPUTS PROGRAMMING	Critical	3	17698.80
60	START TESTING	Complete	3	0.00
70	IN-HOUSE TESTING	Critical	3	9675.75
80	MARKET TESTING	Critical	1	632.05
90	FEEDBACK TESTING	Critical	0	0.00
100	START DOCUMENTATION	Critical	0	0.00
110	BASIC DOCUMENTATION	Critical	0	0.00
120	MANUAL	Critical	0	0.00
130	SAMPLE PROBLEMS DOCUMENTATION	Critical	0	0.00
140	UPDATES DOCUMENTATION	Critical	0	0.00
150	INSTALLATION SUPPORT	Critical	0	0.00
160	TRAINING SUPPORT	Critical	0	0.00
170	UPDATE SUPPORT	Critical	0	0.00
180	FIELD SVC SUPPORT	Critical	0	0.00

                                                         57659.90

Figure 6-29   Earned value report, Software.

```
                    ACTUAL COST INPUT
                    -----------------

Time periods
  1      6800.00    11      0.00    21      0.00    31      0.00
  2      7200.00    12      0.00    22      0.00    32      0.00
  3      9800.00    13      0.00    23      0.00    33      0.00
  4      9800.00    14      0.00    24      0.00    34      0.00
  5     10500.00    15      0.00    25      0.00    35      0.00
  6     13600.00    16      0.00    26      0.00    36      0.00
  7         0.00    17      0.00    27      0.00    37      0.00
  8         0.00    18      0.00    28      0.00    38      0.00
  9         0.00    19      0.00    29      0.00    39      0.00
 10         0.00    20      0.00    30      0.00    40      0.00


   (T)ime period

   (E)nd actual cost inputs

 Press a letter to select an option >


 1730-DO NOT REMOVE WORKFILE DISK PREMATURELY
```

Figure 6-30 Actual cost input, Software.

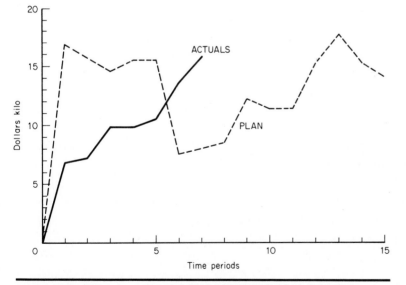

Figure 6-31 Plan versus actual dollars versus time periods, Software.

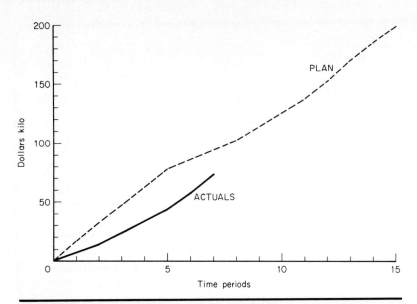

Figure 6-32 Plan versus actual (cumulative) dollars versus time periods, Software.

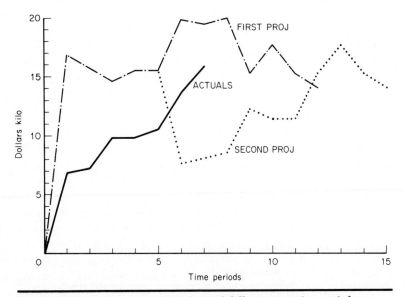

Figure 6-33 Baseline, current, and actual dollars versus time periods, Software.

those finished and partially finished periods. This input screen is shown on Figure 6-30.

The next four figures are examples of graphs that can be generated using the above information. Figure 6-31 shows our 15-month project as estimated on a period-by-period basis in comparison to the actual costs of the project to date. Not all the estimated monies have been used to date, but then, not all of the work has been done to date either. Jobs 70 and 100 are the only ones that are on time (see Figure 6-28). Figure 6-32 is another graph of the same situation but on a cumulative basis. The next two graphs show the original 12-month estimate compared to the 15-month estimate and the actual costs incurred to date. Figure 6-33 compares them on a period-by-period basis and Figure 6-34 compares them on a cumulative basis.

This chapter has shown some of the exciting things the estimator can do with a microcomputer and off-the-shelf scheduling software. There are numerous features not covered; different scheduling applications software packages handle situations in different ways, so if you decide to use a scheduling software package for your estimating, you will want to evaluate those packages available for your computer. In Chapter 7 we will discuss some of the vertical market cost estimating microcomputer software systems that are available for microcomputers.

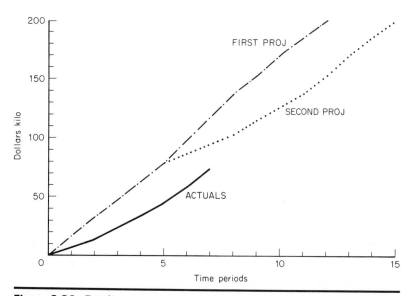

Figure 6-34 Baseline, current, and actual (cumulative) dollars versus time periods, Software.

7

VERTICAL MARKET COST ESTIMATING SYSTEMS

For the purpose of this book, a vertical market or single-purpose cost estimating system is defined as one in which the principal and perhaps even sole use of the microcomputer is for cost estimating. We will discuss two types of vertical market systems here: (1) a microcomputer system in which software and hardware are uniquely designed and sold to work together to the virtual exclusion of other brands or makes of software, and (2) estimating software packages that use all of the computer's capability either for cost estimating or for job costing in accompaniment with other conventional accounting functions such as general ledger, payroll, accounts receivable, accounts payable, sales order processing, purchase order processing, and inventory control.

Almost universally, the vertical market systems for cost estimating are more expensive than the single-purpose or multipurpose software packages discussed earlier (simple user-entered BASIC programs, spreadsheet programs, database systems, scheduling and estimating programs, and integrated software packages). These vertical market systems are, in general, easier for the novice to learn and use because they have been developed specifically for estimating. They require no programming, database structuring, or worksheet structuring skills; usually come with excellent documentation and examples for the specific discipline or profession being served; and are accompanied by varying degrees of quality of continuing support from the software (or hardware and software) supplier. Because they usually address a clientele that is narrower than that covered by generic software packages, and because they require more development effort, they usually cost much more than the other systems discussed previously. But because these vertical market systems can be specifically designed for a given field, profession, or trade, they can contain the specific nomenclature, data, structure, and techniques used in that trade and can fulfill the need for that trade more uniquely and satisfactorily than any other system. (One note about nomenclature: where the project scheduler program discussed in the previous chapter uses the term job as a subdivision of the total project, the systems in this chapter call the job the *total* project.)

Typical Integrated Hardware and Software Systems

Vertical market estimating systems in which microcomputer hardware, software, and continuing supplier support and training are provided with the system can cost from $10,000 to $20,000. If multiple terminals and a network connecting multiple systems are also needed, this figure can easily double. The price includes the computer or computers themselves; the software that runs the computers; complete sets of documentation, training manuals, and other literature; an array of printers; special forms; and technical assistance from the supplier in installing the system. Some integrated hardware and software systems can be leased from the supplier at a cost of 2 to 4 percent of the purchase cost depending on the total system cost and length of the lease.

A typical family of vertical market integrated hardware and software microcomputer estimating systems is marketed by Estimation, Incorporated, of Linthicum Heights, Maryland. Estimation markets two families of systems, one called CONTRACTOR I, and the other named BIDMASTER I. The microcomputer hardware sold with the system contains up to 1 megabyte (1 million bytes) of user memory and up to 20 megabytes of hard-disk storage. The various vertical market options provided with these systems support detailed estimating by mechanical, electrical, and construction contractors and ties in the estimating function with contract billing, inventory control, payroll, general accounting, word processing, time and material billing, job management, and price updating. With this system, the estimator can do "drawing takeoff" estimating using a unique count probe and linear probe, adjust the resulting estimates, and produce bid summaries.

Estimation, Inc.'s systems use two different keyboards, one especially configured for drawing takeoff estimating (shown in Figure 7-1) and a conventional typewriter-style keyboard for word processing and business accounting functions. Figures 7-2 and 7-3 show example templates for the unique estimating keyboard. In addition to pure estimating functions, these systems also perform some design functions that precede estimating such as heating and cooling load calculations for construction and even some premanufacturing jobs such as laying out heating and cooling duct patterns on sheet metal to allow rapid, accurate, and low-waste manufacture of ductwork.

Because of the high degree of sophistication available in this system as a result of maturity and extensive use in the construction marketplace, we will describe below some of the specific trades and job categories covered and some of the system features. As a typical vertical market system, it represents a small segment of the total estimating field of *all* work activities and work outputs. A description of these products will provide the reader with an overview of the things that are currently possible in vertical market microcomputer estimating systems.

The fields, trades, or disciplines in the area of construction estimating covered by Estimation Inc.'s systems are as follows:

1. Plumbing and heating
2. Heating, ventilation, and air conditioning
3. Fire protection

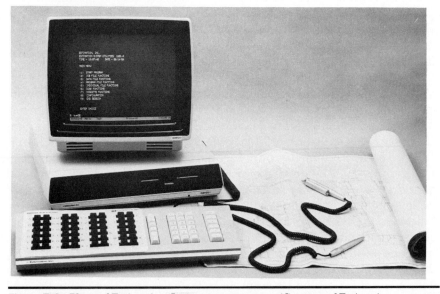

Figure 7-1 Photo of Estimation, Inc. computer system. (*Courtesy of Estimation, Inc., Linthicum Heights, Maryland.*)

4. General mechanical systems estimating
5. General electrical systems estimating
6. General construction estimating
7. Concrete and excavation estimating
8. Drywall partitions and ceilings estimating
9. Carpentry estimating
10. Masonry estimating
11. Roofing estimating
12. Specialty estimating

Estimation, Inc. offers a National Price Service that provides material price updates in selected disciplines twice each month (the company sends the user a computer magnetic floppy storage disk containing the most current prices). Printouts available from the systems include line item by line item printouts of material quantities, material costs, material adjustment factors, labor hours with labor adjustment factors, labor and material category breakdowns, and bid summaries. The systems provided by Estimation, Inc. provide more than the conventional estimating functions. The accompanying time and material billing program sends an

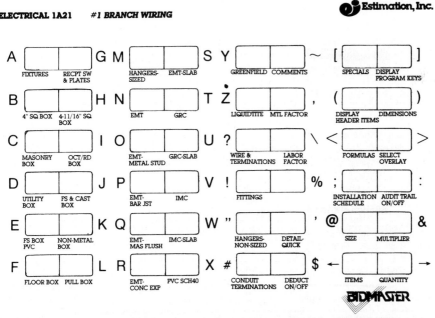

Figure 7-2 Keyboard template, Estimation, Inc. computer system, electrical 1A21 #1 branch wiring. (*Courtesy of Estimation, Inc., Linthicum Heights, Maryland.*)

itemized invoice to the customer of labor and material expended to date; the job management program shows the estimated hours and dollars required, expended, and remaining to date for each part of the job; the contract billing program automatically makes out invoices for completed jobs; the tool inventory program keeps track of expendable and nonexpendable tools and equipment with their present job location; the payroll program calculates and reports complete payroll information (pay rates; hours spent; taxable pay; federal, state, and local taxes; overtime; etc.); and the accounting package program provides income statements and balance sheets each month for the firm's operation. In this respect, the Estimation, Inc. packages perform many of the same functions provided by a vertical market job-cost system which is usually more fully integrated with an accounting (general ledger, payroll, accounts receivable, accounts payable) vertical market software package.

Design Programs That Input to Estimating and Manufacturing

With the recent introduction of several computer-aided design programs for microcomputers, the possibility of direct computer-performed mate-

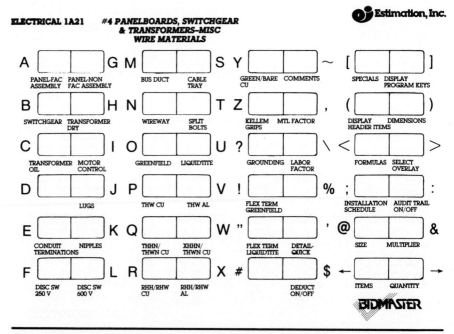

Figure 7-3 Keyboard template, Estimation, Inc. computer system, electrical 1A21 #4 panelboards, switchgear and transformers. (*Courtesy of Estimation, Inc., Linthicum Heights, Maryland.*)

rial quantity takeoff from drawings has become feasible (see Chapter 11, On to Higher and Better Uses). Although Estimation, Inc.'s programs do not go that far at this writing, they do provide several interesting features that tend to more closely integrate the design and estimating functions.

Heating and cooling load estimation   This program calculates heating and cooling loads according to the American Society of Heating, Refrigeration, and Air-conditioning Engineers (ASHRAE) standards for residential and commercial structures. Job characteristics, such as seasonal conditions and number of days and hours during which the structure is occupied, are specified as inputs; evaluation of optimal load reduction is performed by the system and partial loads are analyzed. Once the loads are calculated, the heating or cooling system can be sized and estimated.

Sheet metal material estimation   After drawing takeoff is completed for ductwork, the system calculates the required duct metal gauge and insulation, then prints a layout of blanks to be cut from each sheet of metal. The patterns for each section of duct (including elbows, tees, end caps, transition connectors, offset sections, etc.) are automatically positioned on the metal sheet to reduce scrap and waste. The system even goes so far as to produce a listing of the quantities and descriptions of all job materials, fitting accessories, types of joints, seams, and air-turning vanes and produces a printed, gummed, color-coded identification label to be attached to each sheet of metal as it is cut. A special optical projection system is available to permit scribing of the metal itself to exactly the right size prior to cutting and fabrication. Although the capabilities of this system go far beyond the estimating function, its existence proves that estimating systems can be tied to many of the more repetitive design and manufacturing functions performed in construction and other fields.

Drawing takeoff features   With increasing frequency, microcomputers are using peripheral input devices to speed the entry of data. Estimation, Inc.'s systems use a count probe and a linear probe to speed up the drawing takeoff process in construction estimating. It can be easily envisioned as to how this same technique could be used in estimating other types of work outputs and work activities. The Estimation, Inc. system's count probe is used to touch or mark the drawing or blueprint each time a specific type of component, valve, tee, elbow, etc. is encountered. After entry of a component name and cost, the count probe sends an impulse to the computer each time a component of like type is encountered. The linear probe, on the other hand, has a tiny wheel at its tip which measures distance along a duct, pipe, or wire on the drawing. After entry of the drawing's scale and the characteristic cross-section or size of the duct, pipe, or wire, the linear probe is traced along all linear components of the same type. The computer measures the distance, converts the distance to inches or feet, and computes the cost of the duct, pipe, or wire based on labor and material unit costs that have been entered previously.

One can see how such a vertical market, integrated hardware and software microcomputer system can dramatically speed up the estimating process and relieve drudgery. The real beauty of this and other systems that not only compute the estimate but store it for future modifications and updates is that the minor but inevitable changes that occur in cost estimates can be rapidly made without reinputting all of the data. The change in labor rate, scrap factors, material unit cost, or markup percentage can be easily accommodated with little effort by the estimator. In these updates, it is the computer that does all of the work.

The R.S. Means Company of Kingston, Massachusetts, also markets a vertical market quantity takeoff pricing system (primarily for construction) which uses a digitizer to extract material sizes and quantities directly from drawings. The system, called GALAXY, provides a digitizer integrated with the Means Unit Price Cost Files. For example, say you want to total and cost out all the windows in a 10-story building. First you put your drawing or blueprint on your digitizer. You then select the proper line item number from the Unit Prices Cost File and call it up on the computer. Using the cursor, you outline all the windows in the building, which will give you the total square footage of your window system. The cursor lets you know if you have already included an item and will not count it a second time. When you have taken off the windows, you press a button on the cursor and the total area, the unit price, and the total cost of the window system are automatically computed.

GALAXY can be used with your own cost data or as an enhancement to the Unit Prices Cost File of the Means General Estimating Program and the Square Foot Estimating Program. This same routine can be used for any of the programs. At this writing, other such vertical market estimating systems are being developed or considered for development, and you can expect to see many more work activities and work outputs covered by vertical market estimating systems in the near future.

Vertical Market Software-Only Estimating Systems

Some microcomputer cost estimating applications packages can run on a fairly large number of different computers and do not require their own computer hardware configuration as does the one described in the previous section of this chapter. These software packages often use a significant portion of the microcomputer's memory and storage capacity; require special input or output devices such as microphones, digitizers, printers, or plotters; or are designed for dedicated use of a computer for estimating. These software products are primarily cost estimating systems and are not designed to interface with other accounting elements as are job cost systems which will be discussed later.

Several companies market excellent "stand-alone" vertical market cost estimating software packages that go by different names but have essentially the same features.

Name of software product	*Company and location*
Best Bid	Concord Management Systems, Inc. Greenbelt, Maryland
Cost Plus	Construction Software Systems, Inc. Arlington, Virginia
Data Base/Assembly Estimating CMIS	Construction Data Control, Inc. Norcross, Georgia
ESPRI, Easy Est	Contractors Management Systems Reston, Virginia

These systems have been marketed and used primarily for construction estimating but have sufficient flexibility to be used to estimate the costs of many other work activities or work outputs.

They are based on a database of up to 16,000 items that is purchased or input by the user. The types of work activities and work outputs that can be estimated with these systems depends, of course, on the types of items that are put into the database. For this example we are using construction data items to support construction estimating.

These systems permit the generation of up to 250 assemblies, which are composite labor and material work packages or work elements consisting of up to 20 items (from the database) each. For example, an interior partition assembly could consist of metal studs, metal track, drywall segments, painting, and rubber base molding. These five items are included in an assembly to make it easier and faster to compute interior partition wall labor and material costs by merely taking off the number of linear plan feet of interior partition. An assembly in a nonconstruction activity would be, for example, the research, writing, editing, typing, proofreading, and illustration artwork required for a page of documentation in a technical manual. The page unit costs would be the assembly costs while the typing costs would be an item cost.

Items are cataloged into divisions and subdivisions. There can be up to 16 divisions per job; 10 subdivisions per division; and 100 items per subdivision in the database (16,000 items). The estimator can select from nine cost classes (variously called cost types, cost codes, or cost elements) to permit costs to be categorized into labor, materials, subcontracts, etc. in the final printout reports.

The systems permit designation of up to 100 locations (first floor, second floor, etc.), and global cost adjustment factors can be applied to each or any of the 250 assemblies. Up to 20 different formulas can be used to compute unit quantities and costs. Several of the systems permit input by voice and/or a digitizer to speed up the estimating process. The digitizer works on sonic principles and measures the perimeter of an area, the length of the wall, or the square feet enclosed in an area, and permits the computation of material quantities for complex shapes. The voice input feature permits hands-free operation of the computer. The voice feature is very useful when handling and measuring drawings during the drawing takeoff process used in construction estimating.

The vertical market software-only cost estimating programs are cost-effective because they can be used on an existing microcomputer with little or no purchase of additional hardware. Programmers are not needed to build, modify, or add items to an assembly. Many different preset assemblies can be developed to be used repetitively during the estimating process, and these assemblies can be tailored to fit the specific work activity or work output being estimated at the time it is being estimated. (An item may be easily replaced if the preassigned item does not meet the specifications for the job, and an individual item's quantity within an assembly may be changed from the preestablished assembly quantity.) Since each assembly and/or item within an assembly can be changed during the estimating process, the user has a virtually unlimited number of combinations of assemblies and items. Divisions, subdivisions, and items in the estimating database can all be reviewed on the computer's screen during the estimating process.

All of the systems investigated in this category of software will produce a bill of materials or an item listing that can be used in ordering parts, raw materials, and subcontract work. This development of purchase order information is the time-consuming part of an estimate which the systems minimize. Each item can be factored or adjusted to allow for scrap or waste in keeping with the expected actual scrap, waste, or cost adjustment required for that particular item. This factor can vary between items, assemblies, and estimates. It is not necessary to start from scratch in setting up assemblies each time a job is estimated. Base or typical assemblies may be set up which represent the majority of the work produced by the firm. Then, as estimates are developed, the items to be included in the assemblies can be changed if needed. In closely repetitive work, the estimates for the bulk of the assemblies for each job will already be built and will require little or no modification. As the estimate is produced, a location can be specified for each assembly (i.e., floors, pages, volumes, or phases) and a bill of materials and labor report can be obtained by location. The systems also provide a useful feature of setting up various crews with a given skill or labor mix. A report with the number of crew hours needed by trade is generated and can be adjusted as needed.

All of the systems described here allow the estimate to be built in steps or increments, and it is not necessary to complete the estimate at one sitting. Information is stored on the computer's disk as it is entered, and the estimator can stop at any time and resume the estimating later in the day or week. Several estimates can be in process at one time; the number is only limited to the computer's disk space and to the estimator's ability to mentally adapt to the process of simultaneously developing multiple estimates. Several estimators could be using the same microcomputer alternatively since each job has a name and designation unique to that job.

The Item Database

Normally, a company using the vertical market type of estimating system discussed here will develop their own database while developing their own initial estimates. These data will be gleaned from historical information, current catalogs and price lists, and direct quotes and will be tailored to the company's own work output or work activity. It is possible, however, to purchase or acquire existing databases from the computer software firms servicing like companies in the same industry as a starting point to building your company's own database. As pointed out in earlier chapters, however, this practice should be relied on only initially since it is dangerous to continually use someone else's database to estimate work that your company is going to perform. This practice can lead to a lack of competitive posture in estimating and can harm the realism and credibility of your estimates in the long run.

Screen Display of the Estimating Process

The on-screen displays of these specialized cost estimating software packages are user-friendly and easy to read and understand. The user can list all of the projects or jobs being estimated, view and update the contents of any selected assembly view and update the labor and materials unit quantities and unit prices for any of the up to 16,000 items; copy, erase, or create assemblies or items; and print out a wide variety of estimate reports. The present date is always displayed on the master menu screen and is printed out on all reports produced. This small feature of adding the present date to all major screen displays and outputs is not only desirable but is a must when multiple estimates are being produced. (Nothing is more irritating, confusing, and inefficient than having copies of two updated estimates and not knowing which one is the latest.) The main menu screen also includes the name and "hot-line" telephone number of the software company that sold you the system—a place you can call when or if you run into trouble.

Printed Reports

Five types of printed reports are available: a Unit Cost Report, Division and Subdivision Report, Location Report, Assembly Report, Column Report, and Class Totals Report. The Unit Cost Report lists each item number, description, quantity, unit cost (includes labor, material, and other factored costs such as taxes, overhead, burden, etc.) and total cost. This report gives an "at-a-glance" look at the items that make up the estimate and how that item contributes to the total job cost. The Division and Subdivision Report is a WES breakdown of the items in the total job. This report categorizes the job elements or items into appropriate subdivisions and divisions of work and provides a three-level WES breakout of the costs of the items, subdivisions, and divisions of work. The Location Report sorts out the items by location; and the Assembly Report likewise subdivides the costs into the precontrived assemblies. The Column Report and Class Totals Report break out the cost categories or cost elements (re: material, labor, subcontracts, equipment, etc.) in two different ways. The Column Report lists the cost elements across the top of the page and each column shows the cost element value for each item. The Class Totals Report shows the class or cost element number, description, cost, taxes, markup, overhead, and total cost for each class or cost element.

The specialized cost estimating vertical software package has obvious desirable attributes when it comes to quickly and easily repricing old estimates to accommodate the lag time between the estimating process and actual contract award; updating an estimate with the latest prices; varying the location of work from one place to another by appropriately changing labor rates; and changing the pricing from fixed-price bid to negotiated procurement pricing. Once the initial estimate is prepared, these changes can be made rapidly and accurately in order to meet changing bid or proposal conditions and to outmaneuver the competition. As is the case of most microcomputer estimating systems, the most dramatic benefits come when last-minute additions, updates, deletions, and modifications must be made to accommodate specification changes, schedule slips or extensions, labor pool availability, or material price quotes.

The R.S. Means Company of Kingston, Massachusetts, has a General Estimating Program which is a software program for construction estimating. The program can work on any of the Means Unit Prices Files or on the user's own cost files.

With the Means General Estimating Program you can develop estimating reports for an entire project or any division of the Uniform Construction Index (UCI) format. You can use both your own cost data and crews or the crew data and cost information obtained from Means files. You can override any of the components of a detailed estimate such as crew, productivity, or any of the prices displayed with your own cost data. You can create and update a job file, print any or all of the eight different reports that are available—either bare costs or burdened costs—division-by-division, total job costs, or by division summary. For use in conjunction with the Means General Estimating Program, Unit Prices Cost Files contain the unit prices and productivity factors found in the Means publications: *Building Construction Cost Data, Mechanical and Electrical Cost Data, Repair and Remodeling Cost Data, Residential/ Light Commercial Cost Data,* and *Site Work Cost Data.*

The files give you access to unit prices for work hours, minimum charges, retrofit, remove and reset, interior demolition, masonry, restoration, and mobilization. Use of the Unit Prices Cost Files is an annual subscription service. Each year you receive the up-to-date construction costs for any one of the cost files. Means also has a "square-foot" building construction estimating program supported by square-foot cost files that are updated each year.

A Selected Job Costing System

Job costing systems represent the link between the cost estimating function and the accounting function. There are a wide variety of job costing applications packages on the market and they vary considerably in the degree of estimating they perform. Some are capable of estimating costs from unit price, unit quantity, and productivity data, while others are no more than cost-tracking systems designed to interface with the conventional accounting functions of payroll, accounts receivable, accounts payable, general ledger, and sometimes inventory control. Since this is a book about cost estimating (rather than accounting) with microcomputers, we will address the cost estimating functions of the job costing systems and their capability of tracking actual costs against estimates. In some job costing systems, the estimate is merely an estimated dollar figure inserted by the user for each item. These systems do not help the user develop the estimated number; they merely record this number and it is used as a target or baseline. Actual costs are then recorded and subtracted from the estimated value to arrive at a remaining cost to complete.

In this section we will describe and discuss a job costing system that does some amount of cost estimating, yet provides an interface to the accounting system to permit the recording of actual costs incurred and to allow other accounting functions to be completed such as invoicing and purchasing payments. The system we will discuss is called MICA/JC and is produced by Micro Associates of Port Arthur, Texas. Unlike some other job cost systems, the MICA Job Cost System provides a useful time-oriented schedule report that produces a bar chart showing time sequencing of the various elements of the job. Some of the most useful output reports for the cost estimator are an abbreviated and detailed Job Cost Estimate, an abbreviated and detailed Job Cost Analysis, a Job Profitability Report, and the Job Schedule Report mentioned above.

System Hierarchy

The MICA/JC job cost system has a hierarchical menu structure that makes it easy to operate the system. Each screen display has a code number that permits easy reference back to the well-written operator's manual. [The screen display code numbers are in the form (1-1).] To give you an idea of the depth of the menu structure and the interrelationship of the various screens, the menu structure showing the screen display code numbers is shown below:

```
Job Cost Program (Main Menu) (1-1)
   01. Job File Maintenance (2-2)
        1. Add a Job (2-3)
        2. Edit a Job (2-21)
        3. Delete a Job (2-27)
        4. Display Job Listing (2-29)
        5. Job Status Inquiry and Update (3-1)
        6. Job Cost Reports (6-2)
        7. Transaction Entry (4-2)
        8. Invoice Printing (7-2)
        9. Return to Main Menu (1-1)
   02. Job Status Inquiry and Update (3-1)
        1. Display Job Status (3-2)
        2. Update Job Status (3-4)
        3. Job Close-Out (3-7)
        4. Job Listing (2-29)
        5. Job File Maintenance (2-2)
        6. Transaction Entry (4-2)
        7. Job Reports (6-2)
        8. Return to Main Menu (1-1)
   03. Transactions Entry and Edit (4-2)
        1. Enter/Edit Transactions (4-3)
        2. Print Transaction Proof (4-8)
        3. Post Transaction (5-2)
        4. Job File Maintenance (2-2)
        5. Job Status (3-1)
        6. Return to Main Menu (1-1)
   04. Transaction Posting (5-2)
   05. Job Reports (6-2)
        01. Master Job List (Short) (6-3)
        02. Master Job List (Long) (6-3)
        03. Component Listing (Short) (6-4)
        04. Job Component Listing (Long) (6-4)
```

```
05. Job Cost Estimate (Short) (6-5)
06. Job Cost Estimate (Long) (6-5)
07. Job Cost Analysis (Short) (6-6)
08. Job Cost Analysis (Long) (6-7)
09. Job Schedule (Short) (6-7)
10. Job Schedule (Long) (6-7)
11. Billing Report (6-8)
12. Job Profitability Report (6-8)
13. Job Cost Transaction Ledger (6-9)
06. Invoice Printing and Accounts Receivable Posting (7-2)
07. End of Period Close and General Ledger Posting (8-4)
08. Overall Job File Status (9-1)
09. Job Cost Parameter Maintenance (10-2)
1. Specify General Job Code Parameters (10-3)
2. Standard Component Table Maintenance (10-10)
3. General Ledger Account Code Maintenance (10-15)
4. Initialize Data Files (10-19)
5. Expand Data Files (10-20)
6. Return to Main Menu (1-1)
10. End Program Execution (Returns to Operating System)
```

Developing a Database

One of the first steps in establishing a cost estimate with this system is to develop and enter a listing of standard components. Screens (10-13) and (10-11) in Figure 7-4 show how this is done. Screen (10-13) gives a listing of components that have already been entered. Note that component numbers, descriptions, types, units of measure, cost codes, unit costs, billing basis, and general ledger codes and accounts are provided for each standard component. Also note that the standard component numbering system can be used to create what is equivalent to the assemblies in the previously described estimating system. For example, the foundation (labor, bricks, concrete, and equipment) are coded 121 through 124. This coding, coupled with the type, can be used later to report the cost of the assemblies only if desired. The bottom half of Figure 7-4, screen (10-11) shows the entry form for new components. Three types of components are permitted: (1) master components, which are essentially title categories for assemblies that contain the group of subcomponents which follow in numerical sequence; (2) subcomponents (items), which are associated directly with a master component or assembly; and (3) discrete components, which are items not associated with any master component. The system provides for four different types of billing: (1) not billed, (2) contract billed, (3) markup on cost, and (4) unit priced. Note that the type of billing for each component is specified.

Developing an Estimate

To construct a job cost estimate, general job parameters (title, address, contract number, etc.) are entered and the components that make up the job are selected and entered. Figure 7-5 shows the display screen that is filled out for each job. The top part of the figure shows the screen as it

```
J/C PARAMETER MAINTENANCE      DATE: 10/16/85      STD COMPONENT LISTING  10-13
DISPLAY OPTIONS:  A dvance 25   B ackup 25   H old screen   F1  return to Menu
===============================================================================
                                      COST   COST/   ---BILLING---    ----G/L----
COMP  DESCRIPTION       TYPE UoM   CODE   UNIT    BASIS  AMOUNT    CODE   ACCT
===============================================================================
 100  SITE PREP          M
 101     LABOR           S   HR      1    10.500    M     2.000     46   670010
 102     EQUIPMENT       S   HR      3    50.000    U    75.000     55   721010
 110  EXCAVATION         D   EA      4   750.000    U   975.000     64   800010
 120  FOUNDATION         M
 121     LABOR           S   HR      1     9.500    M     2.000     46   670010
 122     BRICKS          S   EA      2     1.500    U     2.000     19   601010
 123     CONCRETE        S   YD      2    32.000    U    50.000     19   601010
 124     EQUIPMENT       S   HR      3    35.000    U    45.000     55   721010
 130  PAVING             D   EA      4  1200.000    U  1400.000     64   800010
 200  FRAMING            M
 201     LABOR           S   HR      1    11.250    M     2.000     46   670010
 202     RAW MATERIALS   S   LF      2     2.350    U     3.500     19   601010
 203     FINISHED MAT'LS S   EA      2    25.000    U    30.000     19   601010


SCANNING COMPONENT: 204
```

```
J/C PARAMETER MAINTENANCE      DATE: 10/16/85   ENTER/EDIT COMPONENT DATA  10-11


Component Number.............. 0

Description..................
Component Type (M,S,D).......
Unit of Measure..............
Cost Code (0-9)..............
Cost per Unit (estimated $)...
Billing Basis (N,C,M,U).......
Markup or Unit Price.........
G/L Acct Code for Cost.......

ENTER  STD COMPONENT NUMBER       < >  PREV/NEXT      PRESS  F2  TO PROCESS
```

Figure 7-4 Component listing screen and component input screen.

```
JOB FILE MAINTENANCE          DATE: 10/16/85        ADD NEW JOB TO FILE  2-3

                                           JOBS ON FILE:      7 of     10

Job Number.........              Job Type (0-9).........
Job Title..........              Inv. Basis (C;O)....... C
Address............              Acctg Basis (C,P)...... C
City, State  Zip...              Retainage (##.##)% ....    0.00
Contract Number.....             Est. Start Date........
Customer Number.....             Est. Compl Date........
Customer Name.......             Act. Start Date........
Job Manager.........             Act. Compl Date........
G/L Code for Sales.. 240         Act. % Compl...........    0.00
-----------------------------------------------------------------------------
Initial Cost Estimate ($)...      0.00   Initial Contract ($)...      0.00
Revised Cost Estimate ($)...      0.00   Revised Contract ($)...      0.00
-----------------------------------------------------------------------------
                    Current Period      Year-to-Date      Accumulated
                    ==============      ============      ===========
Actual Job Cost ($).....     0.00           0.00              0.00
Total Billed ($)........     0.00           0.00              0.00
Retainage ($)...........     N/A            N/A               0.00

  INPUT DATA     ARROWS  MOVE CURSOR    F2  RECORD DATA    F1  ABORT ROUTINE
```

```
JOB FILE MAINTENANCE          DATE: 10/16/85          EDIT JOB DATA   2-21


Job Number......... 1            Job Type (0-9)......... 3
Job Title.......... PARK CENTRAL OFFICE BLDG   Inv. Basis (C,O)....... C
Address............ 2020 ORANGE AVE            Acctg Basis (C,P)...... C
City, State  Zip... ALTOONA, IA   55566        Retainage (##.##)% ....   10.00
Contract Number..... 84-001      Est. Start Date........ 020184
Customer Number..... 1           Est. Compl Date........ 071584
Customer Name....... JONES BROS. INVESTMENTS   Act. Start Date........ 020784
Job Manager......... JKO         Act. Compl Date........ 000000
G/L Code for Sales.. 14   501030 Act. % Compl...........   45.58
-----------------------------------------------------------------------------
Initial Cost Estimate ($)...  120787.50  Initial Contract ($)...  145000.00
Revised Cost Estimate ($)...  121037.50  Revised Contract ($)...  145300.00
-----------------------------------------------------------------------------
                    Current Period      Year-to-Date      Accumulated
                    ==============      ============      ===========
Actual Job Cost ($).....  22648.08       54609.52         54609.52
Total Billed ($)........  12345.00       38257.49         38257.49
Retainage ($)...........    N/A           N/A              3825.75

SPECIFY  JOB NUMBER     <  PREV   >  NEXT    PRESS  F2  TO PROCESS
```

Figure 7-5 Adding or editing a job.

appears before the job information has been added and the bottom half of the figure shows how a typical input screen might appear after all required entries have been made. Components that belong to the job can either be entered individually or duplicated from another estimate. A typical component input screen is shown on Figure 7-6. Once all the components are entered, an estimate report for the job can be generated.

Output Reports

Figure 7-7 shows an abbreviated job cost estimate report for all jobs currently in the system. If the transactions entered during the job performance result in changes in the estimated or actual component unit costs or quantities, the revised estimated cost will be automatically produced as shown on this figure. Figure 7-8 shows a detailed job cost estimate for job 1. Note that labor and materials or equipment are listed vertically along the left column as separate components rather than on a single row as was the case with the estimating system described earlier in this chapter. This is the only principal difference between the two formats and does not represent a difficulty if you become used to operating with either system.

Provided that actual costs and estimated percent complete values are entered accurately and regularly, the system can produce an accurate abbreviated or detailed job cost analysis report (see Figures 7-9 and 7-10). The detailed job cost analysis report is particularly useful because it shows which components are responsible for the variation of actual job costs from estimated costs. As can be seen from the menu hierarchy, a number of other useful reports are available from the system. Abbreviated or detailed master listing of jobs, job component listings, or bar chart–type job reports can be selected for printout. A billing report, job profitability report, and a job cost transaction ledger report are also available. As in the case with all good cost estimating systems, all screens and printouts contain the current date, which makes it easy to tell if you have the latest figures.

Invoice Generation

Since this job cost system is an integral part of the accounting system, various accounting functions that are associated with the continued progress of the work are made easy. For example, invoices can be generated to obtain progress payments as the work proceeds. Figure 7-11, screen (702), shows how the invoice printing and accounts receivable posting displays appear on the screen for a sample billing situation. Figure 7-12 shows a typical invoice printout, and Figure 7-13 provides optional details that can accompany the invoice. At the same time the invoice is generated,

```
JOB FILE MAINTENANCE        DATE: 10/16/85        ADD JOB COMPONENTS  2-13

                                            COMP. ON FILE:   72 of   100

Job Number.............. 8        Job Title......
================================================================================
Component Number........
Description.............
Component Type (M,S,D)...
Unit of Measure.........      G/L Acct Code for Cost..
Cost Code (0-9)..........     Est. Days to Start......
Estimated Cost/Unit......     Est. Days Required......
Billing Basis (N,C,M,U)..     Actual % Complete......
Markup or Unit Price.....     Date of Status Entry....
--------------------------------------------------------------------------------
           Initial Est  Revised Est   Current    Year-to-Date  Accumulated
           ===========  ===========  ===========  ============  ===========
Qty Units....
Cost ($).....



  INPUT DATA    ARROWS  MOVE CURSOR    F2  RECORD DATA    F1  ABORT ROUTINE
```

```
JOB FILE MAINTENANCE        DATE: 10/16/85        EDIT COMPONENT DATA  2-23


Job Number.............. 1        Job Title...... PARK
================================================================================
Component Number........ 110
Description............. EXCAVATION
Component Type (M,S,D)... D  Discrete comp
Unit of Measure......... CY        G/L Acct Code for Cost.. 66     800030
Cost Code (0-9).......... 4  SUBCONTRACT  Est. Days to Start...... 20
Estimated Cost/Unit...... 5            Est. Days Required...... 5
Billing Basis (N,C,M,U).. U  Unit priced  Actual % Complete....... 100
Markup or Unit Price..... 6            Date of Status Entry.... 030584
--------------------------------------------------------------------------------
           Initial Est  Revised Est   Current    Year-to-Date  Accumulated
           ===========  ===========  ===========  ============  ===========
Qty Units....   2000.00     2000.00      0.00      2040.00      2040.00
Cost ($).....  10000.00    10000.00      0.00     10150.00     10150.00



SPECIFY  COMPONENT NUMBER      <  PREV    >  NEXT    PRESS  F2  TO PROCESS
```

Figure 7-6 Adding job components and editing component data.

the accounts receivable and general ledgers are automatically updated. Each time an expenditure is made on the project, the appropriate accounting function comes into play, and not only is the estimate-to-complete figure and percentage updated but the appropriate bookkeeping functions are performed as well.

At last count, we had records of approximately 40 job costing systems that are available for a wide variety of microcomputer systems. The MICA/JC system is an example of an excellent job cost system that will provide both the estimator and the accountant with the functions needed to effectively and efficiently do the cost estimating and cost tracking functions.

Some Other Types of Job Costing Systems

There are a few other types of job costing systems that bear mentioning here because of their genetic nature and some unique features that are available. Software Solutions of Scotts Valley, California, has a job costing and tracking system that stresses user-defined inputs and outputs. Their system has up to 10 labor files and up to 10 material files and each can contain up to 1000 items. The system permits user-defined overhead rates for each of the 10 labor categories, user-defined escalation rates for up to 20 categories, and a user-defined printout. Instead of preconfigured output reports, the user specifies which data to print by specifying column headings. In this respect the system is somewhat like database estimating (see Chapter 5) with somewhat improved user friendliness.

```
                        AJAX CONSTRUCTION COMPANY

                    JOB COST ESTIMATE ABBREVIATED                      DATE: 10/16/85
                    ================================                   PAGE: 1

========================================================================================================
JOB                                         JOB        -------ESTIMATED COST------- --EST. DATE OF--
NO.  JOB TITLE          CUSTOMER NAME    CONTRACT  MNGR JOB TYPE   INITIAL    REVISED    START   COMPL
========================================================================================================
 1   PARK CENTRAL OFFICE BLDG  JONES BROS. INVESTMENTS 84-001  JKO  COMMERCIAL  :20,787.50  121,037.50  02/01/84  02/07/84

 2   2ND STORY ADD ON   JOHN HARGRAVE     34-002   DDR  REMODELING  26,177.25   26,272.25  03/01/84  03/01/84

 3   PAINT BROWNS ELEM. SCHOOL FT. DODGE SCHOOL DISTRIC 84-901  JKO  PAINTING    17,495.00   17,495.00  02/20/84  02/20/84

 4   SUBCONTR TO WILSON CONSTR WILSON CONTRUCTION CO.  84-501  LLG  SUBCONTRCT  32,296.00   32,296.00  03/15/84  00/00/00

 5   RE-ROOF TOWN HALL  CITY OF FT. DODGE  34-005   JKO  ROOFING    :9,741.50   :9,741.50  03/15/84  03/18/84

 6   SUBCONTR TO REX LUMBER  REX LUMBER INC.  34-550  LLG  SUBCONTRCT  10,750.00   :1,800.00  01/15/84  01/15/84

 7   RE-ROOF MIDDLETOWN SCHOOL DES MOINES SCHOOL DISTR. 84-010  DDR  ROOFING    3,350.00    8,925.00  11/15/83  11/30/83
========================================================================================================
TOTAL FOR ALL JOBS LISTED:                                      236,597.25  237,567.25
```

Figure 7-7 Job cost estimate printout.

REPORT CHARACTERISTICS:

First Job Number to be reported................................. :
Last Job Number to be reported.................................. :

----------COST CODES----------
) - UNSPECIFIED   5 - MISC.
1 - LABOR   6 - OVERHEAD
2 - MATERIALS   7 - COST TYPE 7
3 - EQUIPMENT   8 - COST TYPE 8
4 - SUBCONTRACT   9 - COST TYPE 9

==

JOB NUMBER: 1
JOB TITLE: PARK CENTRAL OFFICE BLDG
CONTRACT: 84-001
CUSTOMER: JONES BROS. INVESTMENTS
JOB MNGR: JKO
JOB TYPE: COMMERCIAL
EST START: 02/01/84
EST COMPL: 07/15/84

COMP NO.	DESCRIPTION	UoM	BILLG BASIS	COST CODE	ESTIMATED COST/UNIT	QUANTITY UNITS INITIAL	QUANTITY UNITS REVISED	ESTIMATED COST INITIAL	ESTIMATED COST REVISED	EST DAYS TO START	EST DAYS TO COMPL
100	SITE PREP										
101	LABOR	HR	M	1	10.500	250.00	250.00	2,625.00	2,625.00	3	14
102	EQUIPMENT	HR	U	3	50.000	40.00	45.00	2,000.00	2,250.00	3	14
110	EXCAVATION	CY	U	4	5.000	2,000.00	2,000.00	10,000.00	10,000.00	20	5
120	FOUNDATION										
121	LABOR	HR	M	1	9.500	410.00	410.00	3,895.00	3,895.00	25	17
122	BRICKS	EA	U	2	1.500	1,200.00	1,200.00	1,800.00	1,800.00	25	17
123	CONCRETE	YD	U	2	32.000	50.00	50.00	1,600.00	1,600.00	25	17
124	EQUIPMENT	HR	U	3	35.000	25.00	25.00	875.00	875.00	25	17
200	FRAMING										
201	LABOR	HR	M	1	11.250	950.00	950.00	10,687.50	10,687.50	50	28
202	RAW MATERIALS	LF	U	2	2.350	8,600.00	8,600.00	20,210.00	20,210.00	50	28
300	SIDING & INSUL.										
301	LABOR	HR	M	1	8.500	640.00	640.00	5,440.00	5,440.00	70	20
302	SIDING MAT'L	SF	U	2	2.750	2,200.00	2,200.00	6,050.00	6,050.00	70	20
303	INSUL MATERIAL	SF	M	2	0.250	3,350.00	3,350.00	837.50	837.50	70	20
400	ROOFING	SF	U	4	3.400	4,500.00	4,500.00	15,300.00	15,300.00	95	21
500	MASONRY										
501	LABOR	HR	M	1	10.500	385.00	385.00	4,042.50	4,042.50	80	24
502	BRICKS & MAT'L	EA	U	2	0.200	7,000.00	7,000.00	1,400.00	1,400.00	80	24
503	EQUIPMENT	HR	U	3	20.000	200.00	200.00	4,000.00	4,000.00	80	24
600	FINISHING	HR	M	4	15.000	750.00	750.00	11,250.00	11,250.00	90	35
700	PLUMBING	HR	U	4	22.500	235.00	235.00	5,287.50	5,287.50	27	38
800	ELECTRICAL	HR	U	4	26.500	385.00	385.00	10,202.50	10,202.50	70	12
995	FICA	NA	N	6	0.000	0.00	0.00	1,870.00	1,870.00	0	0
996	SUTA	NA		6	0.000	0.00	0.00	1,150.00	1,150.00	0	0
997	FUTA	NA	N	6	0.000	0.00	0.00	185.00	185.00	0	0
998	WORKER'S COMP	NA	N	6	0.000	0.00	0.00	80.00	80.00	0	0

TOTALS BY COST CODE:

						QUANTITY INITIAL	QUANTITY REVISED	COST INITIAL	COST REVISED		
	LABOR					3,635.00	3,635.00	26,690.00	26,690.00		
	MATERIALS					22,400.00	22,400.00	31,897.50	31,897.50		
	EQUIPMENT					265.00	270.00	6,875.00	7,125.00		
	SUBCONTRACT					7,870.00	7,870.00	52,040.00	52,040.00		
	OVERHEAD					0.00	0.00	3,285.00	3,285.00		

TOTALS FOR JOB: 120,787.50   121,037.50

Figure 7-8 Detailed job cost estimate report. (*Courtesy of Micro Associates, Inc.,*
Port Arthur, Texas.)

Features that do not appear in some other job cost systems include a special screen format, file, and output report for travel costs; automatic factoring or calculation of a cost as a factor or percentage of another cost or group of costs; provision for including facilities capital cost of money (defense contractors may find this feature especially helpful); and escalation or inflation compounding rates. The escalation-inflation compounding rates range from daily to annually and can be assigned to each cost file and cost element (labor type, material type, travel, and miscellaneous other direct costs). The separate cost tracking feature allows entry of actual cost data, viewing the current status of the job costs, printing of the costs each time they are entered and computation and printout of costs to complete.

Software Resources Center, Inc., of Boulder, Colorado, has a microcomputer cost estimating software package called Summit which has many of the features of the above package but is integrated with a pure job costing and accounting system and it provides other features like: (1) a quote expiration report that provides a list of all quotes that will expire by a specified date and (2) four full levels of detailed breakout made possible by the coding system. Open Systems, Inc., of Minneapolis, Minnesota, has a job cost system that integrates closely with its overall financial management software package.

In our view, at this writing the software industry still has not come up with a truly generic vertical market cost estimating package that does all of the things cost estimators need to do and that takes full advantage of the large storage capacities, increasing random access memory, high

AJAX CONSTRUCTION COMPANY

JOB COST ANALYSIS ABBREVIATED

DATE: 10/16/85
PAGE: 1

JOB NO.	JOB TITLE	CONTRACT	JOB MGR	ACTG. BASIS	ESTIMATED COST	ACCUMULATED COST	% OF EST.	ACT % COMPL	PROJ COST TO COMPLETE	PROJ TOTAL COST	PROJ VARIANCE FROM ESTIMATE
1	PARK CENTRAL OFFICE BLDG	84-001	JKO	C	121,037.50	54,609.52	45.1	45.6	65,201.10	119,810.62	-1,226.88
2	2ND STORY ADD ON	84-002	DDR	P	26,272.25	13,383.15	50.9	48.4	14,239.97	27,623.12	1,350.87
3	PAINT BROWNS ELEM. SCHOOL	84-901	JKO	P	17,495.00	11,171.00	63.9	61.9	6,869.56	18,040.56	545.56
4	SUBCONTR TO WILSON CONSTR	84-501	LLG	C	32,296.00	0.00	0.0	0.0	32,296.00	32,296.00	0.00
5	RE-ROOF TOWN HALL	84-005	JKO	C	19,741.50	10,369.50	52.5	56.3	8,041.26	18,410.76	-1,330.74
6	SUBCONTR TO REX LUMBER	84-550	LLG	C	11,800.00	10,865.00	92.1	100.0	0.00	10,865.00	-935.00
7	RE-ROOF MIDDLETOWN SCHOOL	84-010	DDR	C	8,925.00	9,200.00	103.1	100.0	0.00	9,200.00	275.00
	TOTAL FOR ALL JOBS LISTED:				237,567.25	109,598.17	46.1	46.4	126,647.89	236,246.06	-1,321.19

Figure 7-9 Job cost analysis printout. (*Courtesy of Micro Associates, Inc., Port Arthur, Texas.*)

AJAX CONSTRUCTION COMPANY

JOB COST ANALYSIS DETAILED
=============================

REPORT CHARACTERISTICS:

First Job Number to be reported.................................. :
Last Job Number to be reported.................................. :

------------COST CODES------------
0 - UNSPECIFIED   5 - MISC.
1 - LABOR   6 - OVERHEAD
2 - MATERIALS   7 - COST TYPE 7
3 - EQUIPMENT   8 - COST TYPE 8
4 - SUBCONTRACT   9 - COST TYPE 9
===

JOB NUMBER: 1
JOB TITLE: PARK CENTRAL OFFICE BLDG
CONTRACT: 84-001
CUSTOMER: JONES BROS. INVESTMENTS
JOB MNGR: JKO
JOB TYPE: COMMERCIAL
EST START: 02/01/84
EST COMPL: 07/15/84

COMP NO.	DESCRIPTION	UoM	COST CODE	EST. UNITS	ACCUM. UNITS	EST% UNTS	ACT% COMPL	PROJ UNITS TO COMPL	EST. COST	ACCUM. COST	EST% COST	PROJ COST TO COMPL	PROJ TOTAL COST	PROJ VAR. FROM EST.
100	SITE PREP													
101	LABOR	HR	1	250	245	98.0	100.0	0	2625.00	2550.00	97.1	0.00	2550.00	-75.00
102	EQUIPMENT	HR	3	45	40	88.9	100.0	0	2250.00	2195.00	97.6	0.00	2195.00	-55.00
110	EXCAVATION	CY	4	2000	2040	102.0	100.0	0	10000.00	10150.00	101.5	0.00	10150.00	150.00
120	FOUNDATION													
121	LABOR	HR	1	410	415	101.2	100.0	0	3895.00	3950.00	101.4	0.00	3950.00	55.00
122	BRICKS	EA	2	1200	1190	99.2	100.0	0	1800.00	1740.00	96.7	0.00	1740.00	-60.00
123	CONCRETE	YD	2	50	48	96.0	100.0	0	1600.00	1550.00	96.9	0.00	1550.00	-50.00
124	EQUIPMENT	HR	3	25	25	100.0	100.0	0	875.00	865.00	98.9	0.00	865.00	-10.00
200	FRAMING													
201	LABOR	HR	1	950	393	41.4	38.0	641	10687.50	3840.10	35.9	6265.43	10105.53	-581.97
202	RAW MATERIALS	LF	2	8600	8450	98.3	100.0	0	20210.00	19587.54	96.9	0.00	19587.54	-622.46
300	SIDING & INSUL.													
301	LABOR	HR	1	640	0	0.0	0.0	640	5440.00	0.00	0.0	5440.00	5440.00	0.00
302	SIDING MAT'L	SF	2	2200	2200	100.0	100.0	0	6050.00	5935.75	98.1	0.00	5935.75	-114.25
303	INSUL MATERIAL	SF	2	3350	3350	100.0	100.0	0	837.50	974.30	116.3	0.00	974.30	136.80
400	ROOFING	SF	4	4500	0	0.0	0.0	4500	15300.00	0.00	0.0	15300.00	15300.00	0.00
500	MASONRY													
501	LABOR	HR	1	385	0	0.0	0.0	385	4042.50	0.00	0.0	4042.50	4042.50	0.00
502	BRICKS & MAT'L	EA	2	7000	0	0.0	0.0	7000	1400.00	0.00	0.0	1400.00	1400.00	0.00
503	EQUIPMENT	HR	3	200	0	0.0	0.0	200	4000.00	0.00	0.0	4000.00	4000.00	0.00
600	FINISHING	HR	4	750	0	0.0	0.0	750	11250.00	0.00	0.0	11250.00	11250.00	0.00
700	PLUMBING	HR	4	235	0	0.0	0.0	235	5287.50	0.00	0.0	5287.50	5287.50	0.00
800	ELECTRICAL	HR	4	385	0	0.0	0.0	385	10202.50	0.00	0.0	10202.50	10202.50	0.00
995	FICA	NA	6	0	0	0.0	38.7	0	1870.00	723.81	38.7	1146.19	1870.00	0.00
996	SUTA	NA	6	0	0	0.0	38.7	0	1150.00	444.62	38.7	705.38	1150.00	0.00
997	FUTA	NA	6	0	0	0.0	39.1	0	185.00	72.38	39.1	112.62	185.00	0.00
998	WORKER'S COMP	NA	6	0	0	0.0	38.8	0	80.00	31.02	38.8	48.98	80.00	0.00
	TOTALS BY COST CODE:													
	LABOR			2635	1053	40.0	39.6	1666	26690.00	10340.10	38.7	15747.93	26088.03	-601.97
	MATERIALS			22400	15238	68.0	95.5	7000	31897.50	29787.59	93.4	1400.00	31187.59	-709.91
	EQUIPMENT			270	65	24.1	43.3	200	7125.00	3060.00	42.9	4000.00	7060.00	-65.00
	SUBCONTRACT			7870	2040	25.9	19.4	5870	52040.00	10150.00	19.5	42040.00	52190.00	150.00
	OVERHEAD			0	0	0.0	38.7	0	3285.00	1271.83	38.7	2013.17	3285.00	0.00
	TOTALS FOR JOB:						45.6		121037.50	54609.52	45.1	65201.10	119810.62	-1226.88

Note: the Act % Compl. for Components will be set equal to the % of Accumulated to Estimated cost when not specified by operator.

Figure 7-10 Detailed job cost analysis report. (*Courtesy of Micro Associates, Inc., Port Arthur, Texas.*)

```
JOB COST PROGRAM          DATE: 10/16/85     INVOICE PRINTING & A/R POSTING   7-2

Job Number........ 1                 Rev. Contract......     145,300.00
Job Title......... PARK CENTRAL OFFICE BLDG  PTD Billing........      12,345.00
Contract.......... 84-001            Accum. Billing.....      38,257.49
Customer Name..... JONES BROS. INVESTMENTS   Rev. Cost Est......     121,037.50
Invoice Basis..... C  CONTRACT       PTD Cost...........      22,648.08
Acctg Basis....... C  COMPLETED JOB  Accum. Cost........      54,609.52
Retainage %....... 10.00             Accum. Retainage...       3,825.75
Start Date........ 02/07/84          Actual % Complete..  45.58
Compl Date........ 00/00/00          % of Cost Est......  45.12
=================================================================================
Completion % specified on invoice (###.##)% ... 45.58
Total value of work performed to date.......... 66227.74
Total retainage to date........................ 6622.77
Print your company name on invoice (Y/N)....... Y
Print itemized supporting details (Y/N)........ Y
Terms for invoice payment: Code/Description.... 0
Message to be printed on invoice: line 1....... THANK YOU FOR LETTING AJAX
                                  line 2.......    DO YOUR CONSTRUCTION



ENTER  INVOICE CHARACTERISTICS     PRESS  F2  TO PROCESS    F1  TO ABORT
```

```
JOB COST PROGRAM          DATE: 10/16/85     INVOICE PRINTING & A/R POSTING   7-2

                                       Invoice Number: 1
      [---------Bill To---------]      Invoice Date:   101685
       JONES BROS. INVESTMENTS
                               Project:    PARK CENTRAL OFFICE BLDG
                                           2020 ORANGE AVE
                                           ALTOONA, IA   55566
                               Contract:   84-001
----------------------------------------------------------------------------
    Original Contract Amount................................    145,000.00
    Approved Change Orders..................................        300.00
                                                             -------------
    Revised Contract Amount.................................    145,300.00
    45.58  % Complete to Date                                ==============
    Total Value of Work Performed to Date...................     66,227.74
    Less Amount on Previous Invoices........................     38,257.49
                                                             -------------
    Gross Amount Due this Invoice...........................     27,970.25
    Less Retainage this Invoice.............................      2,797.03
       (Total Retainage to Date =     6,622.77)              -------------
    Amount Due on this Invoice..............................     25,173.22

ENTER  INVOICE CHARACTERISTICS     PRESS  F2  TO PROCESS    F1  TO ABORT
```

Figure 7-11 Invoice printing and accounts receivable posting screens. (*Courtesy of Micro Associates, Inc., Port Arthur, Texas.*)

```
AJAX CONSTRUCTION COMPANY              Invoice Number: 1
1000 ROCKY SHORE DRIVE                 Invoice Date:   10/16/85
DES MOINES, IOWA   55555




JONES BROS. INVESTMENTS        Project:  PARK CENTRAL OFFICE BLDG
                                         2020 ORANGE AVE
                                         ALTOONA, IA   55566

                               Contract:  84-001


-----------------------------------------------------------------------

   Original Contract Amount................................   145,000.00
   Approved Change Orders..................................        300.00
                                                             -------------
   Revised Contract Amount.................................   145,300.00
                                                             =============

   45.58  % Complete to Date
   Total Value of Work Performed to Date...................    66,227.74
   Less Amount on Previous Invoices........................    38,257.49
                                                             -------------
   Gross Amount Due this Invoice...........................    27,970.25
   Less Retainage this Invoice.............................     2,797.03
        (Total Retainage to Date =      6,622.77)           -------------

   Amount Due on this Invoice..............................    25,173.22
                                                             =============


                  THANK YOU FOR LETTING AJAX
                    DO YOUR CONSTRUCTION
```

Figure 7-12 Sample invoice printout. (*Courtesy of Micro Associates, Inc., Port Arthur, Texas.*)

```
Project:  PARK CENTRAL OFFICE BLDG      Invoice Number: 1
Contract: 84-001                        Invoice Date:   10/16/85
                                        Page:           2


                        ***** INVOICE DETAILS *****

-----------------------------------------------------------------------
                    Estimated   Accumulated   % of   Act %   Crnt Period
Job Component  UoM  Qty Units   Qty Units     Est.   Compl   Qty Units
-----------------------------------------------------------------------
SITE PREP
   LABOR       HR     250.00       245.00     98.0   100.0        0.00
   EQUIPMENT   HR      45.00        40.00     88.9   100.0        0.00
EXCAVATION     CY    2000.00      2040.00    102.0   100.0        0.00
FOUNDATION
   LABOR       HR     410.00       415.00    101.2   100.0        0.00
   BRICKS      EA    1200.00      1190.00     99.2   100.0        0.00
   CONCRETE    YD      50.00        48.00     96.0   100.0        0.00
   EQUIPMENT   HR      25.00        25.00    100.0   100.0        0.00
FRAMING
   LABOR       HR     950.00       393.00     41.4    38.0      118.00
   RAW MATERIALS LF  8600.00      8450.00     98.3   100.0     6200.00
SIDING & INSUL.
   SIDING MAT'L SF   2200.00      2200.00    100.0   100.0     2200.00
   INSUL MATERIAL SF 3350.00      3350.00    100.0   100.0     3350.00
```

Figure 7-13 Invoice details printout. (*Courtesy of Micro Associates, Inc., Port Arthur, Texas.*)

speed, high-quality color video graphics, and high-quality printing and plotting capabilities that are now available and becoming available on microcomputers (see Chapter 10, Selecting a Microcomputer-Based Cost Estimating System). At this writing there is still a need for a Lotus 1-2-3 of cost estimating. This generic product should have many advanced features but should at a minimum be capable of a time-oriented look at costs. It should be able to do multiday, multiweek, multimonth, and multiyear estimates; be able to spread costs across the time period where the resources will be expended; and be able to apply escalation, inflation, and the multiple overhead factors that may be encountered through the performance of work at various locations. Many of the systems described in this chapter have most of these features, but a ground-up approach to system software design, programming, and documentation using the latest capabilities of microcomputers will result in an excellent, widely used, standardized system. Look for such a system to appear soon.

CHAPTER 8

CUSTOMIZED MICROCOMPUTER COST ESTIMATING SYSTEMS

By far the most common type of microcomputer cost estimating system is the custom-tailored system. The proliferation of operating systems, software languages, generic applications packages, and hardware brands and options and the lack of a standardized, generic, and easy-to-operate applications software package that can be used in all cost estimating situations has forced companies, universities, individual cost estimators, and government organizations to develop or have developed their own specialized proprietary microcomputer cost estimating software. The competitive nature of cost estimates themselves has hindered the cross flow of information from company to company, from supplier to customer, and from competitor to competitor. Even though the competitive content of a cost estimate does not lie in the methodology or software used to perform the analysis or the computations, organizations have been hesitant to share these programs for the good of all. Therefore, literally thousands of cost estimating software programs have been prepared by their users to match their own accounting systems, estimating techniques, computer hardware configurations, and software languages.

Customized microcomputer cost estimating systems are probably more expensive to the originating and using organization than any other system discussed in this book. We know of some large high-technology firms that have spent $3 to 5 million in developing their own cost estimating and related accounting, cost tracking, inventory or material tracking, and estimating software for minicomputers and mainframe computers; and these same organizations are incurring large (but sometimes hidden or indeterminate) resource expenditures to develop new estimating and forecasting programs for microcomputers. Why, then, do many companies choose to develop their own customized systems?

Customization Is a Key to Utility

Many of the cost estimating software packages being developed for microcomputers are smaller versions of the minicomputer or mainframe computer programs that have been in use for several years in a company. These software packages have been adapted or downloaded to the microcomputers because they were available, the company's personnel already knew how to use them, and because the conversion could be done at a pace commensurate with workload and using in-house engineering and programming skills. Customized systems use the nomenclature, methods, techniques, and sometimes hardware (such as keyboards and monitors) with which the organization is already familiar. An increasing number of customized packages, programs, and templates (especially constructed and formatted data files that work on generic applications packages like spreadsheets and databases) are also being developed from scratch by in-house personnel, modified from programs in the published literature, or developed by consultants or computer software specialty companies. Customized packages have a high degree of utility to the originating and using organization because the software is usually structured for a specific purpose, and, as such, the extraneous operations, time, and training required for adapting out-of-house or off-the-shelf software are eliminated. Since the user and developer of this software are one, there is a greater probability that the software will do exactly the job it is intended to do.

Customization in Cost Estimating and Analysis

There are many areas where customization may be desirable in cost estimating and cost analysis software. These areas are related to: (1) the type of work activity or work output being produced by the software user; (2) the specific number and type of skill categories and skill levels used to do the work; (3) the level of detail required in cost estimates; (4) the time period(s) over which most of the company's work is performed; (5) the skill and experience of the cost estimating group or department; (6) the types and quantity of data that are available to support the estimating process; and (7) the desired interface with other design, engineering, manufacturing, assembly, testing, inspection, inventory control, or accounting functions of the company. Your company must weigh the expense and time required to develop (or have developed) a customized cost estimating system against the benefits to be derived in these areas.

Stand-Alone Versus Integrated Estimating Systems

In the infancy of the cost estimating profession, it was common practice to develop stand-alone cost estimating microcomputer systems. This practice was common because of the difficulty of interfacing the computer software with other software such as engineering or production planning and business software, or because many times these other functions had not been automated or were not compatible with the cost estimating methods used. Stand-alone cost estimating systems were used to develop budgetary estimates, forecasts, and even bids or proposals with no interface or continuing input to the other technical and financial aspects of the work activity or work output. With the realization that budgeting and cost estimating are a vital part of the planning and management process, that cost tracking against the original estimate can lead to better management visibility and performance, and that estimates themselves can improve in accuracy and credibility if supplied with a feedback of actual cost expenditures, more companies are integrating their cost estimating systems with performance and schedule aspects of technical and business systems that support the job once it is started. This integrated approach has been fulfilled in off-the-shelf accounting packages that tie in a job cost function. The best approach in building a customized cost estimating software package for microcomputers is to build in "hooks" or interfaces in any stand-alone package so that it can later be effectively interfaced with other vital project tracking, management, and financial functions. In an organization with any size at all, it is inevitable that you will eventually want to tie in the cost estimating function with these other work management functions, so it pays to provide as much forethought as possible to the future software interfaces that may be required.

One specific area of integration of cost estimating systems with other functions in microcomputers that deserves special mention is the use of the output of computer-aided design programs as an input to the cost estimating process. Packages such as AUTOCAD (Autodesk Systems, Inc.) will produce linear and area calculations that can be used to predict material and labor expenditures for building the product being designed. Although at this writing the design products have not automated the cost estimating function, it is a logical assumption that they will do so in the near future as the drawing information, which is already digitized in the computer, can be used to produce quantities and costs in a fully or nearly fully automated estimating system. As discussed further in Chapter 11, this technique could eventually fully replace the combination manual and automated takeoff procedure discussed under vertical market systems in Chapter 7.

Depth of Estimating as a Software Driver

The advent of the microcomputer itself has had a pronounced influence on the depth or detail of cost estimating performed on most projects. As estimating tools become less expensive, more widely known, and more sophisticated, the level at which estimates are prepared has changed. Where originally cost estimates were prepared at level 2 or 3 in the work element structure (to the system or subsystem level), estimates are now being prepared at the component or even the piece-part level (level 4 or 5). Developers of customized cost estimating systems should seriously consider requiring a capability of summing costs from at least level 4 (the component level). Because of the still-limited data storage capabilities in some microcomputers, there will be a tradeoff in the depth of estimating desired with other factors such as the number of skill categories or skill levels, the number of calendar periods covered, or the number of cost elements included. Where some mainframe computers have estimating software that permits collecting costs from level 7 or 8 in the WES, this capability is seldom used and may not warrant reserving the space to save this much data. If a level 3 or 4 system is chosen because of the limited storage capabilities of your microcomputer, however, you may want to consider providing the coding structure and input sequence that would permit reinputting the top-level results of a level 3 or 4 estimate into the bottom level of *another* level 3 or 4 estimate. This technique will turn your level 3 or 4 WES type of estimating system into a level 6 or 8 system.

Skill Levels, Skill Categories, and Overhead Pools

Other size drivers or specifications for customized cost estimating systems are the number of skill categories and skill levels required in the work force mix, and the number of overhead pools desired. Although many companies use only one overhead pool or rate, some use five or six, one for each major skill category such as engineering, manufacturing, testing, tooling, and quality and reliability assurance. A customized system for your own company can include exactly the number of overhead pools you require or can provide one or two pools for expansion. The number of skill levels within each skill category or overhead pool varies tremendously from company to company, but most companies (80 to 90 percent) will have no more than 16 skill levels per skill category or overhead pool. Selection of a proper number in a customized system will save space for other important information in the microcomputer's estimating database.

Time Periods and Scheduling Costs

Another area where customization of microcomputer cost estimating packages pays off is in the designation of calendar time units and subdivisions that permit the spreading, distribution, or allocation of costs over time. To have a fully responsive microcomputer cost estimating system, one must be able to subdivide costs into the time increments normally used in distributing and allocating or spending dollars as the work progresses. Depending on the size and length of the job, costs can be estimated and budgeted by the year, quarter, month, week, or even day or hour if necessary; but the computer software must be capable of handling the proper time increments. In most instances, it is desirable to have considerable flexibility in assigning time increments, even in highly customized systems. This is because customers sometimes change the way they want costs distributed over time in the cost proposal or bid.

We have seen requests for proposals that call for the costs for the first year of a project to be broken down by month, the second and third year by quarter, and the next 6 years only by year. Because different customers themselves have different accounting systems and fiscal year periods, they are seldom consistent in the means they require in breaking out costs versus time. The differences between fiscal year and calendar year both in the customer's financial system and the supplier's financial system, as well as the fact that these differences often change, make it desirable to have *timing of costs* flexibility in customized estimating systems.

User Friendliness in Customized Systems

User friendliness, or ease of learning and use of the system, is far less important in customized microcomputer estimating software packages than in those designed for the commercial marketplace. In many companies, an extensive training program and apprenticeship is required to become familiar with the estimating system. But along with the microcomputer has come a whole set of nice hardware and software features that, when taken advantage of, can reduce training time for new personnel, encourage cross-training and cross-utilization of existing personnel, and speed up debugging and problem solving. Features such as on-screen menus, the use of function keys and customized function key templates, the effective use of color and graphics in both screen and printout displays, and peripheral input devices such as the mouse, digitizers, light pens, voice input, and touch-screen features can make estimating with microcomputers not only productive and efficient but actually enjoyable and interesting when used effectively. Even though the system is customized and not designed principally for the general public or new user, addition of these nice-to-have features could result in a greater acceptance and use of the system by management as well as by the estimators or technicians who are going to operate the system.

How to Develop a Customized System

Developing a customized cost estimating software package for your company's microcomputers involves the same techniques used for developing any other type of software program or series of programs: the most important part of the process is defining the specifications and requirements of the system. We have discussed some of these requirements and considerations above. Some small programs will undoubtedly be written by the estimators themselves or adapted from the literature to perform routine estimating functions such as those discussed in Chapter 3. Before starting an in-house development, however, be sure to check to see if there is a package available in the open marketplace or in the hands of a software development firm or consultant that can be adapted for your use. There are several sources of information, other than the obvious one of the marketing literature for commercial software packages, that should be searched before embarking on a new development. First, the U.S. government, with its many branches, agencies, offices, and departments, is often willing to help the businessperson in finding predeveloped or modifiable estimating software packages. Government software packages have been developed using taxpayers funds, and, as such, are often available through information dissemination or technology utilization programs or, at last resort, through the Freedom of Information Act. Agencies that do a large amount of cost estimating and budgeting such as the DOD and the three services—the U.S. Army Corps of Engineers, NASA and its space flight centers, the DOE, and many others have data banks, libraries, and computer software facilities designed specifically to help transmit government developed information to the private sector. The Air Force recently purchased thousands of Zenith Z-100 computers and has expressed a willingness to share its generic programs for economic analysis, cost estimating, and other business and engineering functions with its contractors and subcontractors as well as with the general public. Government organizations, of course, can obtain programs from other government organizations at no cost.

Another important source of information and help in developing your company or organization's own customized microcomputer estimating system is the estimating software developer, supplier, or consultant. Many such software companies will provide you with the laborpower, knowledge, and expertise required to develop your own system from scratch. Many such companies already have one or more estimating software systems that they can modify or expand to meet your specific needs. Software packages from this latter category of supplier can be very cost effective because the bulk of the system development has already been done and all that is required is to fund the human and material resources required to match the system to your specific use.

As examples of three specific approaches to customized microcomputer cost estimating systems, the remainder of this chapter describes: (1) a generic work breakdown structure–oriented pricing model, (2) a microcomputer-based integrated cost estimating and financial management system, and (3) technology initiatives economics analysis. These examples are only three of the literally thousands of possible approaches to tailorable or customized estimating systems. They are presented here to give you an idea of the types of things that can be and are being done with customized microcomputer-based cost estimating software packages.

A Work Breakdown Structure—Based Pricing Model

Because of the increasing size, complexity, and duration of work activities and work outputs, the WES or work breakdown structure (WBS) is becoming an increasingly prevalent way of subdividing costs in a cost estimate (see Chapter 2). Originally used primarily for cost estimating of high-technology projects, the WES technique can be applied to any kind or field of work, and it permits the collection and estimating of costs at summary, system, subsystem, or component levels. Because the software itself does not do the estimating but merely collects, correlates, and processes the resource estimates for printout in a final cost estimate or budget estimate report, it is usually called a *pricing* system. One such WBS-WES microcomputer-based pricing system has been developed and is being customized for various clients by John M. Cockerham and Associates (JMCA), Inc., of Huntsville, Alabama. The program is written in Microsoft Basic and operates under the Microsoft Disk Operating System (MSDOS) or the Personal Computer Disk Operating System (PCDOS). It is a typical WBS-WES-oriented system available for customization for various specific applications.

The JMCA WBS Pricing Model can do a large amount of work that can be done with a microcomputer of modest size and capacity. Keep in mind that this type of program estimating software does not provide its own estimate input data as do some more sophisticated models, but it does take the bulk of the drudgery out of pricing a cost estimate.

Customized Programs for Estimating and Financial Management

As is the case with most high-technology advancements, industry in the United States has taken the lead in adopting microcomputers for cost estimating as well as for the other financial and business functions. Federal, state, and local governments have been slower regarding the use of the high-technology microcomputers, but strong industry pressures as well as the desire for increased efficiencies and economies in government have caused an explosive growth in the use of microcomputers and customized microcomputers programs in the thousands of agencies, services, departments, and offices in state and local as well as the federal government. The type of pressure that is continuing to be exerted on government adoption of the latest high technology in computing was evidenced by legislative actions in the United States Senate like the passage in 1984 of a resolution designating October 1984 as Computer Learning Month, and stating: "The use and application of computers is one key to maintaining leadership in the high technology field." This resolution, sponsored by Senator Pete Wilson (Republican from California), cosponsored by 28 other senators, and supported by more than 140 computer manufacturers and software publishers, said, "We must take every opportunity to encourage understanding of computer-based technology through the promotion of innovative learning environments in order to integrate computer technology into our diverse society." These types of influences, pressures, and trends are causing government offices to increasingly adopt and rely on computers in general and microcomputers and customized or off-the-shelf computer programs in specific in almost every corner of the public sector not only for cost estimating but for the related planning, programming, budgeting, and project execution phases of large and small public sector work outputs and work activities.

The number of software programs and hardware systems increasingly being employed in government is phenomenal. To conduct a comprehensive survey of the use of computers for estimating and other functions would be a mammoth task; and any survey would be quickly outdated. To provide a reader with some of the estimating-related uses to which computers are being applied in the public sector, however, we include here only one of the many uses being found for microcomputers in estimating and managing the taxpayer's dollar. The example is in the area of major weapons system acquisition for the DOD, specifically the U.S. Army. The system that will be described is that used by the U.S. Army Materiel

Command, the organization that is responsible for design, development, testing, production, and field support of all Army weapons systems throughout their life cycle. Some of the largest of these weapons systems are managed by the U.S. Army Missile Command of Huntsville, Alabama, which spends about $6.5 billion each year for missile systems and related defense equipment. The Army Missile Command uses the Hewlett Packard 9000 series microcomputer to perform cost estimating, budgeting, pricing, and financial contract management for the weapons systems for which it is responsible.

Early in the concept formulation and system definition phases of a weapons system, the Army solicits ideas and bids from industry regarding new weapons systems concepts and designs. When one of these systems is sufficiently mature to warrant serious consideration for approval, and provided it is determined to be a needed addition to the United States defense posture, the Army prepares an independent cost estimate (independent from contractor or industrial inputs) and a system baseline cost estimate. Using the microcomputer as a tool to handle, compute, and report the numbers, the baseline cost estimate is continually updated, modified, amended, and improved to keep pace with the emerging system definition. Estimates for design, development, testing, and training as well as for production and operational field support are initially made and then kept alive by making the appropriate modifications to the total estimate as the work progresses into the deployment of a weapons system in the field. Even after deployment, detailed cost records and reports are kept on the Army's microcomputers to permit a rapid feedback into the budgeting process.

The principal user of the estimating and financial management system (the Army calls their system the Program Management Control System or PMCS) is the project manager of each weapons system. Through use of the microcomputer-based PMCS, the project manager can

1. Keep track of the baseline cost estimate status and independent cost estimates that are prepared during the project's life cycle.

2. Compare and update budgets for the system based on current estimates.

3. Monitor financial progress of contractors and in-house effort as compared to cost estimates during project performance.

4. Perform cost and price analysis of proposals in preparation for negotiations and contract award to prime contractors.

An early use of the microcomputer is the performance of design-to-cost and design-to-unit-production-cost studies. Because budgets are often limited, the microcomputer's capabilities must be used not only to sum up the estimates of cost of a system, but to slice, reapportion, adjust, and manipulate these costs and the related performance requirements that result in these costs to permit development and production of the system within the desired cost constraints. The Army requires the submittal of cost performance reports, contract fund status reports, and cost and schedule status reports from its contractors for weapons systems. To be able to assimilate, compare, summarize, and understand all of these reports and their potential financial impact on the project without the use of microcomputers would be unthinkable. With the large number of projects underway at one time, the Army Missile Command has found that the use of their standardized PMCS is essential for obtaining a continuing understanding and analysis of the costs of their many projects.

The cost model is operated by a central group that uses several microcomputers on a continuous basis to keep project managers and their staffs informed of their project's financial status and estimates to complete. Microcomputer-generated reports such as the cost and schedule variance trend report shown in Figure 8-1 are produced monthly (or more often if required) to give the project manager, other project personnel, and the agency commanders a visual display of current and projected status. Vital project information such as the original target cost and price, the current target cost and price, the contractor's estimates of cost and price to complete, and the project manager's estimate of cost and

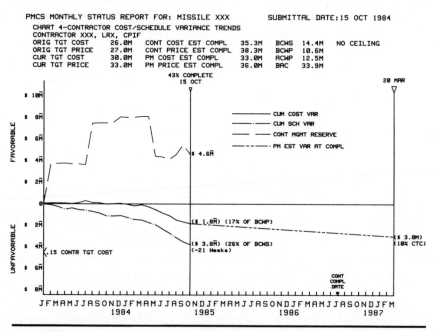

Figure 8-1 Example of monthly financial status report. (*Courtesy of the U.S. Army Missile Command.*)

price to complete. Cost and schedule control system parameters such as the budgeted cost of work scheduled, the budgeted cost of work performed, the actual cost of work performed, and the budget at completion are listed in this report, as well as a fiscal year histogram that plots the cumulative cost and schedule variances, contract management reserve history, and project manager's estimate of variation at completion are all included in one computer graphics plot.

Microcomputer-generated stacked bar plots (Figure 8-2) showing the weapons system production and other costs as portions of the total budget in constant dollars for each fiscal year and the cumulative average for the total project can be produced for any "as-of" date to give a total overview of the project's life-cycle production costs.

In the use of their microcomputer-based PMCS, the Army has come a long way in a short time, due principally to the cost estimating and management capabilities of the microcomputer when supported with the appropriate customized software. Where there once was a major gap between estimating and budgeting, this gap has been narrowed significantly by reducing the time lag between actual reported costs and es-

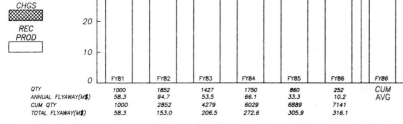

Figure 8-2 Example of fiscal year bar chart report. (*Courtesy of the U.S. Army Missile Command.*)

timated cost generation. Budgeted dollars are now more nearly equal to and consistent with the cost estimates developed and used in the cost analysis and decision-making process. More accurate budgeting means more effective use of resources and a resulting decrease in costs or increase in the value for cost spent by the taxpayer.

Customization to Track Technology Initiatives Against Strategic Requirements

Another customized program that is of interest that (1) includes the fields of cost estimating and budgeting, (2) uses the capabilities of modern microcomputers and applications software, and (3) was prepared for use in the public sector but has similar applications in the private sector, resulted from a small business initiative supported by the U.S. Army's Ballistic Missile Defense Advanced Technology Center. The program is a template or customized application using KnowledgeMan on an IBM Personal Computer Model XT. The program uses the database capabilities of KnowledgeMan to match hundreds of proposals for technological efforts with strategic needs identified by the Army for its future defensive weapons systems programs. The Army calls its technology requirements Strategic Defense Initiatives and wants to fund just the right technology and research efforts to support these initiatives. Cost estimates and proposals for thousands of studies, research projects, scientific explorations, and operations research analyses efforts are made every year by both industry and in-house organizations; and these proposals must be sorted out and matched properly to fit both the funding available and the strategic defense requirements. To assist in this mammoth task, a company named Engineering & Economics Research (EER), Inc., headquartered in Vienna, Virginia, has developed the methodology and microcomputer technology under the Army's small business initiative program. The company plans to market the same technology to the private sector to assist other companies in identifying and selecting the proper independent research and development programs needed to fulfill their long-term strategic marketing and growth objectives.

Figure 8-3 is a sample microcomputer-generated database report containing 103 typical independently proposed technology initiatives that total to over $75 million. Using the microcomputer program, databases of this type can be scanned using multiple criteria to provide the proper mix of technology efforts to support specific long-term objectives. This scanning and selection process uses the microcomputer's capabilities not only to select the proper mix of initiatives to meet emerging needs but also to take into account the timing and evolution of these efforts and the funding profiles required to support them. The technology initiatives can be

CODE	CONTRACT	CONTR	COMPDATE	FUNDING
BM-01-01	DYNAMICALLY RECONFIG. COMPUTER	DCA	12/15/86	400000.00
BM-01-02	INVESTIGATION/ANALYSIS OF BMD ALGOR	TBD	06/30/86	200000.00
BM-01-03	HARDWARE FAULT TOLERANCE	AUBURN	08/31/86	350000.00
BM-01-04	INVESTIGATE/EXPER -RECONFIG. DIAGNOSTICS	TBD	09/31/86	325000.00
BM-01-05	ADV. DISTRIBUTED ONBOARD PROCESSORS	HONEYWELL	06/31/87	1250000.00
BM-01-06	ADOP TECH INSERTION (GAAS)	TBD	09/15/86	425000.00
BM-01-07	OPTICALLY COUPLING NETWORKS	TBD	06/30/85	375000.00
BM-01-08	ARTIFICIAL INTELLIGENCE APP. TO BMD	TBD	09/31/86	250000.00
BM-01-09	ADVANCED COMPUTING METHODS	UAH	06/30/85	325000.00
BM-01-10	ADV. TOPICS ON COMPUTER HARDWARE	LL	09/30/84	250000.00
BM-01-11	MITIGATION OF NATURAL INDUCED RADIATION	TBD	06/30/85	350000.00
BM-01-12	INSTALL HIGH PERF. VLSI DP IN ORBIT	TBD	06/15/88	2500000.00
BM-02-01	DISTRIBUTED COMPUTING DESIGN SYSTEM	TRW,OTHERS	07/15/88	3825000.00
BM-02-03	S/W QUALITY ASSURANCE	ISSI	06/30/86	500000.00
BM-02-03	TRANSPORTABLE LANGUAGE SYSTEMS	AUBURN	06/30/85	475000.00
BM-02-04	DISTRIBUTED SYS ENVIR. AND THREAT SIM.	GRC	10/15/88	2375000.00
BM-02-05	TEST BED DESIGN IMPLEMENTATION	SDC	12/12/86	750000.00
BM-02-06	TEST BED REQUIRMENTS & SPECIFICATIONS	GRC	05/30/85	375000.00
BM-02-07	ARCHITECTURAL DESCRIPTION LANGUAGE	TRW	07/31/87	1450000.00
BM-02-08	REAL TIME MONITORING	CMU	06/16/85	750000.00
BM-03-01	C2 DECISION AIDS	TBD	06/15/87	1675000.00
BM-03-02	WPNS RELEASE/ORDNANCE SAFETY	MITER	06/15/86	325000.00
BM-04-01	C3/BM DEFINITION DEVELOPMENT	MDAC	06/15/85	275000.00
BM-04-02	SETAC	TBD	12/31/88	2000000.00
BM-04-03	INTELLIGENCE REAL TIME APPLICATIONS	TBD	06/15/85	375000.00
BM-04-04	C3 SIMULATION DEVELOPMENT	TBD	09/15/86	1050000.00
BM-04-05	DATA BASE MANAGEMENT	TBD	06/30/85	250000.00
BM-04-06	WEAPONS CENTER STRATEGIES	TBD	06/30/85	375000.00
BM-04-07	BM CENTER STRATEGIES IMPLEMENTATION	UAH	06/15/87	575000.00
BM-04-08	DATA INTEGRATION	TBD	06/15/85	100000.00
BM-05-01	DECENTRALIZED CONTROL	SCT	06/30/85	450000.00
BM-05-02	DISTRIBUTED DATA BASES	UCLA	09/30/87	850000.00
BM-05-03	SOFTWARE FAULT TOLERANCE	U OF FLORIDA	06/15/86	375000.00
BM-05-04	ADVANCED S/W ENGINEERING	U OF CA	06/15/88	1300000.00
BM-05-05	MICROCODE GENERATION SYSTEM	JRS	07/30/86	375000.00
BM-05-06	BM/C3 SYSTEMS STUDIES/RESOURCE MGMT	TBD	06/30/87	1800000.00
BM-05-07	LARGE SCALE NETWORK INTEGRATION TECH.	TBD	03/15/86	300000.00
BM-05-08	SYSTEMS NETWORK INTEGRATION FACILITY REG	TBD	06/30/87	350000.00
BM-05-09	DISTRIBUTED DATA MGMT FOR BM/C3 SYS	TBD	09/30/87	450000.00
BM-05-10	GLOBAL INFORMATION MANAGEMENT	TBD	06/30/88	650000.00
BM-05-11	BM/C3 FUNCTIONS & ALGORITHMS	TBD	06/15/86	600000.00
SA-1A-01	SOVIET CONVENTIONAL BMD ANALYSIS	MIA	06/25/87	750000.00
SA-1A-02	SOVIET DEW BMD ANALYSIS	MIA	07/15/87	400000.00
SA-1A-03	RESPONSIVE THREAT HARDENING	DOE	09/15/86	300000.00
SA-1A-04	STRATEGIC PENETRATION/RED-BLUE STUDY	TBD	06/15/86	150000.00
SA-1A-05	JOINT BMD/BMO RED-BLUE ASSESSMENT	TBD	06/15/88	250000.00
SA-1S-01	RV CONST	DOE	06/30/85	75000.00
SA-1S-02	SETAC THREAT	TBD	06/15/86	150000.00
SA-1S-03	SOVIET BMD ANALYSIS	MIA	09/30/85	100000.00
SA-1S-04	THREAT DEFINITION	SAI	06/30/85	100000.00
SA-1S-05	SOVIET RESPONSES TO NEW INITIATIVES	DOE	05/30/85	50000.00
SA-1S-06	PENETRATION AID & SIGNATURE EVALUATION	TBD	09/15/88	400000.00
SA-1S-07	RV WARHEAD MODELING	CCNL	09/15/88	350000.00
SA-1S-08	OPTICAL THREAT DEFINITION	TBD	02/15/88	150000.00
SA-1S-09	RV MODELING	DOE	09/30/87	1025000.00
SA-1S-10	SAFING,ARMING & FUZING	DOE	06/15/87	750000.00
SA-1S-11	THREAT	MDAC	06/30/87	750000.00
SA-1S-12	MATERIAL ANALYSIS OF FOREIGN RV'S	DOE	03/30/87	150000.00
SA-1S-13	FIO SUPPORT	MICOM	05/31/86	500000.00
SA-1S-14	OFFENSE LAYDOWNS	SAI	06/15/87	450000.00
SA-2S-01	SETAC SYSTEM DEFINITION	TBD	05/31/87	500000.00
SA-2S-02	MISSION ANALYSIS	TBD	09/15/88	1600000.00
SA-2S-03	STRATEGIC ANALYSIS	SAI	09/15/88	1500000.00
SA-2S-04	MISSION/SYSTEM REQ. FOR ADV. CONCEPTS	TBD	06/15/88	300000.00
SA-2S-05	BMD IN PROTRACTED WAR	TBD	03/15/87	750000.00
SA-2S-06	LONG RANGE RESOURCES PLANNING SYSTEMS	SPC	03/15/85	200000.00
SA-2S-07	OFFENSE/DEFENSE RESPONSE ANALYSIS	RRI	03/15/85	300000.00
SA-2S-08	SYSTEM CONCEPT DEF. & PERF. ASSESSMENT	TBD	06/15/85	150000.00
SA-2S-09	DID CONCEPT DEFINITION	TBD	03/30/85	75000.00
SA-2S-10	SIMULATION CENTER	COLSA	06/15/88	3000000.00
SA-2S-11	REENTRY DATA FACILITY	CALSPAN	09/15/88	4500000.00
SA-2S-12	INTEGRATION & POST COMMIT ANALYSIS	TBD	05/15/86	750000.00
SA-2S-13	TERMINAL DEF.RADAR/DP SUPPORT	MDAC	09/15/88	2500000.00
SA-2S-14	OPTICAL SYSTEMS EVAL	NRC	09/15/86	750000.00
SA-2S-15	RADAR CONCEPTS	MIT/LL	03/15/87	1100000.00
SA-2S-16	FACILITIES CONCEPT STUDIES	COE	06/30/86	350000.00
SA-2S-17	PROJECTED TECH. ANALYSIS & PLANNING	TBD	06/30/86	250000.00
SA-2S-18	EXP. SUPPORT/DATA ACQ ANAL & UTILIZATION	TBD	06/30/86	350000.00
SA-2S-19	NEAR TERM BMD ASSETS	GRC	09/15/86	375000.00
SA-2S-20	SETAC SYSTEMS DEFINITION	TBD	06/30/86	400000.00
SA-2S-21	EFFECTIVENESS & PRECOMMIT ANALYSIS	TBD	06/30/86	200000.00
SA-2S-22	DAMAGE ASSESS & GRAPHIC ANALYSIS	ENG. ANAL.INC	09/15/87	650000.00
SA-2S-23	BMD TECH SYSTEM SUPPORT	TBD	06/15/88	4000000.00
SA-2S-24	BMD TOP DOWN ANALYSIS	PHYSICS DYN.	06/30/86	750000.00
SA-2A-01	ACTIVE/PASSIVE DEFENSE	LJI	07/15/88	1000000.00
SA-2A-02	ADVANCED TERMINAL APPLICATIONS	TBD	05/30/85	100000.00
SA-2A-03	HIGH ALT. DEF. TECHNOLOGY REQ.	TBD	06/30/86	175000.00
SA-2A-04	MIDCOURSE ENGAGEMENT SIMULATION	TBD	06/30/87	1050000.00
SA-2A-05	SYSTEM D3 & FUNCTIONAL ANALYSIS	NRC	09/30/86	200000.00
SA-2A-06	ADV. EXO. SYSTEM D3-MULTISENSOR	TBD	09/15/87	250000.00
SA-2A-07	BMD DEW SYSTEM & TECH REQMTS	GRC,SPARTA	03/15/85	150000.00
SA-2A-08	BPI ATP REQMTS ANALYSIS	DRAPER LAB	09/15/86	75000.00
SA-2A-09	NUCLEAR ANALYSIS & TECHNOLOGY ASSESS.	TBD	06/30/86	200000.00
SA-2A-10	NUCLEAR EFFECTS ON OPTICAL PROCESSORS	SCI TEK	09/30/87	250000.00
SA-2A-11	DEW SUPPORT	KAMAN	09/15/88	500000.00
SA-2A-12	DRT CODE IMPLEMENTATION	TBD	06/30/86	550000.00
SA-2A-13	MINOR SCALE DURT EXPERIMENTS	TBD	06/15/86	200000.00
SA-2A-14	JOINT BMD/DIVA NUCLEAR PHENOM ASSESS	DNA	09/15/86	300000.00
SA-03-01	SYSTEMS DEVELOPMENT CENTER	TBD	12/30/88	2000000.00
SA-03-02	C3 TECHNICAL ANALYSIS	TBE	06/15/86	375000.00
SA-03-03	C3/BM THREAT	TBD	06/30/86	400000.00
SA-03-04	TW/AA MODEL	TBE	09/15/87	750000.00
SA-03-05	C3/BM VUL & HARDENING	TBD	03/15/87	475000.00

	75850000.00	Sum
Number of Observations: 103	736407.77	Ave
	50000.00	Min
	4500000.00	Max

Figure 8-3 Technology database. (*Courtesy of Engineering & Economics Research, Inc. These are sample data only and do not represent any real initiative areas or amounts.*)

sorted and organized into a hierarchical categorical structure (essentially a WBS or WES) by subject as shown on Figure 8-4. This database output categorizes the efforts into four levels in the hierarchy: program, project, task, and subtask. The technology item itself represents the fifth level in the hierarchy, so we have a five-level WBS.

There are several major benefits which result from directly relating the costs of ongoing technology advancement efforts which were generated at the grass-roots level to the conceptual systems requirements for new products which results from the top-down approach to planning and estimating. First, and most important, a relevance can be shown between the basic research and the technology funding required to support improved or new work outputs and work activities. This type of microcomputer program draws a thread of rationale between what is needed and what is being done to fulfill future needs. If the correlation cannot be made, then technical efforts and their funding profiles must be changed to establish the required relationship. This technique is particularly applicable when multiple independent activities are being performed in a program to the extent that it will show duplications or overlaps of technical efforts thus reducing wasted dollars and time. Analysis, study, and selection of the proper linkage between technology efforts and future product or system design requirements assure greater correlation and cohesiveness of an organization's activities and greater cost effectiveness in meeting long-term objectives. The speed, security, and adaptability of the microcomputer as shown by EER and others make it particularly adaptable to customization for these types of applications.

Customization with Artificial Intelligence Programs

Texas Instruments, Inc., markets a development tool that lends itself particularly to the solution of problems such as that just described. The software package, called Personal Consultant, is an artificial intelligence software product that can be customized to solve problems of an heuristic nature, that is, where the microcomputer is needed to solve problems involving ambiguous, uncertain, or subjective information. The use of certainty factors allows the system to determine and state the degree of confidence for a particular conclusion. The scheme uses "rules" (up to 400 rules can be used on a personal microcomputer) to establish a user-friendly question-and-answer-style program that solves a problem in much the same way that a person would solve the problem (hence the term artificial intelligence). Personal Consultant is a development package (not a language) that contains all the features necessary for a designer to create a prototype and develop sophisticated commercial

PROGRAM	PROJECT	TASK	SUBTASK	FUNDING
SYSTEMS ANALYSIS/BM/C3				
	BATTLE MGMT/C3 TECH			75850000.00
				32000000.00
		FAULT TOLERANCE COMP.	FAULT TOLERANCE COMP.	7000000.00
		S/W FOR COMPLEX SYSTEMS	S/W FOR COMPLEX SYSTEMS	10500000.00
		WPNS REL & ORD SAFETY	WPNS REL & ORD SAFETY	2000000.00
		BMD COMMUNICATIONS	COMM. SYSTEMS	5000000.00
		NON-COINCIDENTAL DATA SYSTEM	NON-COINCIDENTAL DATA SYSTEM	7500000.00
	SYSTEMS ANALYSIS			43850000.00
		RESPONSIVE THREAT	RESPONSIVE THREAT	6850000.00
			OFFENSE/DEFENSE ANALYSIS	1850000.00
			THREAT	5000000.00
		SYS CONCEPT DEFINITION	SYS CONCEPT DEFINITION	33000000.00
			SYSTEMS DEFINITION	28000000.00
			ADVANCED TECH. STUDIES	5000000.00
		SYSTEMS ARCHITECTURE	SYSTEMS ARCHITECTURE	4000000.00

Figure 8-4 Technology funding summary. (*Courtesy of Engineering & Economics Research, Inc. These are sample data only and do not represent any real initiative areas or amounts.*)

applications that would be difficult and costly using conventional programming techniques. Customization of programs is accomplished by a *domain expert* (someone who intimately knows the software package) who sits down with a *knowledge expert* (someone who intimately knows what needs to be done) and develops a knowledge base for a particular application. Because cost estimating is still a relatively inexact and subjective science, and because it is often desirable to establish ranges of resource or cost expenditures, programs like Personal Consultant are bound to find their way into the arsenal of the cost estimator as a major weapon against overruns, inaccuracies, and cost inconsistencies.

Forms of Customization

As can be seen from the above, customized cost estimating programs can be developed using the techniques of programming from scratch in a computer language, adapting or modifying an existing program, developing a database or template for an existing applications software package, or using artificial intelligence techniques. The technique chosen is usually based on a trade-off between cost and specificity. If you do a lot of cost estimating and want a microcomputer cost estimating program that *exactly* meets your needs and does not have extraneous operations, keystrokes, or formatting that must be done prior to starting your work, you need a customized system. If you prepare cost estimates only occasionally and can live with some inconvenience in operation, an off-the-shelf applications package such as those discussed in Chapters 4, 5, and 6 may be satisfactory. But before you choose, check out all of the options and be sure to determine if what you want is not already available.

Availability of Customized
Public Sector Programs

Customized microcomputer cost estimating software packages developed by federal, state, and local government agencies, departments, and offices are often available to the general public through special agencies of the governments themselves that have been set up to distribute information to the general public, industry, business, and universities. Many times, the public office or agency itself is willing to share software developments as long as security or proprietary interests are not violated. Some of this information can be obtained through the Freedom of Information Act, and others can be obtained through your U.S. or state congressman, senator, or the Library of Congress. The National Technical Information Service (NTIS); National Bureau of Standards; and agency libraries, documentation repositories, and public affairs offices are sources of public sector software programs available at little or no charge to the general business, professional, academic, and industrial public as well as to individuals. Federal or federally supported agencies such as the Federal Software Exchange Center at Springfield, Virginia, or the Computer Software Management Information Center (COSMIC) at the University of Georgia will provide computer software listings, disks, and documentation often for only the handling and reproduction cost.

Since these programs have been publicly funded, and since there are a number of cost estimating and financial packages available through this route, it would be a prudent and cost-effective practice for the potential developer of a customized microcomputer cost estimating software package to check first with these agencies to see if perhaps a usable system has not already been developed at taxpayer's expense and is available to the general public. One notable example is a program called SOFTCOST, which is a software cost estimation model program developed by the Jet Propulsion Laboratory at the California Institute of Technology, Pasadena, California, and available through COSMIC. This program has 2700 source statements and is available at a cost of $300.00 complete with computer disk and documentation! To develop such a system for your own use would cost many thousands of dollars.

9

MICROCOMPUTER TOOLS
FOR THE ESTIMATOR

A full complement of microcomputer tools for the cost estimator includes the computer system unit, the monitor or display screen, the keyboard, and a printer and/or plotter. Many companies sell computers (systems units) without one or more of these vital components and allow the user to select his or her own peripherals. This practice is acceptable for those who are intimately familiar with microcomputer hardware interfaces or those who have some excellent advice available on how to connect the various hardware components, but for the user who knows little about computers it is wise to purchase a matched or preconfigured hardware complement. In this chapter we will discuss each of these major hardware components, describe their functions, and point out the major support features for the cost estimating function. We will also discuss to some degree the interface between software and hardware. (Remember from Chapter 1 that a complete *system* includes both software and hardware.)

First, however, we will discuss some basic computer terms that you will need to know when applying the microcomputer to your cost estimating situation. You will need to know these terms not because you will be using them to design computers but because you will be communicating with those who use language and terminology unique to microcomputers.

Some Computer Basics

Deep within the central processing unit of your microcomputer are *microchips* from which the microcomputer gains its name. Microchips contain thousands of tiny electronic switches that can either be switched on or off. When each switch is off it represents a value of zero and when it is on it represents a value of one. Since each switch can have only two values, it is called *binary,* and the digit that it represents is a *binary* dig*it,* or *bit.* The computer remembers, stores, and manipulates information using bits arranged in the form of *bytes.* A microcomputer's memory or storage byte is usually 8 bits in length. A kilobyte or K is 1024 bytes. If your computer has 64K of random access memory (RAM), that means it can work on 65,536 bytes of information at a time. A megabyte is about 1 million bytes: if your computer has a 10-megabyte storage disk, that means that it can store and retrieve up to 10 million bytes of information on its disk. Information such as computer programs or data can either be stored on magnetic media like disks or in memory. Sometimes programs or other computer instructions are stored in *read-only memory* (ROM) which cannot be erased. If your computer has 16K of ROM, this means that over 16,000 bytes of information have been stored permanently in your computer for use when needed. It is important that the cost estimator's computer have enough random access memory (RAM) to accommodate any required programs plus the data that must be manipulated during program execution and enough storage to keep historical data and other estimates as well as the current estimate that is being developed or updated.

Another important feature of a microcomputer is its *word length.* A *word* in computer terminology, is a string of bits that is handled all at once by the computer when it does its processing. The microcomputer's architecture determines the length (in bits) of word it can handle at one time. Microcomputers exist that use word lengths of 4, 8, 16, and 32 bits. Usually computers that have a large number of bits per word (we are still talking about a microcomputer word and not a text word) are able to compute faster because they handle a larger number of bits at one time. But, as we will discuss later, computation speed is only one of the factors that adds up to computer usage time, so larger-word-length microcomputers are not *always* faster when it comes to the total time required for inputting, computing, and printing out a cost estimate.

A microcomputer *character* is one of 256 alphabetical, numeric, and other symbols. Most of these symbols can be displayed on the computer's screen or on the printer; others are *control characters* or invisible signals to, say, the printer. Each character is represented by one computer byte or word that is 8 bits in length. For example, the capital letter R is represented by the 8-bit binary code 01010010. In this binary code or 8-

bit word, each digit is a one or a zero. The first, third, fifth, sixth, and eighth digits are turned off (0), and the second, fourth, and seventh digits are turned on (1).

An alphabetical or text word, a number, or a combination alphabetical and numerical (alphanumeric) string of characters is formed when two or more characters are placed in a row with no space in between. JOHN, then, is a string of alphabetic characters; 1986 is a string of numerical characters; and JOHN1 is an alphanumeric string of characters. Character codes are usually either 8-bit or 7-bit expressions developed in keeping with a code called ASCII, which stands for *American Standard Code for Information Interchange.*

A computer *file* is a string or set of alphabetical, numerical, or alphanumeric expressions that you are generating, manipulating, or storing at one place on your computer's disk. File names are usually only eight characters long because most computers use eight character designations with a three-character *extender.* The fact that the file title must be squeezed into eight characters sometimes accounts for unusual file names. You have a wonderful opportunity to use your imagination in naming files so that you can remember them. For example, a file containing a catalog of the titles, numbers, dates, and costs of photographic material generated in 1986 could be called SNAPSHOT.086 or FOTO-FILE.86.

A software program called the *operating system* is provided with your microcomputer to make all of the parts work together. The two most common operating systems for microcomputers are the CP/M (*c*ontrol *p*rogram for *m*icrocomputers) operating system and MSDOS (*M*icro*S*oft *d*isk *o*perating *s*ystem). Other operating systems are (1) the UNIX operating system, originally used for larger computers but being adopted for multiuser microcomputers; and (2) the UCSD P-System. Most microcomputers are supplied with one or more *languages* that can be used to feed instructions to the computer. The most common one for microcomputers, one that has already been used in Chapter 3 for simple programs, is BASIC (*b*eginners *a*ll-purpose *s*ymbolic *i*nstruction *c*ode) language. Other common so-called high-order languages are COBOL (*c*ommon *b*usiness-oriented *l*anguage) and FORTRAN (*for*mula *tran*slation). Some other languages that are available follow:

ADA	PL-1
APL	Pascal
C	RPG
FOURTH	SAVVY
LOGO	

A series of instructions or commands to a computer in a language is called a *program* or *software.* You can design your own software if you learn a computer language, or if you learn to follow the instructions of the spreadsheet, database, or other applications package you are using. The glossary of microcomputer terms at the end of this book will help if you run into any other computer terms with which you are not familiar.

In most discussions of computer hardware, the printer is discussed last, and sometimes it is not discussed or described at all. The printer is of great importance to the cost estimator because it produces the final output of the cost estimate which must often be put into an important proposal, cost report, or financial report to management. To make a break with tradition and help restore the microcomputer's printer to its rightful place of importance to estimators, we will discuss the printer first, and then the other microcomputer hardware components.

The Microcomputer's Printer

One of the reasons that the printer is so important to the cost estimator is that printers are often thought of as a peripheral device and, therefore, are often given little attention at the front end of the computer acquisition cycle. Some of the smaller lap-size or briefcase-type portable computers have built-in printers; but these do not produce the large, legible output spreadsheets that are required in proposals and in other important financial documents. In almost every instance it is up to the buyer of a microcomputer to choose from one of the many available printer types, styles, models, and manufacturers. Table 9-1 is a list of 57 companies that produce printers for microcomputers. These companies produce about 250 printer models of various sizes, shapes, costs, speeds, and capabilities.

The first decision the microcomputer owner has to make regarding acquisition of a printer is whether to acquire a dot matrix printer, a character impact printer, or other specialized printer (thermal, electrostatic laser-jet, ink-jet, etc.). The normally more expensive character impact printers use a print wheel or thimble containing cast or pressed metal or plastic character print elements similar to those used on the striker bars of conventional typewriters. Originally, these character impact printers provided a much better print image than other types of printers but were somewhat slower. Perfectionists will still argue that character impact printers give a better image, particularly when used in multiple-carbon-copy systems. However, the dot matrix, ink-jet, and laser-jet technologies are rapidly approaching the quality of the character impact printer, and their speed and flexibility of font style make them desirable for high-quality outputs. Font style can be changed automatically in the middle of a run from conventional print to italics, to boldface, to underlined, to superscript and subscript. For cost estimating outputs, the high quality of character impact printers or of high-technology letter-

TABLE 9-1 Printer Manufacturers

Addmaster Corp.	San Gabriel, CA
Alphacom, Inc.	San Jose, CA
Anacom General Corp.	Fullerton, CA
Anadex, Inc.	Camarillo, CA
Apple Computer, Inc.	Cupertino, CA
Atari, Inc.	Sunnyvale, CA
Axiom Corp.	San Fernando, CA
Azurdata	Redmond, WA
Beehive, Int.	Lake City, UT
BMC	Carson, CA
Bytewriter	Ithaca, NY
Cardinal Scale Co.	Webb City, MO
Centronics Data	Hudson, NH
Commodore Bus. Machines	Santa Clara, CA
Components Express, Inc.	Santa Ana, CA
Computers International	Los Angeles, CA
Coosol, Inc.	Anaheim, CA
Data General Corp.	Westborough, MA
Data Impact Products	Boston, MA
Dataproducts Corp.	Woodland Hills, CA
Datasouth Computer Corp.	Charlotte, NC
Diablo Systems, Inc.	Hayward, CA
Digital Equipment Corp.	Marlborough, MA
Digital Matrix Corp.	Bloomfield, CT
Eaton Corp.	Watertown, WI
Epson America, Inc.	Torrance, CA
Facit, Inc.	Nashua, NH
Florida Data Corp.	Melbourne, FL
Genicom Corp.	Waynesboro, VA
Heath Co.	Benton Harbor, MI
Infoscribe, Inc.	Santa Ana, CA
C. Itoh Electronics, Inc.	Los Angeles, CA
Kanematsu Gosho USA	Bell, CA
Leading Edge Products, Inc.	Canton, MA
Mannesmann Tally Corp.	Kent, WA
Microperipherals	Salt Lake City, UT
N. Am. Industries, Inc.	Hauppauge, NY
NEC Information Systems	Lexington, MA
Okidata	Mt. Laurel, NJ
Olivetti/UPE	Tarrytown, NY
Phillips Peripherals	San Francisco, CA
Primages, Inc.	Bohemia, NY
Printek, Inc.	Benton Harbor, MI
Printer Products	Allston, MA
Printronix	Irvine, CA
Quint Systems, Inc.	Northbrook, IL
Qume	San Jose, CA
Radio Shack	Fort Worth, TX
Santec Corp.	Amherst, NH
Smith-Corona Corp.	New Canaan, CT
Star Micronics	New York, NY
Syntext Corp.	Marlborough, MA
Texas Instruments, Inc.	Dallas, TX
Toshiba	Justin, CA
Victor Business Products	Chicago, IL
Wang Laboratories	Lowell, MA
Xerox Corp.	El Segundo, CA

quality dot matrix, ink-jet, or laser-jet printers is highly desirable. For high quality in dot matrix printers using print wires, look for the one with the most wires (9-wire printheads have started to be replaced with 25-wire printheads) or with multistrike (emphasized or multipass) capability. Emphasized or multipass printing takes more time on most dot matrix printers so you will have to trade off speed with quality. Since character impact printers can only produce a rudimentary form of graphics, the dot matrix, ink-jet, or laser-jet technologies are more suitable for those cost estimators who want to combine graphic presentations with their numerical spreadsheet printouts. Operating systems that permit background printing allow the printer to operate while other work is being done on the computer. This feature may compensate to some degree with the slower output of some printers. The laser-jet printer produces high-quality output at a high speed. An extra buffer can be added to the printer to speed up the total printing process because the printer with adequate buffing capability can keep up with the computer.

The second most important decision to the cost estimator in selecting a microcomputer printer is the width of the carriage (which determines the maximum width of the printout). In our opinion, a 15- or 16-inch-wide carriage printer that will handle standard 11 by 14 inch (11 by 14⅞ inch with perforations) computer paper is a must. Most programs using compressed print on 14-inch wide paper can print up to 220 characters across the page while still allowing ample space for margins. Two hundred and twenty characters across the page will permit the use of 12 monthly columns (one year) containing up to $10 million (with commas, dollar signs, and two decimal places) each month, a vertical total column containing up to $1 billion, and an item description column along the left side of the spreadsheet that is 36 characters long. This allows plenty of expansion capability for estimators who are dealing with large cost numbers. For smaller estimates containing less than $1000 per calendar period, a 24-month spreadsheet with titles and totals can be printed on a 15-inch-wide printer in compressed print.

The use of compressed print, which is not possible on a character impact type of printer, is beneficial even on 8½-inch-wide paper if the legibility of the printout is acceptable for the estimate's intended purpose. Combining compressed print with emphasized or double-strike printing can yield a highly visible, compact, and reproducible estimate output report.

Some of the other characteristics to look for in a printer (or plotter) are as follows:

1. *Alternative character sets or fonts.*   Can the style of print be easily altered?

2. *Printing speed in characters per second.*   Speeds vary from 12 characters per second to 700 characters per second.

3. *Type of paper feed.*   Friction or tractor feeds are available. Tractor-feed systems are more desirable for long runs, whereas friction-feed systems are more adaptable to single-sheet production or short runs. Tractors can be pushers, pullers, or both. Pushers save paper because the sheet can be torn off above the next page to be printed, but they may wrinkle the paper occasionally. Combined pusher and puller is best for a bidirectional feed as used in graphics and some tabular printouts.

4. *Interface.*   Serial or parallel interfaces are available. The serial printer may require a special expansion card for your computer.

5. *Color.*   What colors are available?

6. *Special features available.*   Cartridge ribbons (easily insertable), self-test feature, buffers (ability to hold information prior to printing), single-sheet feeders, bidirectional printing, etc.

Depending on the type of estimates, reports, and proposals you produce, and the quantity or production rate, the cost estimator may even want to purchase *two* printers: a character impact or high- (letter-) quality dot matrix printer for 8½ by 11 inch paper and text printouts and a 15-inch carriage dot matrix graphics or color printer for large spreadsheets and graphs. If both are parallel printers (or serial printers) a simple switch box can be used to direct the computer's output to the right printer. For abnormally wide spreadsheets, there are computer software programs available such as SIDEWAYS that will print huge spreadsheets sideways on continuous-feed nonperforated paper. This solves the problem of getting the spreadsheet (say a 5-year program estimate by months) printed out on one piece of paper provided that the software will print the width) but how you will ever fold up one of these long spreadsheets neatly into an 8½ by 11-inch size report is another problem.

The Keyboard

Turning now from the printer, which is the output device that produces the cost estimate results, to the keyboard, which is the most frequently used input device (other input devices are light pens, digitizers, mice, or touch screens), we see also that there are an amazingly high number of keyboard styles, shapes, and arrangements available to the microcomputer user. It is safe to say that, except for those companies that deliberately copy another's keyboard layout, there is literally no standardization in keyboard design. Except for the relative positions of the alphabet (the standard typewriter alphabetic layout), and the numbers 1 through 9 if a numeric keypad is provided, the interrelationship between the locations of keys is apparently deliberately nonstandard. To the cost estimator, the keyboard layout can be extremely important. The cost estimator should have an immediately available and accessible numeric keypad with the plus, minus, equals, divide, zeros, and multiplication signs located in at least a familiar location with respect to other desktop, handheld, or pocket calculators that he or she uses on a regular basis. A separate set of cursor movement keys apart from the keypad is also a desirable feature to look for. There is also apparently no standard for the location or arrangement of cursor directing keys. We have seen them lined up in different arrangements, in box form, or in diamond form, with the arrows pointing in almost every conceivable direction. The most logical and perhaps the most easily understood and usable is the arrangement that locates the home key in the center of the cursor keypad with the up, down, right, and left cursor keys surrounding the home key like the north, south, east, and west arrows on a compass. Here, a readily accessible and usable location, preferably near the numeric keypad, is desirable. Figure 9-1 is a photograph of the Texas Instrument Professional Computer, which has a reputation of having one of the best and easiest to use keyboard layouts.

There are a lot of other features that you may want to look for in a keyboard, particularly if you type your cost estimate reports or proposals as well as compute them on your microcomputer. Some of these are the *tactile feedback* of of the keyboard that gives you a feel of having pressed the key; a key "click" feature that gives you an audio feedback; contoured positioning and key shapes to fit the fingers, wrist, and hand movements;

Figure 9-1   Photograph of Texas Instruments Professional Computer. (*Courtesy of Texas Instruments, Inc.*)

and small indicator lights that give a status as to whether a key is off or on (like the shift lock key). Many keyboards are separated from the computer system unit to permit comfortable positioning by the user, and some have tilt features to permit positioning at the best angle for typing comfort. Most keyboards are built with sufficient spacing between keys to permit the placement of keyboard templates around the keys to indicate their special functions for specific applications software packages.

The System Unit

The microcomputer's system unit houses the heart of the computer, the central processing unit, and other components such as the power supply, disk drives and controllers, a screen controller, and other components such as special expansion boards for communications, additional memory, graphics, speech recognition, and so forth. It is usually not necessary for the user to become intimately familiar with the system unit except when a feature needs to be added to the microcomputer to enhance its capability. Cost estimators will be concerned with several aspects of the system unit's capabilities as follows:

1. Growth or expansion capability
    a. Memory
    b. Storage
2. Color graphics capability
3. Computation speed

It is important to have or to purchase a computer with adequate memory and storage expansion and growth capability. As more capable applications software packages are developed, they tend to use more of the computer's memory and take up more room on storage disks.

The Microcomputer's Memory

Personal and professional microcomputers usually contain a minimum of 65,536 bytes (64K) of memory, and most microcomputer memories can be increased in increments of 64K, 128K, or 256K up to the design limit of the system unit. Cost estimators should use microcomputers with at least 64K of memory with an expansion capability of up to 128K of memory, and expansion capabilities *beyond* 128K are highly desirable. At this writing, there are microcomputers on the market that offer expanded memory capabilities up to 3 million bytes (3 megabytes). Some of the newly introduced integrated applications software packages require a computer memory well above the 128K value, so the purchaser of hardware must first determine what software packages are going to be used on the computer before sizing the memory requirement.

The Microcomputer's Storage Devices

Storage of information is usually accomplished on magnetic tape or disk. There are two general types of disks: the diskette and the hard disk. The diskette is a removable flat circular magnetic storage device that is rotated like a phonograph record. Diskettes come in various sizes (3.25, 5.25, and 8 inches) and various densities (single, double, quadruple). Some carry information on one side and some on both sides. The hard disk is also a circular magnetic storage device but is usually nonremovable (removable units are available for some computers), rotates at a much higher speed, and stores much more information than the diskette. At this writing there are 5¼-inch hard disks on the market that contain up to 20 megabytes of stored data. The hard disk is housed in a hermetically sealed enclosure, along with its read-write head, to ensure against contamination. Most cost estimators will want a hard disk in their computer system unit because it stores and retrieves information much more rapidly than a diskette and holds much more information in the same space.

Backup "streamer-tape" storage devices are becoming available that will allow the cost estimator to offload all of the information from the hard disk onto one or two continuous tape cartridges. These devices can be used to backup the hard disk contents or to make room for more estimates on the hard disk.

Other System Unit Features

Although microcomputers are so fast in their computations that the computation time is usually a negligible part of the total process of inputting, computing, and printing out or plotting data, there are ways of speeding up the computations when huge amounts of data are being processed. Some computers have *coprocessors* that can be added to the systems unit to speed up operations involving numerical data processing or high-order scientific calculations. Other computers provide faster microchips in their initial structure. In either case, the system unit can handle the degree of computation complexity anticipated by the cost estimator. The system unit can contain a *synchronous-asynchronous* communications option that will allow the use of a serial printer, will permit the use of an external modem for transmittal of estimate data over telephone lines, and will enable the transmission of data between computers. Such options as graphics and color capability, speech recognition and/or generation, internal modems, and local area networking can be added to the system unit for interaction with appropriate software provided by the computer manufacturer.

The Microcomputer's Monitor

The microcomputer's monitor or screen is an important interface with the cost estimator because it can display the input information as it is entered, and it can display numerical and graphic output data before it is printed. The standard screen displays up to 80 characters horizontally and up to 24 lines vertically and ranges in size from 9 inches diagonal for portable microcomputers to 15 inches diagonal for some desktop microcomputers. One of the most important features of the monitor is its resolution. Resolution is a function of the number of dots or pixels that make up the display screen. We consider 200,000 pixels as an acceptable resolution for cost estimating applications that include graphics presentations and 150,000 for applications that include numbers and text only. The number of total pixels on a monitor can be determined by multiplying the number of horizontal pixels by the number of vertical pixels. These horizontal and vertical pixel values are usually supplied by the microcomputer manufacturer in their promotional literature. Color is also a nice feature on a monitor, and a minimum of eight colors (includes black and white) is desirable. For cost estimating programs and cost estimating graphics displays it is not necessary to have a huge amount of color choices, however.

Monitors come with other features such as special glare-reducing coatings, tilt bases to adjust the viewing angle, contrast and brightness controls, and power-on lights.

Documentation

A tangible item that is always required when a computer is purchased is its documentation. The dividing line between hardware documentation and software documentation is indistinct at best because some software is usually supplied along with the microcomputer. Operating systems and sometimes languages and applications packages are often sold along with the microcomputer. Since the cost estimator usually wants to spend his or her time doing cost estimating rather than learning how to operate computers, it is important that the documentation be complete and easy to understand and use. When purchasing a microcomputer, the buyer should look for the following documentation:

1. Computer operation instruction

2. Operating system documentation

3. Separate instructions on each hardware module if supplied by different manufacturers (i.e., printer, disk drives, monitors)

4. Warranty cards and warranty instructions

5. Maintenance manual (sometimes provided at extra cost)

6. Diagnostics diskette (software that checks out the operation of the hardware)

Other Microcomputer Hardware Accessories

Although the keyboard, monitor, and printer are by far the most common microcomputer input-output devices used by the cost estimator, there are a number of other peripheral devices that have been or can be put to use in cost estimating situations. In Chapter 7 we mentioned the digitizer, the count probe, and the linear or distance probe as input devices for drawing takeoff in estimating. The mouse is another commonly used input device that permits ease of movement of the cursor for positioning inputs on the screen and for selecting menu items. The mouse is either mechanically or optically activated by the user's movement of the mouse against a background and contains one or more keys to activate a command once the mouse is positioned properly. Touch screen and light pen devices are also useful for input and may even be better than the mouse because you are working on the same surface (the screen) as the one on which you are actually seeing the results produced. Although light pens have been used mostly for free-form screen artwork and graphics, other applications that may help the cost estimator, such as geometric shape recognition, are in the works. Eventually these input systems may lead to the ability to do cost estimates *as the work activity or work output is designed!* (More about this in Chapter 11.)

If speech input and output are a part of the anticipated applications programs, a microphone and speaker system, along with the appropriate systems unit boards, software, and documentation are required.

Care and Feeding of the Microcomputer

Although modern microcomputers are amazingly reliable and rugged, there are still several precautions that should be taken to avoid loss of in-process or stored data and to prevent damage to the microcomputer's internal components. Some of the environmental hazards to the microcomputer hardware and to the program and data diskettes are excessively high or low temperatures, condensation or moisture, input voltage fluctuations and surges, dust and other foreign particles, static electricity, and excessive shock or vibration.

Temperature

Most microcomputers will operate well in the temperature range of 50 to 100°F and in a nonoperating condition will withstand temperatures as low as −40°F and as high as 160°F without being damaged. Be sure to check your computer's manual to see if there are specific operating and nonoperating temperature limits for your computer and adhere to these. Generally, if the computer operator is comfortable, the computer itself will operate with no difficulty or damage. If the computer has been sitting in a too cold or too hot environment within its nonoperating temperature range, allow sufficient time for the hardware to warm up or cool down to within the operating range specified in your manual.

Humidity and Moisture

Operating humidity should be above 20 percent and below 80 percent. During nonoperating periods the microcomputer should be protected from condensation, dampness, and moisture with a water repellant, antistatic dust cover. A waterproof enclosure and raised floor may be required if the microcomputer is located in a building with a water sprinkler system for fire protection. Alternate fire protection systems such as carbon dioxide or Halon automatic extinguishing systems should be considered as alternatives to water sprinkler systems. The microcomputer location should be segregated from other plant or office operations where steam, dust, or vapors are generated.

Power Spikes, Fluctuations, and Interruptions

To prevent the inadvertent loss of data and possible damage to the machine, there are a number of devices available on the market that will protect the microcomputer from power surges, lightning strikes, and power outages. A minimum requirement should be a power spike protector that guards against sudden power peaks brought about by static, lightning, or cycling of nearby electrical motors or other equipment. These protectors are usually equipped with a circuit breaker and a power-on light to indicate if the circuit breaker has been tripped or not. Standby uninterruptible power systems are also available that will continue to provide power to your microcomputer for from 10 to 30 min after a power outage—long enough for you to save or store any data that are in process and to shut down the microcomputer in the normal shutdown mode. These power systems also have built-in protection against power transients and electrical noise. Some line surge protectors have built-in temperature and humidity indicators to allow you to monitor the microcomputer's environment. Since most microcomputers have built-in protection against certain ranges of power fluctuations, it is best to check with your microcomputer dealer or a consultant concerning the best power spike and outage protection for your microcomputer.

Dust and Static Electricity

A dusty environment should be avoided to protect mechanical components from excessive wear and to prevent arcing of electric circuits. Antistatic dust covers are available to help protect your microcomputer and its peripherals. An antistatic mat can be used (fits under the computer) in areas of high static electricity. This mat is grounded to the ground wire on your power cord. Antistatic antiabrasive wipes are available for cleaning monitor video screens, and an antistatic spray is available for application to floors, carpets, clothing, or any other soft surfaces in the microcomputer's operating area. This static spray eliminates existing charges and prevents new charges from forming. Diskette head cleaning kits are available to remove any accumulated dust from the read-write heads.

Shock and Vibration

If the computer is to be moved or transported frequently, it should be protected against excessive shock and vibration. A microcomputer can be permanently mounted in a van, trailer, or truck if a 2-inch pad of high-quality closed cellular foam is used under the computer base and the computer is secured with an elastic cord that will allow the cord and pad to absorb road shock and vibration. The elastic harness should also have sufficient strength to restrain the computer in the event of a minor collision. (The authors have used microcomputers and their peripherals "on the road" for over 4 years and 100,000 miles with no major hardware failure due to shock or vibration.) When transporting or shipping the microcomputer, a "scratch diskette" or diskette protector should be inserted in diskette drives to prevent vibration of the diskette's read-write heads.

The Diskette: Its Protection (and Precautions)

Flexible computer diskettes should be handled with care to prevent loss of data or mechanical deformation of the material which would prevent reading or writing data to the diskette. Diskettes should principally be protected from magnetic fields to avoid erasure of data. Avoid placing diskettes on or near magnetic devices or machinery or equipment containing magnets or electrical coils such as loud speakers, electrical motors, and even portions of the computer itself (power supplies, printers, etc.). Diskettes can be stored in an area where the temperature stays within the limits of what the computer itself will withstand but must be in the temperature of 50 to 125°F to to operate properly. Do not touch the magnetic surface of the diskette or allow foreign substances such as oil, grease, or dust to come in contact with the diskette's surface. Keep the diskette in the pocket-style jacket it comes in whenever it is not in use. Do not fold or bend the diskette and protect it with a stiff cover or cardboard when mailing it. Label the envelope "Do not bend, fold, or scan" when shipping. Diskettes should be inserted carefully into disk drives to avoid damage or scratching while inserting into the computer. Diskettes should be properly labeled and filed along with a list of their contents to assure that none with valuable data are inadvertently erased.

Data Security

The cost estimator may be particularly interested in the protection of sensitive and competitive cost estimating data. Lockable diskette files are available as are special security boards for insertion into the microcomputer that require a password or series of passwords for access. Generally, however, if the microcomputer area is secure in itself, the data are also secure.

What Brand of Microcomputer Should I Buy for Cost Estimating?

We are not going to attempt to answer the question, "What brand of microcomputer should I buy for cost estimating?" in this book. We will provide you with some food for thought and some checklist-style formats to use in making your decision. At this writing there are over 50 major brands of microcomputers (see Table 9-2), most of which come in several models with varying optional capabilities. All in all, there are at least several hundred microcomputer configurations that would be suitable for one or more of the many aspects of cost estimating. In the volatile and fast-advancing world of microcomputers, new products and brands are being introduced daily, and others are falling by the wayside. Do not be surprised if this list has to be updated frequently. To permit you to do this, we have added a few blanks to the list that you can fill in yourself.

    No matter what brand or model of microcomputer you choose, there

TABLE 9-2   Microcomputers

Altos	Digital (DEC)	NEC	Sperry
Apple	Eagle	North Star	Tandy
Atari	Epson	Olimpia	Teleram
AT&T	Franklin	Olivetti	Televideo
Burroughs	Fujitsu	Osborne	Texas Instruments
Canon	Gavilan	Otrona	Vector
Chameleon	Hewlett Packard	Panasonic	Victor
Columbia	IBM	Poppy (Durango)	Visual
Commodore	Kaypro	Radio Shack	Wang
Compaq	Leading Edge	Sage	Xerox
Compupro	MicroCraft	Sanyo	Zenith
Corona	Mindset	Seequa	
Cromemco	NCR	Sharp	

are several "-ilities" that are important in microcomputer hardware for cost estimating applications: (1) expandability, (2) maintainability, (3) portability, (4) reliability, and (5) flexibility.

We will briefly discuss each one of these features and how they apply to the selection of your microcomputer hardware.

Expandability

As you become more familiar with microcomputers you will notice that, for most brands, new features, software, languages, applications packages, and hardware peripherals are being made available on an almost continuous basis. If you are to keep pace with the competition in developing cost estimates, you will want to add new features, functions, and jobs to your computer's capability long after the initial purchase. As more sophisticated software is developed, this software may require more memory, or storage, or it may require or take advantage of the use of systems unit graphics boards, color monitors, and other peripheral devices for input or output of data. To accommodate these emerging features and functions, the designers of the microcomputer's system unit will have provided one or more *expansion slots* in which to insert electronic printed circuit boards to accommodate new advances in microcomputer technology. Usually (but not always) the computers that have the most expansion slots will do a better job of incorporating new features as they are developed. If you expect to continue to upgrade your computer as time progresses, look for an expansion capability—usually represented by the number of expansion slots in the system unit. The ability to accommodate new features will do much to prolong the life of your computer and will provide the option of keeping pace with technology.

Maintainability

Ease of maintenance and the ready availability of maintenance and repair services are important criteria in the selection of microcomputer hardware. Assuming that you are going to use the microcomputer for the steady production of cost estimates or for rapid response to requests for proposals, it *must* be available and working when needed. Modern microcomputers are remarkably reliable and very seldom need major maintenance and repair work; but the tremendous inconvenience of an inoperable computer warrants close attention to the availability of a responsive service or repair organization. The computer's design itself should be such that internal components can be accessed, tested, and replaced quickly and easily if the need arises. A good maintainable design, coupled with a reliable and rapid-response dealer and repair network, are musts for the microcomputer-armed cost estimator.

Portability

Microcomputer technology has reached a point where tremendous computing power can be packaged into a remarkably small, rugged, and light-weight unit. Although cost estimators do not always need a high degree of portability, the nature of the cost estimator's job itself often requires movement from one job site to another, from one project or source evaluation board to another, or from one office to another. Transportable versions weighing from 18 to almost 60 pounds (without printer) are available for most major microcomputer brands. These single-unit microcomputers are built with special covers, handles, and diskette and cord storage features that make them more easily transportable than the standard multicomponent desktop computer. They have cathode-ray tube (CRT) screens ranging in size from 5½ to 9 inches in diagonal measurement and are built to be especially rugged and reliable. A typical transportable computer is shown in Figure 9-2. Whether these computers are truly portable or not depends on one's definition of portability.

There is a new breed of briefcase-sized or lap-sized portable computers on the market which may be considered by some to be more truly portable than the down-sized versions of desktop computers. These computers weigh less than 10 pounds and have LCD (*l*iquid *c*rystal *d*iode) display screens which take slightly longer to display information than the conventional CRT screens.

The ideal arrangement for an engineer or estimator who travels frequently into the field to gather and compute data and then returns to home base to do in-depth processing and printing of reports is to have *two* computers, one portable and one desktop, that are compatible enough to permit transmission of data between the two. The estimator would then have a choice of working in the field or returning to home base where a more comfortable environment and a faster, larger, and more capable computer exists.

Reliability

Reliability in a microcomputer is difficult to define quantitatively, but the purchaser of microcomputer hardware must at least be assured that the product being acquired has a reputation for reliability. Solicit the opinions of others to obtain a subjective or qualitative measure of system reliability before making an investment in microcomputer hardware. Purchase from a company that has a track record of producing high-quality, reliable products and who will stand behind their product with the required warranties and service.

Flexibility

Depending on the type of cost estimating or cost analysis situation you are in, you may need to have a microcomputer with flexibility of operation. The ability of the hardware to operate using several operating systems and languages would be desirable for those who are developing new estimating methods, techniques, and software, or who are serving as estimating, engineering, or financial consultants to others. Capability of the microcomputer to use several operating systems, languages, and applications packages multiplies the amount of software that is available to your microcomputer and, therefore, increases the number and types of

Figure 9-2 Photograph of Texas Instruments Portable Professional Computer. (*Courtesy of Texas Instruments, Inc.*)

problems you can solve. Also desirable is a microcomputer that permits a smooth transition to more advanced operating systems and applications software.

As is the case with any product, picking out a manufacturer who will support the product with service contracts, hardware updates, telephone hot-line help, and on-the-spot advice is very important. Buying a little-known computer brand at a discount house with no dealer or manufacturer support provided or implied should be reserved for the computer buffs. Pay a little more to get good support, and you will be able to get on with your job of cost estimating. Keep in mind always that the brand name you choose must be capable of running the cost estimating software program you have chosen.

Supplies and Equipment Needed to Support Microcomputer Cost Estimating

If your microcomputer is going to be used steadily in the cost estimating process, the supplies that will be needed are not negligible. Be sure to allot an operating budget to provide various kinds of printer paper, printer ribbons, diskettes, software updates, and maintenance and repair costs.

Pre-printed forms for repetitive work, diskette labels, and "write-protect" tabs are often needed in the organized microcomputer estimator's office. Storage cabinets and files are needed for computer print-outs of past estimates, and diskette file boxes for program diskettes, data diskettes, and backup diskettes. Many estimating offices even have special furniture that places the keyboard and monitor at the proper height for comfortable and efficient usage. A surge protector and/or an interruptible power supply is a must if you are working on valuable data that could be accidentally erased by lightning strikes or power outages.

How to Find Out More about Estimating Microcomputer Hardware

There are several microcomputer buyer's guides on the market that will tell you much more about the many brands and models of microcomputers. A visit to your town's computer dealers; study of one or more of the abundant supply of computer magazines; and attendance at computer, industrial, and business systems trade shows will expand your knowledge about computer hardware. This base of knowledge can then be coupled with the information in the next chapter to assist you in selecting the best hardware tools for your estimating system.

10

SELECTING A MICROCOMPUTER-BASED COST ESTIMATING SYSTEM

We have discussed many different types of estimating systems in the previous chapters. Included in this discussion have been programs written in the BASIC language that you can input, modify, or use yourself; spreadsheet applications programs and templates; database applications, vertical market systems, and customized systems. You might rightfully ask now: "How do I choose between the many avenues offered to get my cost estimating job done most efficiently, effectively, and economically with microcomputers?" As is the case with most choices between alternatives, the answer is not always straightforward and comes only after no small amount of analysis and study.

In this chapter we combine many of the objective and subjective factors into a series of formulas, questions, criteria, and outputs that are designed to assist you in making the decision between the many alternatives offered. In the final portions of the chapter, we have developed scenarios where cost estimators in various aspects of the profession are searching for the system that will best fulfill their needs. Represented in these scenarios are professional estimators in both small and large organizations; estimators who work by themselves or in groups; and estimators in the private sector (business and industry), the public sector (federal, state, or local government services, departments, administrations, and offices), and in the academic community.

The Economics of Microcomputer Estimating System Acquisition

Since the costs of the systems we have discussed vary so widely, the first criterion that an estimator or estimating office should establish before deciding on a set of detailed system specifications is the target budget or price range of the system based on the perceived economic benefits of owning the system. Although some may argue that it is an oversimplification to use only the dollar savings anticipated to arise from the expected labor time savings, such an assumption would be conservative and would stand up under a quantitative analysis (as opposed to the qualitative and subjective goals of "improved efficiency and effectiveness"). To have the computer pay for itself in 1 year would be an arbitrary assumption, but one that most people would feel comfortable with in this age of rapidly advancing computer technology. We will use these assumptions in the interest of keeping the analysis relatively simple and straightforward and will not discuss the time value of money, interest rates, and other factors in this initial analysis.

Since, at the present time at least, the Internal Revenue Service considers microcomputers (and their related software if purchased along with the microcomputer) as 5-year depreciable property, we will use the allowable first-year accelerated capital recovery system (ACRS) depreciation percentages in our analysis, and a 10 percent investment tax credit. The ACRS depreciation schedules for 1985 and 1986 are shown on Table 10-1. The allowable first-year depreciation percentage for 5-year property has increased from 15 percent in 1984 to 18 percent in 1985 and will go up to 20 percent in 1986 and subsequent years unless the tax laws are changed in the meantime. Assuming that the estimating microcomputer system is not obsolete in 1 year (which is highly unlikely even in view of the rapid pace of technology), further significant tax benefits, as well as the continuing productivity increase benefits, will continue throughout the next 4 years.

There are two other assumptions required for our analysis. First, it must be assumed that some transition or training time will be required to acquire, install, become familiar with, and start using the new microcomputer estimating system. Training time (the time period from completion of hardware and software installation until the system becomes fully operational) can be as little as 1 month for the simpler estimating systems to more than 3 months for more complex systems. A typical overall acquisition schedule for a microcomputer estimating system of the more complex variety is shown in Figure 10-1. Experience has shown that it always takes a considerable amount of time to perform all of the steps required to acquire a new microcomputer system and to bring it up to full operational status. Notice that the old mode of operation is continued for

1 month (overlap time) beyond the activation of the fully operational system. The second assumption must be made regarding the amount or percentage of routine operational labor time saved by converting from the old manual or semiautomated method of estimating to the microcomputer method. A conservative estimate says that once the new system becomes fully operational, it will take only 1 hour to do the routine and repetitive parts of cost estimating, where it previously took 4 hours to accomplish the same tasks. Thus a savings of 75 percent for those skills associated with the repetitive functions of cost estimating can be achieved. If the person who was doing these functions was the senior

TABLE 10-1   Accelerated Capital Recovery System

	Allowable depreciation percentages for 5-year property	
Recovery year	For property placed in service during 1985, percent	For property placed in service during 1986 and later, percent
1	18	20
2	33	32
3	25	24
4	16	16
5	8	8
Total	100	100

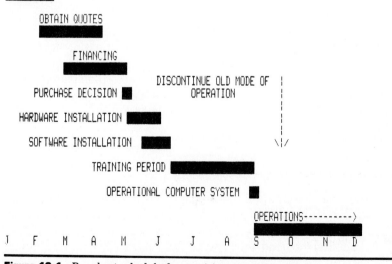

Figure 10-1   Bar chart schedule for acquiring computer system.

estimator, manager, small business owner, or contractor, the labor rate or labor time value for these functions could be high enough to justify acquisition of a very capable estimating system even though the *amount* of work done each month on repetitive estimating functions may be small. On the other hand, larger estimating groups who would expect to keep the microcomputer system operating on a regular or continuous basis could still justify a high-end system even though the composite labor rate of the estimators may be low.

The cost benefits resulting solely from labor time savings, then, can be expressed in an equation as follows:

$$S = \{H*R*0.75 * [12 - (2*T) - O]\} \qquad (10\text{-}1)$$

where S = One year's cost savings (benefits) in dollars
      H = Labor hours per month spent in routine estimating functions
      R = Labor rate of estimator or composite labor rate of estimating group in dollars per hour
      T = Training time in months
      O = Overlap time in months
  0.75 = Empirical factor of 75 percent savings in time through use of a microcomputer estimating system

Note: Training time is doubled in the above equation. This accounts for labor dollars expended for time in training for the crew, *plus* time subtracted from operational computer availability as a result of the training process itself.

Example

A small contractor spends about 5 days (40 hours) each month preparing estimates for new jobs and revised estimates for existing jobs. The contractor's personal time is valued at $25 per hour and the contractor will spend 1 month learning how to use the computer. The computer will be put into service for estimating as soon as the contractor has learned how to operate it efficiently (no overlap time). The cost benefits or savings arising from labor savings, then, for the first year would be

$$S = 40*\$25*0.75 * (12 - 2) = \$7500 \qquad (10\text{-}2)$$

System Price or Budget Versus Cost Benefits

Still assuming that we would like to recover the costs of the estimating microcomputer system within the first 12 months after acquisition, an equation can be written for the system price or budget in terms of cost savings or benefits incurred during the first year. This new equation takes into account the fact that the U.S. government permits a portion of the acquisition to be depreciated during the first year of acquisition and permits this depreciated amount to be deducted from taxable income. It takes into account the fact that the U.S. government has also provided an investment tax credit of 10 percent of the value of the asset to be deducted from the payable income tax for the year of purchase. In recent years, the government has required that the depreciable value of the asset be decreased by one-half of the amount of the 10 percent investment tax credit; the equation takes into account this assumption and includes a yearly maintenance and operations percentage or factor which is a percentage of acquisition cost. The equation for purchase budget is as follows:

$$\text{Purchase budget} = S/\{[1 - I] - [TB*(D1*(1.0 - (I/2)))] + [M]\}$$

$$(10\text{-}3)$$

where S = The savings or cost benefits, in dollars, derived from Equation 10-1

I = The investment tax credit in the form (%/100)

TB = The purchasing individual's or company's tax bracket in the form (%/100)

D1 = The allowable depreciation percentage for the first year in the form (%/100)

M = The annual operation and maintenance cost percentage of acquisition cost in the form (%/100)

Brackets, [ ], and braces, { }, are used in this equation several places instead of parentheses to show the formula's structure more clearly. In an equation used in a spreadsheet formula or BASIC program, these should be replaced with parentheses. The first term shown in brackets accounts for the investment tax credit, the second term in brackets accounts for the benefits from the first year's depreciation (primarily a "cost avoidance"), and the third term in brackets accounts for annual operation and maintenance costs.

Example

Using the above example of the small contractor who does his or her own estimating, we can assume an investment tax credit (I) of 10 percent (10/100 = 0.1); a tax bracket (TB) of 35 percent (35/100 = 0.35); a first year's allowable depreciation percentage (D1) of 20 percent (20/100 = 0.2) assuming that the microcomputer will be purchased in 1986 (see Table 10-1); and an annual operations and maintenance cost percentage of total acquisition costs (M) of 5 percent (5/100 = 0.5). Substituting these values, along with the results of the cost-benefit calculation in Equation 10-2, in Equation 10-3 yields the following calculation:

$$\text{Recommended purchase budget} = \$7500/\{[1 - 0.1]$$
$$- [0.35*(.20*(1.0 - (0.1/2)))] + [0.05]\} \quad (10\text{-}4)$$

which, evaluated, amounts to a recommended purchase budget based on labor savings of $8489.

Comment

Use of this formula will show that companies or individuals that are in higher tax brackets will be able to buy a much more costly microcomputer estimating system with the same cost benefit because of the greater depreciation amount resulting from their higher tax bracket. Companies or individuals that elect to take out a maintenance and service agreement or contract with a dealer or manufacturer will have a much higher M value and, therefore, the equation will show that they must buy a less costly computer for the same cost-benefit value. It should also be noted that the availability of a target or recommended purchase budget not only provides a good measure of what the microcomputer estimating system is worth to the purchaser, but it provides an excellent target point for negotiating the price of the selected system.

Determining System Requirements

Once a recommended purchase budget is derived from a cost-benefit analysis such as the above, the potential buyer of the microcomputer estimating system should survey the market for systems that cost an amount in this price range or lower that will accommodate his or her requirements. To facilitate the matchup of requirements with the budget, the buyer should do two things: (1) answer a set of questions pertaining to the estimating system's specifications and requirements, and (2) price out or solicit bids on three or more systems that will meet these requirements.

The principal questions that the potential user should ask are as follows:

1. How complex is the estimating system that is to be computerized? (How many levels in the WES; how many skills, materials, and other direct categories are required; and how many calendar periods are needed?)

2. Do I want to combine the scheduling function with the cost estimating function?

3. Do I want to combine accounting functions with the cost estimating function?

4. What computer programming or computer operation skills do I have or have available for use in developing and/or operating a system, and to what degree, if any, do I want to use these skills in developing a cost estimating system?

5. Is there a requirement to use existing cost estimating techniques without modification or am I permitted to modify or improve the cost estimating techniques as I computerize?

6. Is there a requirement to use *existing* computer hardware or software that is available within my company or organization or are we permitted to purchase new hardware and/or software?

7. Is there a requirement to interface the microcomputer cost estimating system with an existing system that is operating on a minicomputer or a mainframe computer?

8. Do I want to perform other functions that are not closely related to cost estimating on the microcomputer or microcomputers?

9. Is it likely that the cost estimating function will expand or is it rather static and stable in nature, complexity, volume, and frequency?

Although it is not feasible to quantitatively evaluate the answers to these questions and their impact on microcomputer estimating system costs in a book of this size, we can discuss the general impact of qualitative answers to these questions on system cost.

System Complexity

Cost estimating system complexity will have a strong impact on the microcomputer system's cost. Simple estimates can be accomplished on a small personal or home computer using one of the many available electronic spreadsheet programs. A spreadsheet template such as that described in Chapter 4 can be adapted from the literature, developed by the user, or developed by a consultant. (Each of these three options will result in different costs to the user; each step being higher in cost than the previous one.) The most complex estimating requirements will require the use of vertical market or customized systems. If the calculated cost benefits are great enough, the expenditure for these more sophisticated systems may well be justified.

Combining Estimating with Scheduling

For low-end estimating and scheduling systems, this decision will have less impact on cost than on system capability. Commercially available applications software packages that combine scheduling with estimating tend to have less real estimating capability than the specialized estimating packages or customized templates. The principal reason for this, of course, is that part of the microcomputer's memory and storage capability that would have been used for cost estimating functions is now being used for scheduling. At the higher end of the estimating system spectrum, the added function of scheduling will definitely add cost to the system. The complexity of the scheduling system itself will have a large impact on the magnitude of this additional cost. There are estimating systems that incorporate the scheduling function; then there are scheduling systems that incorporate the estimating function. Because of the trade-offs of microcomputer storage, memory, and speed, the buyer must not only decide whether scheduling is needed, but *how much* scheduling is needed. Generally, projects that take less than 1 year to complete can be accurately estimated without a scheduling system, but multiyear projects or even 1- or 2-year projects can benefit from the combination of scheduling features with the estimating system.

Combining Accounting Functions with Estimating

For some reason, at least at this writing, the accountants and the cost estimators have still not gotten together and decided to fully integrate the accounting and cost estimating functions. Accountants have, in the past, generally associated themselves with keeping track of what has *already* happened while the estimators have focused on what is *going to* happen. As pointed out in Chapter 8, however, there are some good job cost systems that combine some degree of cost estimating with the conventional accounting functions of general ledger, payroll, accounts receivable, accounts payable, and (sometimes) inventory control.

Here, as in the case of the scheduling systems discussed above, the decision comes down to how much true estimating can a combined system accomplish, and will the inputs and outputs be readily recognized and usable by the cost estimator? Until a greater degree of correlation is achieved between the estimating and accounting functions, the purchaser of a combined system can expect to compromise at least on the estimating side of the dual-purpose package. Cost, of course, would be greater in a combined system. But other factors such as speed, flexibility, and interfaces with the scheduling function must also be taken into account. When the estimators are able to project themselves into the future regarding resource expenditures more nearly the same way the accountants have kept track of the past, a fully integrated system will become more feasible.

Availability of Computer Skills

The hidden costs of acquiring a new system, not fully evaluated in the previous analysis, have to do with acquiring the knowledge to select the system in the first place, then acquiring the skills required to operate the system. Looking back to Figure 10-1, you can see that there are several steps in the acquisition process prior to the purchase decision.

These steps involve the study and analysis of requirements; familiarization with the terminology, hardware, software, and acquisition procedures; and, possibly, the preparation of specifications and/or a request for proposal or bid. These steps themselves take time. Time spent costs money. Unless the purchaser is already knowledgeable about microcomputers, the time and money spent on merely *getting ready* to buy a computer can be significant. Then the purchaser must make a "make-or-by" decision regarding computer acquisition studies, programming services, and computer operation services. Doing it yourself may not be the least expensive way, albeit a cost that is not quite as visible and less difficult to justify than hiring a consultant or programmer. The type of microcomputer estimating system developed or acquired should be dependent to a large degree, however, on the computing skills already available or planned to be developed in the acquiring organization. In-house system development skills are highly desirable if the system is going to change, grow, and expand; whereas in-house skills are less important if it is expected that the estimating system will stay static for several years.

Use of Existing Versus New Estimating Techniques

Generally speaking, if one is willing to change, adapt, or modify estimating techniques, methods, and practices to accommodate the capabilities of existing microcomputer cost estimating systems, less money will be spent or required for the new system. Insistence on keeping the old way of doing business will cause system acquisition cost to rise because custom programming may be required to build new systems or to modify existing systems to meet company-unique requirements. As they approach the age of microcomputers, many companies have had to take a new look at their estimating, accounting, and record-keeping systems to take full advantage of the capabilities of the microcomputer. So the microcomputer estimating system acquisition decision not only involves the configuring of a system to meet the requirements, but could result in configuring the requirements to match the microcomputer system's capabilities. It is not that the microcomputer's capabilities cannot meet the requirements, but that the efficiencies gained can be more significant if the microcomputer's full capabilities are exercised. An example would be the use of historical cost data to do cost estimating. If the historical data are stored in the right form, it will be much easier for the microcomputer estimating system to *use* these data in preparing cost estimates. Reformatting the mode and method of historical data storage may force a change in past record-keeping and accounting practices. Willingness to adapt to the new technology will not only save money in implementing a new system but may also result in benefits in other areas that are related to but not integral parts of the cost estimating process.

Use of Existing Hardware or Software

The adoption of new cost estimating methods, techniques, or tools is always accompanied by a decision regarding the interface or interaction of the new procedures and hardware with what already exists and is on hand. Many companies are already doing their cost estimating on mainframe or minicomputers and are beginning to integrate the microcomputer with these larger systems. Factors to be considered in this integration process are (1) software transportability between the larger computer and the microcomputer (the ability to "download" software); (2) hardware compatibility; (3) personnel training required to learn the operation of the new systems; and (4) planned interconnection or intercommunication *between* the microcomputers and a mainframe or host computer. Management is confronted with the difficult decision of whether to hang on to expensive but obsolete equipment by using it in harmony with the new technology or to modify or scrap existing systems in favor of a more optimum and efficient cost estimating and related business and engineering systems computer complex. If several alternative mixes of existing and new systems are possible, a cost-benefit analysis should be performed on each alternative.

Use of the Microcomputer for Purposes Other Than Cost Estimating

The amount of expansion capability and the amount or number of applications software packages needed (both of which affect total acquisition cost) will be affected by planned uses of the microcomputer for functions other than those intimately involved with or related to cost estimating. For example, a small business, a business or engineering professional, or a contractor may want to use a microcomputer for word processing or mailing lists as well as for estimating. For a multifaceted application, vertical market hardware and software systems are not as versatile as a multiuse microcomputer with multiuse applications software packages such as the many integrated software packages now available: Symphony, Framework, Lotus 1-2-3, KnowledgeMan, etc. If the microcomputer is going to be used only part time for estimating, it would be a good idea to combine the estimating use with other related uses that may require other software packages such as the word processing functions required for proposal or bid preparation. (In fact, the proposal preparation process is an ideal place where cost estimating can be combined with other functions in a multiuse computer with a multiple-function software package.)

Allowance for Growth of the Cost Estimating Process

The very availability of the microcomputer itself causes a growth in the number of cost estimates and number of bids prepared. The greater speed and accuracy of the microcomputer as opposed to manual or semiautomated methods results in a capability that usually exceeds its initial workload assignment. In general, the more bids that are prepared, the greater potential there is for more work and greater profitability. As with most high-technology tools and equipment, the workload tends to expand to meet the capability of the machine. In fact, in a healthy growth situation, this phenomenon is desirable. But because of the seemingly endless improvement and expansion of automated business and engineering techniques, the inevitable time will come when expansion of the newly acquired system will be needed. A greater expansion capability usually, but not always, requires a greater initial microcomputer dollar investment.

Matching System Requirements to Price and to the Recommended Purchase Budget

Matching the microcomputer cost estimating system's requirements to the projected or recommended budget usually requires "design-to-cost" techniques which involve preparing cost and price estimates of one or more systems and comparing the prices with the estimated budget. If the expected price of the microcomputer estimating system exceeds (or differs with) the budget, then adjustments must be made in the system's specifications to meet the budget. Through an iterative process, then, a suitable system is identified that meets the minimum requirements of the user. The pricing exercise merely involves the adding up of all of the costs involved with microcomputer estimating system acquisition and operation. In the present exercise where we are evaluating the first-year costs with the anticipation that the system must pay for itself within the first 12 calendar months of ownership, a price sheet such as that shown on Table 10-2 can be used to record all prices and operating costs.

Table 10-2 can serve as a fairly complete checklist of the major cost elements that can be expected to be encountered in the life-cycle ownership of a microcomputer cost estimating system. In scanning this table, it can be seen, even though the microcomputer hardware complement is usually thought to be (and usually is) the highest-cost item in the life-cycle ownership costs, there are many other peripheral costs. These other peripheral costs of ownership can easily add up to equal or exceed the initial hardware acquisition costs.

TABLE 10-2   Acquisition and Yearly Budget Estimate

1. Basic hardware		11 by 14 inch form-feed paper	$
Printer(s)	$	Envelopes–continuous feed	$
Systems units		Blank labels–continuous feed	$
Basic unit	$	Preprinted forms (invoices, etc.)	$
Memory expansion boards	$	Printer ribbon(s)	$
Graphics boards	$	Diskettes	$
Diskette drive(s)	$	Print wheels	$
Hard disk	$		
Communications board(s)	$	4. Maintenance and service contracts	$
Internal modem(s)	$		
Monitor (if separate)		5. Training	$
Color monitor	$		
Monochrome monitor	$	6. Software	
Monitor tilt and swivel base	$	Word processing	$
Keyboard (if separate)	$	Database system	$
		Spreadsheet system	$
2. Miscellaneous hardware and		Integrated software package	$
equipment		Accounting system	$
Static mat(s)	$	Vertical market estimating software	$
Interconnecting cables	$	Customized software	$
Dust cover(s)	$		
Switch box(es)	$	7. Consulting services	
Surge protector(s)	$	Computer acquisition	$
Special computer furniture	$	Programming	$
External modem(s)	$	Management support	$
External disk or tape drives	$		
Uninterruptible power supply	$	8. Insurance	$
Diskette file boxes	$		
Printer stands	$	9. Peripheral input-output devices	
Printer acoustic enclosure(s)	$	Plotters	$
		Microphones	$
3. Expendable supplies		Speakers	$
Paper		Light pens	$
8½ by 11 inch form-feed paper	$	Digitizers	$
		"Mice"	$

Example and Solution

To carry through our previous example of the small contractor who does most of the estimating for the company, we must now define a microcomputer estimating system that fits within the $8489 budget. The pricing exercise may take several iterations, or the price could come within an acceptable range of the projected budget in the very first iteration. Table 10-3 shows the hypothetical results of the iterative exercise to match the computer to the funding target. Notice that the small contractor needed only the printer; the system unit (which included keyboard, dual diskette drives, monitor, 256K of memory, and a three-plane color graphics board); a surge protector; two diskette file boxes; one printer stand; two dozen printer ribbons; a box of 10 diskettes; two boxes each of 8½ by 11 and 11 by 14 computer paper; three applications software packages (word

TABLE 10-3 Acquisition and Yearly Budget Estimate

1. Basic hardware		Preprinted forms (invoices, etc.)	$
Printer(s) (24-pin letter-quality dot matrix)	$1400.00	Printer ribbon(s) (24 multi-strike)	$ 144.00
Systems unit (with 256K, 3-plane, 10-MB hard disk)	$4465.00	Diskettes (4 boxes of 10 each)	$ 116.00
Basic unit	$	Print wheels	$
Memory expansion boards	$		
Graphics boards	$	4. Maintenance and service contracts	$ 40.00
Diskette drive(s)	$		
Hard disk	$	5. Training	$
Communications board(s)	$		
Internal modem(s)	$	6. Software	
Monitor (if separate)		Word processing (including speller and mailer)	$ 495.00
Color monitor	$	Database system	$ 700.00
Monochrome monitor	$	Spreadsheet system	$ 250.00
Monitor tilt and swivel base	$	Integrated software package	$
Keyboard (if separate)	$	Accounting system	$
		Vertical market estimating software	$
2. Miscellaneous hardware and equipment		Customized software	$
Static mat(s)	$	Operating system	$ 40.00
Interconnecting cables	$	BASIC language	$ 40.00
Dust cover(s)	$		
Switch box(es)	$	7. Consulting services	
Surge protector(s)	$ 95.00	Computer acquisition	$
Special computer furniture	$	Programming	$
External modem(s)	$	Management support	$
External disk or tape drives	$		
Uninterruptible power supply	$	8. Insurance	$ 90.00
Diskette file boxes (2 boxes)	$ 60.00		
Printer stands	$ 150.00	9. Peripheral input-output devices	
Printer acoustic enclosure(s)	$	Plotters	$
		Microphones	$
3. Expendable supplies		Speakers	$
Paper		Light pens	$
8½ by 11 inch form-feed paper (2 boxes)	$ 58.00	Digitizers	$
11 by 14 inch form-feed paper	$ 69.00	"Mice"	$
Envelopes—continuous feed	$	Total first-year costs	$8207.00
Blank labels—continuous feed	$		

processing, database, and spreadsheet), computer insurance, and an annual budget for maintenance and repair of $40. The total cost of the microcomputer system is $8207 the first year. The remaining $282.00 can be used to acquire a simple estimating template, or the contractor can elect to build the spreadsheet in house using the spreadsheet system. Simple estimating spreadsheet templates can be purchased for under $200.00.

Qualitative Evaluation of Other Economic and Business-Oriented Benefits and Limitations

In the above example, in an effort to develop a quantitative measure of the value of the microcomputer estimating system to the user, we used only the labor savings and tax benefits to derive an estimated or recommended purchase budget, and this analysis was performed only over the first year of ownership. We assumed that the microcomputer system was paid for on delivery with no finance charges or resulting income tax interest deduction benefits. We did not attempt to quantify many of the other economic and business benefits that will result from microcomputer estimating system acquisition and use. Some of these benefits and characteristics, mentioned generally in Chapter 1, can be qualitatively evaluated and subjective estimates could be applied to obtain a better view of the true savings and benefits, as well as the hidden costs of microcomputer estimating system ownership. Each of these characteristics will be listed below under "advantages" and "limitations" of microcomputers for cost estimating and, where possible, a qualitative impact on cost savings or potential cost expenditures will be indicated.

Advantages

One major benefit derived from microcomputer estimating system acquisition is the remaining depreciation tax credit for the 4 years after the initial acquisition year. Surprisingly, many people do not realize that the microcomputer can be depreciated 100 percent in the 5-year period allowed by the ACRS. This means that, throughout the lifetime of the computer, the total computer costs can be deducted from taxable income. This means that if your tax bracket is 50 percent, the total "delta" or difference in cash outlay between purchasing the microcomputer and not purchasing the microcomputer is only 50 percent or one-half of the purchase price. Essentially, the U.S. government is paying for half of your microcomputer by reducing your taxes over a 5-year period by one-half of the computer's cost to you. If the computer is kept in operation and not sold for the 5-year period, this total benefit will be available to you. If you purchase the computer on time, the finance charges and interest paid are deductible from taxable income. This route would be of benefit to you if you had other alternative investments that could make higher interest rates than those you are paying to finance the computer.

Increased accuracy   The increased accuracy afforded by a microcomputer estimating system may result in significant time (and resulting labor cost) savings. Errors in manual or semiautomated cost estimates can cause time-consuming cross-checking recalculation, can result in underestimates, and can result in overestimates (which can result in a failure to win contracts or bids). The fact that the estimator and/or management can fine-tune the estimate with a minimum possibility of errors at the last minute based on changes in specifications, intelligence about the competition, or inputs from the customer can result in winning rather than losing a competition. Although it is impractical to place a quantitative cost-benefit value on improved cost estimate accuracy, this value could be significant, depending on the current manual or semiautomated method and the present losses resulting from inaccuracies. The microcomputer estimating systems that take historical costs into account can result in greater accuracy because of ease of access to the latest historical costs.

Better utilization of senior estimating knowledge   With many microcomputer estimating systems, the estimating methods, factors, and rules of thumb can be standardized around the methods developed by senior, experienced estimators. Hence, this senior estimating knowledge is available to all estimators in the estimating group. Although it is difficult to quantify the economic benefits of this sharing and dispersion of experience level within the estimating group, the raising of the average experience level of the group will result in much higher quality cost estimates with improved credibility. In most estimating systems, the unit quantities, productivity factors, and some unit prices are stored in the database, and hence made available to less experienced personnel. This saves labor hours for the senior estimators, who undoubtedly are working at a higher unit labor rate themselves. Redistribution of the knowledge within the group allows the estimates to be developed at lower composite estimating personnel labor rates. Allocating repetitive estimating functions to junior personnel allows them to proceed down the learning curve faster and reserves the purely judgmental inputs (such as rules of thumb and cost growth or contingency for factors) for senior estimating personnel.

Better reflection of actual production rates   Many job cost systems, vertical market systems, and customized systems have standardized nomenclature that makes historical production rates more fully understandable. Easy access to history and current production rates minimizes "look-up" time. Job histories can show *why* variances occurred and can be adjusted to account for job-unique inefficiencies. The danger of using outdated or inappropriate historical data is minimized.

Access to most recent unit costs   Data banks, databases, and current lists of material unit prices or unit costs are immediately available and accessible in many microcomputer estimating systems. Since estimating price and productivity databases are customized to the work activity or work output being estimated, these databases can represent company-unique and verified data rather than merely the use of catalog or hand-book data. Inputs from accounting systems can provide updates on unit prices and unit price–quantity relationships.

Limitations

In addition to the advantages and benefits of microcomputer estimating systems, there are also several limitations, cautions, or possible pitfalls to their use. Judicious use of the microcomputer system is needed to avoid these potential detriments to cost estimating credibility, accuracy, and cost effectiveness.

Loss of "feel" for the job   As is the case when most systems are auto-mated, there is a less personal and intimate connection between the estimator and his or her cost estimate when a microcomputer estimating system is used. The computer should not be designed to eliminate the ability to exercise judgment in estimating but should merely reserve the judgmental inputs to those costs that cannot be calculated from existing or extrapolated data. Unique conditions in a work activity or work output may not be obvious or apparent to junior personnel who may be developing the estimate. Too much automation may result in the oversight of some important areas where costs can be cut, profit can be improved, tasks or labor skills can be combined, or duplications eliminated.

Historical cost files may pull through inaccuracies   Anyone acquiring a microcomputer cost estimating system must be fully dedicated to using the system in a way that cost estimates and their historical basis will be kept totally up to date and accurate. Inconsistencies in units, nomencla-ture, and quantities must be eliminated on a periodic basis to prevent inaccuracies from creeping in. The use of an automated system does not eliminate the need for frequent manual checking of estimating system outputs. Labor rates must be the very latest, production factors based on historical data must be the latest available, and unit prices versus quan-tity relationships must be current and accurate.

Introspection as to Why You Want a Microcomputer for Estimating

Before making the final acquisition decision and confirming the selection of a system with given capabilities, the microcomputer estimating system buyer should reevaluate the underlying motivation(s) as to *why* a microcomputer system is being considered.

1. I want to *save time* in doing the routine parts of the estimating process.

2. I want to *develop* new methods and techniques for estimating work activities and work outputs.

3. I want to *analyze* existing or proposed work against possible improvements.

4. I want to *improve accuracy* of existing estimating functions.

5. I want a computer so our business or company will be *up-to-date* in the state of the art and abreast of the competition.

The reason that you want to use a computer for estimating may involve answers to one or several of the above statements. Your answers will be a self-check of the system you are about to buy and how it meets your real requirements.

System Acquisition Scenarios

To provide a set of more specific (but still qualitative) answers to the question, "What type of estimating system should I acquire?" we supply case studies here of seven types of potential purchasers of microcomputer estimating systems.

1. The building contractor who already has a computer that will operate with off-the-shelf applications packages

2. The mechanical-electrical contractor for commercial construction

3. The estimator in a large company

4. The government estimating office

5. The instructor teaching estimating at a vocational or trade school

6. The small businessperson

7. The professional engineer or consultant

The Small Construction Contractor

Bill Wilson is a contractor who builds single- and multiple-family residences, apartments, and some light commercial and business buildings. He operates his business out of his home, and most of his work is subcontracted (about 80 percent). He has a carpentry crew available that he can hire as needed and subcontracts his earthwork, plumbing, and electrical work. He owns an 8-bit home computer with 128K of memory that runs many of the popular applications software packages. He builds about six structures per year. Mrs. Wilson does the bookkeeping for the business manually but would consider a small accounting software package to help her keep track of expenditures and income. What are the options open to Bill with regard to microcomputer estimating systems?

Analysis A lot depends on the capabilities of Bill's present computer and his plans for future business growth, if any. The present computer, with a spreadsheet package, is fully capable of estimating the costs of small structures of the type Bill is building. If he plans to continue at the present construction rate, the small computer may be fully capable of handling his estimating needs if he can build a spreadsheet template or series of templates to do the job. A spreadsheet that could be used for this type of application is shown in Chapter 4. Many of the home accountant or composite general accounting packages that are available for small computers are fully capable of filling the accounting needs for a small home-operated business of this type. The acquisition of spreadsheet and home accounting software, and a dot matrix printer may be all that is required to put Bill in the business of microestimating.

If Bill plans a major expansion of his business within the next year or two, however, he should consider a larger 16-bit computer with 256K of memory. He probably will not need color or graphics capability, or a letter-quality printer, but his larger machine will run software that is much more capable. Many vertical market microcomputer estimating software packages will run on this larger computer, and he will have access to a wide variety of software marketed to his specific business market. Bill should go through a cost-benefit analysis such as that shown earlier in this chapter to see if the acquisition of the new computer will economically justify itself.

The Mechanical and Electrical Contractor for Commercial Construction

The J. T. Jones Heating, Plumbing, and Electrical Company is based in a large city where there is lots of new construction going on. The company has 250 employees and bids on a large number of mechanical and electrical installation jobs each year. The estimating department is supplied with the detailed architectural and engineering drawings, and the drawing takeoff procedure is used to develop quantities of labor and materials for preparing cost estimates. Up to now, the job has been done manually and with the help of desktop calculators and handbooks. Ms. Jones would like to step up her rate of bidding, expand her capture rate for new work, and professionalize and automate her estimating department. What options are open to Ms. Jones?

Analysis   There are essentially two options open to Ms. Jones that depend on how soon she would like to automate the estimating process. The first is to enter the realm of microestimating in a gradual but organized way by (after the proper research and analysis) hiring an estimator or consultant experienced in microcomputers and acquiring one of the network-compatible higher-end microcomputers with a vertical market estimating software package. By having an in-house or continuing subcontracted capability to evaluate, adopt, purchase, modify, or build her own software packages, Ms. Jones has the flexibility to take advantage of emerging estimating software developments. This route toward an eventual customized system for her business will take more time than the second alternative, adoption of a vertical market integrated hardware and software cost estimating system.

The second alternative, described in the first part of Chapter 7, will provide automation of the estimating process at a much faster rate but will reduce the options for going to alternative methods once the vertical market integrated hardware and software system is chosen. In general, it would be better to go to the experienced vertical market integrated hardware and software systems supplier if the Jones company has little present or desired future capability to delve deeply into microcomputers, programming, and cost estimating software systems development. The costs, in the long run, of the two plans are roughly equivalent, with the second plan requiring a much higher front-end investment. We recommend the second option.

The Estimator in a Large Company

Most large companies will already have in-place computerized accounting, record keeping, and estimating systems that conform to traditional skill mixes, computation methods, and company practices, but the estimator may want a readily available personal tool to provide inputs to the master estimating system. Mary Beck has gained approval from her management to spend up to $10,000 for a microcomputer as a pilot project to see if the estimating department can effectively develop estimate inputs for the company's estimating and bidding system. What type of microcomputer should Mary look for?

Analysis   Since the microcomputer may eventually interface with the company's mainframe computer or with other microcomputers in a local area network, hardware and software compatibility with other computers that exist or that are planned in the near future will be important. Mary should acquire a 16-bit or 32-bit computer with a hard disk of at least 10-megabyte capacity and a potential communications capability. Depending on the sophistication of the present company cost estimating system, she may also want to purchase an applications package or set of packages that contains spreadsheet, database, and word processing capabilities. We assume that her first job will be to automate many of the routine tasks of the estimating department that will result in putting the information in a digital form that can either be transferred to the main company's estimating system or printed out in final form as inputs to reports and proposals. Hence, a letter-quality or near-letter-quality printer will also be required. Mary may need some help from the company's data processing department or from an outside consultant in interfacing her microcomputer with the company's mainframe computer or with other microcomputers in the local area network.

The Government Estimating Office

Most government estimating offices do what may more appropriately be called "cost analysis" rather than cost estimating, although some cost estimating is certainly involved. Ken Hawkins has been asked to establish the purchasing specifications for a microcomputer or set of microcomputers and accompanying estimating software for a government office that supports the development of independent cost estimates for budgets and that evaluates contractor bids or quotes. What major considerations should Ken involve in his specification preparation process?

Analysis   First, the microcomputer should have a fairly large storage (disk) capacity because the estimates are going to be large and there will be many of them. But also, he must consider the possible requirement of portability because the microcomputer may have to be transported into source evaluation board areas or into the various project offices being supported by the estimating group. At this writing 20 megabytes of hard-disk storage is available on portable machines, and research is continuing on even larger storage capacities for portables. Because many government cost analysis applications require the development of presentations, a graphics capability is a must. Ken will undoubtedly be developing some of his own software programs or templates using the BASIC language and/or applications packages. He will probably be able to acquire, free of charge from other organizations, cost analysis software that has already been developed (see Chapter 8 for a discussion of available customized systems). He may also need some help from the automatic data processing department or computer services department in developing his own customized systems for use in the source evaluation process.

The Instructor Teaching Estimating at a Vocational or Trade School

Harriet Humphries teaches cost estimating at a 2-year trade school that offers associate degrees in engineering, building science, construction, and manufacturing. She needs a flexible and capable microcomputer to demonstrate the use of the computer in cost estimating situations and needs a convenient and economical way of conveying this information to the students. Her budget will not permit the purchase of a computer to be used by each student or even every other student in the class. What type of equipment and programs are available to help Harriet teach her students about how microcomputers can help in the estimating process?

Analysis With the cost of microcomputer hardware and software continually going down, there are a number of very capable machines available that can do a wide variety of estimating tasks. There are also large-screen data projectors available that cost about as much or even a little less than the computers themselves. Since Harriet does not need a large-capacity hard-disk drive, printer, or a large amount of memory to demonstrate the computer, she may be able to afford a data projector to display what is on the computer's screen to the whole class at once. A graphics package with color added would be an excellent addition and would help hold the students' interest. Harriet should purchase a 16-bit microcomputer with dual diskette drives and a wide variety of software. She needs at least one of each of the following types of applications packages:

1. BASIC language
2. Spreadsheet
3. Scheduling software
4. Word processing

A database system would be optional and would depend on the time allotted for cost estimating instruction. Harriet can develop her own estimating software packages or adapt some from existing literature such as this book, estimating magazines, obtain them from government-sponsored sources, or from her peers.

The Small Businessperson

Fred Weckworth runs a machine and welding shop and wants to develop a detailed estimate and produce a summarized printed estimate for each customer prior to starting each job. He needs a small, economical computer that can print out on 8½ by 11 page showing the quote, and he would like to store each quote for future reference. What is the minimum system that will do this job?

Analysis There are some small microcomputers that have built-in thermal printers that should be investigated by Fred. Several dot matrix printers exist that cost under $200. Fred may want to consider one of the briefcase-size portable computers or merely a small 8-bit system. He may even be able to purchase a used computer at very little cost from a reputable computer dealer or customer. An inexpensive spreadsheet software package may be all that Fred needs to develop his estimates, but he will have to learn how to develop his estimating system himself or get some outside help from a qualified consultant or customer. There are systems available that will do Fred's job with very little investment.

The Professional Engineer or Consultant

Bob Goodrum is an engineering consultant who advises other professionals, small businesses, contractors, estimating groups in both industry and government, and educational institutions on how to apply microcomputers to the estimating tasks in their organizations. He wants a computer that will handle a wide variety and amount of software and that has sufficient expansion capability to accommodate as many future software developments and hardware features as possible. What family of computers should he investigate?

Analysis   At this writing, there are a number of highly capable high-end 16-bit microcomputers that run under two or more operating systems and that have hundreds of applications software packages available. Most of these computers have five to seven expansion slots for the addition of other electronic circuit boards that enhance the speed, memory, and peripheral capabilities of the microcomputer. Some have built-in interfaces that will allow them to be adapted to software written for more advanced operating systems that permit networking with other computers of different brands. Improved microchips are available that significantly increase the speed of computation and the amount of memory available. Bob should consider investing whatever it takes to acquire one of these advanced and highly capable microcomputers as well as the latest in estimating software. Since Bob is advising others how to take advantage of the high technology of microcomputers, he must himself be on the leading edge of technology with regard to the equipment and software library of some of the latest and best applications software packages in order to help his clients to the maximum extent possible. He should be prepared to purchase at least one and perhaps two computers that will run the same software programs and be capable of exchanging data. One could be a transportable or portable computer for use at his clients' offices and the other could be a desktop computer for use in his home office. He will need a letter-quality character-impact or laser-jet printer, a modem, and many of the other features listed in Table 10-1, as well as customized estimating software programs as appropriate. Bob should be prepared to spend from $10,000 to $30,000 to outfit his business with the required microcomputing hardware and software.

11

ON TO HIGHER
AND BETTER USES

There are two basic reasons that overruns, underestimates, inappropriate nonsupportable and noncredible estimates, and inadequate use of cost estimating tools have been prevalent in both the private sector and public sector in the past. The first is a *lack of knowledge* concerning the fact that there *are* reliable and credible estimating tools available, and the second is an *absence of a willingness* by some to *use* the estimates that are produced.

Both of these conditions can be and are being corrected as the technical and business communities are educated to the true nature and content of the cost estimating job. The educational process has been speeded up dramatically by the emergence of the microcomputer as an everyday estimating tool.

The availability of relatively low cost microcomputer estimating tools that can be understood, operated, and sometimes even programmed by the individual estimator and that can quickly produce timely reports that can be more easily understood by management has accelerated and enhanced a more widespread understanding of the estimating process and its impact on good planning, budgeting, and managing of resources. The ability of the microcomputer (with the proper software to access historical data rapidly and use the appropriate parts of these data to develop estimates for new work) has accelerated the feedback process from actuals to estimates and reduced the gulf between present realities and future expectations.

We fully expect the microcomputer to play an ever-increasing role in this important area of closing the gap between the estimator's sometimes errant predictions of future resource expenditures and the accountant's dogged reliance on past and present realities. As the loop between record keeping and forecasting becomes contiguous and smaller as a result of the speed and accuracy of well-constructed software packages, the continuum of financial activity will be smooth, and the visible breaks between past, present, and future more indistinguishable.

At this writing, there are technological advances in the making in the microcomputer field that seem like science fiction even in the late 1980s. Many of these advances have already been introduced in elementary form and others are in the basic research stage rather than the applied research stage. Some of the available and emerging features that are in the near term and that represent a potential benefit to cost estimators are (1) local area networking for estimating, (2) on-line estimating databases, (3) computer-aided design and manufacturing techniques, (4) artificial intelligence for cost analysis, (5) high-speed letter-quality printing and typesetting of estimates for proposals, (6) high-speed color graphics and plotting, and (7) integrated multifunction estimating software packages.

The exciting thing about microcomputers is that, wherever information is available or can be made available in digital form, the estimator can potentially gain access to it through properly constructed software media and this can be done on an individual basis rather than through a large organization or hierarchy. Rapid, on-the-spot communication of information between microcomputers is now available through local area networks, and multimicroestimating systems are feasible. Artificial intelligence systems are becoming available for microcomputers that can even assume some of the judgmental and subjective aspects of the estimator's job through the development of so-called expert systems. The time between computation and publication has been dramatically reduced by high-speed output systems in letter- and book-quality print. Presentations and displays of cost data are improving in quality, color, resolution, and overall eye appeal as a result of the introduction of low-cost, high-speed multicolor plotters and printers. As output quality begins to more closely match that of the commercial artist or printer, additional cost and time savings can be realized in publishing a completed document. We will discuss some of these current and continuing advances and describe some specific ways in which they will benefit the cost estimator.

Local Area Networking for Estimating

The local area network, a network of from 5 to 15 microcomputers, has a sizeable potential to improve the efficiency, economy, and effectiveness of the estimating process in medium-sized and large organizations. The nature of the estimating process lends itself to the use of local area networks. A local area network consists of a single microcomputer, usually with a high-capacity (20 megabytes or more) hard disk that is totally dedicated as a "server." From 5 to 15 microcomputers are linked to this server and can use the hard disk on the server to store, retrieve, modify, update or erase files of estimate information. Access to the hard disk on the server from each microcomputer station depends on the amount of activity between each station and the server. If there is a lot of continuous communication going on between the server and the various stations, access time to the server from any one station may be slow. In most estimating situations, however, the individual estimator works long hours on his or her own computer station before the need arises to access the server. Therefore, more stations can be linked to a server in the estimating function than in other functions (say accounting or banking) and the marginal cost increase to each station resulting from being on a network would be less.

In a local area network configured to perform the cost estimating function, stations are located in the departments that are assigned with the job of estimating the various major parts of the costs. The local area network can take the same form as the WES or WBS, with each level 2 work element responsibility given to a single department or individual. Figure 11-1 shows a schematic of a potential local area network set up to do cost estimates based on inputs from five stations. A five-station network would require either seven or eight microcomputers depending on whether a backup server is desired. One microcomputer is dedicated to the function of server and one is used by the cost estimate manager or proposal manager. The manager would have a letter-quality printer tied to his or her computer to provide final outputs while each station would have a dot matrix printer for estimate drafts, data printouts, etc. A 15-station network would require a total of 18 microcomputers assuming that a backup server microcomputer is desired. Networking and electronic mail software such as Ethernet or Ethermail could be used to establish the communications protocol. Security access codes would be assigned to the manager and to each station operator to allow the manager access to all estimate information and to allow each station access to the estimate inputs.

The operational scenario for the local area estimating network is as follows:

1. The manager establishes the WES names, definitions, coding structure, format, and other vital estimate ground rules, and the manager stores this information on the server with an unprotected access code so each station operator can retrieve it. Each station operator or estimator retrieves the format, coding structure, and estimate ground rules from the file server and starts developing his or her portion of the cost estimate. When draft or preliminary estimates have been completed, the estimators send their draft estimates to the server.

2. When all estimate inputs have been made to the file server, the estimate manager uses the all-encompassing security access code to bring up each estimate input on the microcomputer screen and to review each estimate input.

3. If the manager is not satisfied with an estimate input, he or she sends the estimate back to the file server along with an electronic note concerning the possible modifications, updates, rationale, etc. for the estimate input for later retrieval by the estimator.

4. When all estimates have been reviewed, modified if necessary, and reinput by the estimators, estimate inputs are loaded into the manager's microcomputer and consolidated into a single estimate.

5. The manager can now scan the total estimate on the microcomputer's screen to see if any deletions, additions, or corrections are needed prior to printing out the compiled cost estimate in final form.

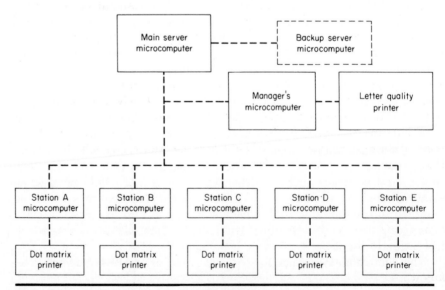

Figure 11-1 Local area network for estimating.

With the use of an electronic mail system and a network-approved word processing package, the estimating network can also be used to send rationale, backup calculations, explanations, and additional ground rules along with the numerical estimating information. This type of network can also be used to put together proposals and bids which contain text material as well as numerical estimate and resource data.

At this writing, it is known that at least two of the Fortune 500 companies are installing estimating and financial systems that perform this type of function, and it is anticipated that many more companies will be installing similar local area network systems in the next several years.

Estimating with On-Line Databases

Through the use of a modem, a telephone, and appropriate communications software, your microcomputer can be used to access public and private databases that contain wage or labor rates, price indexes, catalog prices, exchange rates with foreign currency, and inflation rates. Although the full capabilities of microcomputer communications with online databases has not yet been fully explored or utilized in the estimating profession, the possibilities are innumerable and exciting! Wherever data already exist or can be generated in digital form there is the potential for microcomputer access and use of these data in creating cost estimates. A modem (acronym for *mo*dulate-*dem*odulate) translates the microcomputer's digital binary code into an analog signal of two tones representing either a 0 (off) or 1 (on). The tones travel over the telephone lines in this form and are received by another modem on the other end which converts the signals back to digital form and feeds them to the receiving computer. Communications software helps the user by (1) automatically dialing and logging on to the database, (2) processing the signals so they will be transmitted and received properly, (3) checking for and correcting errors that may occur because of noise or static on the telephone line, (4) keeping track of the time and money spent on the call, and (5) maintaining security of data and programs through the use of access code systems. One to four pages of text or numbers can be transmitted over telephone lines each minute using a modem and communications software.

There are over a hundred major on-line databases available at this writing and many more are becoming available every year. There are databases on business, engineering and science, medical, and a host of other fields. Databases specifically useful to cost estimators represent only a small percentage of these, but many more are becoming available or are in the planning stages. Figure 11-2 is a printout of one of the many thousands of bits of useful information available from on-line databases. It shows the value of the dollar in Japanese yen for the years 1965 through 1982.

Some sample databases that involve economic and financial data are listed below to provide the reader with an idea of what is already available.

Arthur D. Little Online	Management summaries from ADL's market research reports.
BI/Data Time Series	Over 300 economic indicator time series for over 130 countries. Includes production and consumption statistics, balance of payments, demographics, etc.
BLS Consumer Price Index	Consumer price indexes calculated by the Bureau of Labor Statistics.
BLS Employment, Hours, and Earnings	Time series on employment, hours of work, and earnings for the United States by industry. Covers 500 industries in over 200 major labor areas.
BLS Producer Price Index	Contains time series of wholesale price indexes calculated by the Bureau of Labor Statistics for over 2800 commodities.
Commerce Business Daily	Notices from Department of Commerce for government procurement invitations, contract awards, surplus sales, and research and development requests.

```
IMMMMMMMMMMMMMMMMMMMMMMMMMMMMMMMMMMMMMMMMMMMMMMMMMMMMMMMMMMMMMMMMMMMMMMMMMMMMMMMMMMMMM;
:                        Reference Text For: BI/DATA TIME SERIES
LMMMMMMMMMMMMMMMMMMMMMMMMMMMMMMMMMMMMMMMMMMMMMMMMMMMMMMMMMMMMMMMMMMMMMMMMMMMMMMMMMMMMM9
: DDDDDDDDDDDDDDDDDDDDDDDDDDDDDDDDDDDDDDDDDDDDDDDDDDDDDDDDDDDDDDDDDDDDDDDDDDDDDDDDDD :
: DDDDDDDDDDDDDDDDDDDDDDDDDDDDDDDDDDDDDDDDDDDDDDDDDDDDDDDDDDDDDDDDDDDDDDDDDDDDDDDDDD :
: 0105822                                                                          :
: CC=158      JAPAN                                                                :
: IC=EXYR     EXCHANGE RATE OF LOCAL CURRENCY PER US DOLLAR AT END OF YEAR         :
:                                                                                  :
:                        JAPANESE YEN                                             :
:                                                                                  :
: 1982      235.000    1981     219.900    1980     203.000                        :
: 1979      239.700    1978     194.600    1977     240.000                        :
: 1976      292.800    1975     305.150    1974     300.950                        :
: 1973      280.000    1972     302.000    1971     314.800                        :
: 1970      357.650    1969     357.800    1968     357.700                        :
: 1967      361.910    1966     362.470    1965     360.900                        :
HMMMMMMMMMMMMMMMMMMMMMMMMMMMMMMMMMMMMMMMMMMMMMMMMMMMMMMMMMMMMMMMMMMMMMMMMMMMMMMMMMMMMM<

            Now you can read the information we've retrieved.

            Press the SPACEBAR to page down through the text.
```

Figure 11-2 On-line database printout.

Disclosure II	Detailed financials for over 9000 publicly held companies, based on reports filed with the Securities and Exchange Commission. Includes sales, profit, and corporate organization.
Standard & Poor's News	Late-breaking financial news on U.S. public companies, including earnings, mergers, and acquisitions.
EI Engineering	Index to about 2000 significant published proceedings of major engineering conferences, symposia, meetings, and colloquia.
Inspec	One of the largest English-language databases in the fields of physics, electrical engineering, electronics, computers, control engineering, and information technology.
International Software Database	Directory of commercially available software for minicomputers, microcomputers, and mainframes. Over 10,000 listings.

Remember that the above listing represents less than 10 percent of the databases available and that many more are coming on line each year. One can readily see that there is a phenomenal amount of information available to the microcomputer user who has a modem, telephone, and communications software.

On-Line Database Uses in Estimating

Since the development of accurate cost estimates depends on rapid access to the latest prices, productivity indexes, and economic indicators, one can envision how useful a properly configured on-line database could be for the cost estimator. It would be virtually impossible for the estimator to remember, record, and retrieve by conventional means the mass of data that are needed to develop a cost estimate for a complex product or service.

There are four basic types of data that would be feasible and desirable to store in either public commercially marketable or private databases for retrieval and subsequent synthesis into a cost estimate.

1. Labor rate or wage data
2. Catalog prices for materials, parts, and supplies
3. Productivity data
4. Economic trend data (inflation and escalation)

Labor rate or wage data are now available from existing on-line databases of the U.S. Bureau of Labor Statistics or from sources such as Construction Data Services (CDS), Inc., of Washington, D.C., who publish a list of union wages for construction trades throughout the United States. Sample data from the CDS catalog are shown in Figure 11-3 with CDS's permission. CDS plans to make these data available through an on-line database, by December 1985. R. S. Means and MCAUTO, a division of McDonnell Douglas Corporation, have developed a computerized estimating service which includes the unit price information from the R. S. Means publications *Building Construction Cost Data* and *Mechanical & Electrical Cost Data*. The system is based on "work package" estimating and saves time and effort at the takeoff stage.

We envision the eventual conversion of many detailed price lists and catalog entries for product lines into on-line databases. Some vertical market systems, such as pharmacy accounting management systems, already have automatic price updates through on-line access to wholesalers and manufacturers over telephone lines. Rather than going through the time-consuming request-and-bid cycle for standard off-the-shelf items, it may eventually become common practice to rely on a computer link to gain access to the latest prices for raw materials, parts, and supplies. The sophisticated pricing systems already available in many vertical markets allow price discounts, creative pricing volume considerations, loss-leader concepts, and innovative profit-margin-enhancement techniques. These same techniques could be combined with on-line databases to provide a more widespread, multimarket use of computer price updates.

Average productivity data are already available in printed and digital form through such catalogs and databases as the R. S. Means Construction Data. Experienced cost estimators have pointed out, however, that the use of the R. S. Means data alone would very seldom result in a winning bid. This is a logical observation because the predictable result of everyone using the same data would be a narrow or nonexistent spread of cost estimates and their resulting bids. The best on-line databases of productivity data would be in-house databases generated from actual jobs or estimated factors based on new innovations in work methods or procedures. With wage rates and material prices being equal, the primary remaining area for competitive success is in the productivity arena. We recommend a heavy reliance on an in-house database.

Economic trend data, which includes historical and projected inflation and escalation values, and geographic influences on wages and prices are readily available from the Bureau of Labor Statistics database information listed earlier in this chapter.

Once wage rate data, material pricing data, productivity factors, and economic trend data are available through on-line databases, one can start to envision a truly automated estimating system. The software has not yet been developed for such a universal estimating system, but it will not be too many years before this occurs. Microcomputer estimating software development will have to proceed hand-in-hand with database construction to assure that compatibility exists between the purely mathematical summation functions and the data acquisition and selection functions. No matter how automated the estimating process becomes, the inputs of the estimator will still be required because judgments will have to be made such as trading off quality with price, reliability with schedule, etc. But, with on-line databases and well-constructed estimating software packages, the routine part of the estimator's job will be all but eliminated, and the speed and accuracy of producing cost estimates will be improved by at least an order of magnitude.

Computer-Aided Design and Manufacturing

The recent downloading of computer-aided design and manufacturing functions to the microcomputer has opened up a whole new world of possibilities to the high-technology cost estimator. With already digitized information about the *design* of the product or service, the next logical step will be to use this digitized information to compute lengths, areas, volumes, and weights for the purpose of estimating the labor and materials needed to produce the work. AutoCAD, a prominent entry into the microcomputer graphics design field, can compute areas (and, by inference, volumes), but is not a truly three-dimensional system. We predict that three-dimensional graphics design software packages will be available in the very near future and that precise volumes will be able to be computed with these systems. An example of a classic civil engineering problem that can now be solved with mainframe and minicomputers is to balance the volume of cut and fill required for road or railroad construction. With an input of contour lines and elevations, and the desired route and maximum grade, precise volumes of earth or rock that must be moved as well as their average transport distance can be computed with the larger computers. It will not be long before microcomputers can do the same, making available to the microestimator a handy way of computing earthwork and earth-moving costs.

Similar applications in the manufacturing area will permit computation of the volume of metal that must be machined away in order to produce a metal part or component from a block of raw material or a casting. Knowing the amount of material that must be removed and the cutting speeds and rates of the machine tools can result in computed machining times which can readily be converted to machining costs. Tedious drawing takeoff procedures can then be replaced with computer-generated material quantity lists and parts lists developed directly from the computer-aided design. Numbers of rivets, bolts, or other fasteners can be generated from design information rather than hand counting.

STATE	CITY	LOCAL	DOMICILE CITY/ NO. WORKERS	EXPIR. DATE	EFFECT. UNTIL	WAGE BENEFIT	WAGE RATE	H & W	PENS	VAC	APPR	OTHER
WEST VIRGINIA	FAIRMONT	B0984	CLARKSBURG	05/31/85	05/31/83	13.510	11.360	1.050	1.050	.000	.050	.000
	HUNTINGTON	B1353	CHARLESTON 28	05/31/83	05/31/83	13.900	11.750	1.050	1.050	.000	.050	.000
	LOGAN	B0543		05/31/83	05/31/83	14.610	12.460	1.050	1.050	.000	.050	.000
	MORGANTOWN	B0984	CLARKSBURG	05/31/85	05/31/83	13.510	11.360	1.050	1.050	.000	.050	.000
	PARKERSBURG	B1085	CLARKSBURG 20	06/30/85	05/31/83	14.600	12.450	1.050	1.050	.000	.050	.000
	WEIRTON	B0809	STEUBENVILLE	06/30/85	06/30/83	15.170	12.470	1.150	1.500	.000	.050	.000
	WHEELING	B1149	STEUBENVILLE 29	06/30/85	06/30/83	14.970	12.820	1.050	1.050	.000	.050	.000
	STATE TOTALS		194			13.970	11.820	1.050	1.050	.000	.050	.000
	MIDDLE ATLANTIC		2,744			13.965	11.450	.986	1.291	.134	.031	.073
ILLINOIS	ALTON	B0218	CHICAGO 21	07/31/84	07/31/83	16.650	15.300	.700	.600	.000	.050	.000
	AURORA	B0013	CHICAGO	05/31/83	05/31/83	15.820	13.650	.870	.300	.000	.050	.000
	BATAVIA	B0013		05/31/83	05/31/83	15.820	13.650	.870	.300	.000	.050	.000
	BELLEVILLE	B0197	16	07/31/84	07/31/83	15.320	13.650	.550	1.300	.000	.050	.000
	BLOOMINGTON	B0362	16	03/31/84	04/30/84	14.260	12.510	.950	.250	.000	.050	.000
	CENTRALIA	B0019	12	04/30/85	04/30/83	14.135	12.990	.835	1.250	.000	.050	.000
	CHAMPAIGN	B0019		05/31/83	04/30/84	14.135	12.900	.835	.300	.000	.050	.000
	CHICAGO	B0013	260	05/31/83	05/31/83	15.820	13.650	.870	.300	.000	.050	.000
	COLLINSVILLE	B0044	15	07/31/84	07/31/83	15.050	13.050	.650	1.750	.000	.050	.000
	COLUMBIA	B0196	11	04/30/83	07/31/83	19.650	15.000	.800	1.000	.000	.050	.000
	DANVILLE	B0019	DECATUR	07/31/84	04/30/83	17.250	14.800	.650	.800	.000	.050	.000
	DECALB	B0109		04/30/83	07/31/83	15.785	13.120	.800	.900	.000	.065	.000
	DECATUR	B0019	DECATUR 16	05/30/83	04/30/83	17.450	14.850	.650	.800	.000	.065	.000
	DECATUR	B0019	18	05/31/83	05/31/83	16.400	14.020	.650	.900	.000	.065	.000
	DIXON	B0727	6	05/31/83	05/31/83	15.685	14.500	.800	1.100	.000	.050	.000
	E. ST LOUIS	B0100	42	07/31/84	07/31/83	15.820	14.380	1.000	1.300	.000	.065	.000
	ELGIN	B0913	CHICAGO	05/31/83	05/31/83	15.685	14.500	.870	.800	.000	.065	.000
	FREEPORT	B0727	DIXON	05/31/83	05/31/83	16.530	14.750	.800	1.300	.000	.050	.000
	GALESBURG	B0538	14	07/31/83	04/30/83	16.600	14.390	1.000	1.100	.000	.050	.000
	GRANITE CITY	B0397	16	04/30/84	07/31/83	16.520	13.650	.800	1.100	.000	.050	.000
	HILLSBORO	B1084	24	04/30/83	04/30/83	15.490	14.390	.650	.450	.000	.050	.000
	JACKSONVILLE	B0018	14	05/31/83	05/31/83	15.820	14.820	.870	1.300	.000	.050	.000
	JOLIET	B0013	CHICAGO	05/31/83	05/31/83	16.520	14.100	.850	.800	.000	.050	.000
	KANKAKEE	B0751	50	04/30/83	04/30/83	16.250	14.820	.800	2.500	.000	.050	.000
	KEWANEE	B0352	17	05/31/83	05/31/83	16.215	12.670	.800	2.500	.000	.045	.000
	LA SALLE	B1203	50	05/31/83	04/20/83	16.000	14.950	.650	.400	.000	.050	.000
	LINCOLN	B0895	14	04/20/83	04/30/83	16.530	14.830	.800	.850	.000	.050	.000
	MACOMB	B0991	15	04/30/83	04/30/83	16.400	14.850	.650	.850	.000	.050	.000
	MATTOON	B0019	DECATUR	04/30/83	04/30/83	16.380	14.380	.650	1.300	.000	.050	.000
	MONMOUTH	B0538	GALESBURG	04/30/83	03/31/84	14.135	12.950	.800	.300	.000	.050	.000
	MT VERNON	B0021	OLNEY	03/31/84	03/31/84	12.950		.835	.300	.000	.050	.000
	OLNEY	3D021	39	03/31/85	05/01/83	16.415	12.950	.835	1.600	.000	.050	.000
	OTTAWA	B0911	50	03/31/84	04/30/83	14.135	14.070	.700	.300	.000	.045	.000
	PARIS	B0019	DECATUR	04/30/85	04/30/83	16.415	14.850	.650	1.600	.000	.050	.000
	PEKIN	B0231	52	04/30/83	04/30/83	16.720	15.320	.750	1.600	.000	.050	.000
	PEORIA	B0165	85	04/30/83	04/30/83	16.845	15.395	.800	1.600	.000	.045	.000
	PONTIAC	20362	BLOOMINGTON	04/30/83	04/30/83	16.530	13.910	1.320	1.250	.000	.050	.000
	QUINCY	ED018	JACKSONVILLE	04/30/83	04/30/83	15.490	14.390	.650	.450	.000	.050	.000

Figure 11-3 Union hourly wage benefit levels and weighted averages.

UNION HOURLY WAGE BENEFIT LEVELS AND WEIGHTED AVERAGES – CONSTRUCTION TRADES 1983

PLASTERERS TENDERS   # COLA EXCLUDED   * ESTIMATED, SEE TECHNICAL NOTES   @ 1982 RATES

STATE	CITY	LOCAL	DOMICILE CITY/ NO. WORKERS	EXPIR. DATE	EFFECT. UNTIL	WAGE BENEFIT	WAGE RATE	H & W	PENS	VAC	APPR	OTHER
ILLINOIS	ROBINSON	BD021	OLNEY	03/31/85	03/31/84	14.135	12.950	.835	.300	.000	.050	.000
	ROCK ISLAND	BD309	59	05/31/83	05/31/83	15.630	15.430	.500	1.650	.000	.050	.000
	ROCKFORD	BD032	28	05/31/83	05/31/83	15.685	13.020	.800	1.800	.000	.065	.000
	SALEM	BD528	15	03/31/85	03/31/84	14.120	12.950	.835	.300	.000	.035	.000
	SAVANNA	BD727	DIXON	05/31/83	05/31/83	15.685	14.020	.800	.800	.000	.045	.000
	SPRING VALLEY	BD287	100	05/31/83	05/31/83	16.215	13.920	.800	1.450	.000	.045	.000
	SPRINGFIELD	BD477	25	04/30/83	04/30/83	16.500	15.250	.650	.600	.000	.000	.000
	STERLING	BD727	DIXON	05/31/83	05/31/83	15.685	14.020	.800	.800	.000	.065	.000
	STREATOR	BD016	19	05/31/83	05/31/83	15.215	13.920	.700	1.550	.000	.045	.000
	TAYLORVILLE	BD018	JACKSONVILLE	04/30/83	04/30/83	15.490	13.390	.650	1.450	.000	.000	.000
	WAUKEGAN	BD013	CHICAGO	05/31/83	05/31/83	15.820	13.650	.870	1.300	.000	.000	.000
	STATE TOTALS		1,119			16.111	14.041	.798	1.238	.000	.034	.000
INDIANA	ANDERSON	BD023	MUNCIE	03/31/84	03/31/84	13.470	11.530	1.100	.750	.000	.090	.000
	BEDFORD	BD023	INDIANAPOLIS	03/31/84	03/31/84	14.490	12.550	1.100	.750	.000	.090	.000
	BLOOMINGTON	BD023	INDIANAPOLIS	03/31/84	03/31/84	14.490	12.550	1.100	.750	.000	.090	.000
	BRAZIL	BD023	INDIANAPOLIS	03/31/84	03/31/84	14.490	12.550	1.100	.750	.000	.090	.000
	COLUMBUS	BD023	MUNCIE	03/31/84	03/31/84	13.470	11.530	1.100	.750	.000	.090	.000
	CRAWFORDSVILLE	BD024	SOUTH BEND	03/31/83	03/31/83	13.670	11.730	1.100	.750	.000	.090	.000
	ELKHART	BD023	INDIANAPOLIS	03/31/84	03/31/84	14.490	12.550	1.100	.750	.000	.090	.000
	EVANSVILLE	BD023	MUNCIE	05/31/83	05/31/83	13.470	11.530	1.050	.750	.000	.090	.000
	FT WAYNE	BD023	14	05/31/84	05/31/84	15.420	13.530	1.050	.750	.000	.090	.000
	GARY	BD023		03/31/84	03/31/84	14.490	12.550	1.100	.750	.000	.090	.000
	GREENSBURG	BD024	INDIANAPOLIS	03/31/84	03/31/84	14.490	12.550	1.100	.750	.000	.090	.000
	HAMMOND	BD024	GARY	05/31/84	05/31/84	15.420	13.550	1.050	.750	.000	.090	.000
	HUNTINGBURG	BD023	INDIANAPOLIS	03/31/84	03/31/84	14.490	12.550	1.100	.750	.000	.090	.000
	INDIANAPOLIS	BD023	14	03/31/84	03/31/84	14.490	12.550	1.100	.750	.000	.090	.000
	KOKOMO	BD023	MUNCIE	03/31/84	03/31/84	13.470	11.530	1.100	.750	.000	.090	.000
	LA PORTE	BD024	SOUTH BEND	03/31/83	03/31/83	13.670	11.730	1.100	.750	.000	.090	.000
	LAFAYETTE	BD023	MUNCIE	03/31/84	03/31/84	13.470	11.530	1.100	.750	.000	.090	.000
	LAWRENCEBURG	BD023	INDIANAPOLIS	03/31/84	03/31/84	14.490	12.550	1.100	.750	.000	.090	.000
	LINTON	BD023	INDIANAPOLIS	03/31/84	03/31/84	14.490	12.550	1.100	.750	.000	.090	.000
	LOGANSPORT	BD023	MUNCIE	03/31/84	03/31/84	13.470	11.530	1.100	.750	.000	.090	.000
	MADISON	BD023	INDIANAPOLIS	03/31/84	03/31/84	14.490	12.550	1.100	.750	.000	.090	.000
	MARION	BD023	MUNCIE	03/31/83	03/31/83	13.470	11.530	1.100	.750	.000	.090	.000
	MICHIGAN CITY	BD024	SOUTH BEND	03/31/84	03/31/84	13.670	11.730	1.100	.750	.000	.090	.000
	MUNCIE	BD023	26	03/31/84	03/31/84	13.470	11.530	1.100	.750	.000	.090	.000
	NEW ALBANY	BD023	INDIANAPOLIS	03/31/84	03/31/84	14.490	12.550	1.100	.750	.000	.090	.000
	PERU	BD023	MUNCIE	03/31/84	03/31/84	13.470	11.530	1.100	.750	.000	.090	.000
	RICHMOND	BD023	MUNCIE	03/31/84	03/31/84	13.470	11.530	1.100	.750	.000	.090	.000
	SEYMOUR	BD023	INDIANAPOLIS	03/31/84	03/31/84	14.490	12.550	1.100	.750	.000	.090	.000
	SHELBYVILLE	BD023	INDIANAPOLIS	03/31/84	03/31/84	14.490	12.550	1.100	.750	.000	.090	.000
	SOUTH BEND	BD024	38	03/31/84	03/31/84	13.670	11.730	1.100	.750	.000	.090	.000
	SULLIVAN	BD023	INDIANAPOLIS	03/31/84	03/31/84	14.490	12.550	1.100	.750	.000	.090	.000
	TERRE HAUTE	BD023	INDIANAPOLIS	03/31/84	03/31/84	14.490	12.550	1.100	.750	.000	.090	.000
	VINCENNES	BD023	INDIANAPOLIS	03/31/84	03/31/84	14.490	12.550	1.100	.750	.000	.090	.000
	STATE TOTALS		94			13.993	12.061	1.093	.750	.000	.090	.000

Figure 11-3 Union hourly wage benefit levels and weighted averages. (Continued)

Large computer-aided design and manufacturing systems are already bridging the gap between design and manufacturing by developing process plans for the items that have been designed and numerically controlled machine programs from computer-generated drawings. Although microcomputers have not been able to accommodate all of these functions to date, the availability of digitized two-dimensional drawing information can be the stepping-stone toward rudimentary automatic process planning systems. Once the process planning activity is automated (or semiautomated) the cost estimator will have another tool with which to forecast the time-based labor hours and materials required to produce a work output.

Advanced Scheduling-Rescheduling Systems

Before long, one will be able to acquire more sophisticated scheduling systems for microcomputers that will automatically reallocate resources using scheduling algorithms that redistribute resources *within* an activity. The scheduling system (Project Scheduler 5000) described in Chapter 6 will reallocate resources along the time base when one activity is accelerated, delayed, added, or subtracted, but it has no ability to compress or stretch an activity with a corresponding logical redistribution of resources. The estimator will be able to spread resources across an activity in a prespecified way, *and* will be able to stretch or compress any activity (within prespecified percentage ranges) to produce a new resource allocation histogram. The addition of cost and schedule probabilities to network-type scheduling programs, already available in some scheduling systems, will permit ranges of estimates to be developed for alternate program scenarios. Visible display of networks and critical path bar charts on high-resolution color monitors and high-quality printers will permit greater user interaction, quicker response and feedback of changes, and better management presentation potential for these systems.

Artificial Intelligence

At this writing, a family of microcomputer applications software based on artificial intelligence techniques is just being introduced. (Texas Instruments has introduced an expert system called the Personal Consultant for its Professional Computer.) Several years from now, history will undoubtedly show that artificial intelligence, or expert systems as they are called, are uniquely adaptable and applicable to cost estimating situations. The use of rules of thumb developed from experience and the ability to work with ambiguous or uncertain information are examples of capabilities that will differentiate expert systems from conventional microcomputer software applications packages. These are characteristics (uncertainty and ambiguity) that abound in the world of cost estimating. Since cost estimating is a field where subjective or judgmental inputs must be quantified, the artificial intelligence systems will be ideal solutions. These systems require a domain expert, or consultant, who works with a knowledge engineer, or designer consultant, to develop sophisticated commercial applications that would be difficult and costly using conventional programming techniques. The resulting program, or knowledge base, that is developed is then available in a user-friendly environment to serve more inexperienced users. Many of the functions described under "Advanced Cost Estimating Microcomputer Applications" below could potentially use these artificial intelligence techniques to develop specific packages in each general subcategory or discipline area under the general heading of cost estimating. Essentially, the programs that are developed cause the computer to "think like an estimator" using heuristic or judgmental inputs and outputs. The programs permit the user to trace the computer's logic back from conclusion to criteria and assumptions in order to cross-check the output with real experience and to develop or determine the rationale used.

Advanced Cost Estimating Microcomputer Applications

Since much still needs to be done in the area of cost estimating to take full advantage of the capabilities of the microcomputer, it occurred to us to develop and describe a set of criteria for some of the key cost estimating microcomputer applications that will be needed in the future. The description below is a partial listing of the key microcomputer-based estimating functions that will be required by business and engineering professionals to round out this century and to take advantage of the ever-increasing capabilities of the microcomputer.

Building WESs

Up to now, the development of WESs and WBSs has been mainly a hand-done process with little help from the computer. The unique characteristics of the microcomputer that allow the storage, movement, duplication, and interaction of blocks of information will eventually be put to use in the structuring of work within a work output or work activity in a way that subordinate jobs are placed in a correct level and position in the hierarchy and that work element interrelationships are properly diagrammed and coded. Such a program would help the manager or estimator develop detailed nomenclature, coding, definitions, and interactions in a WES. Key inputs, criteria, and outputs follow.

Inputs	1. Each work element name
	2. Each work element description
	3. Each work element code
	4. Relationship with other work elements
	5. *Type* of costs represented (recurring or nonrecurring)
Criteria	1. Number of levels in WES
	2. Number of subelements under any one element
	3. Recurring, nonrecurring, or both
	4. Arrangement (alphabetical, coded, sorted)
Outputs	1. Work element listing
	2. Printout of WES
	3. Printout of work element dictionary

Skill Category and Skill Mix Determination

This program will structure a skill category and skill level hierarchy and mix for an organization and will be able to apply this hierarchy to a specific job or set of jobs. Variation of skill mix with time will be established and labor rate structure will be developed. Key inputs, criteria, and outputs follow.

Inputs	1. Name and composite labor rate for each skill category
	2. Name and labor rate for each skill level
	3. Skill mix ratios and composite rate variation with time
Criteria	1. Duration of job
	2. Business and technical content of job
	3. Interaction with other jobs (staffing constraints)
Outputs	1. Printout of skill category and skill level list
	2. Graphic plot of skill mix with time
	3. Composite labor rates per period

Scheduling and Resource Adjustments

This program schedules activities and resources on a time basis, permitting the acceleration, slippage, extension, omission, or deletion of schedule elements with proportional redistribution of resources when activity lengths are changed. Key inputs, criteria, and outputs are as follows.

Inputs	1. Overall funding profile or constraint
	2. Resource allocations for each activity
	3. Interdependencies of activities

Criteria   1. Duration of job
2. Interaction with other jobs

Outputs   1. Resource distribution by job
2. Histogram (bar chart) showing available versus needed funding

Cost Growth and Contingency Estimation

This program computes the allowance for cost growth resulting from incomplete design and establishes cost contingencies and escalation factors. Key inputs, criteria, and outputs are as follows.

Inputs   1. Number of job elements
2. Cost estimate for each job
3. Skill level required for each job
4. Skill level available
5. Time period for job

Criteria   1. Percent design completion
2. Degree of customer involvement
3. Flexibility of labor base
4. Sophistication of estimating system
5. Track record in estimating
6. Track record in scheduling

Outputs   1. Overall program contingency
2. Overall program cost growth allowance
3. Contingency for each job element
4. Cost growth allowance for each job element

Parametric Estimating

This program accepts historical cost data, selects the most appropriate cost estimating relationship form, and fits historical data to this form for the purpose of developing future estimates. Key inputs, criteria, and output are as follows.

Inputs   1. Cost of each element
2. Time schedule for each element
3. Principal technical parameters for each element
4. Mix of labor and materials for each element
5. Mix of recurring or nonrecurring costs for each element

Criteria   1. Labor- or materials-based cost estimating relationship (CER)?
2. Recurring or nonrecurring cost?
3. Total program time constraints
4. Structure of new estimate
5. Principal technical parameters for new estimate

Outputs   1. Cost-time plot of program
2. Labor and materials costs
3. Recurring and nonrecurring costs

Cost Factor Development and Use

This program establishes resource interrelationships between various aspects of a job. It calculates percentages and direct cost interactions and determines the effect of total direct costs on overhead costs. It develops relationships between labor and material costs for each work element and for the total job. Key inputs, criteria, and outputs are as follows.

Inputs   1. Labor and material cost for each work element
2. Total cost for each work element
3. Total overhead (indirect) costs

Criteria   1. Establish interrelationship structure (see "Building WES" above)
2. Level of significance target value (say 10 percent)
3. Target or straw man job description

Outputs   1. Listing of important factors
2. Sensitivity plots—overhead versus various direct cost elements
3. Straw man cost estimate

Make or Buy Criteria and Determination

This program determines the optimum make or buy position and structure based on a cost analysis of in-house versus out-of-house performance. It determines the degree of premachining, preassembly, or premanufacture of raw materials and parts. Key inputs, criteria, and outputs are as follows.

Inputs   1. Resources (labor and material) versus costs for in-house performance
2. Resources (labor and material) versus costs for vendor performance
3. Previous mix of in-house versus vendor work
4. Schedule variations of in-house versus vendor work

Criteria   1. Funding profile for proposed project
2. Schedule for proposed project
3. Desirable make or buy ratio versus time

Outputs   1. Make or buy structure
2. All-make project costs
3. All-buy project costs
4. Optimum mix project costs

Determining Mix and Magnitude of Independent Research and Development

This program links and relates research and development activities to strategic or long-term goals. It analyzes technology advancement efforts to see if they relate and fit into overall product line and market growth objectives. It flags duplications, overlaps, and omissions of effort and determines the cost-benefit ratio of research. Key inputs, criteria, and outputs are as follows.

Inputs	1. Each technology effort's name and funding 2. Key words to indicate purpose of each 3. Company goals and objectives matrix 4. Schedule for each technology effort
Criteria	1. Range of budgeted to actual technology efforts permissible 2. Funding versus time limitations 3. Amount of duplication permitted
Outputs	1. Independent research and development plan of action 2. Prioritization of technology advancements 3. Estimated funding profile versus budget for advanced research

Profit and Profitability Determination and Planning

This program tracks profit and profitability history and establishes achievable objectives and goals. It analyzes past return on the investment and dissects the profit-producing element to develop a profitability equation. Key inputs, criteria, and outputs are as follows.

Inputs	1. Profit history 2. Return on investment versus time 3. Company financial report balance sheets and income statements
Criteria	1. Degree of reliance on cash flow 2. Degree of importance of future growth 3. Mix of short-term versus long-term profit objectives
Outputs	1. Capital investment allocation 2. Profitability projection 3. Cost reduction initiatives

Purchasing Decision Making (Source Evaluation and Selector)

This program performs a detailed analysis of several bids against an independent internally produced estimate and recommends a bidder with the highest profitability of doing the job within a given fixed target value. Comparison of the vendor's past histories, work hours, materials, subcontracts, and other costs for each element of work or task and identification of major cost anomalies, differences, and drivers. Key inputs, criteria, and outputs are as follows.

Inputs	1. Detailed cost proposal for each bidder
	2. Independently produced cost estimate
	3. Case histories for each bidder
Criteria	1. Scheduled completion date and consequences (in dollars) of a slippage per month
	2. Overall project budget profile
	3. Scoring factors for technical, cost, and schedule performance
Outputs	1. A figure of merit for each proposed bidder
	2. A bidder ranking list
	3. A "probability of completion" factor for each bidder

The above are only a few of the many possible functions and roles that the microcomputer can assume in assisting the estimator, forecaster, and financial planner in achieving the objectives of efficiency, economy, effectiveness, and long-term profitability. In every system discussed or described, the estimator's talent is not only desirable but mandatory. As his of her tools improve in speed, accuracy, capability, and complexity, the estimator's role in exercising sound judgment and professional wisdom increases. With the microcomputer's availability, the estimator now has more time and effort to devote to these ever-increasing aspects of the estimating job. The routine has been supplanted with the unusual, the mundane with the important, and the insignificant with the essential.

GLOSSARY OF MICROCOMPUTER TERMS

Abort To end a program and return control to the operating system, usually when a mistake or malfunction occurs.

Alphanumeric A set of alphabetical and numeric characters.

Analog An object (or variable) that is represented by a physical quantity, such as continuously varying voltage. The physical quantity that represents the variable behaves as some function of the variable. (Contrast with Digital.)

Application A specific program or task, such as sorting employee records, to which a microcomputer solution can be applied.

Application program A microcomputer program designed to meet specific user needs, such as a program that controls inventory or monitors a manufacturing process.

Architecture In the case of microcomputers, the design or organization of the central processing unit (CPU).

Artificial intelligence The ability of a microcomputer to imitate certain human activities such as problem solving, decision making, perception, and learning.

ASCII (American Standard Code for Information Interchange) An eight-level (7 bits + parity) code consisting of control and graphic characters. The code has assigned a binary number to each alphanumeric character and several nonprinting characters used to control printers and communication devices. The binary number (code) assigned to each alphanumeric character is called ASCII code.

Assembly language   A microcomputer programming language whose instructions are codes that represent corresponding machine language commands.

Background processing   The automatic execution of a low-priority microcomputer program such as printing when higher-priority programs are not using the system's resources.

Backup copy   A backup copy is simply a reserve copy of your data and/or system diskette that can be used in case of diskette or system failure.

BASIC (beginner's all-purpose symbolic instruction code)   A higher-level language, similar in structure to FORTRAN but somewhat easier to learn because of a smaller command repertoire and simpler syntax. BASIC was invented at Dartmouth College in 1963 and is probably the most popular language for personal computers.

Baud   A unit of data transmitting and receiving speed, roughly equal to a single bit per second. Common baud rates are 110, 300, 1200, 2400, 4800, and 9600.

Bidirectional   (1) Ability to transfer data in either direction, especially on a data bus. (2) Ability of a printer to print from right to left and from left to right, which helps increase print speeds.

Binary   (1) Number system with only two digits—0 and 1—in which each symbol represents a decimal power of 2. (2) Any system that has only two possible states or levels, such as a switch that is either on or off. This is represented in a computer circuit by the presence of current (equivalent to 1) or its absence (equivalent to 0). All computer programs are executed in binary form.

Binary digit (bit)   The smallest unit of information in the binary system of notation.

Bit   Short for binary digit, which can have only two possible values—0 or 1. It is the smallest unit of data recognized by the microcomputer. All data (letters, numerals, symbols) handled by a computer are digitized, i.e., expressed entirely as a combination of 0s and 1s.

Bit-map graphics   A technology that allows control of individual pixels on a display screen to produce graphic elements of superior resolution, permitting accurate reproduction of arcs, circles, sine waves, or other curved images that block-addressing technology cannot accurately display.

Board   Also circuit board. A plastic resin board containing electronic components such as chips and the electronic circuits needed to connect them.

Buffer   A temporary storage area for data, frequently used to hold data being passed between microcomputer or other devices, such as printers, which operate at different speeds or different times. For example, the screen buffer contains graphic information to be displayed on the video screen.

Byte   A binary element string of 8 bits, usually operated upon as a unit used to represent a character.

CAD   Acronym for computer-aided design. CAD systems employ sophisticated microcomputer graphics technology that include printed circuit design, schematic design, construction drafting, and parts engineering. Representations of products created on CAD systems are sometimes translated directly into physical form through automatic transfer of programmed specifications to manufacturing or production equipment by computer-aided manufacturing (CAM) techniques.

Cathode-ray tube (CRT)   A vacuum tube that generates and guides electrons onto a fluorescent screen to produce such images as characters or graphic displays on video display screens.

Central processing unit (CPU)   Electronic components in a computer that control the transfer data and perform arithmetic and logic calculations.

Character   A single printable letter (A to Z), numeral (0 to 9), or symbol (%, $) used to represent data. Text symbols also include those that are not visible as characters, such as a space, tab, or carriage return.

COBOL (common business-oriented language)   A high-level programming language that is well-suited to business applications involving complex data records (such as personnel files or customer accounts) and large amounts of printed output.

Code   A system of symbols (bits) for representing data (characters).

Command   A user instruction to the microcomputer, generally given through a keyboard, which can be a word, mnemonic, or character that causes a microcomputer to perform a predefined operation.

Compatibility   (1) The ability of an instruction, program, or component to be used on more than one microcomputer. (2) The ability of microcomputers to work with other microcomputers that are not necessarily similar in design or capabilities.

Control character   (1) A character whose occurrence in a particular context controls the handling of data. (2) In the ASCII code, any of the first 32 characters.

CP/M (control program for microprocessors)   An operating system used by many microcomputers.

CPS   Characters per second.

CPU   See Central processing unit.

CRT   See Cathode-ray tube.

Cursor   A movable, blinking marker—usually a box or a line—on the terminal video screen that defines the next point of character entry or change.

Data   Facts, numbers, letters, and symbols stored in the microcomputer. For microcomputer users, data can be thought of as the basic elements of information used, created, or otherwise processed by an application program. Examples of data are employee names, weekly deductions from salary, projected sales, and fuel consumption.

Database   A large collection of organized data that is required to perform a task. Typical examples are personnel files or stock quotations.

Data communication   The movement of coded data from a sender to a receiver by means of electrically transmitted signals.

Data diskette   A diskette containing the user's documentation data. A data diskette does not contain programs.

Data processing   The application in which a microcomputer works primarily with numerical data, as opposed to text. Most microcomputers can perform both data processing and word processing.

Debug   To find and delete mistakes in microcomputer programs or in other software.

Default value   The value chosen automatically by the microcomputer when no explicit choice is made by the user.

Diagnostic   A program that checks the operation of a device, board, or other component for malfunctions and errors and reports its findings.

Digital   The representation of numerical quantities by means of discrete integer numbers. It is possible to express in digital form all information stored, transferred, or processed by a dual-state condition; e.g., on-off, open-closed, or true-false. (Contrast with Analog.)

Directory   A logically organized data structure which holds pointers to access data sets by sequential number or name, usually a directory of all the file names that are located on a disk.

Disk operating system (DOS)   The set of programs that control the microcomputer system and all access to data. It allows the particular application program running on the microcomputer to communicate with the user through the display, keyboard, printer, and other peripheral equipment.

Disk or diskette drive   A unit used to read data from or write data onto one or more disks or diskettes.

Diskette   A flexible, flat circular plate permanently housed in a black paper envelope with magnetic coating that stores data and software. Standard sizes are 5¼ and 8 inches in diameter.

Display screen or display unit   A device that provides a visual representation of data; a TV-like screen. See Cathode-ray tube.

Dot matrix printer   A printer that forms characters from a two-dimensional array of dots. More dots in a given space produce characters that are more legible.

Electronic mail   A feature that allows short memos or messages to be sent to another microcomputer.

Error message   Text displayed by the computer when an incorrect response is typed, which explains the problem and indicates what to do next.

Field   A single item of data, such as a document name. An area in a record (see Record) treated as a unit.

Filename   A sequence of alphanumeric characters, assigned by the user, which can be read by both the microcomputer and the user to store or retrieve a specific file.

Flexible disk   See Diskette.

Floppy disk   See Diskette.

Font   A complete set of letters, numerals, and symbols of the same type style of a given typeface. Examples of typefaces are Baskerville, Century, and Helvetica.

Examples of fonts are Baskerville italic, Baskerville bold, and Baskerville bold italic.

Formatted diskette   A formatted diskette may either be new or recycled. The process of formatting clears all previously recorded data (in the case of recycled diskettes), checks for flawed sectors, and creates a directory that controls the files that may be written on it.

FORTRAN (formula translation)   A widely used high-level programming language well suited to problems that can be expressed in terms of algebraic formulas. It is generally used in engineering and scientific applications.

Function key   A key that causes a microcomputer to perform a function (such as scrolling a designated number of lines) or execute a program. The function each key performs may vary depending on the application software package.

Global   In programming, it is something that is defined in one section of a program and used in at least one other section.

Graphic character   A character, other than a control character, that is normally represented by a graphic symbol.

Graphics   Symbols normally produced by handwriting, drawing, or printing. Synonymous with graphic symbols. (The use of lines and figures to display data, as opposed to the use of printed characters. See Bit-map graphics.)

Hard disk   A disk composed of a magnetic coating applied to a rigid aluminum or ceramic plate. The term is generally used to contrast with diskettes (floppy diskettes) that are flexible, have a slower access speed, and less storage capacity. The hard disk is usually not removable as is the flexible diskette.

Hardware   Any mechanical device that is a part of the microcomputer (the diskette drive, system unit, printer, and so on). (Physical equipment, as opposed to a computer program or method of use, e.g., mechanical, electrical, magnetic, or electronic devices.) Also called peripherals.

Impact printer   A printer that forms characters on paper by striking an inked ribbon with a character-forming element (usually used for letter-quality printers).

Input   As a verb, it means to enter data. As a noun, it means the data entered.

Instruction   In a programming language, a meaningful expression or command that tells the microcomputer what specific task to execute next.

Interactive   Capable of carrying on a dialogue through a keyboard with the user, rather than simply responding to commands.

Interface   An electronic assembly that connects an external device, such as a printer, to a microcomputer.

K   The symbol for the quantity 2^{10} or 1024. The K is uppercase to distinguish it from lowercase k, which is a Systeme International unit for kilo, or 1000 (10^3).

Kb   Kilobyte (1024 bytes).

Keyboard   The set of keys on a terminal that allows alphanumeric characters or symbols to be transmitted when keys are depressed. It inputs text and instructions to the microcomputer.

Large-scale integration (LSI)   The combining of about 1000 to 10,000 circuits on a single chip. Typical examples of LSI circuits are memory chips, microprocessors, calculator chips, and watch chips.

Letter-quality printer   The printer used to produce final copies of documents. It produces typing comparable in quality to that of a typewriter.

Light pen   In microcomputer graphics, a penlike device that can sense light. When it is held up to a CRT it can be used to identify display.

Load   The process of copying a program from external storage, such as a diskette or Winchester disk, into memory of the microcomputer.

Local   Hard-wired connection of a microcomputer to another microcomputer, terminal, or peripheral device such as in a local area network. See Remote.

Local area network (LAN)   Several microcomputers connected together with co-axial cables that can work interactively or use a server microcomputer's disk storage.

Macro   A list of symbols that represents keystrokes. A macro can be constructed and entered into some programs to reduce the number of manual entries that must be made to accomplish a given task on the microcomputer.

Mainframe   A computer that is physically large and provides the capability to perform applications requiring large amounts of data (e.g., for a large-scale payroll system). These computers are much more expensive than microcomputers.

Megabyte (MB)   1,048,576 (2^{20}) bytes.

Memory   (1) The main high-speed storage area in a microcomputer where instructions for a program being run are temporarily kept. (2) A device in which data can be stored and from which they can later be retrieved.

Memory word   The amount of memory that the microcomputer can address at one time. Professional microcomputers usually have 16- or 32-bit memory words.

Menu   A displayed list of options from which the user selects an action to be performed by typing a letter or by positioning the cursor.

Microchip   A microscopic integrated electronic circuit etched on a tiny piece of silicon which is very inexpensive to mass produce and is more reliable and uses less power than conventional discrete circuits.

Microcomputer   A computer which is physically very small—it can fit on or under a desk—and which is based on large-scale integration (LSI) circuitry.

Mnemonic   A short, easy-to-remember name or abbreviation. Many commands in programming languages are mnemonics.

Modem (modulator/demodulator)   A device that converts microcomputer signals (data) into high-frequency communication signals, and vice versa. These high-frequency signals can then be sent over telephone lines.

Monitor   A television-like device that can be used as an output display. (See also Cathode-ray tube, Display screen, and Terminal).

Network   A group of computers that are connected to each other by communications lines to share information and resources. See Local area network.

Operating system   Software that controls the execution of microcomputer programs and that may provide scheduling, debugging, input and output control, accounting, storage assignment, data management, and related services. Sometimes called supervisor, executive, monitor, or master control program depending on the microcomputer manufacturer.

Output   Output is what comes out of a microcomputer. It may be printed on paper, printed on the display, or sent to the diskette.

Pixels (picture elements)   Definable locations on a display screen that are used to form images on the screen. For graphics displays, screens with more pixels generally provide higher resolution. See Bit-map graphics.

Plotter   An image output device that allows the microcomputer to directly control the movement of pens over drafting or graph paper. The plotter is used to produce drawings, charts, and graphs.

Printer   The device that produces a paper copy of a document (hard-copy output). There are two types: dot matrix and letter-quality or impact printers. Unlike a terminal, there is virtually no communication from printer to CPU.

Printout   An informal expression referring to almost anything printed by a microcomputer peripheral device; any microcomputer-generated hard copy.

Program   A series of commands that direct the microcomputer to perform a task.

Program disk   A disk containing the instructions of a program.

Programming language   The words, mnemonics, and/or symbols, along with the specific rules allowed in constructing computer programs. Some examples are BASIC, FORTRAN, and COBOL.

Protocol   A formal set of conventions or rules governing the format, timing, and error control to facilitate message exchange between two communicating processes.

RAM (random access memory)   Memory that can be read and written into (i.e., altered) during normal operation. RAM is the type of memory used in most computers to store the instructions of programs currently being run.

Record   A collection of fields; the information relating to one area of activity in a data processing activity, e.g., all information on one inventory item. Sometimes called item.

Relational character   A character that expresses a relationship between two operands. Common relational operators are $>$ (greater than), $<$ (less than), and $=$ (equal to).

Remote   Not hard-wired; communicating via switched lines such as telephone lines. Usually refers to peripheral devices (e.g., printers, video terminals) that are located at a site away from the CPU.

Reverse video   A feature on a display unit that produces the opposite combination of characters and background from that which is usually employed, i.e., white characters on a black screen, if having black characters on a white screen is normal.

ROM (read-only memory)   Memory containing fixed data or instructions that is permanently loaded during the manufacturing process. A microcomputer can use the data in the ROM but cannot change them.

Screen   (1) The display surface of a video monitor. (2) The pattern or information displayed on the screen. Also called video display, video monitor, video terminal, CRT, video display terminal, monitor, etc.

Scroll   To move the contents of the display up or down by one or more lines, or left or right by one or more characters or cells.

Software   A set of microcomputer programs, procedures, rules, and associated documentation concerned with the operation of microcomputers, e.g., compilers, monitors, editors, utility programs. (Compare with Hardware.)

Sort   Rearranging the records in a file so that the order is convenient to the user.

System   A combination of microcomputer software and hardware that performs specific processing operations.

System unit   Box that houses the microcomputer's system board, disk drives, power supply, and option modules.

Terminal   An input-output device used to enter data into a computer and record the output. Terminals are divided into two categories: hard copy (e.g., printers) and soft copy (e.g., video terminals).

Text   A sequence of characters.

Tractorfeed   An attachment used to move paper through a printer. The roller that moves the paper has sprockets on each end that fit into the fanfold paper's matching pattern of holes.

Upgrade   To expand your microcomputer as new features are developed or as existing features are enhanced.

User-defined key (UDK)   A key that remembers and stores a series of keystrokes, allows the user to save the keystrokes needed to perform a specific operation, and then initiates them in the proper sequence by pressing only one key.

Video display   See Screen.

Video monitor   See Screen.

Video terminal   See Screen.

Winchester disk   A hard disk permanently sealed in a drive unit to prevent contaminants from affecting the read-write head; this virtually eliminates the need for adjustment of the head by field service personnel. The disk is capable of storing larger amounts of data than a diskette.

Word   The greatest number of bits a microcomputer is capable of handling in any one operation. Usually subdivided into bytes. Microcomputers usually have 8-bit (1-byte), 16-bit (2-byte), or 32-bit (4-byte) words.

Word processing system   A system that processes text, performing such functions as editing, paragraphing, paging, left and right justifying, rearranging text, and printing text.

Word-wrapping   The automatic shifting of words from a line that is too long to the next line (lines are broken only at the end of a word).

GLOSSARY OF
COST ESTIMATING TERMS

Best-fit curve   A curve which passes through a group of data values in a manner which best represents the trend of the data points.

Bid   A price quote in response to an advertised announcement or bid request. The bid is usually accompanied by less cost detail and explanatory information than a proposal.

Bond   A certificate indicating a promise to repay a debt at a specified time. Security to guarantee performance or fulfillment of an obligation.

Budget   A statement of the funding amount available for or allocated to a given work activity or work output.

Composite labor rate   The weighted average labor rate for a given work activity, work output, organization, skill category, or time period.

Contingency   An amount of resources allocated within a cost estimate to accommodate unforeseen cost increases.

Cost analysis   The accumulation, organization, and study of costs of a past, ongoing, or projected work activity or work output. Often the cost analysis function is performed to develop inputs, modifications, and rationale for the cost estimating process.

Cost element   An identifiable function or a common group of functions that have been established as a separate resource entity for the purpose of collecting, estimating, and reporting costs. (Examples are labor, materials, subcontracts, travel, and computer costs.)

Cost estimating   The art of approximating the probable worth or cost, extent, quantity, quality, or character of something based on information available at the time. Cost estimating is usually used to develop a price or market sales objective that will assure an adequate profit.

Cost growth allowance   An amount of resources allocated within a cost estimate to accommodate the certainty or high probability of cost increase due to inadequate design definition, expected customer involvement, decreases in productivity, and many other factors.

Cost model   A mathematically and logically ordered arrangement of ground rules, assumptions, equations, and data that permits translation of physical resources or characteristics into costs.

Criteria   The standards against which evaluations are performed.

Critical path   The sequence of events in a work activity that must occur end to end and that establishes the shortest possible time in which the total job can be completed.

Cumulative average learning curve   The plot that shows the cumulative average value for a given learning curve percentage of the dollars or hours required to produce n units versus the n value.

Design-to-cost   The practice of developing a design, set of performance specifications, or a schedule of activities based on an overall target or ceiling budget. Design-to-cost is usually accomplished either by making a series of estimates of work activities or outputs that will fulfill the general need or requirement and selecting the one that most nearly meets the budgetary constraints or by adjusting one or more of the options by changing technical specifications, quantities delivered, delivery schedule, skills used, or quality of materials, parts, and supplies.

Detailed estimate   An estimate that results from the synthesis of cost data from resource estimates made at the lowest possible level in a WES (also called grass-roots estimate, grounds-up estimate, and bottoms-up estimate).

Direct estimate   A judgmental estimate made by an estimator or performer who is intimately familiar with the task being estimated.

Escalation   The increase in resources required to do a job because of design changes, decreases in productivity, undue customer involvement, union benefit changes, inaccuracies in the original estimate, inability to hire new skilled personnel, and other factors.

Gantt chart   A time-oriented bar chart that displays the major schedule-oriented work elements that must be accomplished in order for the total job to be completed on time.

General and administrative percentage   A percentage that is multiplied by total direct and indirect costs to cover general and administrative expenses; includes a company's general and executive office expenses, legal services, accounting, public relations, financial, and other expenses related to the overall business.

Handbook or catalog estimating Development of a cost estimate based on labor productivity factors (labor unit quantities), unit prices, material unit quantities, and peripheral costs supplied in a published handbook or catalog.

Independent estimate A cost estimate prepared by someone other than one bidding for the job, usually the organization that requested the bid or an outside consultant.

Inflation The increase in resources required to do a job because of increases in labor rates, material prices, and overhead costs caused by the state of the overall economy.

Job cost Cost arrived at by a cost accounting method which identifies and collects charges for materials, labor, and allocated overhead in the production of a specific order, a finished unit, or a set of units.

Labor burden The portion of company overhead or indirect costs that is attributable to employees' health insurance, bonuses, paid holidays, paid vacations, sick leave, social security, and pension contributions.

Labor overhead percentage A percentage that is multiplied by labor costs to cover labor burden costs and labor overhead costs.

Labor rates The dollar cost per time of each labor skill category and skill level (otherwise known as wage rate or salary).

Labor unit prices Labor unit prices are equal to labor unit quantities multiplied by labor rates. Hence, the labor unit price is the labor cost per unit of production.

Labor unit quantities The number of labor time units (hours, days, weeks, months) required to produce a unit of output (i.e., welding time per foot; paving time per mile; labor hours per block laid; drafting time per drawing; writing, editing, or typing time per page; etc.) (also called productivity).

Lead time The time allowed or required to order materials, build facilities, produce tooling, etc. so that these items will be ready for use at the proper time to help produce the end product.

Learning curve A curve that results when the dollars or hours required to produce a doubled quantity is derived from the undoubled quantity multiplied by the learning curve factor (learning curve percentage divided by 100). For example, the x (horizontal axis value) and y (vertical axis value) on a cartesian plot for a 90 percent learning curve would be derived as follows:

No. of units	Hours required	
1	100	
2	90	(100*0.9)
4	81	(90*0.9)
8	73	(81*0.9)

Life-cycle costs The total cost of acquiring, maintaining, operating, repairing, supporting, and disposing of a work activity or work output.

Material burden percentage   A percentage that is multiplied by material costs to cover material burden costs, such as receiving, storing, protecting, purchasing, and distributing materials.

Material prices   The costs per unit of material quantity such as dollars per pound or ton, dollars per yard, dollars per board foot, etc.

Material unit prices   Material unit prices are equal to material unit quantities multiplied by material prices. Hence, the material unit price is the material cost per unit of production.

Material unit quantities   The numbers of units of material required for a given amount of completed work (i.e., welding rod usage per inch or foot of weld, tons of asphalt used per each mile of highway paving, number of blocks per foot of wall, number of pounds of sheet metal per foot of ductwork, etc.). These are also called material usage factors.

Milestone   A symbol or designator which signifies the start or completion of a task or work activity, or an important event in the project's lifetime.

Overhead   Costs incurred by a company which cannot be directly attributable to specific work activities and work outputs (also used interchangeably with indirect costs).

Parametric estimate   A cost estimate that is based on statistical analysis and application of historical or actual cost data.

PERT (Program Evaluation and Review Technique)   A means of planning and scheduling a complex set of work activities to assure that each is finished at the proper time and that the overall job is completed on schedule. PERT can also be used to estimate costs versus time, to adjust and level resource expenditures, and to identify trouble spots or potential areas for adjustment in a complex project.

PFD (personal, fatigue, and delay) time   Time expended by personnel due to trips to the restroom and water fountain, telephone calls, unscheduled rest periods, waiting for machine repair or tools, and unscheduled supervisory guidance or training.

Price   The value established for sale of a work activity or work output on the open market.

Process plan   An itemized listing of each task that must be accomplished to perform a job, along with the skills, time, equipment, and material required to do the job.

Production units   The number of pounds, yards, board feet, square feet, gallons, miles, blocks, drawings, parts, pages, etc. to be produced.

Productivity   The number of work units that can be accomplished by a given employee or set of employees in a given time (see Labor unit quantities and Material unit quantities).

Profit   The short-time result of subtracting costs from price. Profit contributes to immediate cash flow.

Profit or fee percentage   A percentage that is multiplied by total costs to derive the profit or fee to be earned on the work.

Profitability The ability of a job to produce profit not only in the near term but to result in continued benefits to the company over a long term.

Proposal A written document that accompanies or contains a cost estimate or bid which describes the work to be done, *who* is going to do it, *how* it is going to be done, *where* it will be done, and *why* the bidding firm should be awarded the contract or given the job. A proposal is usually used in responding to requests for negotiated procurements, while a bid is used for responding to advertised procurements.

Rationale The backup or supporting data and information supplied with or separated from a detailed cost estimate.

Risk analysis The evaluation of a set of conditions to determine the technical, financial, or business risk inherent in the undertaking. Risk can be determined through the use of mathematical models or can be derived subjectively through the use of expert opinions.

Schedule element A schedule element is an identifiable calendar-based segment of the total job that can be identified with a start date, completion date, predecessors, and successors. Also known as a job or activity.

Subcontracts and purchased parts costs The costs of processes, products, projects, or services outside of the producing company or organization.

Takeoff The process of measuring and counting the linear feet, areas, volumes, and number of units of installed parts or subassemblies from detailed drawings in order to develop a detailed time and materials estimate as input to a detailed cost estimate.

Theoretical first unit (TFU) The value of the dollars or hours theoretically required to produce the first unit of production. The TFU value can be derived through the use of learning curve formulas when the dollars or hours required to produce the nth unit and the learning curve percentage are known.

Travel and other direct costs Costs that are directly attributable to the job (travel, transportation, computer services, reproduction services, training, etc.).

Unit learning curve A plot of the dollars or hours required to produce each successive unit versus the number of units produced.

Work activity A type of work that results from the expenditure of labor and materials to produce a nontangible output such as a process or a service.

Work breakdown structure (WBS) A hierarchical family tree that breaks down the major task into subtasks, sub-subtasks, and so forth. Used both in the top-down type of estimating and the bottom-up type of estimating.

Work element An element or subdivision of work. Also variously called a task, subtask, job, or work unit.

Work element structure (WES) See Work breakdown structure. Cost estimate structure or framework. (Used in the bottom-up type of cost estimating.)

Work output A tangible result of the expenditure of labor and materials such as a product or a project.

Work hour A 1-hour period of work for one employee. One employee normally produces 40 work hours in 1 workweek, two employees produce 80 work hours in 1 workweek, etc. Workweek, work month, and work year have corresponding definitions based on their respective time periods.

BIBLIOGRAPHY

Boehm, Barry W.: *Software Engineering Economics*. Prentice-Hall, Inc. Englewood Cliffs, New Jersey, 1981.

Building Construction Cost Data. Robert Shaw Means Company, Inc., Kingston, Massachusetts, 1984 and 1985.

Computer-Aided Cost Estimating System (CACES) Unit Price Book (Volumes I and II). U.S. Army Corps of Engineers, Huntsville, Alabama, 1983.

Computer-Aided Cost Estimating System (CACES) Users Manual. U.S. Army Corps of Engineers, Washington, D.C., March 1984.

"Computer Buyer's Guide and Handbook," Computer Information Publishing, Inc., New York, September 1984.

Fawcette, James E.: "Choosing Project Management Software." *Personal Computing,* October 1984, pp. 114–121.

Foster, Edward S.: "Keeping Your Projects on Time and Under Budget." *Personal Computing,* September 1984, pp. 32 and 41.

Jelen, Frederic C., and James H. Black: *Cost and Optimization Engineering*. McGraw-Hill Book Company, New York, 1983, p. 424.

Job Cost, MICA/JC Job Cost Program Manual. Micro Associates, Inc., Port Arthur, Texas, 1984.

Lotus 1-2-3 Users' Manual for the Texas Instruments Professional Computer. Lotus Development Corporation, Cambridge, Massachusetts, 1983.

Multiplan Software Library Manual for Texas Instruments Professional Computer. Texas Instruments, Inc., Houston, Texas, 1982.

Naisbitt, John: *Megatrends*. Warner Books, New York, 1982.

Ostwald, Philip F.: *Cost Estimating.* Prentice-Hall, Inc., Englewood Cliffs, New Jersey, 1984, p. 369.

Personal Consultant Expert System Development Tools, Texas Instruments, Inc., Dallas, Texas, 1984.

Poole, Lon, and Mary Borchers: *Some Common Basic Programs,* 3d ed., Osborne/McGraw-Hill, Berkeley, California, 1979, pp. 147–150.

Project Scheduler 5000 with Graphics Manual. SCITOR Corporation, Sunnyvale, California, 1984.

Skewis, A. L.: *NES Dictionary.* National Estimating Society, Washington, D.C., 1982.

Stern, Richard, and Hugh Conway: *Handbook of Wages and Benefits for Construction Unions,* Construction Data Services, Inc., Washington, D.C., 1983.

Stewart, Rodney D.: *Cost Estimating.* John Wiley and Sons, New York, 1982, pp. 62–64.

Stewart, Rodney D., and Ann L. Stewart: *Proposal Preparation.* John Wiley and Sons, New York, 1984, pp. 106–110.

INDEX

About the Authors

Rodney D. Stewart, CPE, and *Ann L. Stewart* are president and secretary-treasurer, respectively, of Mobile Data Services, Huntsville, Alabama. Their consulting firm provides computer software development and seminars in cost estimating and microcomputer applications. As manager of NASA's Cost Analysis Office from 1971 to 1981, Rodney Stewart was responsible for NASA cost estimates on engineering work hours and materials for launch vehicles. He has published several articles and books, including *Cost Estimating*, Wiley, 1982. Ann Stewart, a systems writer and microcomputer analyst, coauthored *Proposal Preparation* with Rodney Stewart, Wiley, 1984.